THE PRICE OF PLENTY

THE PRICE OF PLENTY

A History of Meat in America

MAUREEN OGLE

Copyright © 2025 by Maureen Ogle

Parts of this work appeared first in *In Meat We Trust: An Unexpected History of Carnivore America* (Houghton Mifflin Harcourt, 2013; rights owned by author).

All rights reserved.

No part of this book may be reproduced in any form or by any electronic or mechanical means, including information storage and retrieval systems, without written permission from the author, except for the use of brief quotations in a book review.

❋ Formatted with Vellum

CONTENTS

A note to readers — vii

Prologue — 1
Children of Plenty — 3

I. Building an American Way of Meat — 11

Chapter 1 — 12
Carnivore America

Chapter 2 — 35
Out of Sight, Out of Mind

Chapter 3 — 58
Eastern Plots, Western Profits, Beef for Everyone

II: Producers, Consumers, and the Paradox of Plenty — 79

Chapter 4 — 80
What Price Plenty?

Chapter 5 — 107
Mr. Hoover's War; or, How to Fix Prices and Make Enemies

Chapter 6 — 123
Good-bye to All That

III: The Ways and Means of Plenitude — 143

Chapter 7 — 144
Winged Widgets; or, Chicken In Every Pot

Chapter 8 — 164
Go Big or Go Home

Chapter 9 — 184
Going Big: Three Tales

Chapter 10 — 208
Big Doubts

IV: Plenty: Its Pleasures and Its Price — 229

Chapter 11 — 230
"The Greatest Age of Agriculture"

Chapter 12 — 251
Make Mine Biodynamic and Medium Rare

Chapter 13 — 268
Four Stories and Alternative Outcomes

Afterword — 288
Acknowledgements — 291

Notes	293
Bibliography	349
Illustration Credits	407
Index	409
About the Author	421

A NOTE TO READERS

Ours is an age, apparently, of short attention spans. I am thus compelled to note that of this book's 400-hundred-plus pages, its *chapters* — the story you're here to read — occupy fewer than three hundred.

It's not necessary to read any of those other 100-plus pages. Seriously.

At the end of many paragraphs you will see a small number. That's a note. No need to read those; you'll be fine without them.

If you're a notes geek, however, lucky is the geek reading digitally: tap to open note. Finished? Tap anywhere.

(Special note to my fellow historians: in an ebook, the notes are always at the bottom of the page.)

As ever: thanks for reading. I appreciate it.

PROLOGUE

CHILDREN OF PLENTY

The white Europeans who colonized North America's eastern coast in the seventeenth century encountered extraordinary abundance. Immense bird flocks blackened the sky. Rivers and streams ran thick with fish. Shorelines teemed with crab and turtle, and forests with deer, bear, and other game. Above all, there was land, millions of acres stretching off into a distance that would require many lifetimes to map and measure.

Of all the cultural shocks that rattled colonists' psyches, this was perhaps the greatest. They had emigrated from societies where land was scarce and ownership limited. Not so in North America, where land abundance enabled them to develop a meat-centered diet on a scale that the Old World could neither imagine nor provide.

In the earliest years, settlers trapped, snared, shot, netted, and feasted on venison, squirrel, and lobster; pigeon, pheasant, and possum. But they wanted more. Civilized people ate civilized food: beef, mutton, and pork. Civilized people exercised dominion over not just land but animals, too, especially cattle, sheep, and swine.

To the men and women who settled North America, the idea of a world without livestock was as peculiar, and dangerous, as the notion of a world without God. Therein lay the road to savagery.[1]

And Europeans had not traveled halfway around the world to emulate the natives they encountered in North America. According to one chronicler, those "savages" "[ran] over the grass" like "foxes and wild beasts," leaving "the land untilled" and "the cattle not settled." Native villages contained neither pen nor barn.[2]

This lack of "civilized" markers doomed the "savage people." Because they "inclose[d] no ground" and kept no "cattell," decreed Massachusetts leader John Winthrop, they forfeited any claim to the land and its wealth. Instead, white Europeans would rule and use the land to produce meat, thereby demonstrating the superiority of their culture.[3]

Colonists' imported cattle thrived beyond belief or expectation. One South Carolinian boasted that his colony was so "advantageously . . . scituated, that there [was] little or no need of Providing Fodder for Cattle in the Winter."[4]

As for hogs, those "swarm like Vermine upon the Earth," grumbled one man. From north to south, hogs snuffled through forest floors carpeted with acorns and other mast, growing fat on nature's bounty and multiplying to the point of nuisance. But the result was that colonial Americans never wanted for ham, bacon, and sausage.[5]

Livestock translated into tangible wealth that, with good management, multiplied more readily than silver or gold. In Maryland in the late 1600s, one cow and a calf carried as much monetary value as six or seven hundred pounds of tobacco, a third of a year's crop for one man.[6]

Settlers also valued meat for its nutritional qualities. Meat is water, protein, and fat, all of which humans require for survival. More precisely, it is the tissue from which muscle is constructed. Content proportions depend on the age, size, and species of the animal, but a general average is 75 percent water, 20 percent protein, and 5 percent fat.

Nowadays, fat suffers an undeserved bad reputation, but it's one of the body's most efficient tools for storing energy; stored fat fueled early hominids' flights from danger and protected them when food was scarce. Anglo-American colonists also favored meat because it was less labor intensive than foods that required planting, hoeing, and harvesting.[7]

Water, which all flesh contains, nurtures mold and bacteria; meat must be eaten immediately or preserved. Colonists pounded chicken to a paste, stuffed it into ceramic pots, and sealed the container with a layer of fat or oil. They dried beef in the sun, and salted, pickled, and smoked fresh pork. (Colonial diets tended to be porkcentric not only because hogs abounded but because pork is much easier to preserve than beef.)

ABUNDANCE AND DESIRE TRANSLATED INTO MEAT ON THE TABLE. Statistics are hard to come by — the era predated census bureaus and questionnaires — but evidence compiled by historians allows a broad generalization: the average white colonial ate more food, and especially more meat, than anyone on the planet (aside from queens, czars, and other exceptionally privileged persons). Across Europe, a non-royal was lucky to see meat once or twice a week. A typical colonial adult male, in contrast, put away about two hundred pounds a year. (Enslaved people were chronically underfed and ate less of every kind of food.)[8]

Anecdotal evidence supports the estimates. A man who visited Pennsylvania in the 1750s marveled at the abundance of beef cattle. "[E]ven in the humblest or poorest houses, no meals are served without a meat course."[9] Servants accustomed to scraps and scraping by in the Old World assumed and expected hefty meat rations in the New. One visitor recorded an encounter with an indentured servant who had run away "because he thought he ought to have meat every day" and his master refused to cooperate.[10]

Another servant, William Clutton, threatened to strike. It was the "Custom of [the] Country for servants to have meat 3 times a week," but his skinflint master, one Thomas Beale, served only rations of bread and cheese. Officials charged Clutton with mutiny and sedition, but when he was hauled to court, Master Beale's cheapskatery backfired: several people testified that Clutton was a "very honest civill [sic] person." He paid his court costs and walked free, presumably headed back to work and the meat to which he believed he was entitled.[11]

Over time, carnivorous paradise begot lethal legacy. The abundance of meat spawned waste and fostered indifference bordering on cruelty. "The Cattle of Carolina are very fat in Summer," charged one critic, but bone bags in winter because their owners refused to protect them from "cold Rains, Frosts, and Snows."[12]

Settlers dismissed such criticisms, claiming they could spare neither time nor labor to build animal shelters or fencing, occupied as they were with "too many other Affairs." (That their free-roaming livestock placed them on the same plane as the natives they despised was an irony white settlers chose to ignore.) As a result, cattle and hogs scattered their droppings hither and yon, left uncollected because no one would spare the labor to gather and spread them on corn and tobacco fields.[13]

As years passed and settlers exhausted and overgrazed their land, they simply moved on to fresh ground. And why not? In the New World, millions of acres lay just over the horizon.

Thus developed a cycle of destructive extravagance that Americans would pass from one generation to the next.

Abundance of land nurtured an abundance of the livestock that enabled settlers to eat well and to accumulate tangible wealth with a minimal investment of labor. The more livestock a household owned, the more secure its financial future, and the more meat-centric its diet. The more meat-centric the expectations, the more land they wanted, especially for cattle: a single adult bovine required anywhere from five to twenty grazing acres.

Livestock lust fractured communities. William Bradford, Pilgrim leader at Plymouth, Massachusetts, complained that "no man now thought he could live except he had cattle and a great deal of ground to keep them." "[T]here was no longer any holding [settlers] together." They needed "great lots," in order to keep cattle. As a result, his people "were scattered all over the Bay" and their original settlement lay "thin and . . . desolate." Bradford feared cattle lust would bring "the Lord's displeasure" down on them and "be the ruin of New England."[14]

And not only the Lord's. As whites migrated in search of fresh meadow and forest for their livestock, cattle tromped through natives' patches of beans and squash, and hogs rooted up their caches of corn. Some white settlers deliberately set animals loose in order to push Indians deeper into the interior.

A member of the Narragansett tribe voiced a common grievance: Once upon a time the tribe had luxuriated in an abundance of "deer and skins." No more. Now "the English" had stolen the land and allowed "their cows and horses [to] eat the grass; and their hogs [to] spoil [the] clam banks."[15]

"Your hogs & Cattle injure Us," lamented another man in 1666. "You come too near Us to live & drive Us from place to place. We can fly no farther." He begged the Maryland legislature to "let [his people] know where to live & how to be secured for the future from the Hogs & Cattle."[16]

The answer? Nowhere. Courts refused to listen to natives' complaints; colonial assemblies ignored treaties.

Natives in their turn used whites' desire for livestock against their enemy. In encounter after encounter, Indians stole, slaughtered, tortured, and mutilated livestock, because doing so struck at the heart of what it meant to be white and European.

When a group of Narragansetts seized one white man, they forced him to watch as they killed five of his cattle. "[W]hat will Cattell now doe you good?" they asked. Another group warned that they stood prepared to fight. "You must consider," they told their white foes, "the Indians lost nothing but their life; you must lose your fair houses and cattle."[17]

The two years of ambush, torching, and retribution that followed that encounter left seven thousand Indians dead as compared to three thousand whites. But the natives slaughtered eight thousand head of whites' cattle.

Other livestock-driven battles would follow, but whites would win the war. They would convert large chunks of the continent into a livestock trail epic in size and in its demands on the land and its people.

As the decades passed, colonists gradually abandoned hands-off livestock husbandry in favor of more deliberate, commercial production, thanks to two lures.

The first was urban growth along the colonial seaboard. Towns and cities were few, but their inhabitants needed food. The second was the lucrative intracoastal and international trade in barreled meats, available to them because they were British colonials. [18]

In New-York, Philadelphia, and other port towns, commission agents and ship owners dispatched cattle near and far. To the southernmost Atlantic coast colonies, where landowners devoted land and enslaved labor to tobacco, and preferred to let others raise beef on their behalf. To Caribbean-based British and French plantations. To England and Europe as food for growing populations there.

One colonial cattle and hog economy flourished in the valley of the Potomac South Branch River in what is now the northeastern corner of West Virginia.

The area consisted of fertile bottomland suitable for planting, and hills thick with forage grass. In summer, South Branch farmers grew corn in the lowlands while cattle grazed upland. Come fall, they cut cornstalks to the ground, leaving the ears intact, and piled the "shocks" throughout their fields for cattle feed. As stock fed, they deposited manure (including corn; they could not digest the kernels), which provided fertilizer for the next growing season.

Once the cattle had devoured the shocks in a field, hands led them to a new location and fresh stocks, and herded hogs into the first field. The porcines snuffled up the leavings, including the corn kernels, and deposited their own manure.

Settlers planted this corn-cattle-hog complex along the central Atlantic seaboard, modifying it to suit local climate, terrain, and soil.

BY THE TIME WHITE AMERICANS REBELLED AGAINST THEIR COLONIAL overlords, many regarded access to meat, especially beef, as a mark of being an American, an entitlement. To that end, over the next two centuries, they built an American way of meat designed to accommodate this right.

And as we will see, Americans were prepared to pay any price for that American plenty.

I. BUILDING AN AMERICAN WAY OF MEAT

CHAPTER 1
CARNIVORE AMERICA

IN EARLY 1822, ELEVEN-YEAR-OLD PHINEAS T. BARNUM (1810-1891) was hired to help drive cattle from his home in rural Connecticut to New-York City. The boy had heard of the fabled York, as it was then called. No country corner, it was a proper city (population 124,000), situated on an island, no less, and surely full of wonders. Now he would visit.[1]

Off he went with the drover and the other hands. The group likely traveled a heavily trafficked cattle road that ran parallel to the Hudson River, all the way down to King's Bridge, where they crossed from the mainland to the northern end of Manhattan Island. From there they traveled south another ten or so miles along the Boston/Bowery Road to the northernmost fringe of the city, where they stopped at the Bull's Head tavern at Canal Street, the place where livestock sellers and buyers ate, drank, and conducted business on behalf of the stomachs of York.

Barnum's crew settled the cattle in a stockyard, and themselves at the Bull's Head. And then P.T. had five days to explore the city before his crew returned to Connecticut.

He spent the first few days shopping, as Americans did, using coin and barter to obtain (and discard) a variety of items, including a top, a knife, oranges, and firecrackers. Having thus depleted his coin and goods, he devoted the rest of his time to the (free) pleasure that is urban sightseeing.

Among York's attractions were its famed public markets, of which there were nine when Barnum visited. The smallest were conducted in the centers of selected streets, and consisted of a long string of covered stalls and tables. The biggest were grand brick affairs, often two stories and sometimes covering an entire block. Immense openings on all four sides accommodated the thousands bustling through every morning.

The attraction was food. Row after row of stalls, tables, and counters stacked, piled, and covered, with food:

Oysters, lobster, shrimp. All manner of fish. Fresh produce during the growing season; root vegetables in cold weather while supplies lasted. Chickens, pheasants, and other fowl; ham, sausages, and dried beef. Eggs, cheese, butter, and milk (the latter the most perishable of foods).

And fresh meat, especially beef.

Butchers' stalls offered a wonderland of fleshy viand. Beef sides and quarters hung from iron hooks. Piles of steaks and ribs, roasts and loins awaited shoppers. Behind their counters, butchers cut meats to order for customers waiting in line.

Young Phineas was flabbergasted. He'd never seen so much fresh meat — and beef, no less!

He was a country boy, and country folk didn't eat fresh beef. A cow carcass served up hundreds of pounds of meat, too much for a single household, and too valuable to withhold from an urban market whose denizens expected fresh beef every day.[2]

To Barnum's mind and eyes, such "immense quantities of meat" were "incredible."

So incredible that his inner cynic took charge. "What under heaven do they expect to do with all this meat?" Barnum asked a young man who had joined him on his tours around town.

"They expect to sell it, of course."

Barnum scoffed.

"They'll get sucked in then," he assured his older companion, at age eleven already confident in his ability to spot suckers and scams. It was impossible "to consume all that beef before doomsday."

Years later, an older, wiser (and wealthier and famed) Barnum admitted his naiveté. In truth, he wrote in a mid-century memoir, he was the fool. The meat he saw stacked to the heavens was "probably all masticated within the next twenty-four hours."[3]

A CITY MAY SEEM A STRANGE PLACE TO OPEN A HISTORY OF carnivorous America. But it was cities that prompted Americans to make meat on a grand scale, and sell it at an affordable price. From their efforts would come, eventually, all the things many people love to hate now: antibiotics and factory farms; CAFOs and Big Ag and Big Food.

This history of the American way of meat is built on a salient fact: city dwellers don't make their own food. They rely on others to do that for them. The more city dwellers there are, the harder farmers must work to feed them; historically, as urban populations grow, farmers' numbers decline.[4]

To be clear: in 1822, the overwhelming majority of the US population lived in a rural area, and typically on a farm. The nation then boasted 9.6 million inhabitants — roughly the population of 2024 New Jersey, spread over states and territories as far west as the Mississippi River and beyond. Fewer than 700,000 of them lived in a town or city, but they clustered along the Atlantic seaboard from Boston to Baltimore.

In Massachusetts, for example, sixty percent of the population lived in an urban place. Collectively, the residents of New-York, Brooklyn, and Philadelphia represented five percent of the entire US population.

New-York provides an excellent starting point. Think of it as a living laboratory where Americans learned to assemble the acreage, people, skills, tools, and animals necessary to supply a sizable city with fresh meat every day.

In 1822, York was the new nation's largest and most important urban assemblage. Perched on the southern tip of Manhattan Island just off the coast of New York state, it was surrounded by waterways and harbors, including the mouth of the Hudson River, the main passageway to interior upstate New York.

A view of New-York in 1851. When Barnum visited in 1820, the population was centered on the the very tip of the island, in the lower center of the image.

White Europeans had occupied the site since the early 1600s, testament to its strategic and military value. When colonial Americans launched a war for independence, the British were quick to capture and occupy York. After all, having built much of island's fortifications, the Redcoats knew that Manhattan Island was a superb staging ground for their war with the colonials.

After the revolution, the city served, briefly, as the capital of both the United States and New York state. By the 1820s, its financiers, banks, commission houses, docks, wharves, and warehouses were the nation's most significant.

And New-Yorkers could not begin to feed themselves, let alone the thousands who descended on the city daily for business, pleasure, or to begin new lives as Americans.

In the 1820s, the city consumed 150 pounds of *fresh* meat, mostly beef, per person per year. That one dietary demand necessitated the delivery and slaughter of tens of thousands of animals a year. Add in ham, sausage, bacon, and dried beef, as well as eggs and milk, potatoes, onions, and tons of wheat — and the magnitude of urban food logistics becomes clear.[5]

Sourcing and delivering foodstuffs was no small matter in a two-mile-an-hour world. Some cattle arrived by ferry, but most walked to Manhattan from the mainland, herded by cow hands like young Barnum. These days, the drover's trek that he made can be traveled in a few hours (depending on traffic). He and his fellow cattle hands spent days, if not weeks, on the road.

From this distance, it's also difficult to grasp the chronic sense of uncertainty and urgency that anchored these logistics. In the 1820s, both war and the specter of food scarcity were never far from mind. A well-fed city endures siege better than one that is not. A well-fed city is a stable, peaceful city. A starving city is a riotous mob.

Thus the public markets. People needed to eat well, at a reasonable price, because the city's security depended on it. As one historian has phrased it, food was a "public good." Public markets were a fundament of urban security and civil order. The city's charter empowered a Common Council to build and operate such markets, and set their hours, rules, and prices.[6]

A rendering of Washington Market, c. 1851. It sat near the Hudson River, and ship masts can be seen in the background.

And not only the markets. The docks, wharves, and warehouses strung along the Hudson and East rivers were a major entry point for any and all goods coming across the Atlantic. And for foodstuffs arriving from York's hinterlands. Those included Long Island and northern Manhattan Island, where households engaged in "truck" farming, making eggs and vegetables for city people, to New Jersey, Connecticut, and the Westchester region of mainland New York state.

Every day, hundreds of watercraft cruised the region's coastlines and bays, stopping at town landings to collect corn and hogs, eggs and potatoes, beans and greens destined for York. The city's waterways featured a lively, daily parade: row and pole boats, canoes and barges, and sloops specially designed to navigate the often tricky and sometimes treacherous East River. Ferries shuttled back and forth between Manhattan and Brooklyn, which sat across the river on Long Island, and served as a major conduit for York's food supplies.[7]

MOST OF THOSE GOODS WENT DIRECTLY TO MARKET. CATTLE AND hogs, however, followed a different path. They were slaughtered and butchered — processed — into meat. That was the work and domain of the brotherhood of butchers, a close-knit community of white families that had provided York with meat for generations. They clustered together in a neighborhood just south of the stockyards. Butcherville consisted of their homes, kill sheds, and accommodations for tools, equipment, and apprentices.

The male leaders of this tribe were skilled master butchers. Only they were licensed to purvey fresh meats to residents, and only in the public markets. It was they who occupied each market's prime stalls, a benefit granted them by the city. In exchange for that real estate, butchers paid a portion of their take to the city to support market maintenance.[8]

On sale days, the masters were up early to buy stock at the yards. When the market closed at noon, butchers and drovers retired to the Bull's Head to close their deals and talk business and politics.

While the master butcher tippled, his journeymen and apprentices herded the stock to Butcherville, where they slaughtered it, breaking carcasses into sides and popular smaller cuts.

In the wee hours of the following morning, weary apprentices loaded meat onto carts, often hand-wheeled barrows, and headed south to the city and their masters' respective market stalls. They slung sides and quarters over iron hooks, and organized small cuts on the butcher's tables, mostly beef but also mutton and pork.[9]

As unofficial mayors of the markets, butchers often organized events designed to lure custom to their stalls. In early 1821, a Fly Market butcher announced plans for an elaborate display and sale of beef from twenty-one "premium" cattle. To whet the public's appetite, he and his crew paraded the beef in forty decorated carts, one of which carried the silver pitchers the live stock had won at the New York State Agricultural Show.[10]

A few years later, two ambitious young butchers, new to their assigned market, exhibited two seven-year-old "Fat oxen," which they claimed were "superior" to "any thing of the kind ever offered in this market."[sic] The beasts were too large to trudge the streets, so the men herded them to a nearby park for display before they were taken to a killshed for slaughter.[11]

Butchers also promoted their wares and skill with house-to-house cattle parades. Typically, musicians led the way, followed by the host butcher and his cattle, hauled by wagon, the better to both display and protect them. Wagonloads of fellow butchers followed, all dressed in clean slaughtering "aprons and sleeves." The parade stopped at the houses of the host's clientele, and the band struck up brass, reed, and string, the better to encourage the occupants to claim a piece of the beef that was to be.[12]

THESE EXPRESSIONS OF AMERICAN ABUNDANCE WERE NOT LOST ON visitors from abroad. A Scotsman who toured York's markets concluded that Edinburgh had nothing to compare. Like Barnum, he was startled by the quantities of food, and astounded by the sight of "mechanics and cartmen" and other common laborers buying fresh beef for their tables.[13]

In a letter to friends back home, an English immigrant reported that he could "buy the best of meat" at a low price. When one Irishman wrote home with news that he ate meat twice a day, his employer asked why he would lie about the matter; he ate meat at every meal. Because, the man replied, no one back home would believe it.[14]

Newcomers had fair warning: the city's Shamrock Society urged newly arrived Irish to go easy on the meat: their bodies were not accustomed to the American "abundance of animal food." Overindulge, the group warned, and the resulting "diarrhoea" would "throw them on their backs."[15]

One immigrant measured Americans' carnivorous appetites by piles of urban slaughterhouse wastes: "hundreds of calves' heads, large bits, and whole joints of meat," unwanted and unused, except by "street hogs." In "*any other country*," he marveled, all of it "would be sold at some price or other." But in the United States, only "free negroes" would "think of eating . . . head and pluck [organs]" and other lesser parts.[16]

"There are few things in the habits of Americans, which strike the foreign observer with more force," mused one writer, "than the extravagant consumption of . . . meat." "Truly we may be called a carnivorous people."[17]

WHITE URBAN AMERICANS' MEAT CONSUMPTION WAS ABOUT MORE than carnivorous cravings. Easy access to an abundance of beef testified to an American way of life, and the ease with which white citizens pursued life, liberty and happiness. To be a white American was to enjoy foods and fancies that only elites enjoyed elsewhere. Indeed, white Americans regarded the freedom to buy what they wanted as a right.

Nowhere was that more obvious than in New-York. On any given day, the city's docks and shops were piled and stuffed, crammed and jammed, with the latest in European fashion and frivolity. York's thousands enjoyed first dibs on bonnets and scarves and buckles and boots. In America, noted one visitor, even the "poorer class of females" flaunted "a ten dollar hat, [and] a thirty dollar shawl, with silk and lace."[18]

Working men, noted an English tourist, were "extremely well clothed" and made not the "slightest approaches to servility" that he would have expected from such folk back home, where workers tugged their forelocks and all but bowed to their (alleged) betters. White Americans would shake your hand; they would not bow or curtsey.[19]

Boots and ribbons, furniture and mirrors, upright posture and confidence, and meat on every plate: these were the marks of free, white Americans.

A young New-Yorker affirmed that point one day when he snatched a "chinchilla hat from off the head of a negress, stamped on it, and then threw it into the gutter, where it was rapidly borne down the street."

When a startled bystander asked why, the man replied that he had "just paid eighteen dollars for a chinchilla hat for my sister, and I don't mean that any n—ger-wench shall wear one like it, while I know it."[20]

ENTITLEMENT AND A RELENTLESS GROWTH IN POPULATION SWUNG A wrecking ball at York's public markets. In 1820, citizens numbered 124,000. In 1830, 203,000. A decade later, 313,000.

As population pushed north, and away from the island's crowded tip, increasing numbers of Yorkers lived a mile or more from the nearest public market. Citizens clamored for more venues, but the Common Council turned a deaf ear. Each market represented a significant investment in real estate and infrastructure, maintenance and bookkeeping. Every dollar spent on public markets was a dollar that could not be spent on other needs, including a municipal water system, something New-Yorkers craved.

Food prices also soared, as the city outgrew its foodshed and Yorkers competed for foodstuffs with hundreds of new towns in the interior. By the 1830s, the beef that Yorkers ate, for example, often began life hundreds of miles away, in Ohio, Indiana, and other new "western" states, a trek that added to the cost of beef.

The citizenry had little interest in logistics or foodshed capacity. All they knew was that daily provisioning required a longer walk and therefore more time, and cost more, too. And for that state of affairs, they blamed butchers and the Common Council.

Consider the 1830 campaign by the "General Executive Committee of Mechanics, Workingmen, and those friendly to their interests." The group argued that York's hardworking citizens were entitled to buy meat in a free market, preferably one close to home. By restricting beef sales to official markets, the Common Council violated "the just and republican principle . . . that taxation should follow property," not food.[21]

The committee denounced the public markets as a monopoly that imposed unfair taxes on citizens, and argued that the brotherhood was complicit: butchers were required to pay "rent and other dues" to the city, but they passed that expense on to "consumers" as an indirect tax. Who were the consumers forced to pay these "exorbitant taxes?" "We reply all the citizens," the Committee proclaimed.[22]

Other critics noted that the city boasted thousands of skilled butchers, many of them immigrants, far more than the city's official markets could accommodate. But ordinances forbid those butchers from exercising their right to earn "a livelihood for themselves and their families," and "impos[ed] a tax upon [the] time" of residents who lived far from an official market.[23]

In short, the markets were an "odious monopoly." And Americans hated monopolists.[24]

Monopolies, one Yorker explained, granted "exclusive privileges" to "individuals or companies" and transformed "a general right into an exclusive one," thereby depriving others of an opportunity to pursue that path. Worse, having won "sole command" of a good, the monopolist "compels the public to pay twice or thrice as much for it" than if the item were "open and free to competition." Monopolists "take from the many to give to the few."[25]

According to this critic, the mayor and Common Council were

among the worst monopolists. Via public markets, they restricted access to "many of the most necessary articles of comfort and convenience," including fresh beef, which butchers monopolized in collusion with city officials. Thanks to these villains, the price of beef was "excessively increased, and many a poor man deprived of a piece."[26]

The brotherhood of butchers objected.

They were neither "aristocrats," as some critics complained, nor "monopolists." The brotherhood protected New-Yorkers from "bad and unwholesome provisions," such as meat from animals that died of "accident or disease." The butchers' skill and the city's regulations served as bulwarks "against the fraud and impositions of unlicensed and unskillful persons professing to be butchers." Municipal control of meat supplies and butchers' licenses benefited "the whole community."[27]

Citizens voted with their feet. In growing numbers, they abandoned public markets and licensed butchers for (mostly illegal) food and meat vendors in their own neighborhoods.

In the late 1830s, the Common Council ordered an investigation. The men appointed to study the situation threw up their hands in defeat. It was "impossible," they concluded, "to prevent the continual and systematic violation of the Market Laws" that restricted meat sales to public markets.

A few years later, an 1840 Common Council report came down on the side of citizens: the public market's "restrictive features" were "unconstitutional, oppressive, and unjust." Two years later, the Council granted all butchers the freedom to "sell fresh meat in places other than public markets."[28]

For better, for worse, New-Yorkers would now buy beef and other foods free of the city monopoly.

AS FOODSTUFFS TRAVELED LONGER DISTANCES TO FEED EASTERN cities, urbanites recognized the necessity of devising new logistics to feed themselves. In that, they were inspired and motivated by the three-year War of 1812.

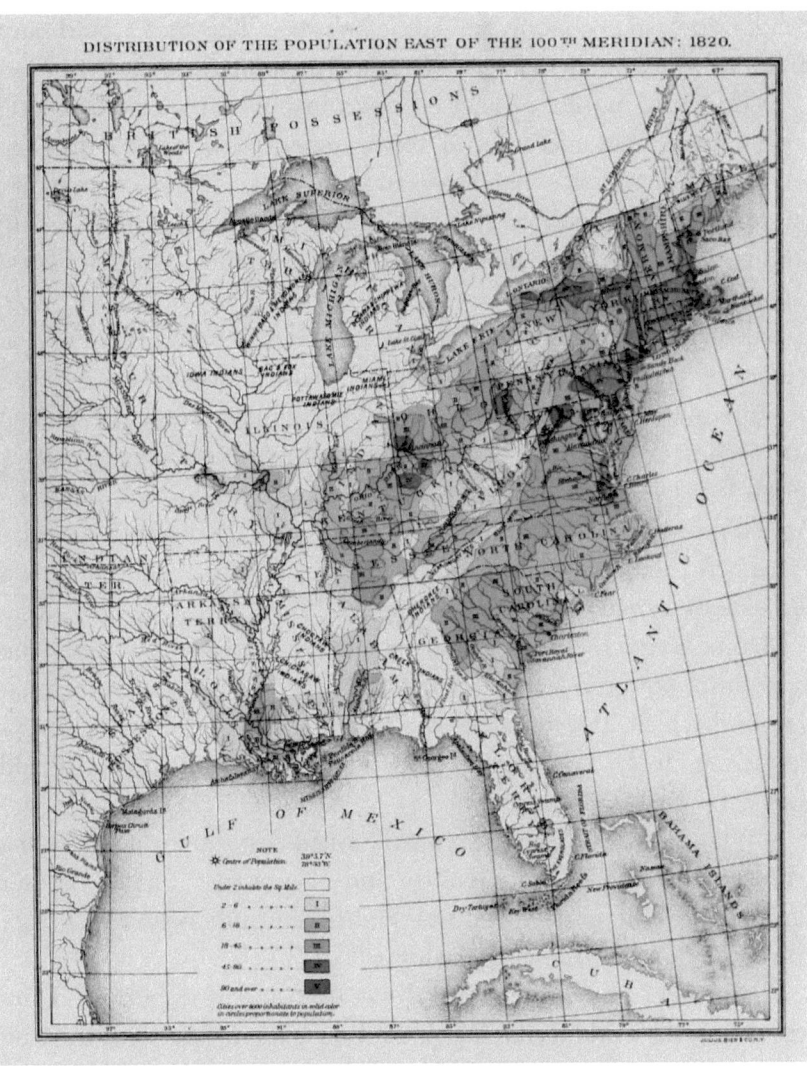

DISTRIBUTION OF THE POPULATION EAST OF THE 100TH MERIDIAN: 1820.

The Ohio River is the spine of the dark crawl of population to the southwest. The Slave Region sprawls along the mid- and lower Atlantic coast. The middle of nowhere coloring on the Gulf of Mexico is New Orleans and vicinity. In the 1820s, Slave Region interests engaged in aggressive occupation of the deep south in order to plant enslavement. A decade later, this map looked quite different.

That event forced Americans to accept a hard truth: they would only be respected by other nations when they no longer relied on those nations. Americans must declare economic independence and build a domestic economy; a "home" market. This idea would have profound consequences for livestock and meat production.[29]

The home market project emerged in the "Greater Northeast" — the dense agglomeration of towns, cities, ports, and farms clustered in the nation's northeastern quadrant. There, merchants, farmers, bankers, elected officials, and others banded together to construct a domestic economy based on agriculture, manufacturing, and commerce.[30]

Agriculture anchored this home market trinity. Agriculture was existential. Without it, people starved. With it, Americans enjoyed the (literal) energy to unload ships, dig canals, keep shops, and operate factory looms. Agriculture seeded manufacturing: livestock hides for leather, cotton for fabric, grain for urban bakeries. Agriculture nurtured commerce and enriched the nation's treasury as exports. According to one observer, the "welfare of the state" and the state of agriculture were one and the same.[31]

Home-market crusaders carried the banner for an American agriculture powered less by brute force than by science and technology, and which incorporated every labor-, time-, soil-saving, crop-improving tool, implement, and idea American minds could conceive.

"Who are the farmer's servants?" asked one supporter. "Not the Irish, nor the coolies, but Geology and Chemistry." Or, as another phrased it, "Chemistry, Natural Philosophy and Natural History constitute the *grammar* of Agriculture."[32]

Reformers were inspired by New-York and its foodshed. Here was a superb, working model of the home market ideal: a thriving urban hub of commerce, banking, and manufacture, fed by a prosperous hinterland where farm families practiced scientific agriculture. Americans would gain true independence by landscaping the nation's interior with hundreds of New-Yorks, thousands of factories, and millions of farms.

"INTERNAL IMPROVEMENTS" EASED THE WAY: OVERLAND TURNPIKE and toll roads, canals and railroads, typically built by combinations of state and private money, and federal legislation that eased the acquisition of necessary land.

The most notable of these internal improvements was also one of the first: the Erie Canal, tailor-made to enhance New-York's role as gateway to and chief entrepôt for the North American interior. According to one happy resident, this "stupendous undertaking" would transform the city into "the Emporium of the Lakes & the ocean." When Yorkers celebrated the canal's opening with a mass parade, a banner on one float reminded celebrants of the point of the pomp: "Internal Improvements are Chains to strengthen the Union of the States."[33]

The Erie was only the beginning. In the 1820s and 1830s, Americans dug three thousand miles of canals. In the thirties and forties, they laid seven thousand miles of railed roads. These improvements connected eastern cities with, for example, grain harvests and livestock in the Ohio River valley, which emerged as the urban east's new foodshed.

The Ohio River flows from its head in western Pennsylvania to the southern tip of Illinois, where its mouth spills into the Mississippi. On both sides lay millions of acres of rich prairie soil and grasses laced together by an extensive riverine system. The Ohio also marked the nation's primary social and agricultural divisions: On its left bank lay slave states with (mostly) agricultural economies that (mostly) rested on enslaved labor. On the right bank lay the free, (mostly) white states of the Greater Northeast's agricultural frontier.[34]

It was there that white migrants by the millions seeded the home market ideal, and elaborated on the colonial corn-cattle-hog complex.[35]

Hogs were central to the Ohio valley's economies. The "principal object pursued at this time," commented an Indiana newspaper editor in 1824, was "to raise a crop of corn and a great number of hogs."[36]

But not just any hogs. Agricultural reformers urged farmers to practice hog "management" that included "regular and systematic feeding" (as opposed to relying on foraging), and "suitable shelters, yards, water, [and] conveniences for breeding." The investment paid off at market: a well-bred, corn-fed hog earned 30 to 60 percent more than scavenger swine.[37]

Getting hogs to market wasn't easy. The drive leader rode on horseback followed by a half dozen or more men on foot who kept the animals in line. Hogs that fell prey to exhaustion were tossed into a wagon that trailed the herd. The day ended at a tavern where the crew corralled the hogs, and cleaned, fed, and watered their horses.

The men cleaned up, too, typically standing in a tub of water for a quick scrub with a broom. "After a slug or two of whiskey," one hand recalled, "we had a supper of hot biscuits with honey or maple syrup and a slab of ham." At daybreak, the routine began anew. Ten or twelve miles a day, for as long as it took to get to market: a week, three, a month or more.[38]

Hog slaughter and pork processing shaped the river's first great white settlement, Cincinnati, Queen City of the Ohio. Also known as Porkopolis. Slaughterhouses and packing plants lined its streets, some mere shacks, others two- and three-story structures, many of them brick.

Hands drove hogs into a pen, packing them tightly so the kill man could walk across their backs as he slammed their heads with a metal sledge-hammer. Others dumped the carcasses into boiling water for soaking, the easier to loosen bristles and hair. Another crew beheaded and gutted what was left. Workers trundled the offal to rendering vats, and hung carcasses on iron hooks.[39]

Cincinnati's market was the world. Ohio-barreled pork, ham, and sausage fed factory workers in England, armies in Europe, and ship crews navigating the seas. British firms set up shop on the Ohio, and German immigrants gravitated to the region; the latter brought Old World butchering skills and cuisine and transformed meat scraps into sausage, and head, feet, and organs into headcheese.

An 1870 rendering of slaughter operations at a facility in Cincinnati. In real life, the place looked nothing like this pristine property.

Hog slaughter gave rise to other urban industries. Hog bristles and hair ended up in mattresses and hairbrushes. Bone became button; blood, dye and ink. And lard emerged as "the very oil that moves the machinery of life."[40]

Lard was a low-cost substitute for butter and other fats. It lubricated the metal machines that were beginning to replace those made of wood. It was central to soap manufacture; Procter & Gamble was born on the banks of the Ohio. It even made light after inventors in the early 1840's perfected a commercially viable method of manufacturing lard-based lamp oil (the market for flammable whale oil promptly collapsed).

CATTLE ALSO CONTRIBUTED TO THE RIVER VALLEY'S ECONOMIES.

On the "cattleman's frontier" of Illinois and Indiana, for example, some prairie cattle kings owned as many as a thousand head. They grazed stock on grass until the animals were two or three years old, and ready for sale to "graziers" who fattened the stock on forage grass, the remains of grain and grass harvests.

Cattle were ready for market at age four to six years. Some went directly to slaughter. But many were purchased by eastern "feeders" who "finished" the cattle on corn, fine-tuning the animals' fat and muscle before sending them to market, at which point their weight ranged from 1,600 to 2,000 pounds.[41]

In those days, drovers like the one who hired Phineas Barnum choreographed the task of moving hundreds, sometimes thousands, of cattle, hundreds, even as much as a thousand, miles from farm to market. Drovers typically walked the animals on rough overland roads that connected the interior Ohio valley to coastal cities and markets.

Some went north to Buffalo, there to travel by canal to cities hither and yon. Some went up and over the Allegheny mountains. On the other side, drovers often sold their haul on the spot to buyers who serviced urban slaughterhouses.[42]

In summer and fall, cattle clogged overland roads, marching two by two, each plodding through tracks laid by those ahead. The bovine multitude could be seen a mile away, wrote one drover, thanks to "long moving lines of rising dust."[43]

Despite the bovines' placid nature, keeping so many cattle in line and in motion was not easy. One drover nearly lost his herd when someone on board a passing steamboat let loose with the vessel's whistle.

The ear-piercing shriek sent the cattle "up the river as if the deuce was in them." The drover galloped after his charges and rode for a mile and a half before he reached the head of the line and calmed the runaways. He'd no sooner restored order than the steamboat caught up with him and the herd, and blasted its whistle again.[44]

"The name of the captain of the boat I knew not," reported the angry drover, "but I wish to caution the public against a man of such mean and disgraceful conduct."

STARTING IN THE 1840s, RAILROADS TURNED LIVESTOCK transportation logistics upside down and inside out, shaping new transit patterns that did not depend on water. Railroads were the great wonder of the age, novel and startling in their speed, size, and complexity. Some lines spanned hundreds of miles, and all carried goods faster than wagons trundling overland roads or steamboats chugging sluggish riverine paths.

They also required considerable start-up capital: In the 1850s, a high-end commercial steamboat cost $60,000, but a railroad company needed at least $5 million just to get started. Some lines boasted capitalization in the tens of millions.[45]

One of the first great byproducts of the railroad age was Chicago. If New-York was the laboratory and model for urban food delivery, Chicago was where Americans mastered the logistics of moving immense quantities of live animals and other foodstuffs long distances.[46]

Chicago the municipality dates to 1830, but the site had been occupied for at least a thousand years: its location on the shore of an immense lake literally connected it to the world, thanks to the Mississippi and other rivers, and the collection of massive lakes that march across the continent north of the Ohio River.[47]

Chicago sat amongst millions of acres of rich soil and an abundance of rivers and lakes. In the 1830s and 1840s, prairie cattle kings, graziers, and feeders relied on Chicago as an entrepôt. Drovers herded stock to Chicago, from where steamboats carried it to Buffalo, and from there to New-York via the Erie Canal.

Chicago, crowed a local newspaper in 1845, was "destined to become the greatest beef market in the United States, if not the world."[48]

The railroads made it happen. From the outset, cattle and hogs factored heavily in railroaders' plans. All things agricultural were important, but livestock, especially cattle, offered a reliable and lucrative category of freight. In the early 1850s, a half dozen or so exceptionally well-funded railroads set out to capture what they could of the livestock and meat industries.

To that end, company owners organized spinoff corporations whose investors included stockyard owners, drovers, livestock commission agents, and meatpackers, the better to squeeze more than just freight rates from cattle and hogs. Such partnerships allowed each of the participants in meatmaking to increase their profits in the growing interior trade in livestock.[49]

By the late 1850s, Chicago boasted an oligopoly in its meat and livestock industries. It consisted of the railroads who backed the city's biggest livestock dealers and yard owners, and the most deep-pocketed of Chicago's meatpackers and livestock commission agents.

For example, the New York Central Railroad, which was cobbled together from smaller roads by a wealthy manufacturing magnate, organized the construction of a thirty-acre stockyard that accommodated 5,000 cattle and 30,000 hogs. That one company's ability to buy large quantities, and pay cash on the spot, hurt smaller yard owners.

So, too, only the largest corporations could afford to invest in the specially designed cars necessary to move livestock from west to east. These entities also built feed-and-watering stations along their tracks, the better to care for four-legged cargo en route, and to pick up more along the way.[50]

In 1864, owners of several of the city's rail and stockyard companies collectively invested $1 million ($278 million today) in the Chicago Union Stock Yard Company, the better to bring order to what had become a profitable but disorganized amalgamation of yards, packing plants, and railroads scattered all over the city. The gates opened on Christmas Day, 1865.

Among Chicago's early movers and shakers was Philip Armour (1832-1901), described by a contemporary as a "man of short legs, a huge trunk, heavy hands, a big head and a ruthless, mighty brain."[51]

Although he is most often associated with meatpacking, by his own admission he was neither stockman nor butcher. "[I]f you showed me a piece of meat," he once said, "I could not tell you what part of the bullock it came from." Instead, Armour made his early fortune gambling on commodities. He was interested in meat for the same reason he was interested in wheat, corn, coal, or gold: it offered opportunities for (legally) manipulating supplies and therefore prices, and thus for earning huge profits.[52]

Armour, who grew up in central New York, earned his first serious money during the California gold rush, when he built sluices that guided water on mined rivers. For this, he reportedly earned $8 thousand dollars; today that's roughly $300 thousand.

In the late 1850s, he landed in Milwaukee, also a Lake Michigan city. It boasted access to raw materials from the region's farms and forests, a robust and diverse economy, and proximity to Chicago.

There, Armour and a partner operated a commission house, selling grain and other provisions. Sensing war on the horizon, the pair bought a warehouse of whiskey, betting that if war came, Congress would raise taxes on liquor. War came; Congress did; the men profited.

In the early 1860s, John Plankinton (1820-1891), a Milwaukee power broker, offered him a partnership in his pork processing operation, the city's largest. Armour promptly impressed the older man by cornering the market in packed pork.

Corners were Armour's special delight, a fact he would demonstrate repeatedly during his life (to the dismay of his competitors). It worked like this: Plankinton and Armour signed "futures" contracts with hog dealers, agreeing to buy pork on a specific date in the future.[53]

At the same time, the two men quietly purchased as much pork as they could lay hands on. When the futures contracts came due, the saps who'd agreed to deliver pork to Plankinton and Armour discovered that there was none to be had.

Except, of course, from P&A, who, having "cornered" the supply, could charge whatever price they wanted.

The partners reportedly earned somewhere between $1 and $2 million from the (legal) scheme; many rivals collapsed under the weight of their costly mistake. P&A used the returns to expand Milwaukee holdings and launch a pork-packing venture in Kansas City, Missouri.

But neither Kansas City nor Milwaukee could satisfy Phil Armour's ambitions. A few years later, he and Plankinton parted ways (theirs was an amicable separation), and he headed to Chicago, where he founded Armour and Company, orchestrated corners, built a pork-processing plant, and acquired a beef-canning facility. And Phil Armour was only getting started. Over the next three decades, he and his "mighty brain" shaped and dominated American meatpacking and much of the nation's fast-growing, long-distance food logistics.[54]

BY THE LATE 1850s, MORE THAN HALF OF NEW-YORK'S LIVESTOCK arrived by rail, and almost certainly via the Chicago-New York railroad/stockyard/slaughterhouse entities.

The city's largest stockyards sat on its waterfronts, and on those of New Jersey directly across the Hudson. New-York also boasted a handful of new "industrial" slaughterhouses that processed hundreds of animals a day, built and operated by many of the same investors associated with railroads and stockyards in Chicago.[55]

Add in hundreds of small killsheds and butcher shops, and the project of herding livestock from docks and rail yards to stockyards and slaughterhouses spawned an endless animal parade.

Pedestrians scattered as cattle — a quarter million a year — plodded through streets jammed with carts and horses, top-hatted lawyers and bankers, servants toting baskets and bags, and shopkeepers standing watch over sidewalk displays. Squealing hogs raced through streets and lanes, forcing pedestrians, carriages, and carts to give way. Drovers used whips to keep them in line, but the more willful swine charged into alleys or through shop doors, chased by boys hired to tackle and drag them back to the parade.[56]

Calves and lambs, prized for their tender flesh, could not be trusted to their own legs or the streets' hazards, so teamsters tossed them onto wooden carts, lacing rope about their feet and necks to prevent them from moving. If a wooden wheel collided with a particularly deep rut or a dried hump of mud, an animal or two might fly out of the cart and into the road.

Then there was the business of converting live stock into meat, a process that cloaked many neighborhoods in a gag-inducing stench. Islands of waste landscaped the alleys adjacent to the butcheries and slaughterhouses.

Legs and heads; hooves, ears, and snouts. Intestines and feces. Piles of stomachs, eyeballs, and brains. Blood and urine coursed along walkways into the streets, then meandered toward the local sewer trench, typically nothing more than a shallow trough running down the side or center of the road.

In spring and summer, the air sagged with a thick blanket of odor. Winter's cold alleviated the miasma but coaxed clouds of steam from the still-warm heaps of entrails.

Even the slaughterers weren't immune. One city butcher admitted that he "often lost a meal" when passing particularly noisome operations.[57]

The rag-and-bone men added to the mix. They collected slaughterhouse wastes, and boiled, steamed, and stewed them into components for glue, lard, buttons, dye, and brushes. They skinned legs, tossing tendons into barrels destined for glue factories. Hooves, the basis of Prussian Blue, went to dye houses.

Butcheries large and small nestled against residential neighborhoods, shared fences with schools, and backed onto churchyards. Throngs of children hung about to watch the work, hanging on every word of the "not very elegant language" of the butchers' world. Critics complained that the young became "habituated to scenes of blood and violence," a gory and three-dimensional nineteenth-century equivalent of the computer games that concern today's adults.[58]

In an earlier day and age, townspeople honored local butchers (when they weren't condemning them as monopolists). Midcentury New-Yorkers, however, regarded them as a literal legal nuisance.[59]

As one resident put it: "slaughter-houses in the very heart of thickly-populated regions . . . taint the air for a long distance about" and transform otherwise "healthful" neighborhoods into "loathsome and unwholesome localities." Should the millennium come, he hoped that those "abominable nuisances [would] be removed entirely" from the city.[60]

But stockyards, livestock parades, and slaughterhouses were only one ingredient in a rich stew of odor, filth, and muck.

Imagine your town — minus piped water. Minus plumbing and flush toilets. Minus sewer systems and zoning regulations.

Imagine block after block of tightly packed wooden structures, each illuminated by candles or oil-filled lanterns. Imagine "tenant-houses": shambling two- or three-story buildings crammed with hundreds of people sharing one or two outhouses.

Imagine animal teams pulling carts, carriages, wagons, and streetcars, and depositing tons of manure each day. Toss in the constant — and bewildering — presence of diseases whose causes no one understood and thus could not prevent: cholera, typhus, smallpox, dysentery, yellow fever, all of which routinely crawled the across Greater Northeast, and up and down the Mississippi and Ohio rivers, carried quickly and efficiently by steamboat and train.

Many urbanites held perfumed sachets to their faces when they were out and about. A scratch of a finger turned to sepsis with unnerving speed and regularity. Penicillin was eighty years away, and the "germ theory" a figment of scientists' imaginations.

Such were New-York and the nation's other midcentury "great" cities. The sheer mass of humanity made its point: if Americans planned to live in cities, they must manage those environments. It was time to re-think the business of making meat. Time to put it out of sight — and out of mind.

CHAPTER 2

OUT OF SIGHT, OUT OF MIND

On October 17, 1866, the owners of the New Jersey Stockyard and Market Company opened the doors of the Communipaw Abattoir. A thousand people showed up for the festivities: retail butchers and meatpackers; livestock dealers and drovers; city councilmen and other local officials.

The facility was the newest addition to a fifteen-acre collection of buildings, stockyards, and rail sidings that sat on the Hudson River in New Jersey, just opposite the southern tip of Manhattan. (Today the area is part of Liberty State Park.) The burgeoning "industrial" area was the work of many of the same people who, months earlier, had opened the gates of Chicago's Union Stock Yards.

The crowd trooped up, down, and around the yards, ramps, and kill floors. They peered into pens outfitted with water troughs and food bins, and examined steam engines, winches, belts, and vats, half listening as company executives touted Communipaw's virtues:

Capacity for twenty thousand cattle, and thirty thousand hogs and sheep (the former greatly outnumbered the latter). The capability to slaughter and dress two thousand head a day, with employees needing but a few minutes to transform a live animal into a market-ready carcass. An attached rendering operation transformed the "fat and refuse" into tallow, lard, and other byproducts.[1]

The event included a demonstration.

The Communipaw abattoir, as seen by an artist from *Frank Leslie's Illustrated Newspaper* shortly after the facility opened.

One man drove a steer onto the killing floor, and another cinched a hind leg with a sturdy rope dangling from an overhead winch. A hard yank upended the beast, leaving its jaw pressed into the ground, its throat taut and exposed. The "sticker" sliced through the animal's neck to the vertebrae. Another employee aimed a water hose at the woosh of blood.

A steam-powered conveyor whisked the carcass to a dressing table, where knife-wielding butchers dismantled it into sides and quarters. Sixteen minutes, start to finish.

Upstairs, efficiency unfolded to the accompaniment of piercing shrieks and rhythmic thuds. Humans herded hogs up a gangway into one of a series of pens, where a man armed with a mallet swung his weapon overhead. Thud. The mallet connected with the hog's skull.

Another man shoved the animal, which may or may not have died from the blow, down a short incline and into a vat of boiling water. The "fisher" crew ringed the vat, prodding the bloody stew with long iron hooks, shoving the hogs toward a revolving wheel that snagged carcasses and dumped them onto the scraping table.

There, a line of men armed with bristle-scrapers attacked each warm hulk, scraping it clean and pushing it down the line. The last man grabbed the beast's hind legs and tossed the carcass on to an overhead hook. One shove, and a pulley system carried its cargo to a duo armed with knife and hose. A quick jab and slice, a swoosh of water, another shove, and what was left of the animal dangled and swayed its way along a conveyor to the hanging room, which could hold thousands of carcasses.

Eventually the guests wandered back to the main floor where waiters had loaded four long tables with platters of ham and beef, bread and butter, fruit and nuts. Quart bottles of German wine stood every few feet along each table. The assembly devoured the lot in a matter of minutes, leaving nothing but "crumbs and empty bottles."

A post-prandial round of speechmaking and back-patting ensued. Thanks to the abattoir's efficient design, raved one speaker, the "entire hog can be saved, economized and utilized, from . . . his snout to the tip-end of his tail," everything "except the squeal." Communipaw, enthused another man, "will doubtless be the great live stock market of New-York City."

Then the president of the city's Board of Health took the stage to remind one and all why they were there.

This "stupendous" project, he told the audience, opened a new era in urban sanitation. The city's butchers could rent space at Communipaw, and thereby eliminate many, maybe most, of the city's slaughter shops. New-Yorkers would enjoy cleaner air and live-stock-free streets. Of this "humane and philanthropic work," he said "nothing in the world excels it in magnitude."[2]

IN THE YEARS JUST AFTER THE WAR OF THE REBELLION (1861-1865), the need for better urban management and more sanitary cities was one of the few matters on which Americans agreed. Over the next three decades, reformers tackled a host of improvements.

They organized centralized water supply and waste systems, the better to eradicate polluted public water pumps; overflowing public outhouses; and the open-air street troughs that served as sewers and typically carried all manner of wastes, from domestic to industrial and everything in between.

They funded urban parks, the better to freshen the air. Some devised ways to improve municipal governance and management. The Women's Christian Temperance Union waged war on urban drunkenness, and "social workers" devoted their energy to helping immigrants and others adapt to urban life in America.

Naturally, urban slaughter and meatpacking came under scrutiny.

Many denounced it as irredeemable: "old-fashioned, clumsy, wasteful," and a "dangerous source of filth." Farmers and country folk expected to live cheek by jowl with cows and pigs, but to a "crowded population," doing so was both "offensive and dangerous." The "nuisances" of meat production "depriv[ed]" urbanites of what they had "an inherent right to enjoy," namely, clean streets and pure air.[3]

Reformers embraced "great central slaughter-house[s]" like Communipaw, outfitted as they were with smoke filters and odor suppressors, conveyor belts and steam engines, and "[operated] under strict superintendence."[4]

It's easy to dismiss such ventures as examples of typical "corporate" manipulation and machination. That they were well-funded corporations is undeniable, but that suited urban leaders. A single entity was easier to deal with than hundreds of small business owners. The modernity of the new abattoir, and the speed with which livestock could be dispatched as meat to consumers, were virtues. Abattoirs promised to remove slaughter and processing from the eyes and noses of the citizenry.

OR NOT.

New-York's butchers wanted nothing to do with Communipaw or any other "great central slaughter-houses."

They denounced it and its ilk as "tyrannical and unjust, and contrary to the spirit of . . . free institutions." And illogical to boot: why, asked one butcher, would the people of New Jersey or "Long Island, or of any other place" welcome what New Yorkers had rejected as "an intolerable nuisance?"[5]

In Chicago, too, butchers balked at the prospect of being herded into a central slaughterhouse. That wrangle landed in the Illinois Supreme Court, where the judges sided with the butchers.

If butchers' shops were nuisances, explained the court, then an official slaughterhouse must also be a nuisance and, by the city's own ordinances, must also be banned. Worse, the city's insistence that butchers work out of a privately owned slaughterhouse was "oppressive, and create[d] a monopoly."[6]

What next? asked the judges. Would the city council grant similar monopolies to sellers of fruit, flour, or vegetables?

Such contests struck at the heart of a fundamental American dilemma: how to balance individuals' rights on one hand, and the public's welfare on the other. No wonder, then, that one such case ended up in the Supreme Court.

The "Slaughterhouse Cases" originated in New Orleans (population 191,000 in 1870). For years, residents had wrestled with the sanitary and health problems that accompany urban life at sea level in a near-tropical climate. Yellow fever paid regular visits, as did malaria, cholera, and other diseases.[7]

The business of making meat exacerbated those woes. The city's butchers (150 of them by one count) routinely tossed carcasses, blood, and other wastes into the city's main water source, the Mississippi River. As a result, putrefied offal clung to the mouths of municipal water-intake pipes. A waterworks employee spent his days "skimming the scum" that collected in the tanks that held piped water.[8]

In the late 1860s, New Orleans residents reached the end of their sanitary rope. They petitioned the city council for a centralized abattoir (a bayou Communipaw as it were). In early 1869, the Louisiana legislature obliged, empowering the Crescent City Live Stock Landing and Slaughter House Company to build a state-of-the-art slaughterhouse and rendering operation.

In an earlier day, New Orleans's white butchers might have cooperated with the project. But in 1869, the wounds of war lay fresh on the body politic.

White southerners resented the end of slavery and the presence of 4 million Black "freedmen." They loathed Yankee "carpetbaggers" who traveled south to either support the freedmen, or to use the chaos to grab profit and power. The Louisiana legislature that granted the franchise to Crescent City consisted largely of northerners and freedmen. Surely, white southerners believed, nothing from that body was legitimate.

The new law, the aggrieved butchers explained, threatened "the personal rights of the masses." We "hold these truths to be self evident," that "every [white] man in this community has a property in his person and his faculties." New Orleans butchers would never "submit" to a law that violated their "natural and constitutional rights."[9]

Such language resonated with white Americans in the years after the War of the Rebellion. Black Americans were now citizens, and in theory equal to whites. But most whites wanted nothing to do with racial equality, theoretical or otherwise. They seized every opportunity to assert white authority and supremacy. In effect, the New Orleans butchers argued that the proposed Slaughter House Company threatened whites' rights.

Lawsuits sprouted like mold after a flood, as butchers, the state, the city, the board of health, and the slaughterhouse franchisees filed suit and countersuit.

The gist of the many cases was this: the state of Louisiana claimed that it possessed the right to protect the public health; an abattoir was one way to do so. The butchers claimed that forcing them to conduct business in a privately owned slaughterhouse violated their rights as defined in the recently ratified Fourteenth Amendment to the Constitution. That addition directly addressed the matter of citizenship, and by extension, rights, and guaranteed "equal protection" for all.

The butchers carried their case to the Louisiana Supreme Court, which ruled against them.

The butchers possessed rights, the judges agreed, but the general "public" had rights, too. It was the job of "the state," in this case the Louisiana legislature, to use its police powers to protect public health. Doing so meant that sometimes some citizens lost some rights, but the majority benefitted in the long run. "Liberty," said the justices, "is the right to do what the law permits."[10]

Undaunted, the butchers appealed to the Supreme Court of the United States. There, too, they lost.

The court ruled that the Louisiana statute neither violated butchers' rights, nor constituted "deprivation of property." Nothing in the state law "deprive[d] the butchers of their right to exercise their trade"; it merely mandated the location where that slaughtering could occur. The public's health and welfare trumped private property and "natural" rights.[11]

JUDICIAL SPARRING CONTINUED FOR YEARS AS CITIES LARGE AND small struggled to create livable conditions — but some in the livestock and meat industries were already considering an alternative to urban slaughter.

Why ship live animals to New York? Why not kill cattle in, say, Chicago, and ship "dressed" beef — whole and half carcasses — east by rail? No need for stockyards and slaughterhouses anywhere near the vicinity of, say, Manhattan Island. And all to the benefit of the public's health.

Two factors fueled enthusiasm for the idea: a new interest in "animal welfare," and an old interest in profits.

The animal welfare angle was promoted primarily by Henry Bergh (1813-1888), a *New Yorker* cartoon waiting to be drawn: thin to the point of being cadaverous, which accentuated his height of over six feet — as did the exaggerated top hats he wore, and his perennial costume of head-to-toe, undertaker black. Wealthy, snobby, rich, and egotistical. A practiced dilettante, he dabbled in poetry and playwriting in between operas, balls, and European tours.

In 1866, at age fifty-three, Bergh discovered his life mission and founded the American Society for the Prevention of Cruelty to Animals (ASPCA).[12]

Bergh found inspiration all around, from the overworked horses that pulled city streetcars, to the animals trudging (or, in the case of hogs, racing) to stockyard and slaughterhouse.

The "tragedy of killing oxen, & other animals is every day performed free of charge to the spectator — the doors of the theatre being always open!" reads an early Bergh complaint to the Metropolitan Board of Health, in this case regarding a 24th Street slaughterhouse. Alas, he wrote, the audience was mostly children. At first they are "terrified," but eventually "the eye and mind of the beholder have become accustomed to the exciting scene — a pleasurable relish!" (The owners told Bergh they kept a whip on hand to keep the children at bay.)[13]

In October 1866, Bergh dispatched three "agents" to investigate the transportation and treatment of livestock coming into New Jersey and Manhattan from Chicago, and followed up with a letter to yard owners demanding they change their ways. In late 1868, he visited Communipaw, traveling incognito. The lengthy letter he wrote to the *New York Times* detailed what he encountered during his "nauseating inspection" of the facility.[14]

Bergh quickly gained national (read: east of the Mississippi River) celebrity as news of his work traveled the country via newspaper and magazine. He inspired George T. Angell to found the Massachusetts Society for the Prevention of Cruelty to Animals, which published *Cattle Transportation in the United States*, an exposé of the inhumane conditions inherent in railroad livestock shipping.

Other prominent voices agreed that change was needed.

According to an 1870 report from the federal Department of Agriculture (founded in 1862), the motion and jostling of the two- or three-day journey from west to east provoked "fear and apprehension" in animals, which led to "chemical decomposition" of muscle fibers. The Department's Commissioner identified "overcrowding in transportation" as a "prolific" source of livestock illness. The "value of stock lost annually from disease is enormous," he wrote, "and threatens not only to decimate our animals, but to expose the human family to ... unwholesome meats."[15]

The editors of the popular *Scientific American* magazine routinely lobbied for shipping dressed beef rather than live animals. The "sudden" transfer from "pasturage" to crowded rail car "produce[d] a feverish state," they explained, that rendered the slaughtered carcass "unfit to eat."[16]

A Boston commission concluded that beef from rail-shipped cattle "endanger[ed] the health of the people," and a physician told readers of the *New-York Tribune* that train travel crushed blood vessels and provoked fever in animals. The meat, he sniffed, is "in a delightful pathological condition when served to the family," every bit and bite as "wholesome" as "liquid scrofula."[17]

The profit angle carried dressed beef over the finish line. During a typical run from Chicago to the east coast, a fifteen-hundred-pound steer lost about two hundred pounds. That was valuable protein that Americans could ill afford to lose given the booming human population.

More to the point, only 50 to 60 percent of a carcass was edible. The rest — bone, hides, offal, and the like — ended up in rendering plants and tanneries to become buttons, leather, and lard. Why spend money to ship what could not be eaten?

Investors were intrigued.

In 1871, the owners of the Western Refrigerator Car Company of Missouri slaughtered cattle "right off the grass" in southwestern Texas, and shipped the beef to St. Louis in ice-packed rail cars. In 1873, the Texas and Atlantic Refrigerator-Car Company shipped one hundred tons of fresh beef from its abattoir in Denison, Texas, to the Erie Railroad's yard in Jersey City, a journey of eight days. A reporter who investigated the delivery described the cargo as being in "excellent condition."[18]

Dressed beef also gained credence thanks to T.C. Eastman, a major player in the livestock/stockyard/slaughterhouse complex. He and partner Nelson Morris (1838-1907) (a Chicago cattle buyer/packer with railroad ties) began shipping live cattle to England in the early 1870s. The project was profitable, but inefficient: the cattle lost as much as one hundred pounds in transit.

In late 1875, Eastman dispatched a load of dressed beef across the Atlantic, cooled en route by a patented refrigeration process. He was soon earning as much as $64 a head profit, a result that precipitated enormous expansion. In 1875, Americans exported 36,000 pounds of dressed beef to England; two years later, dealers were shipping five million pounds a month.[19]

Perhaps the most notable of the early efforts to service consumer markets with dressed beef was that of George Hammond, a Detroit butcher-turned-wholesaler.

In the late 1860s, he launched cold-weather shipments of dressed beef from Detroit to New England. By 1875, he'd moved to Indiana, established the town of Hammond, and built a large-scale slaughtering operation where his employees processed beef destined for wholesalers. But his was a seasonal project, and Hammond served only New England.

It was left to Gustavus F. Swift (1839-1903) to devise a successful challenge to the companies that dominated the movement of livestock from west to east.[20]

G.F., as he was often addressed, grew up on Cape Cod, where his ancestors had landed some two centuries earlier. In the 1850s, he began working at an older brother's butcher shop, carving carcasses and serving customers face-to-face; the pair eventually constructed a crude slaughterhouse on the Cape.

A few years of experience taught Swift that a more profitable future lay in the realm of the middlemen who supplied the cattle he butchered. He began buying cattle, and occasionally hogs, at Brighton, a century-old livestock market near Boston, selling his haul to butchers back on the Cape. By the early 1870s, the Swift name carried considerable heft in his part of the world, and he'd invested in two partnerships with livestock wholesalers, one in Fall River, Massachusetts, and the other in Boston.

But Swift's fortunes were chained to more powerful middlemen in the meat production complex: that intertwined corporate beast of railroads, stockyards, and industrial slaughterhouses.

The cattle he purchased at Brighton typically originated in Chicago. The more miles the livestock traveled, the higher the price Swift paid at the yard, the less profit he earned. He also paid dearly for the privilege: the railroads charged for freight and sawdust, as well as water and feed doled out at watering stations. (Whether the cattle ate or drank was irrelevant; the shipper paid.)

All of it infuriated Swift. Those "simply enormous" fees made other men "immensely rich" at his expense.[21]

The yard owners paid $6 or $8 a ton for hay, for example, but charged cattle buyers like himself $40 to $50 for the privilege of using it. They paid a penny or two per load of cattle bedding, and charged him a dollar a bushel.

Nor did the pain end there. A Boston hog buyer and pork packer learned that the hard way. Like Swift, he resented the fees. Yard managers charged him $1.50 a bushel for corn that sold "right over the fence [for] 35 cents." Frustrated by the pickpocketing, the man built his own yard at Buffalo.[22]

Retaliation was immediate.

When he tried to ship his hogs east, employees held back the stock until noon because it had not been "fed and watered" in the railroad's facilities. By the time his hogs arrived in Albany, the trading day was over. Buyers had long since taken themselves off to the stockyard hotel bar to compare notes and boast of deals over drinks. The rebel's agent was left to wander the deserted stockyard, doomed to take whatever price he could get.[23]

The lesson for Swift and other livestock shippers: Play by the railroads' rules, or don't play at all.

RAILROAD INVESTORS AND MANAGERS WERE PLAGUED BY WOES OF their own. They understood what most Americans did not: running a railroad was literally a losing proposition.

The majority of roads ran through the nation's northeastern

quadrant, but by the late sixties, the number of lines exceeded the available cargo. The ensuing competition for freight and passengers fueled brutal rate wars that threatened to tip the entire edifice into bankruptcy (with a good chance of taking the rest of the nation's economies down with it).

The largest road owners struggled to protect their investments, and to tame what they regarded as the inherent inefficiency of competition.

One common method was the pool: working together as a single unit, a handful of the largest roads "cooperated" to establish freight rates among themselves, the better to prevent rate wars. A handful of big railroaders also devised a livestock "evener" scheme by which they divided available cattle and hogs among themselves so as to "even out" the profits among the member roads.

The arrangements rarely succeeded, depending as they did on voluntary cooperation and mutual trust (both in short supply among railroad titans fighting for survival).[24] But the Big Meat complex argued that their methods injected efficiency into the nation's food systems. Exhibit A: livestock shipping, a "business that moved itself . . . on its own feet and legs."[25]

Suppose a shipper in Chicago arranged with Railroad A to transport five cars of cattle to Philadelphia. On the designated day, Railroad B lured him away with a lower rate. When Train A pulled into Philadelphia hauling five empty cars, the traffic manager telegraphed Chicago to ask why.

Meanwhile, the road manager who received the unexpected cargo telegraphed his Chicago counterpart with urgent questions: Who owned the cattle? What he was supposed to do with them?

In between, "this butcher and that would go to his . . . regular market," discover empty pens and yards, and then "be compelled to run around until he found the cattle." Without established markets and yards, railroad owners argued, without pools and other agreements that stabilized prices and supplies, the system lacked stability and predictability.[26]

"The more you can concentrate this business" into just a few hands, argued one railroad executive, "the less expense it can be done with," and the less consumers paid for meat.[27]

Humbug, replied shippers like Swift.

They believed that "cooperation" was another word for monopolistic collusion. So, too, the roads' watering yards, and their investments in stockyards and slaughterhouses: shippers moving livestock from west to east had few alternatives. Using the rails meant using the infrastructure, and paying rates set by owners who could charge whatever they pleased.

GUS SWIFT WAS NOT INCLINED TO LIVE HIS LIFE AS THE entrepreneurial equivalent of a doormat. In 1875, he moved his family to Chicago and launched a new venture: he would buy and slaughter cattle there, and ship the dressed carcasses east.

Swift would succeed where others failed because he possessed the ability to think like a system; he saw the big picture, and the pesky details, too.

He understood that a side of beef was only one component of a larger whole that included an integrated slaughterhouse and rendering plant; reliable transportation necessary for shipments of perishable products; and a network of wholesalers and retailers prepared to dispose of the product as soon as they received it.[28]

A dressed beef system included: cold cars, warehouses, and the price of ice; livestock producers, commission agents, herders, drovers, and stockyard managers; the line workers who disassembled the livestock; the engineers who designed the packing plants; a host of accountants, sales agents, and office clerks; and the bankers, brokers, and lenders who controlled the money that financed the project.

Swift tackled refrigerated shipping first.

Americans had decades of experience using ice-filled railcars to haul fish, eggs, and produce from one section of the United States to another. The technology was simple — a ventilated rail car packed with ice and salt along its sides and top. It was based on an equally simple principle: warm air rises, cold air sinks. As air chills, it becomes humid and heavy, and drifts down. Ventilation moved the air so that humidity would not saturate the car's contents.

The rest was detail: the beef had to be arranged so that it did not touch the ice, and the car's design simple enough to allow inexperienced hands to add ice quickly during stops en route.

The Union Stockyards in Chicago, 1871. The large building housed the company's offices and other facilities.

In late 1875, Swift contracted with George Hammond to slaughter and ship beef on his behalf, a trial run that allowed him to test Hammond's cars without investing his own funds. He was not impressed, but within a year he had acquired rights to several cold-car patents, and arranged for a Michigan company to build his cars. (Hammond promptly sued him for patent infringement. The court ruled in Swift's favor.)

Swift's next step: develop the necessary rail connections.

Reliable, rapid transit was crucial to his endeavor: the decay of perishable products waited for no delayed train.

From the outset, he planned to launch his empire in New England, where he could take advantage of his extensive network of business contacts. This was also a near-perfect market in which to start, thanks to an abundance of short rail lines connecting cities, villages, and farms.

To REACH THESE MARKETS, HE DECIDED TO SHIP VIA CANADA'S Grand Trunk Railway. It ran along Canada's southern border, and spur lines connected it to Chicago. In the east, the GTR's route sliced through Vermont, providing easy access to New England towns and cities. As a bonus, the Grand's tracks coursed through terrain whose temperatures ranged from cool to frigid for much of the year, thereby increasing the efficiency of his cars.[29]

Railroad and refrigerator cars in hand, Swift turned to distribution. It was imperative that his perishable cargo be unloaded from cold cars directly into ice-chilled storage. Only then could Swift guarantee that his meat would be fresh and appealing to the wholesalers and retailers who passed it to the public.

Here is where Swift's mental file drawer yielded riches. Over twenty years, he had cultivated relationships with New England cattle dealers, retail butchers, packers, and wholesalers. Now he parlayed those contacts into a network of reliable outlets for his sides of beef.

All of it required cash, of which there was never enough. That did not bother G.F. Swift.

According to his son Louis, who co-wrote a fawning biography of his father, the elder man was a "born expansionist" whose "vision" typically "ran far ahead of the money." Using his "persuasive enthusiasm," G.F. "hustled" for loans and "wheedled" funds from anyone who would listen, typically using one loan to pay off another.[30]

Louis Swift's description of his father's money-grubbing sounds a bit like a Ponzi scheme, but it's clear that Swift cultivated trust among lenders. It's also clear that Swift labored the live-long day to build his venture. He raced, as much as one could in those days, from Chicago to Boston, from Maine to Massachusetts to Rhode Island, wooing wholesalers, tinkering with refrigerator cars, and persuading people to part with their money.

It was, wrote Louis, in what is perhaps the only accurate assessment in a book otherwise devoted to hero worship, akin to juggling a "fish-bowl, a cannon ball, and a live rabbit."[31]

AND IT PAID OFF. SWIFT AND HIS BROTHER EDWIN C. SWIFT (1846-1906) launched Swift & Company in January 1878. A year later, their "New England Fresh Meat Express" was delivering hundreds of tons of dressed beef to warehouses in Boston, Lowell, Fall River, and other Massachusetts towns. In dozens of other locations, the Swifts sold beef straight off the railcars to wholesalers who distributed it to another three hundred towns and cities from Maine to Connecticut.[32]

By 1881, the Swifts were shipping three thousand sides of beef a week from Chicago (about a thousand of which were destined for Liverpool, England). The company's infrastructure included five hundred refrigerated railcars; forty-eight "coolers" scattered from New England to Washington, DC; and an assortment of warehouses, depots, and ice "farms" that stretched from Chicago to New England. Their Chicago facility employed five hundred hands, and boasted two steam engines and a "refrigerator" that could hold six thousand carcasses.[33]

Having planted a flag in New England, the Swifts set out to capture the holy grail: New-York City and environs, the nation's biggest meat market.

There Gus would confront the railroad-stockyard bandits who had siphoned his profits with overpriced sawdust and hay. The titans who transported live cattle by train from west to east; who owned the trains that carried the cattle; who owned all or part of the stockyards in Chicago, New Jersey, and New-York. Gus and Edwin Swift intended to repay them in kind.

In the summer of 1882, workmen armed with sledgehammers leveled a collection of aging storefronts and sellers' stalls on a wharf not far from old Washington Market (near the Hudson River just north of where the original World Trade Center stood). On the cleared land, crews built a two-story structure that ran eighty feet front to back, and was reported to be a giant "refrigerator." In early October, workers hoisted a sign into place — G.F. & E.C. SWIFT.[34]

On opening day, the manager offered guided tours to visitors, buyers, and reporters. A "railway" track was suspended from the ceiling. From it dangled wheeled hooks on which to hang carcasses. Swift's refrigerator cars were equipped with similar ceiling-mounted tracks. When Swift cargo arrived in New Jersey, a crew transferred the cars to barges that floated them across the river to the Manhattan warehouse. There, workers aligned the door of the train car with the door of the warehouse, and slid the carcasses off one track and onto the other.

"Everything with us is systematized," a company representative explained to a reporter. Employees relied on telegraphic information that allowed them to respond quickly to local changes in demand and adjust prices accordingly, and do so faster than shippers who hauled live animals. "Everywhere we have located," he said, "our success has exceeded our expectations."[35]

Thanks to such cost-cutting efficiencies, one reporter enthused, the "era of cheap beef" had begun.[36] Another observer commented that dressed beef shipped long distance "has ceased to be an experiment, and . . . become a demonstrated fact." He predicted that Swift, whose unofficial motto was "quick sales and small profits," would "break down local monopolies and high prices."[37]

THE SWIFTS HAD COMPANY IN NEW-YORK. GEORGE HAMMOND tagged along, as did Phil Armour.

During the 1870s, Phil and his brothers had expanded in both Chicago and Kansas City, Missouri. Sometime around 1880, he nosed about the dressed-beef business, but quickly withdrew: he and his employees "did not understand the methods of refrigeration and did not get [the] beef to the seaboard in proper condition." Armour had not understood the system.

He was a quick study. In October 1882, he pronounced himself sufficiently "confident" to "go into [dressed beef] on a large scale," starting in New York City. Read: he had to move, or risk letting Swift and Hammond capture the nation's biggest market.[38]

Armour planned to sell sides of beef, but he also touted "refrigerator" boxes of "small cuts" — tenderloin, sirloin, and so forth, a convenience for shop butchers who typically bought sides and quarters, and watched good beef go to waste because it was insufficiently "prime" for picky buyers. In Chicago, a company spokesman explained, there was "no waste at all." "The blood, the bones, the offal, the hoofs, and the horns are all utilized and made profitable."[39]

Thus the dressed-beef men's equation: Sell direct to wholesalers and retailers. Earn top dollar for the rest of the carcass back in Chicago by converting byproducts to profits.

A newspaper reporter predicted that dressed beef would liberate New-Yorkers from the "abominable nuisances" of butcheries, rendering plants, and "bone-boiling works." Let it all stay out in Chicago "where they rather like such things."[40]

"There can be only one thing left for all the men who have capital invested here in this business," claimed a local meat wholesaler, and that was to "go away." Or, as a less charitable observer put it, "only stupid and sluggish minds" would fail to "heed the signs of the times."[41]

Some applauded the prospect of sweet revenge, especially against the reviled railroad tycoon William "Billy" Vanderbilt (1821-1885).

"There is really no reason on earth," mused one newspaper editor, "why the beef-eaters of New-York should be taxed for bringing hides and horns over Mr. VANDERBILT'S roads all the way from Chicago." He and other rail magnates had grown "fat and comfortable" on the "toll" exacted from consumers. Now, thanks to

Willy Vanderbilt in a glorious 1878 cartoon from *Puck* magazine. The head on the left is that of the man who built the New York Elevated Railroad; on the right is Jay Gould of the Union Pacific Railroad.

Armour, Swift, and dressed beef, "Mr. VANDERBILT sees in his dreams long lines of his stock cars rotting on disused sidings."[42]

The railroad/stockyard/slaughterhouse kingpins retaliated, warning that dressed beef was a danger to one and all. The Swifts and their ilk were "trying to force their beef on the public," charged a spokesman for the old guard. Should they succeed, they would create "one of the greatest monopolies ever known in this country." They would "put on the screws, and make consumers pay whatever price they please" for beef.[43]

Nonsense, retorted a Swift colleague. The brothers were neither monopolists nor "sharks." They were men of business who had developed a "superior system" of supplying beef. Gustavus Swift was a good "Christian" and a "public benefactor" who wanted to "do good rather than evil," in this case by providing Americans with inexpensive meat, and "hundreds" of men with jobs of "good and sure pay."[44]

A Boston reporter took the matter directly to the Swifts themselves. Were they monopolists? he asked in an interview at their offices. Did they fear Vanderbilt and his cronies?

No, Gus replied. His opponents had invested millions building an infrastructure to transport live cattle from west to east, and had earned "gigantic fortunes" doing so. But in the end, what did they have? Stockyards. A few acres of "sheds and fences" that his "refrigerator business" would render worthless.[45]

So, prodded the reporter, would the Swifts back down? Could the "cattle yard railroad ring" stop them?

"Stop us!" Swift reportedly shouted in reply, slamming his fist on his desk. "[N]ot while we have an inch of pocketbook or a drop of blood left!" "We have no fears," he insisted. He and his brother would fight for "their rights, to the last drop of blood."

"We shall fight," Edwin Swift added, "till blood stands four inches deep on the floor!"

There wasn't much to the fight, and the Swifts' confidence was justified.

Statistics document the speed with which the dressed-beef revolution unfolded: In 1880, Chicago trains carried 416,000 head of live cattle and 31,000 tons of dressed beef to eastern markets. Five years later, the number of live cattle had dropped to 281,000, and dressed-beef tonnage had risen to 232,000.[46]

In 1883, the *Boston Journal* reported that three-fourths of the dressed beef sold in that city came directly from Chicago, sixty train cars a week delivering nearly 1.8 million pounds of "bright and sweet" beef. The shipments "materially curtailed" slaughtering operations at the Brighton market.[47]

AMIDST THE *STURM UND DRANG*, IT'S EASY TO FORGET THE POINT OF the project: cheap meat for the millions. Americans wanted beef, and they wanted it because they could afford it. Late-century, white, urban Americans enjoyed a standard of living heretofore unimaginable for the masses.

Credit the "living wage" and hard-won respect for the "wage earner."[48]

Back when P.T. Barnum was a boy, when cities were few and education limited, American cultural values denigrated wage earners. A white man worthy of rights owned property with which his household sustained itself. He was independent. A wage earner, in contrast, was unfree, beholden as he was to others for his living.[49]

That stance could not be sustained. By the 1880s, non-property-owning, wage-earning, white men and women were the norm, not the exception. They were the "lubricant" of the home market and national economy: canal diggers and machine tenders; clerks and bookkeepers; laborers hauling brick and mortar, digging trenches and pipelines. Wage earners, yes, but surely as worthy of rights as property owners.[50]

"Labor," as Americans described this new political and social power, fought excruciating battles throughout the nineteenth century, determined to establish that wage-earning white men deserved the rights accorded to other white men.

But according to Ira Steward (1831-1883), a major figure in the struggle for labor equity, not just any wage. Workers deserved a "living" wage, sufficient to enable an average white urban family to enjoy a modicum of comfort and a bit of money leftover.

After all, Steward argued, they were "not only the great producers," they were also "the great consumers, or ought to be, of nearly all they produce."[51]

He elaborated: Wage-earners owned and rented homes, bought clothing and furniture, and ate "nearly all the food." They "consume the most" and therefore "furnish the most employment" for other workers. A tailor, for example, made clothing, and then spent the earnings on products manufactured by "other mechanics and laborers."[52]

Steward believed that anything less than a living wage constituted enslavement: without a living wage a citizen-worker could not consume, and became a drain on the health and prosperity of society. If the "masses" failed to "increase their use or consumption of wealth," he wrote, eventually "human progress" would come to an end.[53]

Thanks to the surging, late-century industrial economy, millions of white households had money to spend. And millions expected wages and incomes to secure a respectable "standard of living," a way of life that was fifty percent expectation and entitlement, and fifty percent material comfort.

ACCESS TO BEEF FUNCTIONED AS A MARK OF ENTITLEMENT AND A request for respect.

A Boston meat seller confirmed that state of affairs in the 1880s. Among his regular customers was a young seamstress who purchased only tenderloin. One day, he explained to her that she could save money by buying round steak instead. The woman took offense. "Do you suppose because I don't come here in my carriage I don't want just as good meat as rich folks have?" she demanded.[54]

"Even a laborer on the street or a negro will come in and ask for a porter-house steak," groused another butcher. "[N]obody wants anything else."[55]

Americans associated meat, especially beef, with national power and racial superiority. A nation's diet determined whether it would dominate or be dominated. Europeans and Americans were beef-eating masters of the planet. The "rice-eating" Japanese, Chinese, and "Hindoos," however, were an "inoffensive" collection of people from whom not much could be expected.[56]

That's why food and nutrition featured heavily in statecraft. A well-fed populace was a prepared populace, especially the young men expected to fight wars hither and yon. Europeans, for example, invested in public slaughterhouses in order to ensure urban supplies. They eliminated tariffs that hindered the importation of (mostly American) cheap meat.[57]

Meat-as-power also shaped the nascent science of nutrition. If diet determined national might, then it was imperative to know which foods delivered strength and health and, as important, how to wring every last ounce of nutriment from every last inch of soil or, if need be, laboratory. (In 1894, a chemist predicted that a hundred years hence, fields of corn and wheat would be a thing of the past; humans would manufacture flour, meat, and other foodstuffs in laboratories.)[58]

But a mass audience for beef necessitated a massive supply of cattle. For that, the dressed-beef kings relied on ranchers in the Far West.

CHAPTER 3
EASTERN PLOTS, WESTERN PROFITS, BEEF FOR EVERYONE

AT MID-CENTURY, THE FAR WEST, AS AMERICANS CALLED IT IN order to distinguish it from the "west" of Ohio and Illinois, remained almost as mysterious as when federal officials acquired the land in 1803. In contrast to Eastern North America's humidity — trees, rivers, and grasses abound — much of what lies west of (roughly) the hundredth meridian is arid: Little rain. Few trees. Immense mountain ranges dominate much of the terrain.

In 1805, federal officials commissioned Lt. Zebulon Pike (1779-1813) to undertake an extended expedition west and north of the Mississippi-Missouri river systems. There, Pike found millions of acres of "prairie" scarred by "interior deserts," its "barren soil, parched and dried up for eight months of the year." Perhaps, he mused, in time these "vast plains" would become as "celebrated as the sandy deserts of Africa." But the region was "incapable of cultivation" and best left to the "wandering and uncivilized aborigines of the country."[1]

Army civil engineer Stephen Long (1784-1864) reached a similar conclusion during expeditions he led in the 1820s. The expanse between the Missouri River and the Rocky Mountains, he reported, was a "sterile dreary waste," a "Great American Desert" that demarcated the "western limit of our population." Here was a "line of . . . natural defence [sic] . . . so well fortified by nature as to require no artificial structures" or "regular military works."²

The Far West, 1861. As is evident, much of it had been divided into territories — over which federal officials had no control.

White southern patriarchs, on the other hand, were eager to claim southern sections of the Far West, which they viewed as an ideal place to plant both cotton and enslavement. In the 1830s, they lobbied to annex Mexico in order to convert southwestern North America into a vast plantation.

That didn't happen, thanks to the abiding strain of white supremacy that underpins the nation's history. As John Calhoun (1782-1850), southern patriarch *par excellence* and powerful politician (he served as vice-president twice and as Secretary of both State and War), phrased it:

Americans had never "incorporated any but the Caucasian race.

To incorporate Mexico would be the first departure of the kind, for more than half its population are pure Indian and by far the larger portion of the residue mixed blood." "Ours," he wrote, "is a government of white men."[3]

NEVERTHELESS, BY THE LATE 1840s, AMERICANS HAD GAINED TITLE to an additional 1.2 million square miles of the Far West. The parcel included what are now Washington, Oregon, Idaho, and California, as well as Texas and most of the southwest. At the time, those lands were occupied by roughly a half million Native Americans, and US authority existed on paper only.

Of the new acquisitions, California loomed large: in the late 1840s, prospectors struck gold north of San Francisco, a settlement of a few hundred. Eastern money, goods, and people streamed into the bay area, most arriving by via the Isthmus of Panama, an easier, faster route west than overland through the North American interior.

Few found gold but they discovered a landscape and climate worth staying for. San Francisco, one of the world's great natural harbors, was backed by millions of acres of crop and cattle land. By 1860, the city was the nation's fifteenth-largest with a population of 56,000, a number that nearly tripled over the next decade.

Northern California was white Americans' first significant stronghold in the Far West, and the incomers were fiercely protective of what they regarded as theirs. Genocidal violence against non-whites was the law of this new land, where ranchers regularly pooled funds in order to hire "rangers" to hunt and kill Indians. As a gathering of Californians phrased it in an 1853 statement: it was "the duty of every American citizen . . . to exterminate the Mexican race" and any other non-whites.[4]

CATTLE AND BEEF RANKED HIGH ON THE LIST OF THE REGION'S economies, and its California kings were Henry Miller (1827-1916) and Charles Lux (1823-1887).

Both hailed from what is now southwestern Germany, and both emigrated, separately, to the US around 1840. They became acquainted in San Francisco where they each opened retail butcher shops. Miller had grown up in a butcher family; Lux learned what he knew as a slaughterhouse apprentice in New York City. Both married into the same wealthy local family, which gave them access to San Francisco's movers and shakers.[5]

In the late 1850s, the two men organized a partnership devoted to buying, grazing, feeding, and slaughtering cattle. By the 1870s, they owned more than a half million acres of land around the bay, as well as the riverine and irrigation systems that served them.

They were also among the most hated people in California.

Miller & Lux, "the great land monopolists of California," charged one critic, "have succeeded in owning, or controlling . . . the great valley of the San Joaquin from San Francisco to Los Angeles. They can drive their cattle from one end to the other upon their own ground," something the "public cannot do." "If we don't solve this question . . . we will have a bloody revolution in this country."[6]

There wasn't a revolution, but Miller and Lux, and others, demonstrated, decisively, how to raise, graze, and feed cattle on a grand scale in the west, sufficient to serve a fast-growing urban population.

Aside from a small patch of California, at midcentury the United States had little authority in the Far West. Much of it was a war zone as Indian nations battled each other and the handful of US troops on the scene.

ROAMING THE BATTLEFIELDS WERE BUFFALO ON WHICH INDIANS relied for food, blankets, bone tools, and the like. Some 30 to 40 million head ranged across the Great American Desert, herds of such mass "as literally to blacken the prairies for miles" on end, wrote one awed observer, their rumbling bellows echoing like "distant thunder."[7]

Buffalo, like cattle, are ruminants. Over the centuries, their need for food prodded plains ecology toward grasses. They "wintered" without any special food or shelter. The logic was as clear as the western sky: a range that supported millions of bison could support millions of cattle. The Great American Desert could preserve and sustain the American way of meat.

Thus the emergence of a federal policy for the far west: eradicate the buffalo, and thereby starve the Indians, while gaining millions of acres for cattle production.

For a while, buffalo coats and blankets were all the rage in the eastern US, thanks to the fad of buffalo hunting. Railroads hosted shooting events for those who wanted to tour the American Desert and hunt bison, too. Passengers hung from the windows of their slow-moving cars to shoot at the roaming herds.

Although "hunting" may not be the most apt term for prey that conveniently stands still for the kill. "Why," asked one British sportsman, had "an all-wise Providence" created animals "so utterly incapable of self-protection?"[8]

An 1871 rendering of a bison hunt on the Kansas Pacific Railway.

SUCH WAS THE SITUATION IN THE EARLY 1860s WHEN SOUTHERN Americans rebelled, removing themselves from the union.

Northern Republicans, primarily from the Greater Northeast, dominated the Union Congress and seized the opportunity to shape the nation's post-war future. Federal lawmakers passed a Homestead Act to encourage "western settlement." The Morrill Land Grant act subsidized construction of state "land grant schools" for the training of farmers and mechanics. Congress imposed taxes on alcohol and on some incomes; and established standard rail gauges, standard time zones, and a national currency.

In 1862, this Union congress established a federal Department of Agriculture. That marked the culmination of decades of lobbying on the part of home-market promoters in the Greater Northeast. From the 1820s on, congressional southerners blocked every attempt to authorize such a department as an overreach of federal power that violated states' rights. But now they were gone, and both the recent past and the war had convinced many of the necessity for a federal investment in agriculture.

As one of its first projects, Agriculture's staff conducted a census of the Union's food supplies so that officials knew what was available, and where.[9]

The cattle census delivered bad news.

According to the Department's calculations, Americans required 80 head of cattle per one hundred people, but the current ratio was 68 to one hundred. There were not enough to feed both Union troops and civilians. Texans had stopped shipping cattle north, and much of the Union's cattle was on the Pacific coast or in the northern reaches of the Mississippi River valley.[10]

Thus department officials endorsed the *"great law of the movement of cattle." "Cattle must be moved eastward and capital westward to supply the pressing demands of our people."* (Italics in the original.) This "natural law," explained a department analyst, "is most strikingly illustrated in our country" by the "extraordinarily rapid increase of population," and the construction of "great lines of railway for transporting cattle [and] dead meat, hundreds of miles from those regions where they are most cheaply produced."[11]

There it was. Federal affirmation of the need to plant the Far West with cattle.

WHEN THE REBELLION ENDED IN 1865, FEDERAL OFFICIALS redoubled military efforts to secure the west for white Americans, and monied easterners turned their attention to cattle and grazing.[12]

Texas was of particular interest: now that it was back in the union, its cattle could be exploited. Ranchers there had years of experience with range cattle, and with breeding beef cattle. Some Texas cattle headed northeast to stockyards and meatpackers, but in the postwar years, thousands trekked due north, up into the collection of territories that included most of the plains. There, ranchers were building new herds, transforming the Great American Desert into cattle lands.

The trail drives were an extended exercise in misery. A man who drove a herd from Texas to Iowa in 1866 described a litany of woes: eight months of sunburns and stampedes. Long days hunting down skittish, wandering animals, or driving them across rain-swollen rivers.

"Stampeded last night among 6 droves & a general mix up and loss of Beeves," he wrote after nearly four months on the trail. "Men all tired & want to leave. [A]m in the Indian country [and] am annoyed by them believe they scare the Cattle to get pay to collect them."[13]

"Hard Rain & Wind," he noted a few days later. "Big stampede & here we are among the Indians with 150 head of Cattle gone hunted all day & Rain poured down with but poor success Dark days are these to me Nothing but Bread & Coffee Hands all Growling & Swearing — every thing wet & cold."[14]

Joe McCoy (1837-1915) believed that he had a better idea.

McCoy grew up in Illinois, where his family raised livestock. Their specialty was mules, but they also bred and fed cattle, hogs, and sheep. A business acquaintance described McCoy as "a man of hasty temper," a "Mr Know it all" who "never asked any Ones opinion of any act of his or any proget [*sic*]." McCoy's "will & wishes were law," he was "the whole cheese," and the rest of the world mere "skim milk."[15]

That likely explains why, as McCoy put it, he was not "contented to live quietly at home on a good sized, finely improved farm," even one that yielded as much as a quarter-million dollars in livestock a year.[16]

To the west he would go, there to collect Texas cattle for shipment east by rail.

After sealing a handshake agreement with the president of the Kansas Pacific Railroad, he headed to Abilene, Kansas. In the late 1860s, Abilene was a typical, no-account, western town: oozing self-importance and ambition, but more or less devoid of people and profit. According to Joe, the town consisted of a single rail line, a dozen "log huts," one of which was grandly identified as the Bratton Hotel, and not much else.[17]

He fenced a stockyard near the rail line and dispatched messengers to spread the word along the cattle trails: Drive your herd to Abilene and Joe McCoy would ship it east.

Unfortunately, Texas Longhorn cattle carried Texas fever, a then-mysterious disease to which they were immune, but other cattle were not. As longhorns left a trail of dead cattle in their wake, homesteaders begged for help. Territorial and state legislators responded with quarantine zones into which longhorns could not go.[18]

Abilene sat squarely inside one such zone. McCoy, being McCoy, simply ignored the ban. Surely it didn't apply to a big cheese like himself. Locals, however, fought back, using vigilante tactics to protect their herds.

Naturally Joe took umbrage. According to him, Kansas homesteaders were less disease-fearing ranchers than crooks out "to stop the drover by mob violence" in order to "rob or swindle him out of his stock." If the Kansas prairies could speak, wrote McCoy, their tales of "carnage, wrong, outrage, robbery and revenge" would surpass the "annals of the most bloody savages."[19]

Quarantine zones proved to be the least of Joe's woes. Even as he arrived in Abilene, Congress was organizing funding for a transcontinental railroad. Joe's handshake with the head of the Kansas Pacific proved ephemeral, spun into the ether by millions of dollars pouring into the Far West from federal coffers and railroad tycoons.

McCoy was his usual jovial self in describing the end of his trail: Ellsworth, a newer, more western stop on the Kansas Pacific had nabbed "his" cattle. Ellsworthians, he wrote, were "utterly unscrupulous" and "destitute of honorable manhood." These "ghouls," "full of low cunning and despicable motives . . . resorted to every device their fertile brain could conceive" [sic] in order to thwart Joe McCoy and other Abileneans.[20]

EITHER WAY, MCCOY WOULD HAVE DROWNED IN THE FLOOD OF cattle money that washed across the Far West in the 1870s and 1880s. During those two decades, US troops completed the decades-long project to destroy Indian nations, thereby opening land to settlers and investors alike.

Among the incomers were cattle-seeking capitalists from Europe and Great Britain. In the 1870s, epidemics ravaged cattle herds in both regions, and meat supplies were short and expensive. It was those shortages that had fueled the profits of T.C. Eastman, who we last saw shipping chilled, dressed beef to England (and making a small fortune doing so).[21]

Britain's Parliament dispatched two men to investigate the Far West. The scouts returned to London intoxicated by numbers of cattle and visions of wealth. A cattle king, they gushed, "makes an enormous return" on his investment, reaping an "average profit" of "fully 33 per cent."[22]

A correspondent for the *London Times* described western ranching as "riding through plains, parks, and valleys," pleasant jaunts interspersed with livestock "roundups" conducted by "masters and men, well mounted." One promoter claimed that with "good business management," a herd of western cattle returned 25 percent a year. "The cost of both summering and wintering [livestock] is simply the cost of herding," boasted a Wyoming rancher, "as no feed nor shelter is required."[23]

In western vernacular: Round 'em up, ship 'em out. Pocket the profit.

Hyperbolic promises of easy wealth equal a boom. Cowtowns swarmed with multitudes on the make. The editor of the *Laramie Boomerang* described that burg's cattle district as "a young Wall Street" where buyers, sellers, and madmen talked of "millions" as if they were "nickels." Corporate ranching ventures laid claim to cattle lands from the Canadian border to the Rio Grande. Some were legitimate. Others existed only on paper and served as "clever bait," according to a Denver newspaperman, with which to separate "suckers" from their money.[24]

One of the loonier ventures was the one launched by Antoine-Amédée-Marie-Vincent Manca de Vallombrosa, otherwise known as the Marquis de Mores (1856-1896). Born into a lush French family, he married a wealthy New York woman in 1882, set out for the Dakota Territory, and hatched a "ranch to table" scheme, as he called it.[25]

"We propose," he announced, to eliminate "the middleman and send meats direct from the producer to the consumer." There were no details as to how he planned to slaughter enough livestock to compete with Swift and Armour; find buyers for the mounds of byproducts; ship from Dakota to New York City; and still earn a profit. (It's unlikely he wasted much time pondering such trivia.)[26]

Never mind. He dumped his and his wife's money and funds conjured from gullible investors into an abattoir, a byproducts-processing facility, and a town he christened Medora, after his wife.

Morès wasn't much of a businessman, but he was a brilliant publicist. Newspapers around the country regaled readers with updates on the Frenchman ("distinguished scholar, gentleman, millionaire and cowboy"): his conflicts with ranchers who tried to scare him away, one of whom he reportedly killed in a shootout (self-defense, concluded the jury that acquitted him); his home on the range ("an agreeable cross between a Newport cottage and a hunting lodge"); and, of course, his efforts to bring industrial capitalism to the range.[27]

When the end came, the Marquis was dodging creditors, and eventually arrested for fraud.

THE CATTLE BUBBLE WENT THE WAY OF ALL BUBBLES. BY THE EARLY 1880s, postwar western herds had matured, and eastern stockyards ran thick with cattle. Prices, which had soared during the shortages of the sixties and seventies, stabilized and then plunged as a market glut ensued. Dissatisfied investors in New York, London, and elsewhere ordered ranch managers to sell off their stock. A brief financial panic and two brutal winters that killed tens of thousands of cattle in the northern plains spelled disaster for many, but did nothing to alleviate the oversupply.

Small ranchers and corporate cowboys alike scrambled to unload livestock for any price they could get. Yards at Chicago and Kansas City were overrun with "enormous car-loads of . . . cattle . . . pouring in from all directions." Every head that arrived was worth less than the one before it.[28]

"The thing has been overdone, the market is glutted and collapse is imminent," a British agent reported to his superiors. "I have tried everybody [and] every possible means . . . [to] cause a sale by personal favor, commission, etc. . . . There are simply no buyers."[29]

The collapse infuriated a veteran cattle buyer from south Texas, who blamed "men who did not know what they were doing." "I do not think I ever saw a business that was as prosperous," he raged, "that went down as quick and fast, with no confidence left in it at all."[30]

Many victims blamed their woes on the dressed beef men. Rumors of a "Big Three" and a "Big Four" swirled about the stockyards, and drifted through the smoky bars that lined the dirt lanes of Dodge City and other cowtowns. Gossip circulated tales of victims brought low by these grasping fiends.

A startling number of such stories resembled that of a man who was, by his own admission, "entirely unfamiliar with the business." In 1883, he set out for Arizona, hell-bent on grabbing his share of the cattle bonanza. Naturally he found plenty for sale, and he and the cows set out for Kansas City by train.

The dressed-beef barons of that fair cowtown offered what he regarded as an insultingly low price for the animals. Experienced sellers advised him to take the offer, but instead, the would-be cattle king headed to the East Coast. Where he was offered a price beyond insulting. He blamed his woes on the connivance of the "Dressed Beef Trust" and its "local stool-pigeon(s)."[31]

A Texan who suffered a similar experience claimed that the "dressed beef syndicate" earned $15 profit on each head of cattle. "We [ranchers] think that if the slaughterers made a profit of from $2 to $5 on every steer they ought to be well satisfied, and so would we be, and the consumers, too."[32]

Another critic condemned the dressed beef men as a rapacious "monopoly" and a "dangerous power," adding: "They antagonize the railroads, the butchers, the stock yards, the cattle raisers, and the beef consumers; they seem to want the whole earth."[33]

SWIFT AND ARMOUR, MORRIS AND HAMMOND LIKELY HOWLED AT the idea of earning that much profit on cattle or anything else. As had been the case of the early railroad magnates, the packers knew what the public did not: on its own, dressed beef returned almost no profit thanks to layers of expense that stood between the live animal and the shipped carcass.

The cattle that packers bid on in Kansas City or Chicago had already racked up costs. The original rancher took a cut, of course, as did drovers and commission agents who, in turn, paid the hands who'd moved the cattle to market. Those expenses figured into the price on the hoof.

Once purchased, the animal had to be fed and watered until it was time for slaughter. The finished carcass was stored in a refrigerator (that contained tons of expensive ice) before being loaded onto a railcar (also filled with ice) for shipment east, where it was unloaded and stored again.

All of that necessitated an enormous infrastructure of railcars, warehouses, and ice farms as well as office space and thousands of employees. Every step devoured money, but when the final sale was made, it had to be at a price customers would pay. If not, carcasses rotted.

Assuming all the relevant variables aligned — weather, size of the corn crop, global demand, the health of the overall economy — sides of beef returned about one percent profit and usually less. In bad times — if the corn crop failed, if inflation forced consumers to choose between beef and bread — packers lost money.

That slender line between profit and loss explains why the dressed-beef kings obsessed over byproducts. Such profits as there were came primarily from blood, bone, marrow, and hide. Hides, for example, brought a profit almost anywhere in the world. So, too, "oleomargarine," an animal-fat-based butter substitute the packers developed in the 1880s. In short, byproducts subsidized beef.

Such detail was irrelevant to consumers demanding meat, but when prices for steak and ham rose, they blamed monopolies or trusts. That was hardly surprising: corporations, corporate "combinations," and "trusts" spanned the diversity of late-century commerce and industry: railroads, of course, but also oil refining, steel, cottonseed oil, and whiskey. Rope and cord, window sashes and frames. Pig iron, wallpaper, and barbed wire. Stoves, beer, and gunpowder.

Whatever was wrong, whoever was wronged, the villain was invariably a trust/monopolist/corporation.

During the 1880s, thirteen states pondered or passed antitrust legislation. In 1885, the Senate held hearings on alleged collusion in the railroad industry. Witnesses (including Gus Swift) regaled senators with complaints about the railroads' wily methods of dispensing special rates and rebates, and details of their collaboration in setting those rates and rebates. Congress responded by establishing the Interstate Commerce Commission.

IN THIS ENVIRONMENT, THEN, RUMORS OF BEEF TRUST MACHINATIONS were not surprising, nor was the Senate's decision to investigate the "transportation and sale of meat products" by the handful of dressed beef packers engaged in *interstate* commerce. At stockyards, those operations' buying power dwarfed all others. Swift, Armour, and Hammond bought by the tens of thousands of head. Their purchases moved markets and determined prices.

The hearings that began in November 1888 are revealing. Witnesses ranged from small-town butchers to woefully inexperienced, would-be cattle barons (among them the man who trekked cross country in search of a price). Most complained about unfair cattle prices at stockyards, for which they blamed a monopoly, a cabal, a syndicate. A Beef Trust.

Phillip Armour and his brother Simeon begged to differ. Where other witnesses focused on their small piece of the stage — butcher shop, ranch, stockyard — the Armour brothers described an industry international in scope and boggling in its complexity. It was they who tutored their Senate inquisitors in the whys and wherefores of trusts, pools, and corporations.

Phillip regaled the committee with statistical evidence of the global demand for cowhide; discussed taxes that hindered the manufacture and sale of American oleomargarine; and described livestock production in New Zealand, Australia, and South America. He discussed changes in consumer demand in foreign markets. He tallied the amount of beef and mutton imported into the United Kingdom in 1888, as well as the price of tallow in New York City and "oleo oil" in Rotterdam.

Having detailed the complexities of his enterprise, Armour turned to his core business: meatpacking, specifically beef.

He explained that packers stored beef in order to sell it year round at a stable price, a point he illustrated with the example of tenderloin. Packers procured that choice cut during just two months of the year, when corn-fattened cattle from Iowa and Missouri arrived at the yards. If the packers dumped every tenderloin on the market as fresh meat, prices would fall while the supply lasted, and then soar as it dwindled. And then there would be none until the next season.

As to the charges of monopoly, trust, pooling, and the like, the Armours were refreshingly blunt about their intentions. Dressed beef packers "combined" for the same reason as, say, railroads and livestock shippers: if they did not, price wars would drive them to ruin. If they competed against each other, they stood to lose everything.

An 1893 image showing a group of employees making sausage at an Armour plant in Chicago.

What outsiders regarded as collusion, insisted Phil Armour, was simply smart business for men who operated on such a large scale, and who had invested in plant necessary to do so. Their cooperative actions stabilized stockyard prices and meat supplies, and protected their investments, and the jobs those provided.

Simeon Armour, who managed the family's Kansas City operations, detailed the logic of pooling.

Suppose a drover arrived at the stockyard with a herd of cattle. Only half suited Armour's needs on that particular day. The drover, however, insisted on selling the entire herd.

"I want part of those cattle," Simeon explained. "I may go to [another packer] and say 'Here, there is no use of our bidding against each other; I will take half of them and you half.'" The buyer sells his lot; the packers go home happy.[34]

But, he added, there the "cooperation" ended. "We are the biggest fighters, and have the biggest time in cutting each other's throats of any class of business that is done in America." In markets where the brothers competed head to head, he groused, "we are cutting each other's throat all the time in the way of competition. I am sorry to see it."[35]

In short, if meatpackers behaved as railroad men had back in their early years, meat prices would swing up and down and back and forth, making a fickle market even more unmanageable. Left to its own devices, competition devoured itself, leaving only a string of quasi-monopolies to mark its grave.

Cooperation, on the other hand, stabilized market prices and protected packers' investments and profits. Cooperation facilitated the process of turning western cattle into eastern sirloin. Cooperation was good business and good for consumers.

"We do the best we can to buy cattle as cheap as we can," Phil Armour told the senators. "We are here to make money. I wish I could make more. If I knew of any method of making more out of cattle I should certainly do it." And had he "not been a little inventive and enterprising," he wouldn't have made any money at all. "I know I couldn't do it in the old fashioned way," he said.[36]

The dressed beef kings suffered no injury from this, the first federal scrutiny of their affairs. The hearings inspired the passage of the 1890 Sherman Antitrust Act, which had no effect on anyone or any entity. (According to one federal wag, the law was so flawed that "you can drive a herd of cattle through it.")[37]

But the label of "Beef Trust" was now permanently attached to

74   THE PRICE OF PLENTY

the dressed beef titans. In the new century, they would face continued scrutiny, as Americans struggled to manage meat supplies and prices.

IN 1890, AMERICANS WERE STARTLED BY A CENSUS BUREAU announcement that population was so dispersed across the land that the US no longer boasted a "frontier."

That news set off several years of lamentation and navel-gazing. National mythology placed the frontier at the center of the American experience. Josiah Strong, then one of the nation's most influential clergymen, explained that decades of westward movement had honed white Americans' "peculiarly aggressive traits." The task of conquering and occupying the west, said Strong, had "intensif[ied] Anglo-Saxon energy and aggressiveness," and affirmed the "colonizing tendency" of the "race." What was America without a frontier?[38]

That moment of soul-searching coincided with six years of economic depression, the second worst in US history.

Americans regularly experienced short-lived financial panics, but in late summer 1893, and with shocking speed, the seemingly well-oiled home-market machine of credit, labor, supply, and demand screeched to a halt. There were no mechanisms with which to mitigate the wide-spread financial and social distress that ensued. No unemployment insurance (and for most, no insurance at all); no "social security." No government agencies to pick up the pieces.

Businesses and banks failed. Millions were abruptly unemployed. Hobos knocked on doors asking for work and food. Thousands of men marched cross country to ask the federal government for help. For their pains, some died when troops opened fire.

Even as unemployment soared, hundreds of thousands of workers walked off their jobs, demanding better wages and conditions. In summer 1894, fourteen thousand state and federal troops were necessary to end a railroad strike; twenty people died.

The turmoil fostered a belief among many Americans, rural and urban, that big cities were out of control. Soaring rates of immigration fueled the sense of unease: for the first time, a significant number of incomers originated from eastern and southern Europe.

These were not "white" people as late-century white Americans understood whiteness. Most settled in cities, and that, too, triggered fears of urban unrest because so many worked in factories, and factory workers often went on strike. Americans were beginning to link "labor problems" to socialism and anarchism, even communism.

In short, the nation's great cities might be great, but they were also potential crucibles of social upheaval.

THIS LATE-CENTURY COLLECTION OF WOES INSPIRED AN ALL-OUT effort to settle, homestead, and otherwise occupy the west, the better to provide tension-easing outlets for the great cities of the east. Thus far, however, that effort had challenged even the most die-hard western promoter.

Back in the 1880s, failed ranchers blamed meatpackers for their woes, but the truth was that damn near everyone went bust in the west. Year after year, families loaded up and headed west — only to come to grief in its alien landscapes. Time and again, newcomers tried to farm as they had back in Iowa or Illinois. And time and again, most failed. Whatever anyone thought they knew about farming was irrelevant in the arid west.

Plenty of people had tried watering the west. Small homesteaders pooled their resources to build irrigation systems, almost always without success. Others persuaded their state legislatures to fund water projects. Those failed, too: water doesn't recognize borders. It was impossible, for example, for the state of Colorado to dictate how other territories and states accessed and used the mighty Colorado River.

The only successful irrigation projects were ones funded and owned by big land owners like California cattle barons Miller and Lux. That fact, and years of trial, error, and failure, led westerners to one conclusion: only the federal government possessed the wherewithal, legal and financial, to build large-scale, interstate irrigation systems. It was, by default, a hard sell; this proposed expansion of federal authority and revenues horrified many.

That's why in the 1890s, promoters painted a watered west as a release valve for the urban masses. One irrigation advocate explained that the "wage-earners of the East want wider fields for [their] labor . . . The manufacturers of the East want new markets for their wares. Where can either get what they want so fully as by the development of the great arid West . . . ." An irrigated west would support "a greater population than the United States holds today."[39]

An engineer experienced in western irrigation agreed. "The dead and profitless deserts," he wrote, "need only the magic touch of water to make arable lands that will afford farms and homes for the surplus people of our overcrowded Eastern cities, and for [an] endless procession of [immigrant] home-seekers."[40]

Others touted irrigation as a bulwark against western land monopolies. During a discussion of proposed legislation, one congressman argued that unless federal dollars watered the west and opened the land to homesteaders, the nation's "great Western desert will ultimately be acquired by individuals and great corporations for the purpose of . . . grazing vast herds of cattle."

"They will acquire waterways and water rights . . . and become land barons. Then it will be impossible to ever convert [the west] into the homestead lands for our own people or to build up the population of this Western country," he said.[41]

In 1902, President Theodore Roosevelt (1858-1919, president 1901-1909) signed a Reclamation Act whose "central object" was to insure the "settlement of the great arid West by the makers of homes."[42] This was a "poor man's law," he explained, "designed [so] that men of most moderate means might go upon the public lands and . . . obtain homes."[43]

WESTERN CATTLE GROWERS WERE NOT HAPPY. IN THE WAKE OF THE bubble, corporate cowboys and absentee owners had given way to ranch farming that emphasized hands-on grazing and raising hay for winter fodder. Some were family owned; some were corporate ventures run by skilled managers. All were an improvement on the hordes who'd gone west in the 1870s.

And now these stalwarts watched as civilization encroached upon their cattle paradise. In 1889, North and South Dakota, Montana, and Washington entered the union, followed a year later by Idaho and Wyoming; Utah entered in 1896. (Oklahoma joined in 1907; Arizona and New Mexico in 1912.) Irrigation would surely accelerate the flood of incomers, and thus competition for land and water.

Worse, ranchers feared that federal officials would convert grazing lands into homesteads. Nearly all western ranchers grazed cattle for part of the year on public lands, access to which depended on bureaucrats back east. And, too, only federal funds and management could repair the damage done to grazing lands during the great cattle caper, which left the range in miserable condition and rendered some of it useless.

In short, ranchers understood that their lives and work would always be entwined with eastern bureaucrats, and that amiable relations with federal officials were a necessary part of doing business. Ranchers negotiated those relationships via their existing stockmen's associations, which they had organized in order to protect private grazing lands from sheep and rustlers.[44]

The USDA was equally interested in ranchers. Secretary James Wilson fretted about the tepid growth of the nation's cattle herds, which were not keeping up with the human population. Nor were he and Department colleagues pleased with the quality of western cattle; entirely too many were bottom-of-the-barrel "scrubs."

Interstate meatpackers cultivated relationships with both the Department and western ranchers. Armour, Swift, and the others had launched their ventures in the early 1880s, just as cattle prices stabilized and then plunged. From that episode, they learned hard lessons about their dependence on cattle producers. They, too, fretted over the preponderance of scrubs, and begged for "modern" animals with high meat yield and standardized bodies.[45]

The steady downward drift of cattle receipts distressed the

owners of the Chicago Stockyards. They approached western livestock associations, the big packers, and the USDA with a plan to host an annual national livestock exposition at a Chicago exhibition hall. The event would feature competitions, prize cups, and monetary rewards, carrots to encourage farmers, ranchers, feeders, and breeders to improve their stock. In a separate hall, the USDA could host displays, demonstrations, and posters, the better to teach attendees about the role of livestock production and meat in Americans' lives.[46]

The Exposition brought producers, packers, marketers, and the USDA into close partnership. (The Exposition Board included a Swift and an Armour.) Both buoyed and challenged by these actions, the makers of livestock and meat welcomed a new century.

II: PRODUCERS, CONSUMERS, AND THE PARADOX OF PLENTY

CHAPTER 4
WHAT PRICE PLENTY?

In the early moments of the new century, there were few places more entertaining and awe-inducing than the nation's cities. Some had populations well over a million, inspiring a new kind of architecture with a new name: skyscrapers, these many-storied buildings were called.

Cities were home to new technologies that bordered on the miraculous. People could talk to others located far away by using a box on a wall. Sit in front of a screen and watch seemingly real people chase train robbers and rescue damsels in distress. Push a button or flip a switch: voila! electric lighting. The bright lights and thrilling "rides" at Coney Island and other pleasure parks amused millions.

The great wonder of the age: a wheeled vehicle powered by an "internal combustion" engine. In 1900, the automobile was a rarity and largely for the deep-pocketed. By 1920, nine million such vehicles were clogging city streets.

The most significant aspect of the urban landscape was obvious and thus easy to overlook: the sheer number of people eating well and living materially comfortable lives. Here was the home market in full bloom, although the agricultural aspect of the project was mostly out of sight and mind.

Coney Island, New York. 1908.

The New York of 1920 would have astounded and delighted its inhabitants of 1820, who would have appreciated this new generation's manner of pursuing life, liberty, and happiness.[1]

FOOD WAS CENTRAL TO THE EXCITEMENT OF URBAN AMERICA. Never had so many enjoyed access to so much food, and so much variety. This historic abundance was provided by a shrinking number of farmers, and enjoyed by a citizenry more ignorant about the means of food production than any previous generation.

"We are no longer a nation of farmers living in sight of our food supply," wrote one observer. "The journey between us and [our] food supply, once only as long as from our own field and garden to our back door, has been lengthening year by year."[2]

For better, or for worse, interstate meatpackers played a central role in lengthening that journey.

Collectively, those packers, especially Swift and Armour, had amassed thousands of refrigerated rail cars. They owned networks of warehouses chilled by mechanical refrigeration (born in the early 1880s). They latched on to motor trucks early and often.

Because they were so well positioned to gather and deliver perishables, no group did more than they when it came to organizing and managing food logistics and long-distance shipments of foodstuffs.

For example, the packers invested in eggs, cheese, and butter. These refrigerated protein alternatives to beef and pork balanced the ups and downs of livestock supplies and meat retail prices.

They planted roots in California in order to serve that region's commercial farmers — "growers," they called themselves — who clamored for reliable, speedy transport to carry tomatoes and lettuce, grapes and oranges, plums and more to eastern markets. Packers responded by building west-coast canning facilities where they packed those items and more, including fish, shipping them in packer-owned railcars.

Packer byproducts made billiard balls, chess pieces, buttons, sandpaper, and fertilizer. Beermakers purchased packers' isinglass, and used it to clarify lager. Thyroid and thymus; stomach and pancreas; blood and spleen: all could be turned to profit in the production of tonics and elixirs, or used in tanning and fabric manufacture.

A bemused commentator observed that packers sold beef and pork simply "for the purpose of getting them out of the way" so as not to "hamper the conjurer ... in his tricks" with the rest of the animal's body. And no matter how many byproducts the packer-magician pulled out of his hat, he eyed his cattle and hogs "with distrust," suspicious that the animals were "keeping something back" that might otherwise be turned to profit.³

A delightful rendition of the Beef Trust at work.

THERE WAS ANOTHER EXPLANATION FOR THE PACKERS' PENCHANT FOR diversification: declining meat consumption. Americans' per capita ingestion dropped from 142 pounds in 1900 to 136 in 1920.⁴

As we will see shortly, high prices, especially for beef, forced millions to curtail their input. But the sheer abundance, novelty, and variety of foodstuffs, and reasons to eat them, also lured Americans away from meat.

Changes in early-twentieth-century restaurant culture offer a window into ways in which diets and dining options changed. Eating away from home was not new, but in the nineteenth century, it was confined primarily to the rich and the poor.

In big cities, people living in cheap housing rarely enjoyed the convenience of a conventional kitchen. Residents of such crowded neighborhoods relied on food carts and street stalls, bought bread from bakeries, ate prepared foods from immigrant-owned "delicatessens," and grabbed quick meals at diners, coffee shops, and saloons.

The monied urban elite occupied the other end of the spectrum. For the Astors and Carnegies, Armours and Swifts, dining out often involved wearing precisely appropriate clothing, hats, and gloves, while seated at elaborately set tables in rooms filled with lush furnishings, soft music, attentive waiters, and menus written in French.[5]

The rising middle class was conspicuous by its absence. Many could afford housing with kitchen included. Many shuddered at the notion of eating in public. They disdained the ostentatious rich, and abhorred the idea of rubbing shoulders with factory workers in greasy coffee shops serving questionable food.[6]

As the century ended, those views were challenged by urbanites, including a growing class of salaried workers putting new skills to work in all manner of non-manual labor, from the use of new typewriting and calculating machines to shorthand and accounting. Men and women who migrated from farm were eager to leave old farmways behind. Why cook at home when you could be out on the town, making a city life of your own?[7]

Restaurateurs jumped at the chance to lure the salaried middle away from their home tables, and experimented with format and atmosphere, seeking a middle ground that would appeal to this middle class.

Cafeterias, for example, offered the ultimate in cost-control. These bare-bones chains prepared mass quantities of food in warehouse-like kitchens. Drivers delivered it to outlets where employees broke it down into single portions. No table service, no servers, no printed menus. Choose your food and carry it to your table.[8]

Some restaurateurs opted to specialize, serving only breakfast, for example, or only fried chicken. The ground beef burger, arguably the most American of foods, quickly dominated this subsector.[9]

Regardless of format, eating away from home broadened and enriched Americans' foodways. It was also, however, a useful reminder to meatpackers that humans only have one stomach: in the process of sampling culinary wonders, more Americans relegated meat to an afterthought.

FOOD FADS ALSO CONTRIBUTED TO AMERICANS' ADOPTION OF NEW dietary customs. According to one historian, the options included "intensive chewing diets, one-food diets, low-protein diets, all-meat diets, raw food diets, yeast-free diets, forced feeding, fasting, and others."[10]

Vegetarianism, long confined to an infinitesimal bit of the population — more health cult than fad — waltzed into the mainstream, thanks in large part to John Harvey "J.H." Kellogg (1852-1943), who snatched this particular ism from relative obscurity and deposited it in the laps of the masses.[11]

During his adult life, Kellogg was famous, respected, even idolized by many. He was obsessed with human health, especially digestion, and shared his knowledge with the world via multiple books and his famed Sanitarium in Battle Creek, Michigan. Over many years, thousands traveled there seeking relief from "erroneous habits of life," such as smoking, drinking, and meat eating.

According to Kellogg, meat destroyed human health, consisting as it did of "the dead matter and waste matter of another animal." His vegetarian Battle Creek System ruled the table at the Sanitarium.[12]

Not everyone could afford a stay at the Sanitarium, but millions could follow the System by eating Kellogg's Corn Flakes, or one of the other non-meat, easily digested foods manufactured by the Kellogg family (those were the responsibility of J.H.'s younger brother Will Keith Kellogg (1860-1951). Bare minimum, they were easier to prepare than steak and eggs. Tired of corn flakes? Try Shredded Wheat Biscuits, made by Kellogg competitor C.W. Post.

"[M]any persons imagine they can get 'strong as an ox' by eating beef," read one Shredded Wheat advertisement. "The ox gets

86 THE PRICE OF PLENTY

his strength from eating grass and cereals. He doesn't eat meat. He is a strict vegetarian. Pound for pound there is more muscle-making, brain-building material in Shredded Wheat Biscuit than in beef, bacon, or eggs."[13]

None of that was true, but in an age of mostly unregulated advertising it also didn't matter. What did matter over the long haul was that Corn Flakes and Shredded Wheat entered households and stayed there, as did a host of other breakfast cereals that competed for Americans' stomachs and food dollars.

FOR ALL THEIR AMUSEMENTS, NOVELTIES, AND PLEASURES, EARLY-century cities continued to nurture fear and dread. Many Americans viewed them as epicenters of social evils that threatened the nation's stability.

For example, the "labor problem," as it was dubbed, lived on as workers battled for living wages, safer working conditions, and an eight-hour day. Reformers continued their crusades against urban crime, prostitution, gambling, and intoxication. The anti-saloon campaign proved enormously popular: these alleged houses of ill repute lined city streets, and public drunkenness was endemic.[14]

This general fear of urban disorder was exacerbated by a dramatic surge in urban food prices that began in the late 1890s and only ended in the late 1920s.

A few numbers: from 1900 to 1910, retail food prices increased 20 percent; the "commodity price index," a new federal measure, rose 21 percent; the price of farm products, whether for food or fiber, 38.8 percent. Beef and pork prices were particularly hard to swallow. Bacon's wholesale price, for example, marched up 130 percent; mercifully, its retail price only rose 70 percent.

Why? Soaring urban population, of course, in the US, but also around the world, and thus demand for agricultural products. Every ton of wheat that left the country was a ton of wheat that could not feed Americans. Demand for foodstuffs increased, but supplies did not thanks to declining yields on worn-out soil; the only way to increase output was by applying expensive fertilizers. Farmers relied on animals for power, and planted millions of acres in the oats necessary to feed them.

The silver lining? Thanks to the chronic supply/demand imbalance, American farmers enjoyed record incomes. Millions of rural families ordered goods from the Sears, Roebuck catalog, and adopted an "urban" style of living on the farm. (More or less: until the 1930s, most rural Americans lacked running water and electricity.)

Urbanites complained constantly about the "high cost of living," as it was dubbed (the good ol' HCL), and often blamed farmers for their woes: if farmers were earning record incomes, surely they could afford to charge less for their crops and livestock. Otherwise, they were simply gouging city people.

THERE'S A NAME FOR THE RELATIONSHIP BETWEEN THE PRICES consumers pay and the prices farmers earn. Agricultural economists dub it the "paradox of plenty," or the "surplus problem." Farmers are known to refer to it as the "pain of plenty."

Put simply, those who produce food and those who consume food have opposing interests. Producers benefit financially from scarcity; consumers benefit financially from abundance.

When demand for, say, beef outstrips supply, beef's retail price goes up. There's not enough to go around. Stockgrowers earn handsome rewards; consumers grouse about high prices.

The reverse is also true, as we saw during the 1880s cattle boom and bust: if stockgrowers produce an exceptionally large class of marketable cattle in a given year, animals flood the stockyards. Meatpackers pay rock-bottom prices, and urbanites cheer. Cattle producers, alas, go home broke.

In the early twentieth century, urbanites mostly groaned — and protested and boycotted. They demanded low-cost food, especially meat, and plenty of it.

Economists and policymakers supported those demands. Indeed, they were adamant on the point. Not only *should* consumers be able to buy both beef and shoes; they *must* be able to do so. The nation's economic health depended on consumer activity.

In 1907, a noted economist described consumer spending as the "new basis of civilization": a living wage plus disposable income plus a commendable material standard of living equaled human progress. Or as a federal official phrased it a few years later, the "great buying public" was the "stimulant to both consumption and production."[15]

Diagrammed (crudely), the idea was:
living wage → consumption/demand → manufacturing+goods → jobs → living wage → repeat

Reality is the inevitable wrench in the machinery of theory. Economies are susceptible to vagaries of nature and human behavior. Almost anything can throw an economy, and thus wages, out of whack: drought, crop failures, livestock epidemics, labor strikes (the tool by which the living wage was won); war, flood, and famines thousands of miles away.

Put another way, a consumer economy functions efficiently and predictably only when the living wage is buffered against nature and *forces majeurs*. Regardless of "what happens," consumers must be able to consume.

One way to shield income and encourage consumer spending is by "fixing" prices for everyday basics. To that end, early-century urban voters supported efforts to remove "utilities" — water, electricity, sewer systems — from the free market. Public ownership sheltered those expenses from the whims and greed of corporations and private enterprise.

Credit is another way to insure that consumers consume. Nowadays most adults carry a card that grants credit, but in the early twentieth century, personal credit was rare. That changed, as economists applauded the value and virtue of consumer spending. In the 1920s, General Motors launched the General Motors Acceptance Corporation (GMAC), which provided low-interest loans to credit-worthy borrowers so that they could buy motor trucks and automobiles.

But the cornerstone of a consumer economy, and the motherlode of disposable income, is food.

Food is one of the few items that every human needs. The less households *must* spend for food, the more money they *can* spend on, say, cars and shoes. Keep food prices low, and consumers will keep the world spinning 'round.

The obvious question is *how*. Given the paradox of plenty, how is it possible to keep food prices low and guarantee that producers profit?

THE LONG ANSWER IS STILL PLAYING OUT ACROSS MORE THAN A century of technological, political and cultural events that affect and shape food production and prices.

The short answer is: federal authority and policy. Starting at the turn of the century, Americans built an agricultural infrastructure that accommodated consumers and rewarded producers. The results include the juggling act known as "farm subsidies," as well as the most contested and controversial aspects of contemporary farming such as immense feedlots and hog barns and the use of antibiotics and other drugs.

At the federal level, it was left to the Department of Agriculture to orchestrate and conduct this far-reaching project.

In the years after its 1862 founding, the Department amassed an extraordinary body of knowledge relevant to agriculture. Its interests ranged from livestock nutrition to range grass management; from ornithology to pomology; from seeds and forestry to chemistry, statistics, and engineering.[16]

Department executives systematically captured everything and anything connected to feeding people, including the sciences of nutrition and "home economics," both of which left indelible marks on American society.

An example: When middle class Americans began dining away from home, the Department promptly pulled the burgeoning restaurant industry into its embrace. Its experts urged restaurateurs to focus on simple menus that featured "the right combination of calories, protein, vitamins, [and] minerals" served in a homey, welcoming atmosphere. They taught restaurant owners to operate like factories and think like accountants, controlling costs with tested recipes, portion control, and standardized inputs such as bread slices, eggs, and steaks of uniform size and quality.[17]

In all of this, the Department pursued a single goal: maximize the nation's agricultural abundance, and conquer the paradox of plenty.

We can begin our journey through that quest by looking at consumer reaction to high prices, and cattle producers' reaction to low prices, from the turn of the century to the outbreak of WWI. As we'll see in the next chapter, that war was pivotal to Americans' understanding of the problem of plenty, and its price.

I. CONSUMERS, BOYCOTTS, AND THE BEEF TRUST

In late 1901, beef prices suddenly shot up, and then continued marching upward into the new year. In late March 1902, the editors of the *New York Herald* began running a series of explosive articles that detailed the machinations of the Beef Trust, the alleged instigator of these high prices.

"BEEF TRUST SQUEEZES POOR FOR $100,000,000" announced the headline of the first installment. The trust "dominat[ed]" the nation's food supplies by using "despotic and aggressive" tactics that "killed" competition.[18]

Its members practiced collusion in a secret office somewhere on Madison Avenue in New York City. The trust controlled the stockyards, cheated livestock producers, fixed prices for steak, and woe betide anyone or anything that tried to stop it.

Readers who stayed with the story — and who could resist? — learned that the trust controlled 75 percent of the nation's egg and poultry supply. Swift executives had "secretly" stashed 43 million eggs in cold storage, which they planned to release or hold "as suits their convenience in manipulating the market."[19]

Agriculture Secretary James Wilson (1835-1920; secretary 1897-1913), himself an Iowa farmer and livestock producer, tried to set the record straight. Cattle and hog feeders, he explained, used corn to fatten and finish stock for market. High-price corn equals high-price beef and bacon. In 1901, corn yields were poor, and so corn's price was high. "Cattle and meat," he explained, "like all other commodities, have to follow the laws of supply and demand."[20]

A 1906 illustration. Among his products are "Potted Poison, Chemical Corn Beef, Bob Veal Chicken, Tuberculosis Lard, Decayed Roast Beef, Deodorized Ham, Embalmed Sausages, [and] Putrefied Pork."

Logic and facts be damned. The *Herald's* exposé was reprinted in hundreds of newspapers and read into the *Congressional Record*.

Union employees in New York pondered a thirty-day boycott of meat. In Newark, New Jersey, workers striking for higher wages blamed the Beef Trust for their troubles. Meat retailers boycotted their wholesalers on grounds that those middlemen were perpetrators of the Trust's schemes.[21]

"Among the homes of the workingmen on [New York's] West Side," reported the *Tribune*, "the effect of the rise in the price of a meal is painfully apparent." "Families which have been accustomed to having meat on the table twice a day are now forced to get along with a meat stew once a day." A city restaurateur told a reporter that he had "stood it about as long as I can without losing money." He planned to raise prices, having been "forced to do so by the unreasonable men back of the Trust."²²

Lower East side residents discuss the boycott.

Five weeks after the *Herald*-inspired furor began, protests turned violent. Kosher retail butchers on Manhattan's Lower East Side announced a two-day boycott of meat wholesalers, during which they would close their doors to shoppers.

That infuriated neighborhood residents, who were already reeling from the assault of high prices. On May fifteenth, some five thousand women staged a series of coordinated attacks on butcher shops and any customers fool enough to buy meat in them. They smashed shop windows and "hurled" meat out into the streets.²³

The nightmare scenario of food-shortage-driven urban upheaval had become reality. Something must be done.

NO POLITICIAN WANTED TO BE KNOWN AS THE ONE WHO TURNED cities into battlegrounds. In the heat of the moment, President Theodore Roosevelt launched a legal assault in hopes of lassoing both the Beef Trust and the high cost of living. He ordered Attorney

General Philander Knox to open an investigation into the allegations aired by the *Herald*.

Thus began a years-long game of cat and mouse as federal and state courts tried using antitrust laws to break the Beef Trust on behalf of consumers. Time and again, legal efforts came to naught. Court cases dragged on interminably, doing nothing to improve prices in real time. Worse, the 1890 Sherman Antitrust Act remained a model of flabby political expedience. It did little to clarify the distinction between mergers and trusts, or between corporations that were simply large and those that monopolized industries.

Moreover, although the Constitution granted Congress the authority to "regulate commerce . . . among the several states," a right the Supreme Court affirmed in 1824, neither Sherman nor any other law had defined "interstate commerce."

Suppose a packer bought cattle at the stockyards in Kansas City, slaughtered them there, and then shipped the beef to Indiana. Where did his "commerce" end? Missouri? Or Indiana? Who or what ought regulate his business? Missouri? Indiana? Congress? Federal authority only? State and federal? For that matter, what was the difference between "commerce" and "manufacturing"?

Who knew? And because no one knew, lawsuits proved useless as a weapon against high prices.

For example, in a lawsuit inspired by the *Herald*'s reports, a judge forbid packers from fixing prices and engaging in "combination" — unless it was necessary to do so. The ruling also allowed the packers to withhold meat from the market as needed in order to "prevent the over-accumulation" of "perishable articles."

In short, the decision affirmed the point Phil Armour had made during the 1888 Senate hearings: making and selling perishable foodstuffs for a national market was complicated; the usual rules of buying and selling did not always apply.[24]

And so it went. Perhaps the best that can be said is that these years of courtroom wrangling proved a useful laboratory for exploring the ways and means of Sherman. Much legal experience

94   THE PRICE OF PLENTY

was gained by attorneys arguing their way through the antitrust maze.

COURT CASES CAPTURED THE PUBLIC'S ATTENTION, BUT AS A DEVICE for taming the good ol' HCL, they were a bust. The Department of Agriculture, on the other hand, specialized in fighting high prices and the paradox of plenty.

Secretary Wilson had taken office in 1897 with the intention of making American agriculture the envy of the world (it was already the world's largest such economy).

He envisioned the Department as a university staffed by scholars building a science-driven agriculture, and to that end assembled a remarkable cadre of scientists, economists, engineers, and statisticians. Many of these men and women were graduates of land grant schools, and eager to devise a modern agriculture that would parallel, in utility and efficiency, a factory floor or corporate bookkeeping department.[25]

"We [shall] have no useless American acres," Wilson said in 1905. "We will make them all productive."[26]

To that end, USDA staff studied and analyzed every aspect of agricultural practice, from tilling and harrowing to barn design and bookkeeping techniques (at the time, few farmers kept financial records). They tested and evaluated new farming technologies, and taught farmers how to use them.[27]

So, too, the Department's partners, the land grant schools and the agricultural experiment stations attached to them and funded by state and federal coffers. Staff at the Illinois Experiment Station, for example, studied barn use to determine the most efficient layouts, and experimented with concrete-paved floors (the better to remove manure) and "self-feeding" boxes that allowed cattle to eat when they wanted. Such ideas reduced labor costs, improved efficiency, and brought more profit to growers.[28]

As ever, the USDA devoted considerable attention to livestock and meat, from breeding operations to food on the table. For example, staff spent years and considerable money tracking and eradicating Texas fever and other livestock diseases. In 1904, the Department began conducting experiments in livestock breeding and feeding, work supported by its Veterinary Division and Bureau of Animal Industry. In 1910, Secretary Wilson established an Animal Husbandry Division, and expanded livestock research facilities by purchasing 475 acres of land near Beltsville, Maryland, for that purpose.[29]

CATTLE DREW PARTICULAR ATTENTION IN THE EARLY CENTURY primarily because there weren't enough of them. Starting around 1900 and continuing for fifteen years, beef prices rose because even as the human population soared, cattle populations plateaued.

As high prices drove consumers away, the impact rippled through the production process: the feeders who finished cattle stopped buying from the stockgrowers, who then culled their herds. Those actions drove supplies down and prices up, and the cycle continued for years: once culled, a herd needs seven years to rebuild.

Determined to break this cycle and increase herd size, in 1908 Secretary Wilson ordered the Bureau of Animal Industry (BAI) to study the matter. The report issued in late 1909 provides a fascinating look at the whys and hows of the high price of meat.

Staff began by collecting retail meat prices in fifty cities around the country. After running the numbers, they learned that the mean retail price of beef was 38 percent higher than the wholesale price, and that lesser cuts of beef carried a higher wholesale price than prime cuts.

"Indeed, the rule is quite general that low-priced beef is marked up twice as much relatively as high-priced beef is. In other words, . . . poorer people pay nearly twice the gross profit than the more well-to-do people pay," the report noted.[30]

But why the gap between wholesale and retail price? Meat retailing was one reason. In most of the cities studied, retail butchers significantly outnumbered the available clientele. That "multiplication of small shops is a burden to consumers and no source of riches to the small shopkeepers. When twenty or more small shops divide the retail business" in an area better "served by one large shop," shopkeepers paid high overhead in order to capture a small group of consumers, who then paid high prices for their food.[31]

Urban entitlement also explained the gap. According to the report, city people "want delivery of goods, perhaps by special trip, and this requires at least one man, horse, and wagon. They want the market man also to send a man to their dwellings to take orders." And often as not, all this just for a single pound of beef or bacon.[32]

As to the paltry growth in cattle numbers, the report blamed federal public land policies and rising land costs, especially west of the Mississippi River. As ranchers had feared, eastern bureaucrats had reduced grazing acres in recent years, and banned the miles of fences that made western grazing easier. In response, stockgrowers culled herds.

Moreover, the millions of Americans who migrated to the watered west typically eschewed livestock in favor of "quick cash crops" like wheat, hay, or oats. "[C]heap beef is not the product of high-priced land."[33]

The report emphasized two main points.

First, since 1900, beef consumption had declined (and would continue to do so for years). The analysts noted the irony: the USDA had significantly expanded Americans' dietary options. But humans only have one stomach; when food was varied and abundant, "some meat must be displaced."[34]

Second: the nation's human population had risen a whopping twenty percent from 1900 to 1910 alone, but the number of cattle and hogs barely budged.[35] Higher meat prices were inevitable.

The report ended on an ominous note: Retailers were profiting. Middlemen were profiting. Packers were profiting. The only group not profiting: livestock producers. That was especially true for cattle, which were "barely as valuable as they were nine to fourteen years ago."[36]

In January 1910, not long after the Department issued the report, simmering consumer aggravation bubbled over. Two groups separately but simultaneously called for a national meat boycott.

In Ohio, a factory foreman encouraged his co-workers to boycott beef; most signed on — and so did thousands of others around the country. In Washington, DC, a group of residents organized the National Anti-Food Trust League. Many of them worked in government; some were members of congress; some were angry spouses struggling to make ends meet. They, too, urged Americans to boycott meat.[37]

Over the next two months, boycotts spread across the United States. Said one angry consumer, "The country has grown and the demand has increased, but the production has remained stationary" because farmers were "getting money too easy; that's what is making the trouble." "They lie abed until 9 now and [then] take an automobile ride."[38]

AFTER THE RIOTOUS 1902 RESPONSE TO HIGH BEEF PRICES, THE threat of urban unrest alarmed officialdom. In late 1910, as food prices continued to march upward, a Senate committee opened hearings into the baffling ways and means of the HCL. Expert witnesses opined on a number of explanations, from tariffs to the price of gold to the eight million immigrants who'd entered the country in the previous decade.

Ultimately, the Senate committee's final report to Congress focused on two general categories of causation.

The first was Americans' sense of entitlement. Consumers wanted cheap meat *and* access to the era's panoply of consumer goods. According to the report, "consumers are demanding a much higher grade of article than was the case a few years ago." They want "expensive" cuts of meat, and commercial "creamery" rather than hand-churned "country" butter; fresh laid eggs rather than ones held in cold storage. One frustrated egg dealer described an order he received: "five cases of eggs, not over three days old, all white," and uniform in size.[39]

As Secretary Wilson had explained during his testimony, many urbanites lived in "flats," and food came the nearest shop. They thought nothing of 'phoning the butcher for home delivery of "20 cents' worth of meat." What urbanites failed to grasp, said Wilson, was that such niceties weren't free.[40]

The second cause of high prices was agricultural, especially the exorbitant cost of land and labor.

Wilson was blunt about the latter. "The lure of the city, a bigger [wage] at the factory, the lure of the sidewalk and electric lights and the theater and the [shined] shoes — all of those things have taken the boys away from the farm."

As a result, farmers struggled to find labor. In the first ten years of the century, wages for full-time hands and seasonal labor rose 45 to 75 percent, depending on crop and region. (Wages typically included cash, rough lodging in bunkhouses, and three squares a day.)[41]

Rhetoric and hearings had the usual effect, which is to say none at all. Food prices climbed; consumers complained. Eventually so did cattle producers, who were fed up with being at the bottom of the meat-making totem pole.

II. THE STOCKMEN STRIKE BACK

Western cattle producers, whether ranchers or feeders, had long felt snubbed. Even into the twentieth century, many Americans viewed cattle ranching with skepticism; as a "temporary stage in the evolution toward a more developed western society." According to one naysayer, there was no "country on the globe and at no period of the world's history has any nation or people who devoted themselves exclusively to stock-raising ever risen much above semi-barbarism."

Even Teddy Roosevelt, who'd enjoyed his own ranching experience in the 1880s, viewed "the men who guard and follow the horned herds" as advance scouts who laid the way for progress and "the settlers who come after." Ranching, he opined, was suitable for "vigorous, primitive pastoral peoples," adding that the rancher "shows more kinship to an Arab sheik than to a sleek city merchant or tradesman."[42]

When ranchers weren't busy being primitive pastorals, they were monopolists grabbing the west for themselves. That was the line taken by reclamation boosters: without irrigation, cattle kings would steal all of the public acres. Better to water the west and settle homesteaders who would bring civilization to the wilds of cattle country.

As far as ranchers were concerned, homesteaders were parasites whose encroachment made it ever more expensive to grow beef cattle. Which is why western ranchers and other cattle producers organized early and often. It was either exercise strength in numbers, or be run over by federal bureaucrats and homesteaders.

For some years, western cattle producers' primary organization had been the American National Live Stock Association (ANLSA), which, despite its name, was western- and cattle-centric. And when members gathered in early 1914 for their annual convention, they were angry, and ready to fight. What they did at that gathering would eventually demolish the Beef Trust.[43]

The ranchers had reason to be upset. Several months earlier, Congress had lifted tariffs on both cattle and beef in hopes that Canadian cattle and South American beef would drive down retail prices in the United States.

Stockgrowers had begged Congress not to do so, explaining that the Beef Trust's reach extended to South America, where trust members had acquired cattle herds and built some of the largest, most efficient packing plants in the world. But Congress went ahead because consumers were grousing, and "[e]very bureaucrat became a mouthpiece for Argentine and Australian beef and mutton," railed one ANLSA member.[44]

Worse, when the tariffs were lifted, "timid" stockgrowers reacted by culling herds and dumping their cattle on the market. The resulting glut drove down the prices ranchers could get for their animals, and reduced the nation's already scanty cattle supplies — with no effect on the retail price of meat, which failed to drop "not even by the fraction of a cent."

Who wouldn't be angry?

But tariffs weren't the only topic on cattlemen's minds that year. Channeling the USDA, one speaker at the Association's meeting charged that retailers were killing the beef industry with inefficiencies and high overhead. The retail "cost of beef, pork, and mutton" had "lost all connection with stock-yard values of cattle, hogs, and sheep."[45]

What infuriated him most, however, was that no matter what happened to stock producers, interstate meatpackers never suffered. They had "so systematized [their] business as to insure a small, but certain, percentage of profit" and thereby "immunized" themselves to "trade vicissitudes." It mattered not the least to them, he added, that once beef left the packing plant, costs "pile[d] up" as it wended its way through an inefficient "distribution process."[46]

Then Nebraska cattle producer E.L. Burke rose to launch a fiery attack on the Beef Trust; its reverberations would be felt for years.

Burke charged that meatpackers used their control of livestock marketing to neuter the law of supply and demand. They'd long owned trade newspapers and warehouses and so forth, but in the previous decade they'd constructed multiple stockyards and packing houses west of the Mississippi — in Denver, Oklahoma City, and other locations. As matters stood, as soon as a cow left range or farm, it entered a realm controlled by packers, where the law of supply and demand did not apply, and livestock producers were powerless.

He challenged his colleagues to fight back. If cattle producers wanted to survive and thrive, they must focus on "economy, elimination of waste, co-operation, and improved methods."[47]

But, said Burke, "We have a right to demand and expect the strongest kind of co-operation from the packers, the stock-yard companies, the commission men, and the railroads." He backed that claim with unassailable logic: "They are all in the same boat with us. If the producer of the raw material goes down, all the balance go with him."

Before members adjourned for the year, the ANLSA president, Henry A. Jastro, appointed a committee to investigate these allegations.[48]

IN JULY OF THE SAME YEAR, AN EPIC OUTBREAK OF HOOF-AND-MOUTH disease began in Michigan and quickly spread to the Chicago Yards. Before it was conquered the following year (in May 1915), it spread to twenty-two states, mostly in the east. The epizootic necessitated multiple quarantines, including major yards, and hindered livestock sales and meat production for months.[49]

July 1914 was the same month that war erupted in Europe and Asia, and combatants in England and France pleaded with the US for food. That year, roughly 37 percent of the nation's wheat crop left the country. Packers ramped up their shipments abroad, as the French in particular clamored for cattle and beef.[50]

And yet, in 1914, stockyard prices for "finished," corn-fed cattle plunged.

How could that be? The war had boosted demand. The nation's cattle supplies already lagged well behind normal demand. Hoof-and-mouth disease had sent cattle numbers even lower. How could fed cattle prices possibly go down?

The explanation was (and is) simple: in the face of high retail prices, meatpackers eschewed high-priced, corn-finished beef in favor of low-grade beef from grass-fed range cattle. The allies at war also sought low-cost range beef. No one wanted prime fed beef.

Cattle feeders, however, were more inclined to believe the explanations provided when Live Stock Association members gathered again for their annual meeting in March 1915 (two months later than usual, thanks to hoof, mouth, and war). The committee that President Jastro had appointed a year earlier reported on its findings. The news was grim.

The committee's chair, A.E. de Riqles of Denver, laid out the details.[51]

The Beef Trust owned large packing facilities and multiple stockyards, and effectively controlled livestock marketing west of the Mississippi River. They owned most of cattle cars, and some rail lines that hauled livestock. They owned banks and credit operations that specialized in dispensing livestock paper, often the only source of loans for stockgrowers. Livestock commission agents, ostensibly representatives of cattle sellers, sold cattlemen's stock for prices set by packers. Packers also financed and controlled much of industry media, too.

Put simply, at market, stockgrowers had zero bargaining power. They had to take the price that packers set. If the law of supply and demand appeared to be broken, that's because it was.

1909 photograph of the Chicago Stockyards. It provides a good sense of the horizontal scale of the thing (all that urban real estate!), as does the immense Armour sign in the background.

OVER THE NEXT FEW MONTHS, DE RIQLES'S COMMITTEE SET IN motion a plan for action, one that required federal involvement.

Working with Colorado's governor and the Speaker of that state's House, de Riqles asked Agriculture Secretary David Houston (1866-1940; secretary 1913-1920) for a meeting with department "experts" to discuss the possibility of "organizing cattle growers." In late May, three USDA agents arrived in Denver, and met with Live Stock Association members as well as "high officials, members of congress, prominent bankers, stockmen, business men and farmers."⁵²

That gathering led to a special ANLSA convention in July 1915 in Denver, called to discuss plans to "break the control of the livestock industry" by the "packer trust." The attendees included a committee appointed by Colorado Governor Carlson; local bankers and business owners; Charles Brand, who directed the USDA's Office of Markets and Rural Organization, and a half dozen other Department employees.⁵³

After two days of closed-door discussion, the group voted to ask Secretary Houston for a federal investigation. Congressional approval would take months, so the Live Stock Association asked that in the interim, the USDA host a conference open to those associated with the business of making and distributing meat. Perhaps a "frank presentation of all the facts from all parties interested" would enable the industry as a whole to devise a "reasonable remedy" to the problem.⁵⁴

In mid-November 1915, the USDA's Charles Brand hosted said conference. The 124 registered attendees included six packer representatives, eight USDA employees and a Department solicitor; two dozen members of the Association of Freight Traffic Managers; executives of the major stockyards; two men representing the Master Butchers of America (the retail side); land grant faculty, and members and officers of the ANLSA.

Brand opened the gathering with a reminder that the "interests of the consumer must be protected and safeguarded," and then turned to floor over to de Riqles, who rose to plead the stockgrowers' case.⁵⁵

The law of "'supply and demand,'" he began, "has ceased to have very much to do with the matter of price-making."⁵⁶

In "recent years," explained de Riqles, cattle feeders had routinely experienced "frequent and violent fluctuations in prices" that could not be attributed to supply and demand. "A drop of $1 per 100 pounds in a couple of days can hardly be explained on that theory." He blamed market turmoil on the "centralization of the buying power into the hands of fewer large slaughterers."[57]

As an example, he told the audience about the "disastrous losses" western feeders experienced from June 1914 to June 1915. That period coincided with the hoof-and-mouth outbreak, but that event primarily affected cattle moving *east* from Chicago; for months, eastern sellers and buyers "were not in the market."

According to the law of supply and demand, prices paid for cattle *west* of the Mississippi River should have been sky high.

They were not, said de Riqles, because the Beef Trust controlled the marketing apparatus west of the river, thanks to their ownership of yards, packing plants, rail sidings, and the like. Controlling cattle prices was just another day at the office.

He also explained that cattle producers competed directly with the packers for financial credit because the Trust owned many of the institutions that extended it. Most of the available credit went to packers; cattle growers "naturally [took] second place," and paid a higher rate. "Livestock paper" was typically granted for two to three months, and due in either fall or spring. But because packers owned the credit they dispensed, it "would not be difficult to manipulate" offerings in order to bleed debtors.[58]

The stockgrowers, he reiterated, did not seek to destroy or "revolutionize" the packers. "Our large cities" could not be fed, and stockmen could not sell "without these great central markets and large slaughtering plants." "Our desire is to eliminate or minimize the effect of certain evils and practices which have crept into the present system."[59]

He closed by presenting the ANLSA's proposal for leveling the playing field.

Stockmen wanted a five-day market, rather than the two to three days available at present. They wanted the USDA to publish market statistics and prices. They asked for public abattoirs at public yards; a ban on packer control of "stockyards and other instrumentalities"; a ban on allowing commission agents to serve both sellers and buyers; and federal and state oversight of yards and packers.[60]

While most attendees were sympathetic and supportive, the six packer representatives had little to say. The secretary of the American Meat Packers' Association (AMPA) explained that they had been willing to make a "formal statement," but the invitation "did not mention any specific packing-house problems to which we could address ourselves." The packers' business was "highly departmentalized. We did not know what you wanted to discuss."[61]

But even when asked directly to comment on a topic, Armour vice-president Arthur Meeker declined. "I really did not come here to talk; I came to listen."[62]

The packers' feigned ignorance would prove lethal. The stockmen interpreted it as a face slap, an overt display of disrespect. Live Stock Association president Dwight Heard was "exceedingly sorry" about the lack of packer participation. His membership was desperate for a "frank" discussion. As the group's special committee put it, when it came to "getting closer to the packing-house people," the Brand conference was a failure.[63]

IN EARLY FEBRUARY 1916, HOWEVER, THE ANSLA's EFFORTS received an unexpected boost. William P. Borland (1867-1919), a Missouri congressman, asked his colleagues to authorize a Federal Trade Commission (FTC) investigation in to the affairs of the Armour, Cudahy, Hammond, Morris, Sulzberger, and Swift companies. The choice of the FTC was deliberate: stockmen wanted nothing to do with another Department of Justice, antitrust go-round, and unlike the USDA, the FTC had subpoena power.

Borland told his colleagues that "conditions in the cattle feeding business in the west [had] grown steadily worse" because of the Beef Trust's grip on the stockyards where cattle were marketed. The situation was "abominable," and not only for livestock producers. Packer power meant an "empty cupboard for many wage earners and the pauperization of thousands of tenant farmers. No more vicious and high handed conduct can be imagined than to take advantage of the present war situation to squeeze the American farmers."[64]

In April, a House Judiciary subcommittee held hearings to

weigh the pros and cons of the requested investigation. Among those who testified were four members of congress, a former Secretary of the Interior who was also an ANLSA member, the president of the National Live Stock Exchange, the governor of Virginia, and a host of livestock growers and feeders from around the country.

The packers were there, too, and this time they spoke up.

Armour vice-president Meeker charged that it was "perfectly evident" that "this agitation, or campaign, like all its predecessors, is based not on facts" but "suspicions."[65]

The problem was that outsiders didn't understand how packing worked. "We often buy cattle," he said, "knowing we are going to sell the beef at a loss, and often lose money, but the next week we hope to have better luck." When asked to explain what "economic laws" guided such behavior, Meeker said there were none. "If we tried to apply economic laws, we would not do business."[66]

"I think the fact that we conduct our business on [a] small margin of profit," he sniffed, "should be proof . . . that it is not conducted illegally. One is not in business to do business illegally for a small profit."[67]

There are "a million people in this country engaged in the business of producing live stock," he added, "whose chief interest, naturally, is to get as much for their cattle as they can." And "there are a hundred and one million people" whose "interest is to see how cheap they can buy their beefsteak, and their purchasing power determines the price."[68]

In early December 1916, the House Judiciary Committee recommended that Congress fund an FTC investigation. Two months later, President Woodrow Wilson (1856-1924, president 1913-1921) ordered the Trade Commission to investigate "the production, ownership, manufacture, storage, and distribution of foodstuffs," with particular attention to "manipulations, controls, trusts, combinations, or restraints."[69]

Two weeks later, food riots erupted in a number of cities. In early April, the US entered the ongoing war.

CHAPTER 5

MR. HOOVER'S WAR; OR, HOW TO FIX PRICES AND MAKE ENEMIES

From the moment it began in 1914, the European war had exacted a toll on the neutral United States, primarily in the form of higher food prices; month after month, ever upward the cost of eating rose.

The denizens of the Brownsville section of Brooklyn, New York, felt the pain daily, theirs being a working-class neighborhood where food devoured 50 percent or more of household income. But in February 1917, the price of basics — onions, potatoes, cabbage, and bread — abruptly jolted higher, sometimes as much as thirty percent a day. In the month's third week, overnight the price of potatoes and onions more than tripled, rising from five cents a pound to eighteen.[1]

Furious neighborhood shoppers blamed the dozens of pushcart peddlers who supplied the pricey produce. The peddlers typically bought from food brokers and wholesalers, and naturally they set their retail prices based on what they'd paid their middlemen, a detail that mattered little to the thousands trying to feed their families.

At mid-morning on February 19, one shopper realized she could not afford even the meager amount of food she needed. She'd had enough. She shoved the vendor's cart onto its side. As onions and potatoes rolled into the street, she raced away, clutching her precious haul.

A pushcart market in New York City in 1915. This one appears to be located under an elevated railway.

When the peddler protested, dozens of women surrounded him. As word spread and morning turned to afternoon, more women showed up. By evening, more than a thousand were marching through shopping districts, overturning carts and stalls, and dousing foodstuffs with kerosene to prevent them from being sold. The next day, five hundred women descended on City Hall, demanding to speak to the mayor: "We want bread! We starve!" they chanted.[2]

Over the next few weeks, demonstrations spread across the country. Police shot a man during a Philadelphia riot.

"We don't want their oleomargarine," complained one protestor. "I could buy butter once on my husband's wages — I don't see why I shouldn't have the same to-day." "There will soon be a revolution in this country," the leader of Feed America First told a reporter in St. Louis. "The railroads and trusts are back of these high prices. When the people get together they will soon force the hands of these magnates."³

A member of the Federal Farm Loan Board directed a stark warning to Agriculture Secretary Houston: "We shall have in this country a political revolution, if not something worse, unless the question of the furnishing of foods to the people at the lowest possible price is taken up."⁴

A trio of Senators urged their colleagues to act "at once." "Conditions prevailing throughout the country . . . are amazing," and "we should have the courage" to confront them, argued Senator William Borah (1865-1940, R-ID). "What these suffering poor want is food and nothing short of that will answer." The "question of the food shortage" was "of the gravest moment."⁵

The "increase in the cost of living," added Senator George W. Norris (1861-1944; R-NE), "cannot continue without . . . bringing ruin even to those who are most prosperous. If we are going on in the way we are . . . ultimately, there must come revolution. Those who are hungry and cannot make a living are increasing by thousands as the cost of living goes up. Hunger knows no reason. It was the cause of the French revolution."⁶

ON APRIL SIXTH, PRESIDENT WOODROW WILSON, RECENTLY SWORN in for his second term, added a new reason for food prices to climb: he asked Congress for a declaration of war. Congress obliged. The "question of the furnishing of foods" could no longer be avoided.

Wilson, it must be noted, had little knowledge of agriculture or how prices were made, and had no understanding of the paradox of plenty, a fact revealed by his solution to the high cost of food: "We ought to raise such big crops that circumstances like the present can never recur," he said in a November 1916 speech. (Agriculture Secretary Houston gently suggested that the president avoid making any similar statements.)⁷

In spring 1917, the "question of the furnishing of food" was second only to military matters. Wilson asked Congress to create a federal body to manage domestic food supplies and prices on one hand, and organize and ship foodstuffs to the allies on the other. The director of this body should enjoy total control of the nation's food supplies.

This was a stunning request. Suspend the laws of supply and demand? Use federal authority and revenues to meddle with markets? Did the emergency of war warrant turning "the market" over to federal management?

For the next few months, Congress debated the nature of constitutional and congressional authority. In August 1917, Wilson signed the Food and Fuel Control Act, which, among other things, established a wartime United States Food Administration (USFA).[8]

Wilson had not waited for Congress. Three months before the bill landed on his desk, he assigned the job of Food Administrator (FA) to Herbert Hoover. It was he who would raid the nation's food stocks in order to insure that American troops and the Allies had enough to eat; keep food prices low for homefront consumers; and guarantee producers that they would profit.

Hoover (1874-1964; Commerce Secretary, 1921-28; president 1929-1933) was the logical choice for the job.

When the war broke out in 1914, he had hastened to Europe to organize a "relief" committee to provide food and necessities for refugees driven from their homes by invasion. Hoover gained considerable renown for that effort, which by any measure was a spectacular success. By the time he returned to the US in spring 1917, he was arguably one of the most famous people in the western world.

By training and temperament, he was an engineer, a term that in his mind included everything from designing mines and bridges to orchestrating food-supply logistics. Politically, Hoover was a devoted small-government Republican. He favored cooperation and volunteerism, which he dubbed "associationalism": governance and policy-making somewhere in between laissez faire, "invisible hand" capitalism, and overt, hands-on interference.

But this was war. And war, according to Hoover, warranted

government interference in economies and markets. If markets ran "free," and supply and demand unchecked, the masses would starve while the wealthy and the black-marketers reaped rewards.

He was also haunted by the recent Russian revolution, which he described as a "food riot" on the part of the "starving thousands" stirred to violence by a "radical and pacifist element." It was incumbent upon the United States to prevent the food shortages, high prices, and anger that provoked revolutions. "If through any failure of ours, we should bring about this situation among our western allies or among our people, there will rest upon us the responsibility for a failure of civilization and government larger than has ever rested upon a nation."[9]

Hoover intended to be master of his new domain. If appointed "to control the food supply of the United States," he told a reporter, his first task would be "to cut off every official and every theorist. There must be, above all, no professors on this job." Nor, he added, would he "be shackled by anybody in the Department of Agriculture."[10]

HOOVER'S FIRST JOB WAS TO GET CONSUMERS ON BOARD. His Belgian relief work taught him that Europeans were mentally prepared for war because they were "disciplined" in the practice of "simple living." Americans, however (according to Hoover), were undisciplined and practiced high living.

"We have gone for a hundred years of unbridled private initiative in this country and it has bred its own evils," he opined, one of which was "the lack of responsibility in the American individual to the people as a whole, the unwillingness of personal selfishness to sacrifice to national interest."[11]

And so he bullied, pleaded, cajoled, and nagged his countrymen to embrace a more frugal, efficient way of life, and support the war with a "psychology of conservation." Make do with less.

One example: Hoover asked citizens to avoid eating in restaurants. Most homes, he pointed out, boasted the "machinery of feeding": sinks, iceboxes, ovens, an experienced cook, and the like. A trip to a restaurant "duplicate[d]" that machinery. Worse, when Americans dined out, they ate "twice as much" as at home. Eating away from home was inefficiency incarnate, and a waste of food. Eat at home, he urged the nation, where "the gospel of the clean plate . . . must become universal."[12]

A US Food Administration poster, 1917.

He insisted that they change their diets. The troops and Allies were first in line for "concentrated foodstuffs — grain, beef, pork, fats, and sugar." But the nation had "a great surplus of potatoes, vegetables, fish, and poultry." Fill up on those, urged Hoover, and leave beef and pork to the troops.[13]

Persuading the public to eat fish and eggs was child's play compared to his main job: generating surpluses of those "concentrated foodstuffs" so that he could remove millions of tons of them from domestic supplies without creating shortages that would send prices out of control.

Indeed, Hoover's plan depended on surplus production: it was imperative that the US have "enough" of everything for itself and its allies. Should surpluses pile up, he planned to palm those off on to the allies — at prices set by him.

AS WE WILL SEE, THIS APPROACH TO SURPLUS RAISED EYEBROWS among those who understood how agriculture worked. It also met with pushback from allies, who, despite their desperation, resented forking over cash for the sake of serving as a food dump. (The Lord who managed Britain's wheat supplies described Hoover's "shifty hangdog manner" and "general craftiness of manner and phrase" as "discourteous and extremely unsavoury.")[14]

But Hoover was not one to ask for advice — he gave, he did not receive — and he pressed forward with construction of a food-dispersing machine.

Meatpackers were central cogs in the project. Hoover came into the job with neither respect nor fondness for packers. As far as he was concerned, they were a lying, cheating trust of middlemen. He found them "very difficult to deal with," although he conceded that they had a natural upper hand simply because because they "operat[ed] in large units."[15]

But he needed them. As Food Administrator, his success depended on access to transportation, warehouses, refrigerated rail cars, and established supply chains. The meatpackers had plenty of each.

But Hoover also knew that his clout and current events gave him a good hand, too. He needed what they had to offer, but his hand included the lucrative contracts he dangled before them: a promise to purchase at least forty percent of their output, which he would sell to the US military and "neutrals."

For the price of a federal operating license. No license, no war contracts. He also limited the Big Five's return on capital invested to nine percent, which angered the packers, who demanded ten percent. In response, Hoover played one of his strongest cards: A reminder that the Federal Trade Commission was engaged in a deep dive into their most intimate financial affairs. Was it perhaps in their best interest to cooperate with the Food Administration?

And if that didn't work, he played the patriot card and ordered them to do what was best for the country. "We have a good example in the condition of Russia where radical public opinion was allowed to go rampant . . . resulting in the entire collapse of property values."[16]

To their credit, the packers contributed above and beyond. They ramped up plants, abandoned handsaws for "power band saws," and installed technologies that enabled employees to process two thousand cattle a day, and fill 20,000 cans a day with meat products, such as corned beef hash (about 180,000 pounds a day). The packers also contributed glycerin, potash, and sulphuric acid, all of which were used in munitions manufacture, and supplied the government with glue, soap, and fertilizer.[17]

The Food Tsar, as Hoover was known (but not to his face) never entirely trusted the packers, but at the end, he praised them for providing "an indispensable service" during time of war. In the first half of 1918, Americans exported 1.5 billion pounds of beef and pork, "fresh, cured, and canned."[18]

IF INTERSTATE MEATPACKERS WERE ONE COG IN HIS MACHINE, farmers were another. Perhaps because of his general ignorance of matters agricultural, Hoover regarded its practitioners as an irritating but necessary nuisance en route to low food prices for consumers and big shipments to allies. In return, farmers made his life hell.

There were so many of them, all clamoring for different things. What was good for cattle feeders was bad for corn growers. What was good for wheat farmers was bad for corn. What was good for cotton growers was bad for hog farmers. As for rice (which Hoover begged Americans to substitute for wheat), who knew?

Hoover was primarily interested in wheat growers (whose story parallels this one) and hog farmers. The latter provided Hoover with a crash course in the complexities of agriculture and the paradox of plenty.

Hogs were central to his agenda: they provided cheap, easily processed protein that shipped well, and their short life cycle facilitated the process of scaling production up or down as needed. He urged American farmers to "raise hogs, and more hogs, and still more hogs."[19]

That they should be rewarded for their output was an afterthought to the engineer-in-chief. Only when others pointed out the problem of profit did Hoover come up with a plan, one based on the work of Henry C. Wallace (1866-1934), an Iowa farmer and publisher of an influential agricultural weekly (and a persistent thorn in Hoover's side).

Over many years working with corn and hogs, Wallace had tracked a stable relationship between hog production and corn prices. When the price of one hundred pounds of live hog equaled or exceeded the price of (approximately) eleven bushels of corn, farmers fed hogs. When hog prices fell below that threshold, they raised corn.

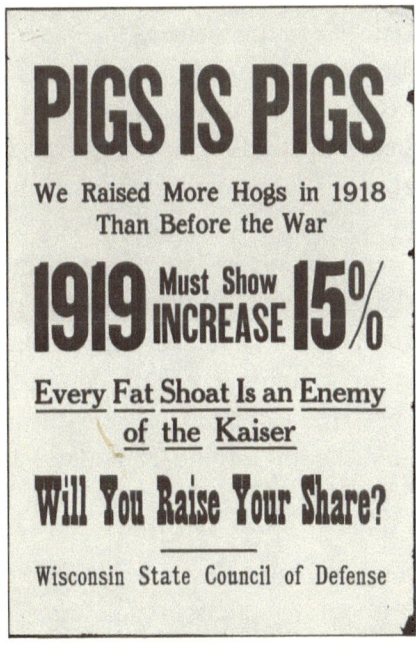

A 1918 plea for more hogs.

Using the Wallace ratio, Hoover assumed eight months to fatten a hog; calculated the average price of corn over eight months; multiplied that number by eleven; and bingo!: hog producers would enjoy "absolute assurance" of a fair profit.

Or not. Hoover's tidy calculations ignored a crucial factor: the cost of production. When his advisory committee pointed this out and demanded a corn/hog ratio of 14 to one rather than 11 to one in order to cover production costs, Hoover accused them of "exploit[ing] the country" during a time of war.[20]

Nor would he offer a price guarantee. He explained that he could do so only if that price was backed by a $1 billion fund from "responsible quarters" (i.e., Congress). (An institution where, it should be noted, Hoover was not particularly popular.) Joseph Cotton, a Wall Street lawyer who, for reasons no one understood, chaired Hoover's Meat Division piled on, warning hog farmers that Hoover's plan was "not a guarantee backed by money. . . . It is a statement of the intention and policy of the Food Administration which means to do justice to the farmer."[21]

Negotiations between hog producers and Hoover's minions dragged on for two months. Farmers were convinced, rightly, that Hoover favored consumers and meatpackers. He did so because he feared the "disturbances" that could erupt if consumers decided they were paying "too much" for basics. As one of his advisers phrased it, there were "ninety million consumers in this country" who were "entitled to be heard" on the subject of prices.[22]

For his part, Hoover became increasingly impatient with the hog farmers. For "certain members of our community," he fumed, money was the only "inducement" to help the war effort. "The German farmer in the name of the Fatherland supports a nation two-thirds as large as ours . . . on an area" the size of Texas, he wrote.

"If we cannot find this same devotion" in a democracy "without compulsion and without payment in guarantees, I, for one, am prepared to . . . accept autocracy for Democracy will have demonstrated its inability to defend itself."[23]

Hog farmers held firm, and in the end, Hoover agreed to a ratio of 13/14-to-1, and agreed to exercise "full control" over exports and military buys in order to insure that price (a glib statement that meant nothing given that he already exercised "full control" over everything related to food). He also promised to keep the packers in check.

But it was clear he never understood the paradox of plenty. Henry Wallace lamented the Food Tsar's ignorance. "From every side," he wrote, "people beset [Hoover] to hold down the cost of living," but neither Hoover nor "the people" "understand that if the cost of food products is held down below the cost of production, the farmer can not continue to produce." Making more of "the thing," whether hogs or corn, meant consumers paid lower prices and farmers went broke.[24]

AND THAT WAS JUST DURING HOOVER'S FIRST SIX MONTHS IN OFFICE. The winter of 1917-1918 nearly broke him and the nation.

In early December 1917, rail service snarled and came to a halt from coast to coast. Cargos could not move, and because they could not, there were no empty cars to haul the next cargo in line. Coal, already in limited supply, sat on rail tracks for days on end, so long that it often froze during the course of its sluggish travel.

Then in early January 1918, two dozen barges carrying precious coal sank after crashing into ice. A week later, a ferocious blizzard shut down the midwest. The Commissioner of Immigration foiled an alleged plot by Italian anarchists to steal food from warehouses and depots around the country. The president of Cornell University warned of an impending famine, and some cities took the drastic step of capping retail food prices.[25]

Cattle and hog feeders seized the moment.

Convinced that their woes were due to the Beef Trust and Hoover's inept meddling, they launched an attack on the Food Administration and its head honcho. Their vehicle was a series of February 1918 Senate hearings to determine how, if at all, the nation ought to increase the production of wheat and meat.[26]

A. Sykes (1861-1939), president of the Corn Belt Producers'

Association, was the first to address the Senate Committee on Agriculture and Forestry.[27] He was blunt: when Herbert Hoover established minimum sale prices for hogs, his calculations failed to include the cost of producing said hogs.

Livestock producers were also angry that their fates were being determined by an engineer and a Wall Street lawyer who'd likely never been near a feeding operation in his life. Indeed, none of Hoover's advisors was a "practical farmer," who would have told him and Cotton that a price pulled from the air was of no use whatsoever.[28]

"If the Government is going to regulate prices at all, gentlemen," Sykes told the senators, "it must regulate all prices or it must not regulate any prices, and it must regulate these prices with a view to the cost of production." The "farmers of this great American Republic," he added, "feel that they ought to have some voice in at least arranging their own business and saying how it shall be conducted and how these markets shall be fixed." As matters stood, only "patriotism" kept them going, because they were making no profit on their labor.[29]

The executive board of the American National Live Stock Association (ANLSA) turned out in force for the hearings (and preceded that appearance with a White House meeting with President Wilson). Speaking on behalf of the members, Dwight B. Heard, a powerful stockman from Arizona, told the Senators that the price of livestock feed was sky high, thanks to war and drought.

The price of feed, explained Heard, was "determined by the law of supply and demand," but the prices paid for cattle and hogs were "controlled by the Food Administration in the interest of the consumer." Add in the railroad crisis, and a "material increase" in the cost of farm labor, and livestock feeders were going broke, literally.[30]

Heard and other ANLSA members resented the hypocrisy. "While the meat producer sees his industry in serious danger . . . he finds labor amply protected and receiving liberal returns, and the meat packers. . . and producers of steel, copper, flour, sugar, lumber, and many other commodities make liberal profits." A livestock producer "naturally feels that he is entitled to fair returns."[31]

Another Association member told the senators that both Hoover and President Wilson had urged livestock growers to produce to the maximum. At "diverse times and in different ways," and weaving a "fine-spun argument," they had "assured" producers of "a reasonable profit." Somebody "had the power to put prices down, and whoever had the power to put them down has the power to raise them."[32]

E.L. Burke, the firebrand whose 1914 speech inspired the ANLSA to seek federal help, piled on. "The Government from the start, ignoring the cost of production, has controlled prices in the interest of the consumer."[33]

But, he added, the Food Administration, loathed though it might be, represented a "link between the old and the new order of things." In the old days, packers controlled the market; in the new order, producers must get a fair shake. Wartime price controls, said Burke, must become "permanent."[34]

The "better they do it and the more they learn during the war . . . working out the problems connected with it," the better positioned the nation would be when "the time comes for handling them for good."[35]

Eventually Meat Division chief Joseph Cotton showed up. The audience had already enjoyed a few laughs at his expense (he was an expert in watered stock, but knew nothing about live stock), and he made no friends during his brief time at the witness table. "I want to impress upon you once more that the main work of the division is to get beef and hog meat on certain ships and going," he said. The Food Administration's work "must go on, no matter who gets hurt."[36]

THE DAYS WORE ON. MORE WITNESSES TESTIFIED. AND THEN ON March 15, Committee Chairman Thomas P. Gore (D-Ok) asked Henry C. Wallace the only question that mattered.

Wallace was in the middle of a detailed presentation, complete with charts and graphs, explaining that recent wild price fluctuations at stockyards were anything but the "stable" prices Hoover had promised producers.

Chairman Gore interrupted to ask a "lengthy" question. "Is it possible to stabilize prices without stabilizing the factors of cost that go to make up the price?"[37]

"Is it possible," he mused, obviously thinking aloud, to "stabilize the price of hogs without stabilizing the rent of land, the rate of interest, the wages of labor, the price of corn, and the other things that go to make up the total cost of the hog?" In order to stabilize, say, agricultural labor wages, was it also necessary to stabilize the price of board, lodgings, and clothing? Or, he wondered, "is the ramification of that process infinite, and isn't that what makes it an impossible" project?[38]

At that point, another senator jumped in with a less philosophical inquiry, and Wallace carried on with his charts and graphs. But some minutes later, he returned to Gore's queries.

Yes, said Wallace, "unquestionably" once begun, a stabilization cycle is endless. But in his mind, the main problem was the fundamental gap between producers and consumers. Wallace elaborated with a telling example from recent upheaval in the dairy industry.

In response to fluctuating prices, Chicago milk producers staged a general strike. City officials established a commission composed of producers and consumers, and charged them with determining a fair retail price for milk.

The committee's *producers* based their price on the costs of production, such as the price of "corn, hay, silage, mill feed, etc." Alas, on this committee, producers were outnumbered by consumers, who rejected this "perfectly sound way" of calculating prices. The urbanites decided that milk should cost 12 cents a quart, and then "juggled" the numbers until 12 cents finally tumbled in to place.

One of the senators didn't get it. *Why* the juggling? "Well," replied Wallace, "the people in Chicago, Senator, thought that milk ought to sell for 12 cents a quart retail," and so that was the price, production costs be damned.

The "great trouble," Wallace explained, was the "attitude of the representatives of the Government." They regarded farmers as simply another "organized business" and proceeded accordingly: meet with representatives; discuss the grievance/ask/demand; come up with an agreement; voila! "the trouble is over."

But in agriculture, he said, there were few or no "representatives." The term "farmer" covered a lot of territory, so to speak. You could no "more commit the farmer to a general policy through a few representatives," said Wallace, "than you can fly to the moon."

AS USUAL, HOOVER TOOK THE CRITIQUE PERSONALLY AND LAUNCHED a counterattack.

In his role as Food Administrator, he was responding to "the total economic dislocations imposed by the war." The Allies were buying goods on behalf of 120 million people. On the home front, the USFA was buying supplies for two million troops. It was "absolutely impossible" to meet such needs by relying on "normal commercial agencies." As a result, the federal government, via Hoover's office, was in effect a temporary "gigantic monopoly."[39]

It was "an actual physical fact," Hoover explained, that "this one gigantic buyer dominates the market" by both "making and influencing prices." He recognized that economists and theorists had "never contemplated" this kind of "price-fixing," and certainly not on this scale. But the global situation demanded that "Government must necessarily regulate the price," and economists must abandon cherished textbook "theories" and "procrustean formulas of supply and demand."[40]

All of it — designing the machine, managing it, defending it — took a toll. No matter what Hoover did, his "impossible job" inevitably made someone unhappy. If it wasn't the haranguing and (in his mind) near-persecution from a mostly hostile Congress, it was the nonstop wrangling and "eternal opposition" between producers and consumers, who forced him to wage a constant battle to "balance" the rights of those two parties. Whose rights to a fair profit mattered most? Whose price was the right price? Whose price was fair to whom?⁴¹

Market meddling also left his small-government mind ill at ease: "Whenever you begin to tamper with a normal course of commerce you have to keep on tampering," he explained. And tampering and tampering, on and on, in an endless Sisphyean struggle to make a perfect market that produced perfect prices.⁴²

Don't be surprised, Hoover told one correspondent, to "hear that I have 'cracked up.'"⁴³

HE DIDN'T, BUT FOR BETTER OR FOR WORSE, THE USFA SERVED AS A laboratory for exploring ways to sustain a consumer economy. Certainly the war provided an extended exercise in federal involvement in affairs economic, industrial, and agricultural.

But the war years also demonstrated agriculture's significance to the economy, the gross national product, and civil order. In the wake of the war, Americans would elaborate on those lessons, forge a new kind of agriculture, and explore ways to insure both profits for farmers and low-cost food for consumers.

CHAPTER 6

GOOD-BYE TO ALL THAT

TWO VIGNETTES FROM THE 1920S ILLUSTRATE A PIVOTAL LESSON OF the Great War: Americans could do without meat.

THE FIRST TAKES PLACE IN 1923. WITH MEAT CONSUMPTION IN FREE fall, the National Live Stock and Meat Board (NLSMB) decided to fight back. The Board, which consisted of meat packers (intra- and interstate) and producers of an assortment of livestock species, launched a wide-ranging campaign to promote meat.

The Meat Board sent lecturers hither and yon, placed pro-meat articles in newspapers and magazines, and bombarded teachers with instructional material. Industry representatives touted meat's virtues via radio (the nation's newest communication medium). During "Meat for Health" week, the Board's publicity arm cranked out 3 million pieces of literature, including pamphlets, advertisements, and posters for windows and meat wagons. Paid speakers hosted informational programs at butcher shops and grocery stores.

As part of the project, the Milwaukee Meat Council, a local group of packers and retailers, hired an actor to portray a caveman, presumably because such a figure epitomized brute strength and good health. He strolled up and down one of the city's busiest streets, carrying a club and wearing a "shabby mane and beard, bear skin, [and] sandals." A sign on his back read "I EAT MEAT."[1]

Fun on the sidewalks of Milwaukee.

THE SECOND OCCURS IN 1926. THE NEW YORK CITY BOARD OF Education banned frankfurters from school lunchrooms, declaring such sausages as "unsuited" to students' nutritional needs: children filled up on this "heavy" meat, and then "neglected to eat green stuff."[2]

Meat people were outraged. A butchers' trade magazine

denounced the attack, and praised the frankfurter because it provided "the most nutriment for the money." Having taught children that frankfurters were "unwholesome," students carried that message home, and their mothers banished sausages from "the home table."

The decision to take it off school menus, sighed one manufacturer, "puts us back ten years, at least."

The Department of Agriculture, patron of both franks and the green stuff, defended sausages as "wholesome, appetizing and economical." Served with bread and a drink, "they provide lunches that are hard to beat when time is a factor and the pangs of hunger are to be fully satisfied."[3]

AS WE'VE SEEN, MEAT CONSUMPTION DROPPED YEAR AFTER YEAR, AND for many reasons. One of them was the Board of Education's "green stuff," which contained the newest in nutritional science: the vitamine, as it was originally dubbed.

The identification of the vitamin complex was the work of scientists around the world in the late nineteenth century. They were convinced that foodstuffs contained an X factor; a component other than protein, carbohydrates, and fat. Scurvy, for example, could be cured only with certain foods, especially citrus fruits. Why? What did citrus contain that, say, beef did not?

In 1910, a Japanese scientist described what he called a "vitamin complex," and two years later, a chemist in London affirmed the role of amines in nutrition. In 1913, American researchers, including two at Wisconsin's land grant school, identified a life-essential amine in milk fat, Vitamin A. Here was "incontrovertible evidence" of a "hitherto unsuspected nutrient indispensable for health and . . . the maintenance of life."[4]

Over the next few years, scientists decoded vitamins' mysteries and their implications for nutrition. The USDA and its partners studied vitamins from every conceivable angle, from their role in human nutrition to the benefits of vitamins for livestock. Department agents helped restaurateurs, hospitals — and school boards — incorporate the "Newer Nutrition" into the foods they served.

The nation's thousands of magazines and newspapers piled on, often relying on information from USDA bulletins and press releases. Writers praised the virtues of spinach, lettuce, tomatoes, and other once-lowly foodstuffs.[5]

"Feed your body vitamins," urged a typical essay in 1919. The body demands these "Unknowns," "mysterious substances that have defied chemical isolation and analysis, but which have a powerful and determining effect on growth."[6]

Meat consumption would never be the same.

VITAMINS LURED CONSUMERS AWAY FROM STEAK AND BACON, BUT high prices continued to drive them away in hordes. Unlike previous years, however, neither packer nor stockgrower nor herd size was to blame in the 1920s. Instead, the fault lay in food wholesale and retail. Those were mired in inefficiency and nineteenth-century logistics that were wholly unsuited to modern urban landscapes.

Most Americans still shopped for food the way their grandparents had: dry goods like flour and spices at one store; perishables such as potatoes, onions, and apples at another; meat from a butcher shop. Shop owners bought merchandise in small lots from multiple food jobbers, each of whom carried a narrow line of goods. Thus the traffic jams, as multiple vehicles made multiple stops to deliver multiple small orders to multiple shop owners.

Delivery wagons and trucks converged on warehouse and market districts via narrow streets built decades earlier. A single truck parked at a warehouse could block access to an entire street, forcing others to idle their horses and engines in side streets. All the while, grapes and lettuce, potatoes and onions, hams and steaks suffered whatever weather blessed that day.[7]

A USDA report calculated the inefficiencies. Suppose a wholesaler bought a carload of lettuce totaling 320 crates. A typical jobber purchased 1/16 of that load; a retailer 1/320; and the consumer "one head or 1/7,680 of a car." Each subdivision of the original carload added to the final retail price.[8]

A slightly upscale grocery store in 1920.

The urban grocery business was often the refuge of the incompetent and inexperienced. A study of Oshkosh, Wisconsin, revealed that grocers there included a policeman, a shoemaker, and a musician, which, claimed one analyst, was why so many retailers failed. In Louisville, Kentucky, a third of grocers failed after a year; in Buffalo, New York, 60 percent went under.[9]

A consumer economy based on low-cost food necessitated a revolution in food retailing. Chain grocery stores, which offered a nearly miraculous alternative, began appearing around 1910, but in the 1920s, their numbers expanded significantly.[10]

Chain grocers celebrated the pleasures of food shopping, offering clean, well-lit shops, wheeled carts, low prices, and, thanks to self-service, maximum convenience. Shoppers were free to browse the array of foodstuffs, from (green) produce to canned goods. In contrast to small neighborhood grocers who sourced their goods from wholesalers and brokers, chains ordered directly from manufacturers, and in large quantities. Bulk buying meant lower retail prices.

Food manufacturers benefited, too. By dealing with a single grocery chain rather than hundreds of individual retailers, they reduced bookkeeping and accounting expenses, to say nothing of costs associated with sales and delivery.[11]

IN THOSE EARLY YEARS, HOWEVER, EVEN THE CHAINS STRUGGLED TO tame meat retailing, which was its own special quagmire.

Tens of thousands of small retailers sold meat; no one knew the exact number, but best estimates placed it at around ninety thousand. Some were well-managed speciality stores staffed by skilled butchers. But the majority were holes-in-the-wall with no refrigeration and incompetent proprietors. Add in meat peddlers hawking from wagons, and mom-and-pop stores that sold a few groceries and meats of questionable origin, and meat retailing was a poster child for inefficiency and the high price of meat.

According to a study of Chicago's five thousand meat markets, a quarter of new butcher shops closed in the first year; sixty per cent did so after three. That "short life and high turnover" forced meat-packers, jobbers, and wholesalers to deal with a "constantly changing" clientele, which devoured salesmen's time, necessitated excessive paperwork, and translated into higher prices for consumers.[12]

Moreover, meat retailing thrived on deception. Butchers sold goat for lamb, horse for beef, beef suet for pork sausage, and end cuts for center pieces. "Clean-up men" and pseudo-butchers lured customers by advertising "exceptionally high-quality meats" and selling ones "of the most inferior quality." Many butchers, the study noted, attached weights to the underside of scales so as to cheat every customer who walked through the door.[13]

Meat even confounded chain store executives. They were confident that they could bring skill, integrity, and proper storage to meat retailing. But as one put it in 1930, "[c]hain store merchandising is founded on control," and meat's unwieldy carcasses, and fat, gristle, and bone made it a difficult beast to tame.[14]

An executive with A&P, the nation's biggest grocery chain,

begged the nation's meat makers to whip meat into shape so it behaved less like itself and more like canned peas: a uniform, compact, manageable product. "It is now possible to buy bread already cut in slices," he argued, so surely it was "logically and economically" possible to offer consumers pre-packaged meats.¹⁵

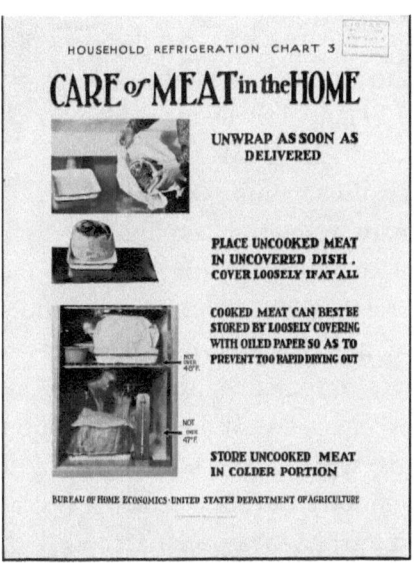

The always on-the-ball USDA had something for every occasion. In this case, the lessons are from the Department's Bureau of Home Economics. 1929.

IF ONLY IT WERE THAT SIMPLE. "THE PACKAGING OF COFFEE, crackers, cereals is child's play compared with packaging of fresh meats," marveled one reporter. "A whole new technic must be worked out."¹⁶

Even when packaging succeeded, customers weren't sure what to do with it. One retailer recounted the day an angry customer marched into his store and demanded a refund for a package of bacon she'd bought three weeks earlier. The meat was spoiled, she told the man. The puzzled grocer asked her where she'd stored it. On top of her ice box, she replied, but that "should be of no significance" because the bacon was in "a 'sealed package' and should not require special care." (Presumably the woman's refund included a quick lesson in packaging and refrigeration.)[17]

SUCH WAS THE PUBLIC FACE OF MEAT IN THE TWENTIES. BEHIND THE scenes, turmoil ruled, as two separate but connected events upended the lives and work of meatpackers and livestock producers alike.

The meatpackers' turmoil began first.

In early 1918, Senators William S. Kenyon (1869-1933, R-IA) and John B. Kendrick (R-WY, 1857-1933) urged President Woodrow Wilson to nationalize the interstate meatpackers, and introduced a Senate resolution urging the transfer of packers' companies from private to public ownership. In theory, the measure would break the trust's grip on the nation's food supplies, increase packer competition, and drive down food prices.

The idea wasn't as startling as it sounds. Just a few months earlier, during the winter of wartime transportation chaos, President Wilson had authorized the United States Railroad Administration to commandeer the nation's railways. Now the two senators asked to do the same with interstate meatpacking.

Initially, their ask went nowhere, hardly a surprise given the pressures of war and general suspicion of government ownership. But it gained new life when, in mid-summer 1918, the Federal Trade Commission (FTC) delivered a report castigating the interstate meatpackers in rich detail.

Recall that in early 1917, and in response to stockgrower pressure, the president had ordered the FTC to analyze the nation's food systems. To that end, FTC staff combed through millions of pages of packers' records, memos, and letters, and heard from dozens of witnesses.[18]

The result was everything stockgrowers and anti-corporate/antitrust interests had hoped for: six volumes of excruciating detail, often in the packers' own words, about the ways in which they managed and manipulated more or less as they pleased. It appeared to confirm anything and everything that anyone and everyone had ever suspected about the Meat Trust. (Careful readers, however, noticed that many conclusions were based on flimsy evidence, and that much of what the packers did was legal.)[19]

The FTC's director added his own warning: this handful of corporations was intimately, multifariously entwined in the nation's food systems. So entwined, he charged, that barring intervention, "actual control of the nation's food supply" by "five packers . . . [was] entirely probable."[20]

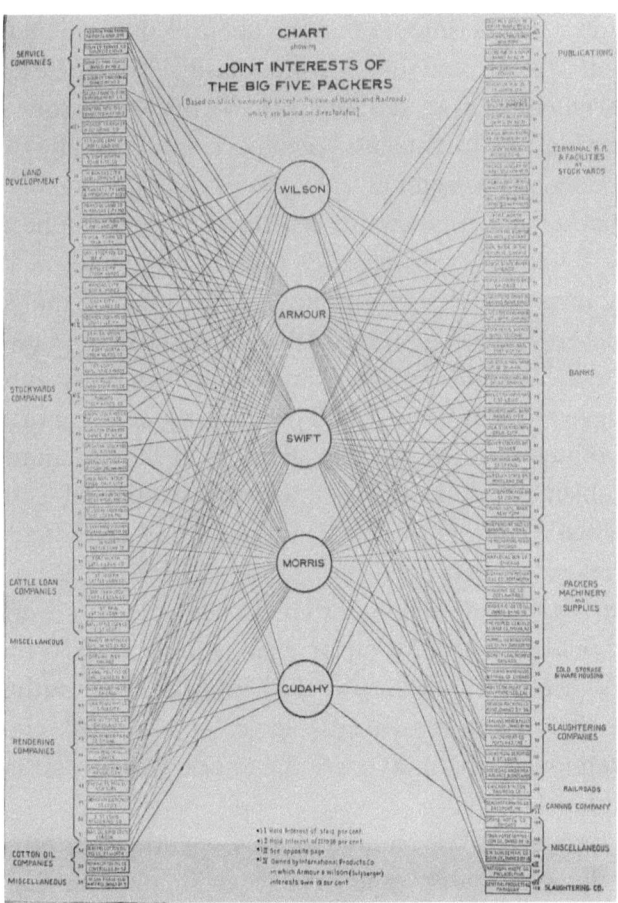

A diagram from the FTC's report on the packers. They were deeply involved in the nation's food systems. The chart is equally difficult to read in its original form, so many were the links.

Which was precisely the point the American National Live Stock Association had made two years earlier.

Thanks to the FTC report, the nationalization scheme was on the table. By early 1919, both House and Senate were deep into testimony and debate about the merits of *Government Control of the Meat-Packing Industry*, as the hearings were titled. A subtitle elaborated: "A Bill to Stimulate the Production, Sale, and Distribution of Live Stock and Live-Stock Products, and for Other Purposes."[21]

Naturally, skepticism and outrage abounded: surely nationalization paved a road straight to communism. Nonetheless, a clear consensus emerged from the hearings: Virtually everyone opposed nationalization of interstate meatpacking; virtually everyone supported federal oversight of it.

The packers fought back. In February 1919, as the hearings got underway, Thomas E. Wilson (1868-1958), president of Wilson & Company meatpackers and a prominent member of the American Meat Packers Association (AMPA), presented an unexpected proposal to the members of the Kansas Livestock Association.

He suggested that packers and producers join forces in a permanent committee that would meet monthly to handle mutual grievances, problems, and needs. Such a demonstration of cooperation might persuade Congress to back away from formal federal supervision of packers' affairs.

Wilson explained that in order for the plan to work, stockgrowers would first need to create a single organization that represented all livestock producers and enjoyed "full authority" to represent their interests. Packers spoke and lobbied via AMPA, Wilson reminded the audience. Livestock producers needed a similar national entity.

Thus organized, Wilson argued, packer and producer could "sit down at the same table" and engage in "intelligent, fearless and unselfish" discussion and, in theory, present a united front to federal officials. (No doubt some in the audience wondered where Wilson was four years earlier, when livestock producers had begged packers to sit at the same table.)[22]

AMPA's self-interest was obvious. And its timing was terrible. Or calculatingly cruel.

Even as Wilson proposed this alternative to federal oversight, even as House and Senate hearings contemplated packer nationalization, livestock producers were mired in a horrific agricultural price collapse that was sweeping them into foreclosure on a daily basis. The packers knew that producers were desperate; perhaps they assumed desperation would drive them into the packers' embrace.

This "price toboggan," as one historian described it, would last for years, and led, eventually, to agricultural subsidies and other government manipulation of markets. Our concern here is with the triggering event.[23]

During the war, President Wilson, Herbert Hoover, and the USDA urged agriculturalists to produce as much as possible. Even when the war ended, Hoover explained (repeatedly), American farmers would need to support postwar rebuilding abroad.

Agriculturalists obliged. Millions mortgaged and borrowed in order to buy more land and livestock, to build barns and silos, and purchase feed, fuel, tools, fertilizers that boosted yields, and draft animals (still the primary source of farm power).

Wilson, Hoover, and the USDA miscalculated. When the fighting stopped in November 1918, US military officials and foreign countries promptly canceled contracts.

In a matter of weeks, corn prices fell 78 percent. Wheat dropped by half. As beef exports plunged, cattle prices collapsed. In the first quarter of 1919, the price of finished beef cattle dropped 25 percent, and the price of low grade 15 percent. Feeders stopped buying cattle; western stock producers culled herds.[24]

Desperate to find buyers, and earnings with which to pay their debts, producers dumped crops and livestock on the market. As always, the ensuing glut pushed prices off the cliff. Rural banks failed. Rural populations declined as residents fled to cities in search of stability.

And no matter how low prices sank, farmers kept producing, glutting markets, and destroying any chance of making a profit.

Such was the situation when AMPA proposed a partnership with livestock producers. Perhaps in a different year, the livestock crowd would have dismissed the packers. But producers were desperate, and in March 1919, AMPA members and representatives of multiple state, regional, and national livestock organizations gathered to discuss the proposal. The livestock attendees tentatively endorsed the proposition; their respective memberships would make the final decision.

Thomas Wilson, never one to miss a chance, took that as a yes and a done deal, and dispatched press releases to that effect.

A rude awakening arrived in the form of Wyoming Senator John B. Kendrick, one of the masterminds behind the packer nationalization effort.

Kendrick was a long-time cattle producer and member of the ANLSA. In 1919, he also happened to be the association's president. And he wanted nothing to do with a joint packer-producer committee on which producers would be a minority. More to the point, he told his colleagues, a committee could not begin to "destroy the absolute control" of the packers. Only legislation would accomplish the job.[25]

Livestock producers, neck-deep in crisis and collapse, got the message. In May 1919, they organized a national Committee of Fifteen composed of representatives of every major livestock association. No packers allowed.

BY THAT TIME, THE PACKERS' PLOT HAD THICKENED. IN SPRING 1919, Congress removed nationalization from its agenda, thanks to the nation's first Red Scare of the century. The Great War had formally ended, but in its wake a number of countries, including Russia, experienced violent turmoil involving various isms. Many feared the poison would wash on to American shores.

A rash of postwar labor strikes exacerbated that fear. According to the press, and millions of Americans, the strikes were likely the work of Italian anarchists, or Bolsheviks eager to deliver the US to Russia and communism. In April, federal officials uncovered a bomb plot. In June, activists detonated bombs in eight cities. The man who targeted the home of US Attorney General A. Mitchell Palmer died in his own explosion. (Palmer was not hurt, although his house was badly damaged.)

Palmer, a man with presidential ambitions, launched a full bore assault on Bolshie Bogies, ignoring the constitution in the process and creating a Justice Department unit that morphed into the Federal Bureau of Investigation a few years later. The Sedition Act of 1918 provided easy mechanisms for deportation and censorship. The Senate delved into alleged communist-sponsored activities.

The image of wild-eyed, bomb-throwing anarchists running amok in streets and factories was too much to bear. Almost overnight, public opinion condemned anything and everything that smacked of socialism, nationalization, or communism.

And congress scurried away from even a hint of nationalization. Members even questioned the validity of the FTC report on grounds that some of the staff involved were socialists. An Indiana senator demanded that the report's authors be investigated for "sedition and criminal anarchy." The ensuing internal witch-hunt included sifting through the trash at the homes of several FTC staff members.[26]

Alas, the packers' relief was short-lived. That summer, Palmer took a break from hunting Reds to open a new investigation into meatpacking, one he planned to base on the FTC's damning pages.

The packers cried uncle. In autumn 1919, they agreed to divest all of their non-meat-related holdings, including stockyards and media, and to use their cold-storage facilities only for meat. In exchange, Palmer dropped the case.[27]

The packers had signed away their collective past. The Beef Trust was no more.

THAT MOMENT WAS NEARLY OVERSHADOWED BY ANOTHER EVENT: THE November launch of a national farmers' organization, the American Farm Bureau Federation (AFBF). "[N]o longer," crowed one celebrant, would the "American farmer weakly submit to being the scapegoat of either capital or labor."[28] As its first act, the Bureau would force Congress to sign on to federal supervision of the packers.

The Bureau's history is rooted in the USDA. In the first decade of the twentieth century, Department agents organized "extension" services, the better to dispense USDA expertise to farmers in, say, Texas or California. Working with groups or one-on-one, USDA county agents taught the latest in farm management practice, from planting to tilling to bookkeeping, helping farmers use science and technology to produce better crops and higher profits.

In response to this outreach, many farmers organized county "bureaus," the better to learn from and cooperate with their assigned USDA agent. The term "bureau" was intentional: bureau members were decidedly businesslike in their approach to farming, and bureau conjured busy, businesslike ventures. County bureaus proliferated after 1914, when Congress approved regular funding for extension activities. The ranks of agents swelled markedly after the US entered the war in 1917: the USDA and Food Administration assigned all manner of new duties to these men and women on the ground.[29]

In December 1918, members of the National Association of County Agricultural Agents approved a resolution urging county bureaus first, to organize state bureaus, the better to represent county interests, and second, to bring the state bureaus together in a national bureau.[30]

And so it came to pass that in November 1919, a collection of bureau delegates formally launched the American Farm Bureau Federation. A spokesperson assured the public that Bureau members were "unqualifiedly in sympathy with the government's determination to suppress radicalism, and lend our full support to all effort to rid this country of Bolshevism and all other anarchistic tendencies."[31]

In March 1920, the AFBF opened an office in Washington, DC (Bureau headquarters was in Chicago), and dispatched agents to the halls of Congress in order to "establish points of contact with the government and with business organizations." And in June, the livestock producers' Committee of Fifteen voted to turn its work over to the Farm Bureau, explaining that the "character of the federation and the personnel of its officiary give promise."[sic][32]

EVENTS SOON PROVED THE WISDOM OF THAT DECISION.

In summer 1920, agricultural prices collapsed to previously uncharted depths.

In autumn, farmers produced the biggest corn crop in the nation's history; most of it went to waste. One measure of its market value: a Kansas town opted to buy corn rather than coal for its winter heating needs.

Heading into winter, the Chicago Union Yards recorded their largest receipts since opening in 1865, as livestock producers unloaded every four-legged creature they had. The prices paid didn't begin to cover their costs of production, let alone make a dent in their debts.[33]

Farmers begged for assistance. New Treasury Secretary David Houston was unmoved; it was not the government's job to provide funding for farmers. The Federal Reserve Board also dismissed the pleas: there was no cause for alarm. The current circumstances were "inevitable and unavoidable consequences of the economic derangements" of war.[34]

So, too, the powerful US Chamber of Commerce: "depressions in agricultural sections . . . are neither so lasting nor so severe as those in industrial centers." The "farming community can furnish its own subsistence and tide over bad times."[35]

Here was stark evidence of one of farmers' biggest complaints: second-class treatment. Neither Treasury nor Reserve Board had any qualms about dispensing credit and assistance to other industries, but balked at doing the same for agriculture. What did the Chamber think kept its commerce going? Wishes and dreams?

Rural districts seethed with rage. In joint hearings of the House and Senate Agriculture Committees, a Nebraska farmer warned that out west, the price collapse had fertilized "a bumper crop of bolshevism."[36]

THE AFBF SEIZED THE MOMENT. THE NEW SESSION OF CONGRESS that opened in early 1921 was marked by "conspicuous lobbying," as angry, but organized agriculturalists swarmed Capitol Hill. Eastern members of Congress, mostly oblivious to rural rage, were startled and somewhat disdainful of the farmers clamoring for attention. The Bureau was undeterred. "We do not lobby. We present facts. We get the will of our people and lay it before Congress."[37]

In April, Bureau leadership steered farm groups through a ten-day lobbying spree in Washington conferring with, among others, new Secretary of Commerce Herbert Hoover; new Agriculture Secretary Henry C. Wallace; the Governor of the much-hated Federal Reserve Board; the head of the Federal Farm Loan Board, and the chair of the Interstate Commerce Commission.

In May, Gray Silver, the AFBF's chief lobbyist, organized a Congressional Farm Bloc composed of senators and representatives from farm states. The Bloc was adamantly bi-partisan and prepared to ignore party politics in order to transform their agenda into law. (Their colleagues were not amused.)[38]

Organized pressure paid off in June, when House members approved a measure that imposed federal oversight on packers and stockyards. An opponent described the bill as "a government oligarchy of socialism," but livestock producers were jubilant.[39]

From there, House members moved on to matters related to appropriations, and the Senate promptly moved to adjourn: DC is soggy hot in summer, and few wanted to dither while the House tinkered with the nation's money.

Farmers were infuriated, interpreting adjournment as a way for Senators to dodge the packer regulation bill approved by the House. To the astonishment and rage of many, the Senate Farm Bloc defeated the resolution to adjourn. No one would go anywhere until House and Senate both passed a packer/yards bill.

On August 15, 1921, after almost seven years of lobbying by livestock producers, President Harding signed the Packers-Stockyards Act, which placed interstate packers and most stockyards under the supervision of the Department of Agriculture (where they remain today).

THE VICTORY DID LITTLE TO STANCH THE BLEEDING. IT COULD NOT prevent crops from rotting in fields, or deter stockmen from culling herds. Nor did it assuage the growing political unrest in the mid- and far west.

Utah Senator Reed Smoot (1862-1941, R-UT) warned that a "radical wave" had "swept the Middle West" and sparked "an uprising of farmers because of intolerable conditions." Farmers were "ready to strike at anyone." Senator William E. Borah agreed. Anyone who did "not understand that there is practically a political revolution on," was obviously "totally blind."[40]

Apparently the blind included President Warren G. Harding (1865-1923, president 1921-23). When he opened a National Agricultural Conference in January 1922, he repeated the party line: in the current crisis, legislation could "do little more than give the farmer the chance to organize and help himself." Channeling Commerce Secretary Hoover, Harding argued that voluntary cooperation was the best way, the only way, to stabilize prices and produce profits.[41]

Had the conference been held two years earlier, its Committee on Marketing would certainly have assented and returned a resolution espousing the virtues of voluntarism and cooperative marketing. Not in 1922.

In its report to the full body, the Marketing Committee asserted that when producers earned less than "the cost of production," federal officials should "reestablish a fair exchange value for all farm products" relative to the prices of "other commodities."[42]

The statement was written by George N. Peek (1873-1943), co-owner of the recently-failed Moline Plow Company, which went under because broke farmers couldn't afford to buy what Peek and his business partner Hugh S. Johnson (1882-1942) sold. The pair channeled their frustration into a plan to stabilize agricultural prices and insure farmer profits.

They proposed that the federal government purchase surpluses of various commodities, thereby removing them from the market and creating a scarcity. As prices rose, officials would release surplus to the domestic market. Any surplus not finding a minimum domestic price would be sold by the government on the global market.

The idea of crop withholding was not new. Since 1905, some in agriculture had favored the "Joseph Plan" of holding surpluses in order to wait for higher prices. In 1920, Henry A. Wallace (son of Henry C.) had proposed a similar plan, which the USDA's then-secretary Edwin T. Meredith endorsed in his 1920 annual report.[43]

The Peek-Johnson plan incorporated complex mechanisms to achieve the intended outcome; indeed, it was so complicated that few admitted to understanding the details.

But supporters understood its gist: the problem in American agriculture wasn't Beef Trusts or disorderly marketing or sloppy retailing. The problem was surplus, and agriculturalists' seemingly inherent need to maximize production at all costs. The savviest cooperative marketing in the world would not convince agriculturalists to voluntarily withhold harvests.

The current crisis drove the point home: in the mid-1920s, the only reason farmers finally stopped glutting markets was because they'd run out of the cash or credit necessary to plant another field, raise another crop of pigs, or feed another beef cow.

The Peek plan was a clear indication that at least some in agriculture were ready to leave the past behind if doing so would resolve the paradox of plenty. How to do so was not yet clear (and a century later, it still isn't), but at the time, those in search of a new way forward agreed on three main points:

First, Americans must manage agriculture in ways that satisfied both consumers and farmers, or the nation could expect food-related social unrest.

Second, farmers were entitled to profit from their labor, and to economic "parity," as some called it, with urbanites. Those who practiced agriculture ought not be punished when supply and demand parted ways. They should be rewarded for feeding the millions.

Third, the paradox of plenty — the problem of surplus — was baked into agriculture. It would never go away. For decades, farmers had depended on exports to absorb surplus. The end of the war had shown the folly of that tactic.

Over the next few years, as the agricultural depression worsened, and rural communities crumbled, Congress pondered legislative solutions that used federal dollars and authority to manage markets. The most successful of these was the McNary-Haugen Act, a variant of the Peek-Johnson Plan (the two men helped write the bill), which proposed a complex formula that allowed the USDA to manage surpluses by paying farmers to withhold crops, and/or by selling surplus on global markets.[44]

Congress passed versions of McNary-Haugen twice in the twenties; twice President Calvin Coolidge vetoed it. Many Americans were (and still are) horrified by the prospect of government meddling in the "free market": using taxpayer dollars to circumvent marketplace mechanisms paved the way to socialism, communism, or worse.[45]

BUT IN THE 1920s, AGRICULTURALISTS AND THEIR PARTICULAR experts also explored an alternative route to farmer profits and agricultural stability: factory farming.

In the US, factories had long epitomized efficiency. Thanks to inexpensive, mass-produced goods, millions of Americans owned more than one shirt or coat and multiple pieces of furniture. So enamored were Americans of the factory ideal that they embedded it in everything from grocery shopping and housekeeping to manufacturing and roadbuilding. Agriculture, however, in the felicitous phrase of one historian, was the nation's "last great nest of chaos."[46]

Nor was the idea of factory farming new. In the 1890s, the director of a federal nutrition research program argued that because modern urban societies depended on "a cheap and abundant food-supply," farmers ought to apply to agriculture the "principle which has proved itself true . . . in the factory."[47]

Under Agriculture Secretary Wilson, the USDA's emphasis on farm management and economics pointed the same direction. Factorylike scale and efficiency in field and barn would reduce farmers' costs of production. The less money farmers spent to grow corn or feed cattle, the more profit they would earn when it came time to sell. Efficient farms would keep food prices down and foster a healthy, productive workforce (and stave off anarchy, socialism, and other evils).

And, too, the recent war had affirmed the necessity of a stable, profitable agricultural economy. As one observer put it in 1922, "When a nation depends on [others] for its food," relationships with those others inevitably devolve into "either subordination or control. Whether a nation becomes a dependent or dominant nation depends upon the ability of its agricultural population to provide for the whole population."[48]

Unless agriculture became "Fordized," many voices argued, Americans would be reduced to the status of Asian rice-eaters, the worst imaginable fate for an industrial (and racist) society.

High time, then, to transform agriculture from a backward beast into a systematized model of mechanized efficiency. An agricultural economist conceded that in the short run, "industrial agriculture" might "have a demoralizing effect" on some rural Americans. Over time, weak, unproductive farmers would leave the land. Those who remained and practiced factorylike management would enjoy "a higher standard of living" — and make enough cheap food to maintain the health of the consumer economy.[49]

Two decades (and a depression and another world war) would pass before factory farming reached full flower in the form of, for example, livestock confinement and the use of antibiotics and hormones. But in the 1920s and 1930s, farm-as-factory shaped the birth and success of a new meat industry. Devoted to mass-producing chickens for table meat, the "broiler" trade mapped a path to agriculture's future.

III: THE WAYS AND MEANS OF PLENITUDE

CHAPTER 7
WINGED WIDGETS; OR, CHICKEN IN EVERY POT

In the story of the chicken-meat "broiler" industry, it's obvious which came first: the egg.

Eggs are efficient packets of protein that can be transported long distances, and offer nearly infinite utility, making them valuable to human beings. In the nineteenth century US, millions of farm families made eggs by the billions. In rural communities, eggs functioned as currency, both in the barter system that remained common for much of the century and as a household's "surest source of cash in emergencies."[1]

Those eggs require hens, about which a few facts are worth knowing. Hens lay eggs. That's what they do. They don't need a rooster's input. When the rooster is involved, the egg output is fertilized and hatches. Left to their own devices, hens are most productive in spring and summer.

That was when hands culled the hatch of cockerels — young males — as soon as those could be identified, sending them to market, the makings for summer fried chicken. In autumn, farmers supplied shoppers with the makings of hearty soups and stews: worn-out hens, aged roosters, and males kept on hand to raise to "roaster" size (about four pounds).

Seasonal meat birds went to market live. Urban poultry butchers sold pot-ready birds, for a price: the task of converting a feathered carcass into edible meat requires a fair amount of labor. Thrifty shoppers bought vendors' undressed carcasses, examining them for clues to a bird's age and health. Spurs, for example, indicated an old male. Spoilage was impossible to disguise: poultry flesh greens as it decays. "Green-strucks" were for those with the smallest of purses.[2]

As the "old times" (barter) gradually gave way to the "modern" (cash), and small towns to skyscrapers, demand for both eggs and laying hens multiplied dramatically.

Curious minds and eager entrepreneurs tried breeding better laying hens, for example, and invented devices that enabled commercial hatcheries to handle eggs by the thousands, even the tens of thousands. Poultry experts took up the cause at the USDA, land grants, and experiment stations.[3]

Here is where the bird came first. Between eggs and Americans' plates stood poultry disease. Chicken flocks incubate disease; they are germ and bacteria factories. The bigger the flock, the higher the mortality rate.

Scaling up egg production necessitated scaling up hen production, which meant scaling up outbreaks of poultry disease.

Was there a way to organize large hen flocks so as to mitigate disease? A major source of disease was the very soil in which chickens foraged, leading one poultry expert to ask:

"Why do we need [chicken] yards?" "Is there any need whatever of wasting good land, plus the cost of fences and maintenance, upon yards or outside?"

The year was 1907; food prices were high, and urban growth hastening across the land. Why not take hens off soil? Why not confine them?[4]

Such questions gave rise to the "colony" system: coops on wheels, and thus easy to move from one spot to another. Sized to accommodate no more than one or two dozen birds, a few hands could readily move the little caravan from place to place in search of fresh soil.[5]

A stationary variant allowed growers to raise masses of birds on relatively few acres in coop "trains," sometimes a half mile long.

The traincars were narrow, rectangular boxes with doors at both ends and wall openings for light. The interior was divided into two rows of pens that ran the length of the car, each sized to hold only a few birds. An aisle in the middle and open doors at each end provided efficient access to hundreds of birds, who could be managed by relatively few hands.

By 1910, some commercial growers, especially in climates with mild winters, had amassed flocks as large as ten thousand. They supplied eggs to "big chicken factories," where electric incubators produced chicks by the thousands. In 1913, a "mammoth" Texas operation hatched a chick every twelve seconds, every day, all day.[6]

An admiring visitor to one such factory reported that "baby chickens are [now] manufactured by artificial processes from the raw material in great industrial plants that are as different from the old-fashioned poultry farm as any factory is different from any farm." The "modern pure-bred hen [is] an egg machine," the observer wrote, and the "chicken industry has become industrialized."[7]

Chickens for meat? Not so much.

In the early years of the new century, commercial producers of "broilers" — two pound chickens grown for meat — were few and far between, and found almost exclusively in proximity to the dense populations necessary to make such ventures profitable.

These growers marketed hand-raised, specially fattened meat birds, such as the "Philadelphia" broiler (born and raised in southern New Jersey). An enthusiast explained that such birds boasted "better flavor" than yard birds, and a juicy texture, thanks to a protein-rich diet. Growers confined the chickens in order to prevent "violent exercise" that "hardened muscles." They were also, he added, "often beyond our pocketbook."[8]

Indeed. A Philly broiler cost 50 cents a pound; in today's money, a two-pound bird would cost $22.

Another broiler industry catered to the nation's fast-growing Jewish population, thanks to two million immigrants who arrived between 1880 and 1914 and settled primarily in cities. Observant Jews did not eat pork, and although many embraced the American passion for beef (a rarity in the old world), chicken was central to Jewish diets and cuisine.

One kosher poultry market emerged in and around New York City, where the majority of new Jewish arrivals landed. Another centered in and around Petaluma, California, a long-time producer of eggs and hens for nearby cities. The region's poultry and egg production expanded in the late century, thanks to the arrival of Jews who emigrated to the US via eastern Russia and China.[9]

A third broiler project was largely the work of the Swift and Armour companies, who had long trawled midwestern farms in search of eggs. (Both companies, you may recall, were charged with "hoarding" eggs in order to jack up prices.)

As the century turned, executives turned their attention to chickens as meat. In the first decade of the century they built midwestern feeding stations: one-story warehouses filled with "batteries": stacked rows of wire cages sized to hold four or five birds, and equipped with attached troughs for food and water. For ten days to two weeks, the chickens fed on ultra-rich, fattening diets of corn, oats, and buttermilk.[10]

Employees accelerated the fattening process with cramming mechanisms. Imagine a wooden tripod equipped with a foot pedal and a rubber tube attached to a bag of feed. An operator shoved the tube down the bird's throat and then pressed the pedal to force food from the bag into its gut. "Under the machine system," explained one man, they "have to eat, and they must take on flesh. Then there is no waste of food."[11]

When birds weighed two pounds, plant employees slaughtered them, leaving head, feet, and innards intact. They scalded the carcasses to ease the removal of feathers, and froze them, a process that required three to four days. Then they packed the product in wooden crates for shipping or freezer storage.

These were not cheap chickens, not with so many layers of processing and distribution piled on. Swift's clientele included high-end hotels and restaurants, posh resorts, railroads that offered first-class dining services, and caterers that specialized in serving what one broiler industry analyst called "swell spreads."[12]

Realistically, those were the only available options, and not only because of price. Hotels, restaurants, and other such entities that served large quantities of food typically owned what average consumers and shopkeepers did not: large, electric-powered, mechanical refrigerators and freezers.

Even that high-end market was a gamble. "It is a remarkable fact," commented one observer in 1904, "that with all of their resources . . . the big meat packers have never been able to profitably enter the chicken trade, even at the present high prices."[13]

Still, he could read the writing on the chicken coop wall, and predicted "an expansive future for chicken meat and its trade." If producers could hatch eggs and raise layers by the thousands, surely the same could be done for broilers.[14]

As far as the USDA was concerned, "industrial" broiler production was a sound proposition, and the main obstacle was knowledge. From 1900 to 1915, the Department and land-grant Experiment Stations expanded poultry-related research.

As important was the body of work coming from the then-new science of genetics, the study of how and why biological traits (like feather color) pass from parent to offspring. Geneticists studied living things, and chickens were ideal subjects: inexpensive, small, easy to handle; they matured in weeks rather than months; their reproductive cycle was short; offspring developed not in a womb but in a separate container, the egg.[15]

By 1920, research in the US and elsewhere had produced an immense body of poultry science that translated into breakthroughs in the management of poultry behavior, nutrition, and disease. Here was information that could be used to increase egg yield and hatchability, for example, or to control common poultry diseases.[16]

The USDA/land grant nexus was especially interested in confinement. Experienced poultry growers knew that confined hens lived longer, and laid more and healthier eggs, than free-ranging birds, not least because growers could quickly identify and remove sick birds before disease wiped out the flock.

The downside was significant: confined birds developed rickets, or "leg weakness," as farmers called it. It crippled afflicted birds, preventing hens from laying and chicks from maturing. Science to the rescue: In the early 1920s, researchers discovered that birds fed with vitamin D would grow and lay with little or no natural light.

That "phenomenal" discovery, raved one expert, unlocked the door to poultry production based on "specialization and the application of factory methods." Large-scale chicken production was now possible.[17]

From the outset, broiler production was viewed as manufacturing rather than farming. In its early days, funding came primarily from manufacturers of commercial livestock feed, such as Quaker and Purina, and from investors who wanted in on the ground floor of what many assumed would become a large, profitable industry. In this scheme, the people who raised the chickens were viewed as factory workers, rather than as farmers.

We can understand that process by turning to Delmarva, as it is known. This spit of land between the Atlantic Ocean and the Chesapeake Bay encompasses the borders of Delaware, Maryland, and Virginia. Its economy was primarily agricultural: farmers grew produce and fruit for urban markets along the east coast. In the 1920s, it served as the launching pad for commercial broiler production.[18]

Delmarva was convenient to the USDA's Beltsville, Maryland, livestock research campus, the Department's Washington headquarters, and the tri-state land grant schools and experiment stations. All of them funneled science, information, and expertise to

Delmarvans. In effect, the region served as a laboratory where Department officials tested new methods of poultry and egg production, and taught the willing how to make eggs, layers, and broilers efficiently and profitably.[19]

To be clear, many peninsula households raised chickens and sold eggs at market, as did millions of households around the country. But the USDA encouraged Delmarvans to incorporate science and scale, system and method, into their work with hens and eggs. To grow in a business-like manner that could be tracked and measured, predicted and improved.

In the early 1920s, an outbreak of poultry paralysis swept through the region's flocks. This common virus activates only when birds are fifteen to twenty weeks old. Once paralysis sets in, the bird's utility is zero. No doubt guided by advice from USDA staff, hen growers and egg producers shipped young hens north as broilers; that was the only way to extract profit from otherwise doomed birds.

The returns were immediate and positive. New York City alone, with its millions of Jewish residents, needed all the meat chickens it could get.

The experiment persuaded many Delmarvans to raise broilers rather than laying hens. They received priceless assistance from the USDA and the tri-state land-grant complex in a remarkable collaboration that aimed to build, from scratch, a science-based broiler industry capable of making millions of pounds of poultry meat a year. Experts shared advice on everything from wiring coops for electricity to use of battery cages to the need for scientifically engineered commercial feeds — no scraps and bugs for these birds.

Indeed, commercial livestock feed was built into the collaboration. In recent years, its manufacturers had incorporated as much "science" as possible into their feeds; partners, as it were, in the USDA project of increasing productivity. Companies like Purina hired agents who worked on the scene, coaching Delmarvans through the process of commercial poultry production. The agents organized "loans" of both chickens and feed to families who agreed to raise birds to market weight, using the company's feed.

Exactly
the Right Feed
for Battery Brooding or Winter Broilers

BATTERY brooding will appeal to the poultryman who appreciates the fact that profits can be swelled by use of modern, scientific methods.

To the same type of mind, the advantages of Quaker Ful-O-Pep Chick Starter will be apparent. Especially, as a battery feed.

For Quaker Ful-O-Pep Chick Starter can be used with minimum work, and every assurance of the most satisfactory results. Battery feeding is a most critical test for a feed. And Ful-O-Pep can't be beaten!

First, it's the famous oatmeal chick mash, and oatmeal by every count, is a supreme food for baby chicks. With the oatmeal are combined cod liver oil, cod liver meal, molasses, proper minerals, proteins — just the right balance to build bones, blood and sound organs. Ful-O-Pep feeds and the Ful-O-Pep method of feeding reduce or eliminate feather pulling and cannibalism.

Batteries have proved to be an excellent place for starting pullets for two or three weeks. Ful-O-Pep Chick Starter is giving exceptionally good results in battery feeding and does not have to be changed when the chicks are put on the floor.

If you want to know how successful battery brooding can be, if you want winter broilers that get the top prices, follow the Ful-O-Pep Method. Mail the coupon below. See the Quaker Dealer near you.

Quaker
FUL-O-PEP
CHICK STARTER
THE QUAKER OATS COMPANY, CHICAGO, U. S. A.

BUY QUAKER FEEDS IN STRIPED SACKS

A 1930 advertisement for one of Quaker's many chicken and egg products. This one features battery brooders.

After selling the birds to the buyer of their choice, growers paid off the feed company loan — and immediately borrowed more.

In the 1920s, most Delmarva broiler growers were, and remained, household ventures. But those seeking scale experimented with ways to make as many birds as possible. Doing so necessitated input from USDA agents who helped navigate the disease and logistical maze. But expansion and scale was predicated on a "producer," often a corporation, who organized funding and distribution, and contracted with others to grow the broilers.

In that sense, some Delmarva broiler makers were producers, rather than growers. Producers organized capital; growers fed chickens. The latter were factory hands, as it were, making feathered widgets. Such an industry, the Department hoped, would bring efficiency, centralization, and systemization to broiler production, and maximize productivity.

As Delmarva's broiler output grew, buyers connected with New York City's kosher poultry markets began scouting the scene, often contracting in advance for a grower's entire output. Truckers, both local and from the kosher suppliers up north, hauled chickens far more efficiently than trains.[20]

Thanks to the available expertise and easy credit, broiler production quickly became a sizable regional industry. In 1925, for example, Delaware's growers sent 50,000 chickens to market. A year later, they sent a million. In 1932, six million; forty million in 1940.[21]

In the late 1930s, investors elaborated on the new industry by constructing processing plants on the peninsula. After all, why ship live birds? It was more efficient, and profitable, to slaughter them on Delmarva, and ship carcasses north.

Early processing plants were hardly high technology. After hanging the birds by their feet on chains suspended from an overhead conveyor, workers slaughtered and drained them, and then scalded the carcasses. Some plants de-feathered mechanically: the dead birds tumbled around a rotating drum lined with wax-coated rubber fingers that tugged feathers loose.[22]

THE BROILER INDUSTRY EXPANDED DRAMATICALLY DURING THE Great Depression (1930-1939) and World War II (1939-1945; US 1941-1945), especially in northeastern Georgia.

Like most southern states, Georgia's population was largely rural, and its economy primarily agricultural. And in the 1920s, like most southern states, Georgia's agriculture was a pit of chaos and despair, ripe for repair and transformation.[23]

For decades, cotton had been the state's primary cash crop, "the only farm product that is clothed with the dignity of collateral," as one observer admitted. Typically, white and Black field hands grew cotton on land owned (typically) by whites. Hands began the growing season by "borrowing" seeds, tools, and foodstuffs from local landowners and "furnishing merchants" (who were often one and the same). Invariably, come harvest, there was not enough to pay the debts accrued months earlier. This cycle of debt stalled rural Georgia in a rut of declining returns and rising debts.[24]

In the 1920s, the situation became intolerable. The postwar agricultural crisis hit cotton growers hard. A cotton boll weevil infestation exacerbated the misery. Sharecroppers sank deeper in debt, praying that landlords would not evict them. Landowners and merchants defaulted on loans. Banks shut their doors.

In desperation, the state's Department of Agriculture promoted chickens and eggs in much the same way that the USDA had done at Delmarva. The state's urban population had doubled since 1900. Why import eggs from, say, Iowa, when Georgians could raise their own? Why raise cotton when eggs and birds paid more?

Georgia's Agriculture Department and land grant school provided expertise and technical assistance. Funding and other support came from local bankers and merchants, and the ever-present commercial feed manufacturers. Swift executives announced plans to build a processing plant for making their "buttermilk" birds.

Railroads organized "car-lot" sales for poultry growers, sending special trains to collect rural poultry to sell in bigger markets. Families flocked to depots carrying chickens in "every conceivable container — cotton baskets, orange crates, crocus sacks, boxes and coops," sometimes in lots as small as "three or four."[25]

The effort provided tangible success in short order. In 1919, the state had zero hatcheries; by 1924, there were 41. Georgia farmers, cackled a reporter, were "outwit[ting] the boll weevil" with "modern poultry houses and raising thorough-bred fowls." "Nothing but the automobile craze," claimed another journalist, "ever struck a country so forcibly as the poultry industry has. At the rate it's going, poultry growers will be as numerous as Ford owners within twelve months."[26]

But three or four birds hauled in orange crates and crocus bags was not what the nation needed. When the Great Depression slammed into Georgia's economy, it set the nascent chicken meat industry on a path toward industrial broiler production.

A 1926 ad for Purina Chick Startena, appropriately steeped in vitamins.

WHEN THE DEPRESSION BEGAN, HERBERT HOOVER WAS PRESIDENT. In theory, this should have been his moment. He'd spent decades thinking about and experimenting with ways to manage crises. Alas, the scale and speed of the collapse overwhelmed the Engineer-in-Chief. Associationalism and cooperatives could not fix what ailed the nation. By the early 1930s, a third of Americans were (famously) unhoused, unfed, and unemployed.

In 1932, the largely white electorate (which now included women) replaced Hoover with Franklin D. Roosevelt. FDR possessed an abundance of charisma and political acumen, and a sufficiency of intellectual curiosity. He also knew how to read the room, as it were, and from his perspective in March 1933 when he was inaugurated, what mattered most was that he do something. Anything.

FDR and his cadre of advisors, experts, and intellectuals framed the catastrophe as one of underconsumption: Americans weren't buying enough stuff. The president's solution was to prime the nation's economic pump: get Americans back to work so that they had money to spend.

That was the point of the alphabet soup of agencies organized during his first months in office. The Works Progress Administration (WPA) and the Civilian Conservation Corps (CCC), to name two of many, created jobs that provided paychecks. Workers built park facilities, bridges, and roads. They constructed an aquarium in Key West, Florida, and painted murals on post office walls. The TVA (Tennessee Valley Authority) employed thousands, and delivered electricity for the first time to a broad swath of the rural south.

Agriculture lubricated the pump. In periods of social instability, stable food supplies are existential. In Europe, food shortages and high prices had fueled eruptions of the dreaded isms, including fascism and Nazism. If food prices and unemployment rose in the US, there would be hell to pay in the form of boycotts at best and food riots at worst.

As important, however, FDR identified farmers as consumers first, and farmers second. Broke farmers were non-consuming farmers, and there were, in 1932, millions of broke farmers. FDR also grasped what Hoover never did: farmers would not produce for free. Why go broke on behalf of the urban millions?

Thus the plan: get agriculture on its feet first so that this group of consumers could spend money that would prompt factories to open so that the rest of the nation could get on its feet.

In May 1933, he signed the Agricultural Adjustment Act (AAA). The legislation created an Agriculture Adjustment Administration (also AAA) to stabilize the price of commodities such as cotton, corn, hogs, and tobacco.

As needed and necessary, the Adjustment Administration would remove selected commodities from the market, creating artificial scarcities that would drive up the price. Affected commodity producers would receive a "benefit": a cash payment from the federal government, "compensation by the rest of society to farmers for their service in supplying goods and raw materials."[27]

By late 1933, hundreds of thousands of rural households had received at least one check. Here was cash to pay debts, purchase supplies, and buy manufactured goods like shoes or gasoline, thereby providing work for shoemakers, sales clerks, refinery workers, and gas station attendants.[28]

FDR's NEW DEAL ARRIVED IN GEORGIA IN SUMMER 1933, WHEN USDA agents paid Georgia's white landowners $8 million dollars to plow up their planted cotton fields; the ensuing shortage would drive up the price. Although the direct impact of this mandate varied from farm to farm and region to region, overall it marked the end of cotton culture as it had been known and practiced since the 1860s.

Among those caught in the turmoil was Mary Tallulah Dickson Jewell Loudermilk of Gainesville, Georgia. Situated in the northeastern corner of the state at the foothills of the resort and tourism regions of the Carolina Mountains, the town had a population of 8,600 in 1930. Tallulah, as she was known, owned the Jewell-Loudermilk Warehouse Co., a typical "furnishing" operation, purveying seed stock, commercial livestock feed, fertilizer, and basic farm tools. When regional agriculture suffered, so did her income.

And after the USDA showed up with its $8 million, nobody needed what she was selling.

Her son Jesse (1902-1975) had spent the 1920s in Florida working as a surveyor during that state's real estate boom. But

Florida was a canary in the coal mine that was the great depression, and when that boom went bust, Jewell headed home to Georgia.[29]

Tallulah suggested that he turn part of her warehouse over to chicken feed and chickens. Perhaps those would sell.

Trucking chickens, 1938. It's worth noting the driver likely traveled unlit dirt roads for much of the journey.

A commercial feed manufacturer, also struggling, provided Jesse with a line of credit. A company agent helped him establish a modern bookkeeping system, and accompanied Jewell on tours of the countryside to recruit families willing to "grow" chickens on his behalf.

Jewell loaned birds and feed to his growers, and when the chickens were ready to sell, he trucked them to Atlanta and other regional urban markets, sometimes live and stashed in wooden crates, sometimes slaughtered and packed in ice. After selling the birds, he paid his growers their share of the profit, minus the loan of chicks and feed.

In every case, Jewell, the producer, studied markets and organized funding and sales. His growers grew according to his instructions. The underpinnings of the infant operation, however, were federal and state subsidies, both direct and indirect.

In 1935, for example, the USDA launched the Poultry

Improvement Program, a well-funded commitment to the study and control of poultry disease. TVA-generated electricity proved a boon for chicken growers: they used electric lights to keep birds awake longer so they would eat more and gain weight faster. Conversely, when markets were glutted, growth could be slowed by turning off the lights. Electricity also powered automated watering systems that allowed growers to raise more chickens with less labor.[30]

Broilers got Jewell and Georgia through the worst of the depression. In 1934, Georgia producers put 400,000 broilers on the market. In 1939, they marketed 1.6 million. One newspaper reported that in some Georgia counties, the "fuzzy down of the baby chick has all but ousted the fleecy lock of the cotton boll from its pedestal as chief money crop."[31]

THEN CAME 1939, AND A NEW WAR IN EUROPE AND ASIA. Technically, the US was neutral; in practice, President Roosevelt took no chances.

He quietly placed the nation in an unofficial, low-level state of emergency, and laid plans to supply arms to England and its allies. In spring 1940, FDR organized a Council of National Defense Advisory Commission that included a Division of Price Stabilization and a Division of Consumer Protection. Manufacturers of weapons, ammunition, and other war materiel signed federal contracts, cranked up their factories, and hired thousands of workers.

Jesse Jewell knew an opportunity when he saw one. As federal and military officials began soliciting bids for foodstuffs, Jesse gassed up his REO truck and headed to Washington, hoping to persuade military buyers to send a contract or two his way. They were persuaded.

When the US entered the war in late 1941, federal officials reserved pork and beef for the troops. Broilers stayed home to fill the void. To that end, the government effectively commandeered poultry production at Delmarva for the duration of the war. The USDA launched a "Grow More Poultry Program"; the public feasted on chicken fixed every which way; and military buyers grabbed as much as they could for men and women stationed stateside. (Turkeys, however, were shipped to troops for morale-boosting Thanksgiving and Christmas feasts.)

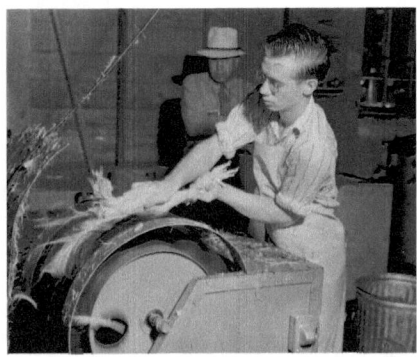

The war produced a host of time-saving devices and techniques in broiler production. This electric plucker was one of them. The manufacturer claimed it could pluck as many as 1,000 birds a day. From 1941.

Jewell rode the wave thanks to his federal contracts. It helped that for the time being, Delmarva was dedicated to military rather than civilian production. It also helped that he owned various "phases" of production, including a hatchery, feed dealership, and processing plant. By "stacking one phase on top of another," he reduced production costs, and balanced his earnings.[32]

Not that it was easy. For example, he was required to subject carcasses to a high-temperature scald (at a temperature established by USDA research), and to ship birds frozen and packaged in precut pieces. The scalding equipment initially increased production costs by 50 percent, but it replaced human labor, which was in short supply: between 1937 and 1941, thirty percent of Georgia's agricultural workers abandoned farm for factory. If Jewell wanted to fulfill his contracts, automation was a must.[33]

At every step, federal and state assistance subsidized Jewell's expansion. Faculty at land grant schools and extension programs contributed research in the form of new freezing techniques and disease management strategies. The USDA and military staff offered engineering expertise and cut red tape, pressuring equipment manufacturers to honor nonmilitary contracts such as those from broiler processors.

Georgia broiler production soared: 17 million in 1943; thirty million in 1945. But the assistance infuriated small operators who couldn't (or wouldn't) shoulder the necessary expense to go big. One man complained that the system was "arranged to help big business and discourage little business."[34]

He was right. A Georgia extension agent explained that the "trend toward fewer farm people, larger farms, and a larger output per farm worker would tend toward a more prosperous rural economy in Georgia." As wartime Secretary of Agriculture Claude R. Wickard phrased it: there was no room or time for "little farms for little people," or those who regarded "agriculture as a way of life" rather than a business.[35]

GETTING AMERICANS OUT OF RURAL AREAS WAS EASY ENOUGH, thanks to the war. From 1940 to 1944, 6.6 million adults left the nation's farms, a migration that translated into serious labor shortages.

On the Delmarva peninsula, six poultry processing plant owners asked federal officials for war prisoners, promising to build a suitable camp to house them. Locals put some three thousand POWs to work in fields, chicken houses, and processing plants.[36]

One consequence of federal input and demands was an often chaotic broiler market. The Grow More Poultry Program sounded good on paper, but the federally mandated price ceilings often left growers short changed, literally: officials established a price for the broiler, but did nothing to stabilize the price of, say, chicken feed or chicks. A ceiling price that sounded good to a suit in Washington, DC, often translated into a loss on every bird for beleaguered growers.

Nor did the Office of Price Administration (OPA), the agency charged with keeping prices under control, deter a black market so brisk that it stalled federal efforts to put chicken on home front tables.

"Chiselers" swooped down on Delmarva, offering as much as twelve cents a pound above the federal price. Locals often obliged, illegally, and why not: as the price of chicken feed soared, they needed the extra money just to keep making chickens. Federal troops patrolled the main road in and out, stopping trucks to search for chickens. If a driver had birds but no official papers for them, soldiers seized the chickens and hauled them back down the road for shipment on a federal truck.

That was relatively easy on the peninsula: there was only one highway out of town. In Georgia, on the other hand, locals were experienced black marketers; they kept moonshine flowing during the dry 1920s. Truckers black-marketed chickens with impunity and ease, thanks to their knowledge of local roads. Federal troops failed to stop the flow. There were too few of them, and too many chicken smugglers traveling roads unmapped and hidden from sight.

A black market in beef and pork flourished, too. It was so easy. Millions of ranchers and farmers grew livestock, and there were thousands of small, intrastate meatpacking houses whose owners had little state oversight. "In this economic labyrinth," a reporter mused, "the meatlegger finds easy pickings" in the "stock raiser with itching palms."[37]

A California butcher abandoned any claims to ethics. "I gotta make a living and I gotta keep my customers satisfied," he confided to a reporter. "Every morning I make the rounds of four black-market outfits. In one I say to the guy 'I'll bet you $25 you can't get me a side of beef.' I lay the cash on the table and I always lose the bet. What the hell would you do?"[38]

He had plenty of customers: unemployment was at zero, and there wasn't much to buy. Why not pay hefty prices for illegal meat? "Los Angeles aircraft workers pay $1.95 a lb. for steak," noted an observer, "then display their prize like a Prohibition college boy showing off his flask; Manhattan housewives happily fork over 80¢ a lb. for beef liver."[39]

THE TRUTH IS THAT DURING THE WAR, AMERICANS ATE AS WELL AS they ever had, and far better than everyone else on the war-ravaged planet. The reasons were many: a perfect combination of sun and rain, half million new tractors, double the number of combines. Record crop yields and livestock numbers. In the first half of the 1940s, farmers' average incomes rose from $245 to $655; net farm income jumped from $2.3 billion to $9.2 billion, a new golden age of agriculture.[40]

A staggering 100 million pounds of surplus butter lay waiting for use, more than twice the output of a normal year. In spring 1944, the War Food Administration reported an "unmanageable" glut of eggs and potatoes. Officials quickly organized a National Potato Week, followed by a National Egg Week, in hopes that "the nation would rush to buy."[41]

As for meat, there was plenty. In 1939, Americans ate 133 pounds per capita of beef, pork, and lamb; in 1945, they consumed 145 pounds. The last time they'd downed that much was in 1924. Poultry consumption marched to record highs: In 1939, 16.6 pounds of poultry per person landed on the nation's tables. In 1945, Americans dished up a record twenty-five pounds.[42]

From 1942. Even in the midst of war, Americans had plenty to eat, as evidenced by the well-stocked cold cases in this store.

The depression and war affirmed Americans' sense of entitlement, and enshrined consumers and cheap food as the prime movers of the nation's many economies. FDR regarded access to food as a right, not least because ample food supplies ensured civil stability and thus national security. His New Deal stimulated and fostered consumer activity. During World War II, federal officials enlisted shoppers as home front warriors, urging them to monitor prices and report retailers who violated price control regulations.

Organizations of "citizen consumers" demanded the same rights, recognition, and protection granted to other interest groups, such as labor, agriculture, and business. Meatless Mondays were a wartime duty, but they were because citizen-consumers believed that they would, eventually, receive benefits from cooperating during food rationing.[43]

But that guns-and-butter stance begged an important question: How to reconcile the conflicting appetites of business owners bent on free markets and high profits; workers demanding high wages to buy consumer goods; shoppers insisting on cheap food and plenty of it; and farmers charged with providing such food while also enjoying the same high consumer spending as everyone else?

Americans would wrangle with that question for the rest of the century, but in the immediate aftermath of the war, the agricultural establishment — about to be renamed "agribusiness" — concluded that the need for low food prices and high farmer income required total commitment to "Fordized" farming.

CHAPTER 8
GO BIG OR GO HOME

ACCORDING TO A 1956 ROPER POLL, MANY AMERICANS REGARDED pork as "less nourishing" than beef or poultry, and more fattening than both. They associated beef with "athletes, bankers, [and] slim and beautiful women," and pork with "poor people, truck drivers, [and] large families."[1]

That's one reason why beef consumption jumped ten pounds in the 1950s, and why, for the first time, beef topped pork as Americans' favored choice of meat. Another is affluence. Historically, beef intake rises with income, and the roaring postwar economy (driven in part by the "military-industrial complex") pushed earnings up even as food prices remained low.

King Beef fostered midcentury clichés: suburbanites grilling burgers at backyard barbecues, white-collar workers downing three-martini lunches punctuated with steak. The nation's millions of "war babies" (aka baby boomers) gobbled commercial baby foods like strained beef; in the early 1950s, Swift alone sold thirteen beef-based toddler delights.

Sales of canned beef products skyrocketed. For those, manufacturers relied on grass-fed range beef: tough, stringy meat that is tastiest when cooked for long periods and paired with herbs, spices, and other ingredients. Perfect for the meat sauce and meatballs in Chef Boyardee Spaghetti.

And for canned beef stew, canned corned beef hash, canned tamales and chili, and even canned "sandwich steaks" (precooked steak slices ready to meet bread). Or for Kri-Pi, a meat pie sold in two cans taped together to make a single package; dough in one can, "meat, vegetables and gravy" in the other.[2]

"Our products are like cake mixes and canned soup," explained a happy purveyor. "They're selling well because housewives are looking for quick, easy ways to fix food."[3]

MIDCENTURY AMERICANS SNAPPED UP THESE DELIGHTS AT A NEW kind of store. The supermarket was a great wonder of postwar America, so much so that federal officials adopted it as the poster child for capitalism and the American way of life during the Cold War (1947-1991) against communism.

Supermarkets were born in the Depression 1930s, when a handful of independent stores opened in the suburbs of eastern cities, or in industrial zones where empty warehouses abounded. These "supers" offered free parking, high-volume sales, high product turnover, and low labor costs.

Initially, the differences between supers and chain stores were two-fold: the original supers were stand-alone and independently owned; and their offerings dwarfed those of the average chain store, both in number and variety. But as the depression wore on, some chains adopted the supermarket mode of retail.

The USDA embraced the supers as vehicles for devising and conveying postwar food policies, and for keeping food prices low. Chain supers provided roadmaps to consumers' minds, a tool with which to track, read, interpret, and respond to consumer behavior, an increasingly important field of study for the Department.[4]

The supers were also quick to accommodate fresh meats.

In the 1940s and 1950s, and thanks in large part to war-based research, new packaging materials replaced the clumsy cellulose/cellophane packaging of the 1920s. Manufactured from polyvinyl chlorides, these transparent sheets could be stretched and molded around irregular cuts and pieces, lengthening the shelf life of fresh meats. By the 1960s, odor-free, self-service supermarket meat departments had become common.[5]

Supermarkets bore no resemblance to grocery shops of old. This is an outlet of the Giant chain in 1958.

The emergence of supermarket chains drew meatpackers and livestock producers into a tight, sometimes uncomfortable, triad. Retailers wanted packers to provide multiple cuts of meat, in more or less uniform size, in a variety of grades and standards. Packers in turn urged stockmen to strive toward uniformity in their market-ready stock.

In the western US, where urban populations grew dramatically after the war, supermarket chains upended conventional producer-retailer relationships. Some chains operated their own packing plants, the better to keep costs down. Some contracted with cattle feeders to make beef for their stores. Some even owned cattle feeding operations.

THE MIDCENTURY HOTEL, RESTAURANT, AND INSTITUTION INDUSTRY (HRI) emerged as the nation's biggest dispenser of meat products. In postwar America, food sold or served in places other than home or retail occupied an enormous chunk of the food landscape.

The Institution segment included hospitals, medical research, and care facilities, which mushroomed after the war; the masses of young people in school lunchrooms and university and college dining halls; federal and state prisons; airports and airplanes; corporate and factory cafeterias.

It also included the military, whose capacity and capabilities loomed large in the postwar psyche and economy. Korea. Southeast Asia. West Germany. The Iron Curtain. Military bases in the US, and "peacekeeping" missions around the world. All of it necessitated building an infrastructure to support and feed troops dispatched hither and yon.

The Pentagon alone dished up thousands of meals a day — and the Pentagon didn't want two thousand random pieces of chicken a day. It wanted two thousand that were uniform in quality, weight, and shape.

If the I in HRI pressured livestock producers, packers, and processors, so did H, the hospitality segment. Postwar white Americans enjoyed a level of mass affluence new in human history. The large middle-class enjoyed disposable incomes, forty-hour workweeks, and access to interstate highways that allowed them to travel long distances for short vacations. Cities like New York and Los Angeles saw hives of visitors piling into hundreds of new hotels: for business, for pleasure, for conventions and conferences. Chain hotels placed huge for orders for properties scattered coast to coast.

"R" stood for restaurants. Urban growth, cheap cars, and disposable income spawned restaurants by the hundreds of thousands. Many were chains; many were devoted to "fast food." By the mid-1960s, fast-food chains numbered four hundred, and the segment grew 79 percent in the second half of that decade. The two hundred largest chains operated more than forty thousand outlets.

The most famed was McDonald's. It grew from one shop in 1955 to 228 in 1960, and thereafter opened about a hundred outlets a year. By 1970, it was the sixth-largest food server in the United States, after the army, the USDA, the navy, Kentucky Fried

Chicken, and Marriott Corporation. But even the Mr. Steak chain, dinky by comparison, dished up 150,000 steaks a week, all of which had to look and weigh the same.[6]

AMERICANS' ABUNDANCE STOOD IN PAINFUL CONTRAST TO MOST OF the rest of the war-ravaged world. In the immediate aftermath of World War II, millions in Asia and Europe faced starvation. Low crop yields and a series of brutal winters left many hungry, as did floods in China, and tsunamis in India.

A relief agency attached to the new United Nations reported that in just one Chinese province, five million people faced imminent starvation from a diet that consisted of "wild leaves and stems and roots." The Italian premier warned that his nation was on the "eve of starvation." Herbert Hoover, who had made food aid a major part of his life's work, was more specific: "It is now 11:59 on the clock of starvation."[7]

This was a human tragedy, one of the four horsemen. The powerful in Washington, DC, interpreted it as a threat to national and global security. An American general serving in occupied Germany was blunt about food's role in postwar security. Forcing citizens of war-torn nations to choose "between being a communist on 1500 calories and a believer in democracy on 1000 calories" would "pave the way to a Communist Europe."[8]

President Harry Truman (1884-1972; president 1945-1953) affirmed that point in his 1949 inaugural address:

"More than half the people of the world are living in conditions approaching misery. Their food is inadequate. They are victims of disease. Their economic life is primitive and stagnant. Their poverty is a handicap and a threat both to them and to more prosperous areas." Truman asked Americans to "help the free peoples of the world . . . to lighten their burdens." Only democracy, he said, "can supply the vitalizing force to stir the peoples of the world into triumphant action . . . against their human oppressors [and] their ancient enemies — hunger, misery, and despair."[9]

The logic was emotionally satisfying: The US was free and capitalist. The Soviet Union and People's Republic of China were unfree and communist. Americans must feed humanity so that humanity would not turn despairing hearts and empty stomachs toward authoritarian governments. Feeding the world was an American obligation.[10]

Within limits. When the Korean War (1950-1953) began, Truman assured Americans that there would be no rationing, no shortages of gas, tires, meat, or anything else. They would enjoy both guns and butter.

THE IMPLICATIONS FOR AGRICULTURE AND LIVESTOCK PRODUCTION were many and significant.

On one hand, federal officials promoted the American "family farm" as the antithesis of Soviet, state-run, collective agriculture. Supermarkets and family farms embodied an American ideal: free people producing an abundance of food for free spenders.[11]

On the other hand, postwar geopolitics transformed *factory* farming into a patriotic imperative. If food could win wars, hot or cold, American farmers must do everything necessary to support the cause. There was no time to dally, no place for laggards.

Too many farmers persisted in "standing still" and relied on the "methods of their grandfathers," wrote a reporter summarizing a hearing on agricultural underemployment. Smart farmers were "moving forward" into factory-like farming. It was imperative that they focus on scale and efficiency, and think like factories. Those who refused, who eschewed scale and efficiency imposed a "heavy burden" on the nation.[12]

Science, cheap fuel, and hubris were part of the postwar farm package.

A plant breeder who began his career in the 1950s recalled that he and his colleagues assumed that science would "dominate the universe," and that supplies of "very cheap energy" would never run dry. That combination bred a McCarthyist "mood of intolerance" among scientists; human and scientific "arrogance" spawned an "intellectual wasteland." "I was . . . the most arrogant bastard that you want to run across," he said later.[13]

This is what federal policy wanted to eliminate: run-down farms where people still used human labor rather than machine.

In short, postwar national security interests raised the stakes for agriculture, and imbued food policies with new significance.

Republicans and Democrats agreed on the basics: Farmers were entitled to a fair return for their labor. Consumers were entitled to low-cost food and lots of it. Satisfying both groups required federal involvement.

When it came to devising policies, however, the two parties disagreed. At midcentury, Democrats wanted to continue along the consumer-oriented path laid by the 1933 Agricultural Administration Act. Republicans argued that government's only job was to facilitate individuals' access to free markets.[14]

When Republicans captured the White House in 1952, Dwight D. "Ike" Eisenhower (1890-1969, president 1953-1961) deftly merged his party's hands-off stance with Truman's plea to feed the world. His device was Public Law 480, a mechanism for off-loading American agricultural surpluses as "foreign aid" intended to prevent other nations from sliding into Communism.

This is what the USDA wanted farms to look like.
Except with the hogs more confined.

All of it — patriotic necessity, science, cheap fuel, an insistence on low-cost food — inspired some of modern agriculture's most contentious practices, including livestock confinement, hormone- and antibiotic-laced livestock feeds, big-breasted hybrid chickens, and ownership of the entire production process (known as vertical integration).

ANTIBIOTICS

To understand how antibiotics ended up on the farm, we need to look (briefly) at barnyard nutrition.

Single-stomach animals like chickens and hogs are healthier and reach market weight faster when their diets contain "animal protein factor." APF is precisely what the name implies: proteins from animals rather than plants. Think fish meal, cod liver oil, "tankage" (rendering byproducts). But those ingredients were expensive. If scientists could unravel the mystery of APF, they could synthesize less expensive substitutes.

World War II raised the stakes of this research. Americans imported cod liver oil from Norway, and fish meal from Japan. As long as war raged, those supplies were beyond reach. University, corporate, and USDA laboratories (all short-handed as scientists and graduate students headed off to war) attacked the problem of APF with new vigor, conducting feeding trials with sweet potatoes and other plants, as well as vitamins, minerals, amino acids — anything that might replicate the effects of APF.

But this was no time for "repeat[ing] feeding trials for five successive years before conclusions are drawn," argued an experiment station researcher. The emergency of war demanded "newer and more effective research." He urged his colleagues to study the work of biologists, chemists, and geneticists, whose research focused on the fundamental, physiological processes of life.[15]

How, precisely, did growth happen? What internal mechanism caused plants, for example, to reach for sunlight? "The ultimate objective" of such work, explained one scientist, was "growth control." If humans understood the mechanics of growth, then they could manipulate it, and perhaps even encourage "abnormal growth."[16]

Colchicine, for example, a substance derived from the crocus plant, was thought to be a growth accelerant. In 1940, a scientist at the University of Pittsburgh injected it into chicken eggs. The birds that hatched grew "abnormally large" combs and wattles, and males crowed three months earlier than usual.[17]

In the end, the answer to "what is APF?" arrived in the late 1940s, and via the liver and pernicious anemia rather than the crocus and colchicine.

Pernicious anemia gradually cripples its victims by attacking their nervous systems. Prior to 1950, it was a deadly global scourge that could be cured or alleviated only with hefty doses of liver — a half-pound or more a day — or injections of liver extract, both of which were expensive. (Nor, it must be admitted, was the prospect of consuming a half-pound of liver a day particularly inviting.) If scientists could unravel the liver's secrets, they could conquer pernicious anemia.[18]

That happened in 1948, when researchers identified liver's antianemia ingredient and dubbed it vitamin B_{12}. It could be manufactured at low cost using byproducts from antibiotics manufacture. Two years later, a different team discovered that cattle fed with *synthesized* B_{12} grew markedly faster than ones fed B_{12} extracted from liver. Nor did it take much: about an ounce of antibiotic per ton of feed.[19]

The discovery blew "the lid clear off the realm of animal nutrition," noted the editors of a farm magazine.[20]

Feeds laced with a synthetic vitamin-and-antibiotic product cost less to manufacture than those based on fish meal or tankage. Livestock who ate it reached maturity faster, so growers spent less on feed. For broiler producers like Jesse Jewell, the combination produced a 10 percent trifecta: chickens that ate antibiotics needed 10 percent less time to reach market weight; they needed 10 percent less feed; and mortality rates dropped about 10 percent.

This left "animal nutritionists gasping with amazement, almost afraid to believe what they had found." Farmers would "[n]ever again" have to contend with the "severe protein shortages" that plagued them during World War II.[21]

From the perspective of both farmers and consumers, antibiotics were as valuable as tractors, combines, and agricultural subsidy programs.

The USDA used posters like this to encourage producers to think modern.

HORMONES AND DIETHYLSTILBESTROL

Hormones are central to the process of growth and aging, and many early- and midcentury scientists used them in their research. The synthetic hormone Diethylstilbestrol (DES) was especially popular because it was manufactured with cheap coal tar derivatives. That low cost included a hidden price: all hormones, natural or synthetic, are potentially carcinogenic, but DES is about three times more powerful than natural hormones, and unlike natural hormones, its residues linger in the body.

In the 1970s, it would be banned from use, but at midcentury, few found fault with the substance. It was a hormone, and hormones are related to growth, and DES was cheap, so scientists employed it in lab research; manufacturers added it to breast enhancement creams; physicians prescribed it to pregnant and menopausal women.

Why not livestock?

In the early 1940s, a poultry scientist at California's College of Agriculture (now University of California–Davis) implanted DES pellets in roosters. The birds' combs shrank, and they sprouted "female feathers and a layer of fat." Their ordinarily "stringy" flesh "became light and tender." A few years later, the Food and Drug Administration (FDA) approved DES pellets for use as a chemical castrator implanted in birds' heads or necks. Processors typically removed those parts of the carcass; in theory, there was no danger that the pellets would end up in human stomachs.[22]

But DES found its primary residence in the cattle barn.[23]

Bovines are ruminants; they have multiple stomachs. They don't chew their food so much as moisten it to ease the trip to stomach number one, the rumen. It harbored immense colonies of microorganisms, but how did those transform roughage into carbohydrates? Was it possible to increase or improve rumen efficiency?

In the 1940s, bovine nutrition research flourished in Corn Belt laboratories such as the one at the Ohio State University Agricultural Experiment Station.

There, Wise Burroughs (1911-1986) and his team of scientists shared a laboratory with a nine-month-old Hereford named Christopher Columbus. A 1948 visitor to the laboratory described Chris as an exceptionally "happy" and healthy animal — despite the fist-sized hole in his flank. In the name of science, Burroughs and his colleagues fed Chris combinations of feedstuffs and then scooped them from the rumen for analysis.[24]

The scientists' inputs included urea (nitrogen-rich and converted to protein in the rumen) and molasses (which sweetened the mix and added carbohydrates). They experimented with plastic pellets, which generated friction and boosted rumen efficiency.

Corncobs, a cellulose-rich roughage, offered a tantalizing line of research. Cobs piled up by the billions on American farms; if those could be used as cattle feed, livestock producers would save money.[25]

Burroughs's work with corncobs intrigued Roswell Garst, an Iowa hybrid corn producer (who, in 1959, would host visiting Soviet premier Nikita Khrushchev). Garst had conducted his own corncob experiments, and concluded that cattle fed with cobs and cornmeal fared as well as those that ate shelled corn, allowing him to halve his feeding costs. Eager to know more, Garst urged officials at the land grant Iowa State College (now Iowa State University) to hire Burroughs.[26]

By 1951, the scientist was ensconced in an Ames laboratory, studying digestion thanks to a research grant from the Iowa-based Rath Packing Company, and where he used sheep rather than cattle: sheep are also ruminants, and they cost less, ate less, and were easier to manage than cattle

Burroughs dosed one test group with DES, perhaps inspired by scientists at Purdue University, who had fed it to both cattle and sheep. Burroughs assumed that sheep dosed with DES would grow faster than those in his control groups. He was wrong. Regardless of what they'd eaten, both groups grew at the same rate.

The only feed common to all his test subjects was clover hay, so Burroughs prowled the pages of scientific journals and learned that livestock forages such as clover and soybeans contain estrogenic substances. In February 1954, Burroughs announced that DES-laced feeds, properly applied, would provide cattle the same growth boost that antibiotics gave chickens and hogs.

By early 1955, 2 million cattle were ingesting Stilbosol, a premix manufactured and marketed by Eli Lilly and Company, which held five-year, exclusive rights to the patent. An agricultural magazine reported that one ounce was sufficient to "fortify" rations for 2,800 head of cattle; that tiny dose translated into "an extra half ton of beef." DES was "the bright hope of feed dealers and cattle feeders alike."[27]

"Amazing? You bet it is!" enthused a writer for *Farm Journal*.

"Nothing has ever hit the meat-animal business with the impact of stilbestrol," he opined, not even antibiotics.[28]

CONFINEMENT

The idea of confining livestock was not new. In California, for example, cattle ranchers and feeders tinkered with it in the early twentieth century. Many paved their feedlots in order to use tractors and blades rather than shovels and shoulders to spread manure where it was needed (instead of where livestock deposited it).

In the thirties and forties, the broiler industry's success with confinement inspired broad interest among livestock producers and the experts who served them. A study at Iowa State College, for example, revealed that during wet weather, cattle struggling to maneuver in mud burned enough calories to lose as much as three pounds a month. That loss turned expensive feed into a "complete loss" in the account book. Animals on a paved lot experienced less weight loss and fewer injuries. Profit margins increased by as much as $10 a head.[29]

"You can't afford a muddy barnyard," a reporter told readers of one farm magazine. "If yours is, it's costing you plenty."[30]

Hog farmers were especially receptive to confinement. It would enable them to automate feeding and exercise control over animals' diets, something that was impossible when hogs ran on pasture. Confinement also reduced mortality rates by protecting hogs from predators and weather.

The experience of one Iowa farmer demonstrates the appeal of confinement. Every year, he lost pasture-based swine to dysentery. In the early 1950s, he adopted antibiotic-laced feeds in hopes of improving mortality rates. The drugs made no difference. An agent from Iowa State College explained that his soil teemed with parasites and bacteria. So the farmer emulated the broiler industry and moved the hogs indoors. He significantly reduced loss from disease.[31]

Confinement also protected investments in expensive breeding stock. As HRI and supermarket buyers became increasingly specific in their demands, many farmers invested in breeds engineered to produce specific animals; leaner hogs, for example. Some bought "Specific Pathogen-Free" stock: animals bred and born in sterile environments. Farmers were loath to let these animals run free.

Confinement encouraged specialization. A Wisconsin hog farmer decided that instead of raising hogs from birth to market, he would focus on inseminating and farrowing sows, and sell the offspring — "feeder pigs" — to others. Thanks to confinement, he could breed sows and sell feeder pigs year-round. Demand was so high that he contracted with other farmers to produce feeders for him.

Confinement also saved labor, which was scarce on the ground. An Illinois hog farmer reported that thanks to confinement, he'd reduced his labor hours by half even as he doubled his output. "You don't have to go to confinement feeding . . . to stay in the hog business, but it surely takes a lot of the drudgery out of raising hogs!" he said. His two sons applauded the move: both were in college; both planned to come back to the farm; neither wanted the "drudgery" of old-fashioned farming.[32]

HYBRID POULTRY AND VERTICAL INTEGRATION

Starting in the late 1940s, A&P and the USDA sponsored a series of "Chicken of Tomorrow" competitions that rewarded poultry breeding innovations. The point of the exercise, its holy grail, was a better *meat* bird. Thousands of breeders and growers participated. The winning companies profited beyond expectations: by 1950, nearly 70 percent of the 625 million chickens raised for meat descended from winning Chicken of Tomorrow bloodlines.

The new chickens were "all white meat, tender and delicious." They were meaty and big-breasted; they boasted hefty drumsticks; and they arrived at maturity faster and on less feed than any birds in history. They converted feed into meat more efficiently than cattle, and nearly as efficiently as that master of conversion, the hog.[33]

Supermarket chains loved the hybrids, and adored their price. Chicken was an ideal "loss leader": advertise chicken at rock-bottom prices, and shoppers lured in by that would stick around to load their carts with higher-priced goods. The more dependent the chains became on that strategem, the more they pressured Jesse Jewell and other processors to supply cheap broilers.

In turn, those enormous supermarket poultry orders enticed newcomers to raise broilers; most lacked the experience needed to navigate the industry's ups, downs, and necessities. In the 1950s, the result was a decade of overproduction, poor quality broilers, and the onset of an obnoxious cycle: the more broilers glutted the market, the more chains snapped them up for use as loss leaders.

One grocer complained that when a competitor across town sold broilers for, say, 29 cents, "we've got to sell at 29 or lose our customers for everything else we sell in the store." The glut, complained a merchandiser for one major chain, "starts the price-cutting sale cycle all over again and everybody gets hurt!"[34]

Broilermakers also accommodated the supers' demands by pairing hybrid chickens with vertical integration, the practice of controlling every "phase" of production, from hatchery to processing plant, and "stacking" the phases within a single company. Supporters claimed that vertical integration improved efficiency and reduced costs without subsidies or other government intervention.[35]

Jesse Jewell was the king of vertical integration, which was one reason he thrived in the gold-rush mentality of postwar broiler making. He had long owned his own processing plant and hatchery. In the early 1950s, he organized a partnership with Pillsbury Flour Mills Company: Pillsbury built a feedmill in Gainesville and leased it to Jewell, who used it to manufacture his own feed, and earned a royalty on every pound of feed sold to other buyers.[36]

He balanced basic broilers with "value-added" products. Those included chicken sticks (a variant of the popular 1950s fish stick), chicken pot pies (the crusts came from a factory he owned in Alabama), and chicken-based frozen TV dinners.

"Integration has made chicken the cheapest meat on the market," Jewell said, "and we want chickens to stay cheap." Analysts applauded Jewell and other integrators: they were more business-oriented and "cost-conscious" than traditional farmers who operated on "a smaller scale."[37]

Jewell also shifted costs to his growers. In his mind, broiler growing was a part-time job, something a family could fit in around other employment. But he also demanded that growers constantly add newer, better equipment, such as automated feeding systems. He drew new contracts that based payment on feed efficiency.

Growers believed they were getting the short end of the stick. In 1957, the House Select Committee on Small Business held hearings in an effort to make sense of the industry's mayhem and the growers' complaints. The committee heard from chain stores, broiler producers, feed dealers, and growers.

In his testimony, Jewell blamed the chronic glut on the ubiquitous feed manufacturers, who lured new growers with promises of big profits. He also charged that supermarket chains' demands for cheap chicken were making the situation worse. All he could do was integrate his parts and pieces and hope for the best. He had to go big or go home.[38]

Growers disagreed. They complained that they were hired hands rather than farmers. But for better or for worse, that was precisely the goal: to make the farm function like a factory. Broiler growers were the equivalent of assembly line workers, the broiler being their widget.

Nor were they alone. Commercial vegetable and fruit farmers typically raised crops under contract for food processors who required produce of uniform size and grade. And as some argued, every farmer who participated in a federal subsidy program was, in effect, a contract producer.

"As a whole," commented one analyst, "agriculture stands alone as the only major industry that still clings to its glorious past and holds out for a 'free price.'" In time, another predicted, integration would "revolutionize the production of animal products." Contract farming would be the norm rather than the exception.[39]

THE USDA'S DECADES-LONG PUSH TO MODERNIZE AMERICAN agriculture had come to fruition. Among those who experienced that process was John Davis (1904-1988). He grew up on Corn Belt farms, first in Missouri and then in Iowa. During his childhood, his family relied on horse-drawn plows and cultivators, and a steam-powered thresher (which they shared with neighbors). They butchered and processed their own hogs.[40]

He graduated from high school in 1923, a moment when the farm crisis hammered even relatively prosperous farm families like his. By then, the Davises were farming in central Iowa, not far from Iowa State College. The proximity allowed Davis to attend school and help on the farm.

But after earning a bachelor's degree in economics, he, like so many other young rural Americans, migrated away from the farm. During the 1930s, he watched the Great Depression unfold as a small-town Iowa schoolteacher. In summer, he headed to the University of Minnesota for course-work, earning a master's degree in agricultural economics in 1935.

Davis never returned to farming. Instead, he accepted a series of white-collar jobs, including two stints at the USDA, in a career influenced by Herbert Hoover's ideas about associationalism and hands-off help. In 1954, he accepted a position at Harvard Business School, where he directed an agriculture program.

By that time, the fifty-year-old Davis had spent his entire life immersed in agriculture. His variety of vantage points inspired a simple, but powerful, observation: agriculture could not be isolated from the rest of the economy. Davis argued that viewing "agriculture as an industry in and of itself" made sense a century earlier when most Americans lived and worked on the land. In the mid-twentieth century, that perspective was both foolish and short-sighted.[41]

Modern farmers delegated the tasks of "storing, processing, and distributing food and fiber" to "off-the-farm business entities," like trucking companies and grocery chains. A different set of "off-the-farm" companies manufactured the inputs on which modern farmers relied, whether tractors and combines, or antibiotics and poultry cages.

Together, this triumvirate — agricultural production, processing-distribution, and input manufacturing — constituted one of the largest components of the nation's economy. Davis and collaborator Ray Goldberg calculated that in 1954, consumers spent $93 billion on agriculturally based "end products and services" — food, paper, restaurant tabs, textiles, and so forth — a figure that did not include dollars spent to grow, process, manufacture, or distribute food and fiber.

According to the pair, the triad's weakest link was agriculture. Its individual units — farmers — lacked the power and information needed to make market decisions. Input manufacturers and output processors, in contrast, executed financial and production decisions based on internal factors largely under their own control. The price a farmer paid for, say, a tractor was based on factors controlled by the manufacturer, not the farmer, and the price had nothing to do with crop and livestock prices.

Over time, Davis and Goldberg explained, the market stabilized this "cost-price" squeeze, but always at the expense of farmers and the taxpayers who subsidized them. The more subsidy programs that Congress created to protect farmers, the more those programs entangled other members of the triad. Manufacturers of grain silos, to use a simple example, had a vested interest in ensuring that farmers produced surpluses that needed to be stored in silos.

The authors also distinguished between farmers who practiced "commercial" agriculture, and "low-income" farmers who did not. Marginal farmers worked the land but would not or could not commit to thinking like a factory; they contributed nothing substantive by way of food and fiber. As a result, society lost "the value of their productive potential."

Worse, policymakers and politicians invariably characterized the "farm problem" in terms of those two poles — commercial farmers on one end and marginal farmers on the other — rather than seeing the two as connected to each other, and to the other two arms of the triangle that formed the complete picture.

Until and unless Americans grasped the complexities of providing food and fiber for a non-agricultural population, and the intimate connection between agriculture and the economy as a whole, and until they made hard choices about what constituted a "viable" farm, the agricultural problem would never be solved.

Put simply, Americans could not afford to conceptualize agriculture as an enterprise distinct from the rest of the economy. Davis and Goldberg urged Americans to frame the production of food and fiber as "agribusiness." If that meant abandoning adulation of the "family farm" and rethinking the myth of the sturdy yeoman, so be it. Only then would the nation come to terms with the fundamental conundrum of how to satisfy an urban majority, sustain a consumer economy, and feed the world, too.

CHAPTER 9
GOING BIG: THREE TALES

THREE INTERCONNECTED STORIES OFFERS INSIGHT INTO THE GO-BIG mentality of the postwar period: the experiences of a multigenerational cattle-feeding family; the emergence of contract farming and confinement as standard practice; and the reinvention of meatpacking by Iowa Beef Packers and others.

I. THE MONFORTS OF COLORADO

At midcentury, there was no better place to go big than on the range. The Monfort family did just that when they built a "beef factory" in northern Colorado.

Charles K. Monfort (1870-1930) and Pella J. Phipps Monfort (1873-1959) met and married in Illinois. Son Warren (1892-1978) made three. C.K. taught school, and the family operated a small farm near Charleston, Illinois. In 1906, the elder Monfort retired from teaching, and two years later, the family migrated west, buying an acreage near Fort Collins in Weld County, Colorado (1910 county population 39,000).[1]

By western standards, the state's northeastern quadrant was an exceptionally attractive location. High plains summers are hot but dry; the winters, moderate (relative to, say, the midwest or the northern plains). It was also well watered, thanks to irrigation and the Cache la Poudre River, which cut an east/west slash across the landscape. The area boasted superb rail connections to all parts of the US, and the flat terrain invited road construction: early-twentieth-century homesteaders typically arrived by train or car rather than ox and wagon.[2]

In 1910, Colorado boasted 799,000 people; half lived in an urban place, most of them in the northeastern quadrant's four cities: Denver (pop. 213,000 in 1910), Boulder (9,500), Fort Collins (8,000) and Greeley (8,100). The latter three were home to state colleges; Fort Collins housed the land grant school, Colorado State College of Agriculture and Mechanic Arts (now Colorado State University).

Beyond these towns, the economy was largely agricultural. Cattle, sheep, and potatoes were common; sugar beets supplied sugar factories, a major local industry.

The Monforts took up chickens and eggs, breeding White Leghorns and selling branded "Strictly Fresh Eggs from Monfort Ranch" to local grocers. Chickens were C.K.'s particular passion. He promoted their production as both a way of life and a business, and participated in local farmers' institutes and poultry societies.

Indeed, all three Monforts organized their lives around agriculture, chickens and eggs, and an impressive array of clubs and organizations devoted to agriculture. The family embodied the USDA ideal: educated, business-minded, and open to new ideas and new modes of farming.

In 1918, C.K. and Pella sold their first ranch and purchased 80 irrigated acres about two miles north of Greeley. There, Charles continued to raise chickens, but he and Pella leased most of the land to son Warren and daughter-in-law Edith, to use as they saw fit.[3]

WARREN HAD GRADUATED IN 1914 FROM THE STATE NORMAL School of Colorado in Greeley (now the University of Northern Colorado). He spent a year teaching school in Sterling, Colorado, but in spring 1916, a year before the US entered the world war, he enlisted in the Army, hoping for a post in aviation. He failed the eye test, but he was good material. His tour included work as a mechanic and staff sergeant, and when the war ended in 1918, he was enrolled in officers' training school. In early 1919, he married (Lillian) Edith Shrum (1890-1972). She was from Omaha, and Phi Beta Kappa in college, from which she graduated in three years.[4]

By some accounts, Warren was not enamored with teaching. That's easy to believe if only because it's hard to imagine Warren Monfort doing anything other than working long hours outside with animals and plants. Indeed, based on available evidence, Warren and Edith entered marriage assuming a life centered on family and farming. What kind of farming, precisely, was not clear at the outset, but they did what Monforts always did: they consulted with experts, in this case CAC faculty, and the local extension services and experiment station.

That resulted in a plan to practice "permanent agriculture" based on row crops, crop rotation, and livestock. The Monforts also agreed to open their operation to visitors as a "model" of the USDA ideal in action. Extension agents, CAC faculty, bankers, and land developers used the operation as an example of how to thrive in northeastern Colorado.[5]

The "Monfort rotation plan" included alfalfa, beets, and federally certified seed potatoes. The family fed a few sheep and about two hundred head of cattle. For livestock feed, they relied on local grain and hay, as well as beet pulp and other crop wastes.

In 1920, the couple invested in a Ford truck, the better to haul beets and hay. After Warren modified it to suit the terrain and his needs, it became the farm's most useful tool. On a model farm, pistons replaced literal horse power (and freed up land on which to grow something other than horse feed).[6]

Model the Monfort farm might be, but it wasn't easy, especially given their reliance on sugar beets, their primary cash crop. To break even, they had to harvest at least twelve tons of beets per acre. At the time, moreover, the domestic sugar industry was in great turmoil thanks to foreign competition. "During the 20s," Warren said later, "we thought we would go under about every year, but somehow we managed to hang on."[7]

SOMETIME DURING THE MID-TWENTIES, EDITH AND WARREN abandoned permanent agriculture for cattle feeding. Presumably they had run the numbers and concluded that on the arid Colorado range, cattle made more sense than conventional agriculture.

Specialization didn't mean simpler or easier. The new venture required cattle-buying skills and knowledge of breeding and feeding. They would need to master the logistics of feeding thousands of head at a time, and the equally complex logistics of shipping cattle to market. They would have to contract for feedstuffs, employ skilled veterinarians, and hire hands knowledgeable in the ways of cattle.[8]

The goal was to compete with Corn Belt cattle feeders back east, so to speak, in Iowa, Illinois, and thereabouts. In the 1920s, most of them still practiced "in/out" feeding: when corn was abundant and its price low, they bought and fed cattle. When corn prices were high, they sold it for cash, and bought fewer cattle or none at all. They also only fed seasonally, because livestock gained little weight during midwestern winters; slipping and sliding on snow and ice burned calories.

Put another way, midwestern cattle feeding was a sideline, and the quality of Corn Belt beef ranged across a broad spectrum.[9]

Warren and Edith had a better plan. Thanks to Colorado's relatively temperate climate, they could feed and market cattle year round. They planned to invest in high-quality cattle stock in order to make high-quality beef.

Their feedstuffs included beet pulp and corn silage; the latter is the entire corn plant — kernels, cobs, leaves, and stalks — chopped fine. Local farmers grew the corn on contract for Monfort, who provided them with hybrid seed and fertilizer at cost. Monfort employees made silage right in the field thanks to company-owned mechanical choppers, and then dumped it back at the feedlot in one of three "pit silos."[10]

The Monforts' organizational and business model lay "across

the mountains" in California. "Out there," Warren explained, "they didn't have to unlearn anything such as we do in changing from the small farm feedlot" to a factorylike, automated operation.[11]

But the family hewed close to USDA gospel. Its ideals and philosophy, pamphlets and bulletins guided their path. Consider Warren's words at a 1930 Northern Colorado Economic Conference organized by CAC's extension service.

Cooperation and association, Warren explained, were the foundation of "efficient and orderly marketing," a phrase much beloved by the USDA. He encouraged feeders to think about their operations as businesses. Too many still treated feeding as a winter occupation, for example, taken up only "after the rush of fall work." A more profitable approach was year-round feeding, including "economical summer feeding."[12]

He urged his peers to practice Hooverian associationalism; to "associate" and "develop close cooperation" "in all matters relating to the welfare of the cattle industry." And not just locally, but with feeders elsewhere, and with the "range producers" who supplied the livestock that feeders fed.

Still, all of it was a risk, especially during the agricultural crisis of the 1920s. But Warren thrived on risk — others described him as an "aggressive" businessman — so why not?[13]

THE FAMILY GAMBLE PAID OFF. SALE AFTER SALE, YEAR AFTER YEAR, Monfort cattle brought record prices at auction, and earned ribbons and trophies in competitions. By the late 1930s, the family's "beef factory," as they called it, was finishing 4,000 head a year. A specialized, large-scale operation yielded profits.[14]

By that time, the Monforts' three children were following their own USDA-approved paths. From grade school on, Margery (1920-1988) committed to the "home" part of the USDA equation, whether through 4-H and extension projects and clubs or by helping her mother organize social and civic activities. After graduating from college, she took a job as a county extension agent, bringing USDA ideals to rural homemaking.

Richard (1923-1944) and Kenneth (1928-2001), on the other hand, were all in on cattle. Cattle morning, noon, and night.

In early 1936, 13-year-old Dick "electrified experienced stockmen" when he submitted the highest bid for a load of Hereford feeder stock at the prestigious National Western Stock Show in Denver. By the time he graduated from high school, he was raising more than a hundred head, a mixture of Hereford and Angus stock.[15]

Kenny was right behind. When he was eleven, one of his fat steers was named Grand Champion at the 4-H Weld County Junior Fair. A few weeks later, he won the same award in the 4-H competition at the state fair. (Dick showed the fair's overall grand champion.) And a few months after, Kenny electrified his own crowd at the National Western when his entry won Grand Champion Steer.[16]

"Boy, am I happy!" he told a reporter. "I sort of felt all along that Slit Ear was going to be a grand champion," he added. "He ate so much."[17]

War came in late 1941. Warren chaired both the Weld County Meat Board and its county trucking committee, dispensing permits and quotas for slaughter, and reviewing applications for trucks (in short supply everywhere.) In between he made beef at the factory: 6.5 million pounds in 1942; 7 million in 1943. That was about the same time that Kenny, age fourteen, and Dick, age twenty, established Monfort Brothers beef company.[18]

In early 1944, in a live, on-air, radio presentation, the Skelly Oil Company presented the Monforts with its Skelly award, a promotional gimmick designed to make good copy for radio, and goodwill for Skelly. In this case, the company recognized the family for its "agricultural superiority." Warren "doesn't farm in the usual sense," the host explained to listeners. "His job is principally to take the field products of many farms and convert them into choice human food — beef."[19]

Richard wasn't there. He'd enlisted in the Army Air Force in late 1942 (unlike his father, he passed the eye exam). While Skelly honored his family, Air Navigator Lieutenant Richard Monfort was in England, awaiting orders.

"We have a front row seat for the big show," he wrote to a friend back home, "and from what General Jimmy Doolittle says we have a lot of work to do before things start. Every possible chance we get we'll be out tearing at the enemy. I am in one of the best squadrons here."[20]

Two weeks after the Skelly ceremony, military officials notified Richard's wife, Viola Swanson Monfort, that he was missing in action. Two agonizing months later, the family learned that he was dead, shot down over Germany.[21]

EDITH, WARREN, AND SIXTEEN-YEAR-OLD KENNY CARRIED ON. Financially, the war years were good, albeit maddening. The Office of Price Administration (OPA), for example, one of many bureaucratic nuisances in those years, was notorious for rules "so complicated that it is impossible to operate," and equally impossible to obey. In 1946, Warren pled guilty to breaking some OPA regulation or other. The $1,000 fine devoured less time than wading into the morass of an appeal.[22]

That regulatory environment may explain why, in 1946, he bypassed the conventional feedlot-to-auction route to market, instead selling eight thousand cattle on contract to wholesaler National Food, a subsidiary of a Chicago-based grocery chain that also owned a Denver packing company. With this move, noted one reporter, Monfort had shifted from "speculative feeding" to "commercial feeding."[23]

In late 1949, Kenny dropped out of Colorado A&M, where he majored in livestock nutrition; married Patricia Ann McMillen; and joined Monfort Beef. Away went father and son into the go-big fifties.[24]

Ken Monfort was born for business. He paired an exuberant personality with an imposing presence, not least because he stood nearly six and a half feet tall. (In later years, the company's Japanese customers adored him: here was the Marlboro man come to life.)

Intelligent and curious, he kept one eye on business in his feedlots, and the other fixed on events national and global, contemplating the way in which monsoons in India or labor strikes in Milwaukee might affect his Colorado cattle. He had a mathematician's brain, and an endless fascination with turning ideas and opportunities to profit. He was famous (or infamous) for his indifference to his surroundings, known for wearing two different shoes or the same shirt many days in a row.

The chain-smoking, coffee-loving Kenny (a small mountain of disposable cups obscured the back seat of his car) loved his work. His ambition at least equaled that of his father. Warren Monfort had always been "a heck of an asset to the industry," mused a neighbor, but "when the young fellow came along he just went ape."[25]

The family entered the 1950s with a decidedly "go big" mentality. Demand for cattle feeding was about to explode, thanks to a sharp decline in acres available for grazing.

All told, from 1930 to 1950, federal officials closed off 45 million acres of grazing land, converting those to other uses. During World War II, for example, the Pentagon commandeered thousands of western acres for use as airfields, bases, and weapons testing grounds. Military development and affiliated industries attracted workers who needed housing, streets, stores, and so forth. When the Grand Coulee Dam went into operation in 1942, grazing lands were watered and converted to wheat. Wheat fields and suburban tracts grew where cattle once roamed.[26]

What's a cattle rancher to do? Reduce a cow's time on the range from two or three years to one year, that's what. As Warren explained to a reporter, thanks to fewer grazing acres, "more of the growing period will have to be in feedlots" like the Monforts'.[27]

In Greeley, the family remodeled and expanded in order to accommodate younger cattle and more of them. They automated the feeding process, and configured feed formulas designed for cattle of various ages. They installed floodlights in the yards, the better to encourage 24-hour feeding on the part of the lots' twenty-two thousand cattle.[28]

The Monforts also integrated vertically. In 1951, they built a 400,000-bushel grain elevator on the Union Pacific rail line in central Nebraska. That arm of Monfort Beef was the domain of Margery Monfort Wilson and husband Lloyd Wilson, a longtime employee. The Wilsons bought and stored grain for the Greeley feedlots, and sold wheat and corn to their Nebraska neighbors. The family also installed buying agents "at strategic points" in several plains states, the better to buy livestock.[29]

Farming, Warren told a local Kiwanis group in 1958, was no longer a "way of life" but "a highly capitalized, mechanized 'big business.'" It was "much larger and more complex . . . than our fathers ever dreamed of," he said, and speculated that someday "good swine producers may be feeding hogs in air conditioned quarters."

He also extolled the virtues of vertical integration. "In the efficiency race," he said, "the white meat [broiler] industry has put on a show that would make some other industries green with envy."[30]

Next step: build a packing plant.

IN THE 1950s, WARREN AND KENNY WERE TROUBLED BY THE LACK of buyers in the vicinity. They were "at the mercy" of the ten meatpackers then operating in the Denver area. Three were owned by a national grocery chain, which also fed its own cattle and had no need for the Monforts'. Four were owned by national packers, who had their own feeding arrangements. Three were local independents. None wanted what the Monforts had to offer.[31]

They tried, and failed, to persuade a national packer to build a plant in Weld County. "Most of the big packers would go as far as Denver," Ken said later, "but just wouldn't consider a plant in Greeley."[32]

So they turned to Plan B: build their own facility. Ken envisioned one sized to handle their cattle, and a business model centered on HRI. He had no interest in consumer-focused products like canned beef stew and TV dinners, and the accompanying complexities of retailing, advertising, and the like. Individuals shopped by brand and label; hospitals and corporate cafeterias did not.

The slaughterhouse they opened in spring 1960 bore little resemblance to older, nineteenth-century plants. It flowed horizontally rather than vertically; the kill-and-cut operations took place on the ground level. The kill floor was washed by natural light, thanks to an expanse of green glass on the building's north face.

Carcasses arrived at work stations via an automated, ceiling-suspended rail-conveyor. Workers stood on adjustable platforms so they could move up, down, and around a carcass with a minimum of bending or stooping. Another conveyor removed wastes to a rendering operation in the basement. The hides landed there, too, deposited into two circulating, automated brine tanks that cured them in six hours.[33]

Two factors shaped the plant's design.

First, it accommodated unskilled labor. Ken wanted his workforce "to be from Greeley, not only to help local people but to get men who would stay with us." On the Monfort slaughter line, an employee made one or two simple cuts before moving the carcass on to the next person, who added more cuts.[34]

The second factor driving the plant's design was byproducts or, more accurately, the lack of them. Synthetic body soaps and detergents had replaced ones made from animal fats. Lard was an antique curiosity in an age of calorie counting and convenience foods. New drugs and commercial fertilizers eliminated the need for hog thyroids and dried blood. Hide values plunged thanks to plastics and other new-age materials. Shoes, purses, and furniture? Manufactured using anything other than leather.

Without byproducts, Ken had to make every inch of both plant and animal pay its way. Thus the flexible platforms and overhead conveyor, thus the wash of natural light: he aimed to eliminate every and any inefficiency and unnecessary expense, from the number of steps workers walked, to the number of light bulbs that illuminated the plant.[35]

In the early days, the operation "was something less than a howling success," thanks to recalcitrant machinery and his own inexperience. But he managed and learned and plodded along, chugging coffee and puffing cigs, pondering ways to "add value" to basic beef.[36]

It didn't take long. In early 1962, he announced plans to build a "breaking" facility. There, employees would dismantle and carve — "break," in industry jargon — whole and half carcasses into "primal" cuts: flank, loin, and the like, to be sorted and packaged in vacuum-sealed bags, and then packed in boxes for shipping.

The lure was profit: shipping primal cuts in stackable boxes lopped $3 to $4 off transportation costs.

So BEGAN THE BOXED-BEEF REVOLUTION, A PIVOTAL MOMENT IN THE American meat industry inspired by the constant pressure to keep food prices low.

Consider the traditional path that fresh beef traveled from a meatpacker to, say, a chain supermarket. The packer shipped whole or half "swinging carcasses" by truck or train to a warehouse. There, butchers broke the carcasses into primal cuts, boxing them for delivery to individual stores. At the stores, union butchers unloaded the inventory, and cut, wrapped, and packaged it for placement in self-service cases.[37]

Every step drove up the retail price. According to a 1966 study, workers handled a beef carcass an average of nineteen times: five at the packinghouse, eight by middlemen, and another six at the chain-store warehouse. Hauling, shipping, and handling equaled "shrinkage": a carcass lost 2 percent of its bulk within forty-eight hours of leaving the packing plant. The (average) nine-day transit from slaughterhouse to grocery store subtracted 5 percent of its weight.[38]

Then there were union wages and work rules, which were many and iron-clad. In Chicago, to name one example, union butchers employed at grocery stores stopped work at six p.m. No fresh meat could be sold until they returned the next morning.

Add in the equipment — slicers, power-driven saws, refrigerators and freezers — and selling beef in-store was not cheap. Fresh beef returned minuscule profits, at best, but gobbled about 60 percent of a meat department's labor costs.

Grocers begged Monfort and other packers to render efficiencies at slaughter. An industry analyst urged packers to stop thinking of carcasses as commodities. Carcasses were a "vehicle for selling services" such as boxed beef. Only then would they "reap the . . . true profit which the market offers."[39]

THE MONFORTS LISTENED. BY THE LATE SIXTIES, THEIR OPERATIONS looked like the set of a science fiction film. A reporter who visited in 1966 marveled at what he found.

A "touch of the Old West" was delivered by Monfort veterinarians who ambled through the lots on horseback to monitor the well-being of sixty thousand head of cattle. Otherwise the ambiance was more suited to astronauts than cowboys.

One building contained an electronic device that looked like a "control board at the Cape Kennedy missile site." Employees fed it punch cards that contained vital information: minutely calculated feed formulas for the company's livestock, whose daily diets required a thousand tons of alfalfa, corn, meat scraps, vitamins, minerals, antibiotics, and hormones.[40]

To the tune of "clicks and clatters," the machine read the cards and transmitted data to a second machine housed at a nearby silo, a three-hundred-foot-tall structure subdivided into vertical bins, each containing one ingredient. Electronic signals tripped the bins' gates, releasing feedstuffs into trucks equipped with rotating drums that mixed the ingredients en route to the feed bunks.

When a driver neared a bunk, he flipped a switch that opened the drum, spilling its contents onto a conveyor belt connected to a feed trough, ready for the cattle that milled about the Monforts' three hundred acres. When the cattle were thirsty, they served themselves, using their noses to trip an automatic fountain fed by underground pipes.

Inside the packing plant, the action revolved around a giant electronic control board, the heart of the facility's "automated electronic beef handling system."[41]

The dispatcher needed only to push a button to send a specific carcass — whose weight and meat ratio met the buyer's specifications — to, say, rail fifteen. There it hung awaiting the rest of the buyer's order. When all the items had arrived, a click sent them rolling to the loading dock or the breaking room.

In the latter, one crew broke the carcasses into primal cuts, and another packaged the pieces. Some beef was packed in boxes dosed with carbon dioxide that chilled the contents. Some was bagged in vacuum-sealed plastic film before boxing.

Kenny explained his beef factory's success this way: the "only way to stay alive in this business is to continually improve your efficiency."[42]

To which the folks at the USDA said: amen.

II. CONTRACTS AND CONFINEMENT

In the late 1940s, Swift built a hog slaughter facility in North Carolina. Executives assumed that urban growth was about to explode in the east (they were right), and they wanted to be ready to capitalize on it. The region didn't produce enough corn to feed hogs on a large scale, but the climate enabled year-round production, and North Carolina offered cheap land and labor, and proximity to the East Coast's metropolitan markets.

From day one, supply issues plagued the operation. Despite the region's historically porkcentric diet, commercial hog production was rare in southern states; landowners preferred cash crops such as cotton and tobacco. Haphazard local hog farming translated into erratic supplies of mediocre hogs for Swift.

Taking a tip from the broiler industry, company executives purchased quality sows (bred to specification) and leased those to (white) farmers who agreed to feed at least fifty animals according to contract specification and to sell the offspring to Swift.

"Inherent in all this are the principles of the industrial production line," commented a reporter in 1959. "The businessman at one end of the line ships out standardized pigs to farmers who'll feed them according to a set pattern." Regular production schedules stabilized supplies and prices, and provided consumers with "cheaper, better pork."⁴³

Contract hog farming quickly leapfrogged from the southeast to the Corn Belt, ushered in by commercial feed manufacturers.

As ever, midwestern hog producers practiced in/out feeding. As ever, any ten Iowa hog feeders raised hogs on ten different types of feed, and ended up with ten lots of livestock that varied in weight, musculature, fat, and marbling. Specification buyers like Armour and Swift, Safeway and A&P, Howard Johnson and Marriott didn't want pork grab bags. They wanted carcasses with specific ratios of lean to fat at a specific price.⁴⁴

In those days, their dream hogs often came via feed manufacturers. For example, one manufacturer provided "technical assistance" to growers who signed detailed contracts that stipulated every detail, from feed formula to breeding stock to the design of breeding pens and farrowing huts. The payoff: the feed maker pre-sold the hogs on contract at a premium price to packers seeking uniformity and quality. As in the broiler industry, the grower worked in the field; the producer worked in an office.⁴⁵

"This is the beginning of a revolution in swine raising," raved a Missouri slaughterhouse owner who was determined to transplant the model to his state. An agricultural consultant advised doubters to keep an open mind. "If you don't want [outsiders] to take over your traditional product," he said, "don't spare the horses." Translation: Modernize your operations.⁴⁶

CORN BELT CATTLE FEEDERS GOT THE SAME MESSAGE. IN 1959, A Federal Reserve analyst delivered a blunt assessment: large-scale, efficient western feeders like the Monforts were driving the "small, one-or-two-carloads-a-year Corn Belt cattle feeder out of business."⁴⁷

A western meatpacker affirmed the point, noting that specialist feeders focused on "only one aim and that was to produce an animal of desired quality as quickly and as economically as possible." By comparison, Corn Belt cattle feeding practices were "wasteful and unscientific."[48]

A Missouri man got the message: "As in most any business, the fellow who produces the cheapest will stay in." If he and other Corn Belt cattle feeders hoped to survive, they would have to put "beef feeding on a factory basis." That included confinement.[49]

One Michigan cattle feeder invested in confinement because he couldn't "afford to pasture cattle on high-priced Corn Belt land." From the 1950s on, urban growth and new highways gobbled midwestern acres. Confinement enabled farmers to increase herd size, and turn increasingly valuable pasture to other uses, such as grain crops.[50]

Confinement also mitigated the impact of the Corn Belt climate as producers built facilities that included heating, cooling, and ventilation technologies. Doing so allowed feeders to market year-round. "We were getting killed selling twice a year," said an Iowan who moved his cattle into confinement. "Now we're marketing every month, averaging the ups and downs, and making money."[51]

Two Indiana brothers who shifted cattle from pasture to confinement weren't complaining. They reduced feeding time from four hours to just fourteen minutes a day, and cleanup from three hours to twenty-four minutes. Thanks to those efficiencies, they upped the number of cattle they fed from 82 to 257.[52]

A South Dakota cattle feeder had no regrets about his shift from pasture to confinement. "You should have been here last winter to appreciate fully what it means," he told a reporter, referring to storms that left a "17-inch snow pack." While other feeders' cattle lost weight navigating wintry terrain, his enjoyed "good gains."[53]

"He's got what I call a beef factory for the 60s!" said his neighbor down the road. "Slickest set-up I ever saw." The push of a button fed 300 head in a half hour on a "complete ration" of "silage, corn, protein pellets, [and] molasses," thoroughly mixed so that "every mouthful . . . [was] alike."[54]

Hog farmers were especially enthusiastic about confinement. Consider an Illinois man who marketed about seven hundred head a year, feeding them with corn he grew. In the 1950s, subsidies and confinement caused him to reconsider. "I analyzed my work schedule," he said, "and found that raising corn brought me in only 10 per cent of my income, but took 50 per cent of my time. That was the turning-point of my farming career."[55]

He rented his corn acres to another farmer, increased his hog herd, and invested in automated augers that carried feed from bins to mixing floor to hog pens. By 1960, he'd upped his output to seventeen hundred head and was aiming for two thousand. "With 700 hogs, my gross ran about $30,000," he mused, and he'd "had to work as long and as hard as any farmer." By "modernizing," he doubled his gross and "with far less work."[56]

One convert reported that confined hog farming required "more power, more interest, and more insurance," and the "tax assessor was there before the roof was even on." But he had no desire to go back. He was making more money, and his operation was easier to manage and more comfortable for him and the animals.[57]

"It boils down to our being able to take better care of more total cattle with less labor," said one Iowan. "At the same time, the cattle are doing better. How can we go wrong?"[58]

Make no mistake: farmers who eased their workloads weren't lazy; they were realistic. The labor shortage would never end, and even hands who could be persuaded to get on board weren't interested in the sunup-to-sundown, seven-day work-weeks of the past. Many people believed that confinement would lure a younger generation of farmers.

Confinement could not cure all ills, and no one expected it to do so. But for many, it was a welcome departure from the past.

THERE WAS A DOWNSIDE TO CONFINEMENT. "YOU NEED SOME KIND of manure handling system," noted an Indiana man, "or it'll drive you nuts."[59]

In the fifties, most farmers who practiced confinement used a tractor and blade to push the stuff to one side. When the pile warranted attention, they loaded it onto a truck to spread on fields or sell as fertilizer. Others borrowed a European solution: using a hose, they "float[ed]" solids into a pit, pumping the goop into a tank every few weeks before hauling it to a field.[60]

In the early 1960s, a new idea swept the countryside. The manure "lagoon" was promoted by Ralph Ricketts, an agricultural engineer at the University of Missouri. His research revealed that ordinary pond bacteria could digest hog wastes, leaving "hardly a whiff of foul odor, flies, or even sediment."[61]

Manure lagoons quickly spread from Missouri to other states. When two *Farm Journal* reporters investigated in 1962, they found more than two hundred hog-farm lagoons in Missouri, and dozens more elsewhere, from Pennsylvania to Illinois, from Kentucky to Utah to California.

Not everyone was convinced. "How stupid can you folks get, anyway?" asked a reader of one farm magazine. Why would anyone "dump manure into lagoons, and thereby destroy organic matter, rather than put it back into the soil?" he asked. "Lagoons, the magic way to get rid of manure? Better say: Lagoons, the magic way to poverty!"[62]

"You can call it a lagoon if you like," groused another man. "For my money, it was an open, stinking, septic tank. Nobody would go near it."[63]

By the mid-sixties even enthusiasts were questioning the magic. Research indicated that a successful lagoon (regarded by many as an oxymoron) required more land than most farmers were willing to sacrifice. The US Public Health Service calculated that an anaerobic lagoon required seventy-eight cubic feet per hog. A truly odor-free pit required nine acres (about the size of seven football fields) per thousand hogs.

Even then, a reporter warned, lagoon operators "faced all the problems of a sanitary engineer operating a sewage works for a town of 1,000 people, without the engineer's training and staff."[64]

The sprawl of urban growth also provoked resistance as millions of new home owners experienced a whiff of modern farming. A reporter who investigated manure odor litigation in 1965 found that nearly all the complaints lodged against farmers came from residents of new housing developments. "It's the number of animals being kept in one place that's doing it," explained an official with the Illinois Department of Public Health.[65]

"You've got a stick of dynamite in your hands if enough people living near you decide they don't like your barnlot smells," warned a reporter for one farm magazine. "They can close you up!"[66]

According to another observer, farmers were "caught in the middle": consumers "demand[ed] more red meat" even as they insisted on "less pollution from its production."[67]

The clash between manure management and urban opposition raises an obvious question: Why didn't governments — county, state, or federal — act to ban confinement operations?

The answer is deliciously ironic.

In the 1960s, in response to voter demand, Congress passed laws aimed at curbing pollution of air, water, and soil. One bill required states to establish pollution standards with the goal of forcing polluters, especially farmers, to reduce environmental contamination.

Among the recommended livestock "waste-management" technologies: confinement. An Ohio State University professor of environmental engineering explained that there was "no question but that a lot of the livestock industry is ultimately going to have to go to enclosed systems."[68]

And so the new model of livestock production — confined, large-scale, automated — thrived and spread.

In the early 1960s, 61 percent of grain-fed cattle came out feedlots of fewer than one thousand. A decade later, only 35 percent of fed cattle came from such small lots. During the sixties, some 400 giants produced half the nation's fed cattle, and the number of feedlots dropped from 164,000 to fewer than 120,000.[69]

The number of hog producers dropped, too. In 1950, 2.1 million American farmers sent hogs to market, the majority of them raising fewer than a hundred head of hogs a year. Twenty years later, the nation's hog farms numbered fewer than a half-million.

III. Iowa Beef Packers and the New Meatpacking

MEATPACKING LOGISTICS WERE ALSO SHIFTING. AT MID-CENTURY, the industry moved decisively to the west and south, the better to find cheap land. New packers like Monfort had little use for old ways of processing meat. The new age demanded hyper-efficiency. No company delivered that better in the 1960s and 1970s than Iowa Beef Packers, Inc. (IBP), the brainchild of Andrew D. "Andy" Anderson.

Like Ken Monfort, Anderson was a commanding figure: six-foot-four, typically attired in blue jeans and cowboy boots, shirt, and hat. He was talented, ambitious, and best described as a serial entrepreneur: as soon as he launched one venture, he was itching to tackle another. In his case, success inevitably bred success, and he never lacked for investors. "Andy's a genius," said a colleague. "He has an idea every 15 seconds, some realistic and some unrealistic."[70]

Anderson's association with meatpacking dated back to the 1930s, when he worked at a West Coast slaughterhouse. In the early 1950s, he and two partners opened a packing plant in Boise, Idaho, which they sold eighteen months later. Anderson stayed to manage the plant, but when the new owners sold it to Swift in the mid-fifties, he left for his home state of Iowa and Denison, a small town in the western part of the state. There IBP was born.

It's not clear why Anderson landed in Denison, although it's possible that he'd read an advertisement that the town's Chamber of Commerce placed in the *Wall Street Journal* in 1956: "DENISON, IOWA. With every natural advantage for industry, offers excellent sites and build-to-suit plans! If you, Mr. Industrialist, are planning expansion or relocation, INVESTIGATE DENISON, IOWA NOW!"[71]

The postwar years had not been kind to Denison and the surrounding area. Some farmers were under- or unemployed; a damaging drought had wreaked havoc on corn crops; the growth of western feedlots had hammered local cattle feeders.

Some three hundred farm families left Crawford County from 1940 to 1956. Nearly every issue of the local newspaper included at least one full-page advertisement for a farm sale. Fewer farmers translated into fewer patrons for Denison businesses. The *Journal* invitation was born of desperation.

Not long after he arrived in town, Anderson proposed building a hog packing plant that would utilize livestock from area farms. Town boosters promoted the plan: "A farmer a day is moving away; Let's build the plant and help him stay!"[72]

Local residents invested $300,000 in the venture, and Anderson obtained a matching amount as a loan from the federal Small Business Administration (established in 1953).

Crawford County Packing Company opened its doors in spring 1958. A year later, the shareholders, all of them locals, sold CCPC to Consumers Cooperative Association, a thirty-year-old farm cooperative with more than $100 million in assets, including oil wells and a refinery. Shareholders earned a 123 percent return on their investment, not bad for a small-town venture and confirmation that Andy Anderson knew how to turn ideas into profit.

True to form, a few months later, Anderson launched Iowa Beef Packing. Within weeks, Crawford County residents had invested $400,000. (Five years later, many backers were millionaires several times over.)

Anderson supplemented this investment with a "government participation service" loan from the Small Business Administration: of the $350,000 requested, the Denison Federal Savings and Loan would provide 10 percent, and the American taxpayers the rest. The money paid for 140 acres west of town, a site that included plenty of water (the operation would consume millions of gallons a year) and abutted a line of the Illinois Central Railroad.

As he had with the hog slaughterhouse, Anderson designed this new plant to achieve maximum efficiency and accommodate minimal skill. Slaughterhouse workers stood on adjustable platforms; an overhead conveyor system transported carcasses from the kill room to refrigerator, truck, or railcar. IBP relied on unskilled local labor and focused on one product: fresh beef for HRI. "We don't believe in highly complex situations," explained an IBP executive.[73]

The company's buyers purchased cattle directly from farmers and feedlots, no auctions or stockyards necessary. When a buyer completed a transaction, he used an in-car radio to relay the animals' weights and prices to a dispatcher back at the plant. Production managers used that information to decide when they needed more cattle, when buyers should pull back, and whether the buyer's price was in line with that day's needs. Line managers always knew exactly how many cattle were headed their way and when those would arrive. Cattle were slaughtered within hours, and often minutes, of their arrival.

The company motto was "Think Money."

At IBP, everyone, from cattle buyers and janitors to line workers and Anderson himself, clocked in six days a week. Anderson drove the point home by adopting green (the color of money) as the unifying theme of the company's public face. Inside and out, the packinghouse and office walls were green. So were the carpets. Secretaries sat at green desks and cranked out letters and memos on green typewriters.[74]

Green thinking paid off. By the end of the first year, employees were slaughtering a thousand cattle a day, and IBP had acquired a second plant in Fort Dodge, Iowa, where Anderson installed a state-of-the-art processing line.[75]

In October 1963, IBP went public — testimony to the demand for a new meatpacking model. By 1964, IBP was the tenth-largest packing company in the United States and on *Fortune* magazine's 500 list. Two years after the initial offering, an IBP share was worth sixty-three times its original value. In the late 1960s, IBP followed Monfort into boxed beef, with the goal of breaking the "chains of history that . . . confined the retailing of meats to the dark ages."[76]

IBP's primary claim to fame, however, was its war on union workers. Anderson and his colleagues made no secret of their loathing. "We're trying to revolutionize beef packing," said a company spokesman. "The union is trying to prevent this." IBP executive Currier Holman packed a tear-gas gun, boasting that "business as we pursue it here at IBP is very much like waging war."[77]

During a months-long strike that began in 1969, persons unknown toppled the towers that anchored IBP's in-house radio communications system. An arsonist destroyed the home of a company executive. A gun-wielding striker wounded a secretary who was believed to be providing information about the union to her bosses. She survived, but the shooter killed her sixteen-year-old sister.

In mid-April 1970, after fifty-six bombings, two hundred tire slashings, more than twenty shootings, and one death, the strike ended. IBP agreed to pay 20 cents more an hour than the union had originally asked for.

IBP's ruthlessness also led to a collision with the Mafia. Anderson and Holman coveted the east coast market. But most grocery chains there employed union butchers, who relied on mafia connections to prevent the incursion of job-killing boxed beef from moving east.

Andy Anderson consulted with one of the country's biggest broiler producers, a man who'd managed to break through the mob in New York. The chicken man's advice was simple: Pay the bribes; it was the only way in.

Bribes opened doors but Currier Holman, by then IBP's president, stumbled into the snare of an ongoing federal investigation into Mafia-union connections. A jury convicted him of conspiracy. "I never bribed anybody in my life," Holman told a reporter. "It's all a damned lie."[78]

He got lucky: the judge viewed Holman as a "victim of the extortionate practices" of the very people he had bribed. There were, he told Holman, "few people in American business who would have acted differently in these circumstances." Holman avoided jail, IBP paid a $7,000 fine and, it should be noted, went right on paying the bribes necessary to win grocery contracts.[79]

THE BEST EVIDENCE OF THE NEW PACKERS' SUCCESS CAN BE measured in the declining fortunes of the old meatpacking kings, especially Armour, Swift, and Wilson & Co. Unlike their new competitors, the old guard was chained to unions and to "ancient and obsolete plants."[80]

Armour's Chicago operation, for example, consisted of 7.6 million square feet of floor space in 121 buildings spread over eighty-seven acres. Inside, beef slabs hung from iron hooks, and workers moved from carcass to carcass. Employees shoveled offal and tossed hides into wooden handcarts, trundled their loads to an elevator, waited for a car, boarded, pushed the cart off at the designated floor, unloaded it, and then retraced their steps, this time pushing an empty cart.[81]

The cavernous curing and refrigerator rooms stood idle. New curing and smoking methods had reduced processing from two months to as little as thirty minutes. The "Turbo-chill" technique sliced 25 percent off the time needed to chill a carcass to the required sixty degrees.[82]

The giants struggled to adapt. They pulled out of Chicago (the Union Stockyards closed in 1971), and sold off urban slaughterhouses in favor of new or newly remodeled plants in rural locations. "We're going to spend several million dollars to replace our 1910 plant in Oklahoma because we can't afford not to," said a spokesman for Wilson. "With wage rates the way they are now, we can't go on paying people to wait for elevators."[83]

But as one onlooker put it, the old guard "moved from very big obsolete plants in the city to very small obsolete plants in the country." Union workers resisted innovations that eliminated jobs, whether in plant layout, processes, or machinery. When Swift built a new plant in, say, Fort Worth, it looked different from its aging one in Chicago, but it "worked" the same.[84]

The old-timers even dragged their feet when it came to the meat itself. Armour and Swift balked at the idea of frozen meats, let alone boxed beef, because their union employees resisted.

Even when they manufactured value-added products, they were too timid to venture far. In the 1960s, for example, Swift developed "compressed bacon bars" that American astronauts carried into space. What should have been marketing rocket fuel instead stayed under wraps because, as one employee said, "Suppose the moonshot fails and those guys die up there." The astronauts didn't, but Swift's opportunity did.[85]

Such failings made the old packers an attractive takeover target in the '60s and '70s, usually by conglomerates with no experience in making meat. Some scoffed. "What meat packing assets are best equipped for," an analyst told a reporter, "is the luring of lambs to slaughter."[86]

Ken Monfort had little sympathy for his older brethren. "After World War II," he said, when they "should have modernized, they didn't. When they should have changed location, they didn't." So he and IBP and other revolutionaries seized the moment, and demonstrated that "money [could] be made in modern plants, operated well, in the right locations." "The big packers," he said, "follow us now, rather than lead us."[87]

Go big, or get out of the way.

CHAPTER 10
BIG DOUBTS

IN 1953 MORE THAN A THOUSAND SHEEP DIED UNDER MYSTERIOUS circumstances in Utah. Angry stockmen blamed their losses on nuclear "fallout": radioactive residue from a nuclear bomb explosion, in this case via a Nevada weapons test site. The Atomic Energy Commission denied the charge. But a year later, fallout from a Pacific Ocean bomb test coated a Japanese fishing boat. The crew of twenty-three became ill; one man died.

Not long after that, Americans learned that nuclear fallout had tainted food and milk supplies via the radioactive isotope strontium-90.[1]

Then there was the Nightmare Before Thanksgiving. In early November 1959, the Department of Health, Education, and Welfare (1953-1979) announced that some of the nation's cranberry crop was contaminated with aminotriazole, an herbicide and known carcinogen. Most Americans celebrated that holiday season cranberry-free.[2]

And when it wasn't aminotriazole, it was *Salmonella*, of which midcentury food processing produced a bumper crop. Processors manufactured enormous quantities of everything from frozen TV dinners to dried milk to boxed cake mixes. One careless move at just one factory, an epidemiologist explained, could spawn an "infection that [could] spread throughout the country."[3]

THE POSTWAR YEARS WERE ONES OF EXCITEMENT AND WONDER — television entered American homes — but Cold War and the creation of mind-boggling, planet-destroying weaponry laced those years with fear. So did toxic cranberries and tainted milk.

Meat production and processing were repeatedly implicated in the stream of news about dangers in land, air, and water.

Exhibit A: the broiler industry, where *Salmonella* was endemic. In 1956, for example, investigators traced an outbreak of salmonella infection to chicken salad prepared at a plant in Atlanta, Georgia, a facility involved in previous food poisoning cases.

No wonder. Every inch of the plant was contaminated, as were its employees and the carcasses coming into it. In a disturbing testament to the anger that followed, the investigators' report noted that "discouragement of plant personnel became so marked that, surreptitiously, the cartridges were removed from a gun kept in the plant for protection of payrolls."[4]

Around the same time, USDA analysts discovered that salmonella was also endemic in cattle feedlots, carried by stock coming out of Texas and other southern states. A likely source was the livestock-feed manufacturing industry, whose practitioners dotted the post-war south in order to service cattle, hog, and chicken feeders. Those factory-like plants were as susceptible to contamination as any that processed human foods.[5]

Even more shocking was the fallout from passage of the 1958 Food Additives Amendment, an addition to its mother bill, the 1938 Federal Food, Drug, and Cosmetics Act. This new addition was inspired by concerns about food processors' free hand with "additives," man-made and natural. Mystery ingredients, charged critics. (What *did* all those unpronounceable words mean?) The amendment required food processors to test new additives before using them, and its Delaney Clause banned the use of known carcinogens.[6]

After the passage of the new amendment, and out of an abundance of caution, USDA officials commissioned a committee to survey the nation's meat supplies for evidence of "additives" or chemical "overflow." Employees at various USDA divisions and bureaus, including the Meat Inspection Division (MID), pored over years of relevant data in order to assess the situation.[7]

The news was . . . bad.

According to several years of MID records, "residues of DDT and related materials" (read: chlorinated hydrocarbons) were "an almost universal contaminate" of the nation's food supplies. A series of emergency laboratory tests of current slaughterhouse samples delivered more bad news: on average, a beef cow's body contained "shockingly high" levels of pesticides.[8]

Agriculture Secretary Ezra Benson (1899-1994, secretary 1953-1961) concealed the reports.

Benson believed that additives made American food "the safest, cleanest, and most wholesome in the world," and President Dwight Eisenhower agreed: chemical additives were necessary in order to "produce adequate amounts of safe and wholesome foods and protect them from deterioration without chemicals." Chemical contamination was a price Americans paid for cheap food.[9]

From a political perspective — and these were, after all, political animals — the best reason to lose the report in a file drawer was to avoid alerting the public. Pesticide- and DDT-tainted beef would not go over well.[10]

MEAT CONSUMPTION CAME INTO QUESTION THANKS TO NEAR-PANIC about both cancer and heart disease.

First, there was an alleged midcentury heart disease epidemic, as officials reported a sharp increase in cases. Actual evidence was (and is) shaky: recent medical advances enabled physicians to diagnose more cases of heart disease because they had better tools with which to categorize and identify it; and because more Americans were living long enough to suffer ailments that afflict aging hearts.[11]

But some experts blamed Americans' diets. According to an

especially shaky theory, Europeans experienced a decline in heart attack and heart disease rates during the 1940's, thanks to a wartime diet low in protein, fat, and calories. At the same time, disease rates rose in the US, where diets contained an abundance of all three. That was enough to convince the easily persuaded: people living in "poor" countries experienced fewer heart attacks than affluent Americans. Therefore, rich diets and rich people reaped rich numbers of heart attacks.[12]

Ancel Keys (1904-2004), a media-savvy scientist, popularized this view. He claimed, based on evidence that ranged from sketchy to nonexistent, that high-fat diets elevated serum cholesterol. That led to atherosclerosis ("hardening of the arteries"), which led to heart attack, an equation dubbed the "diet-heart hypothesis." Therefore, he concluded, fat is bad. Meat contains fat; therefore meat is bad for your health.[13]

Many scientists challenged his claims (and decried his lack of evidence), but Keys understood that he who controlled the medium, controlled the message. His talent for explaining complex ideas in simple language appealed to journalists, who dutifully reported theory and conjecture as fact. In 1961, editors at *Time* magazine solidified both Keys's reputation and his ideas by putting him on the magazine's cover.

Then there was cancer, described at the time as one of the "principle diseases of mankind," and noteworthy as the nation's second-leading cause of death.[14]

No one knew why some became sick and others did not. According to experts, cancer could be sparked by almost anything. Specialists calculated that 15 percent of diagnoses were likely due to environmental causes. During a Congressional hearing, an official with the American Cancer Society described the disease as "an all-pervading biological problem of baffling complexity." Treatments were few and some were as deadly and debilitating as the illness itself. Post-diagnosis life expectancy was short.[15]

Cancer. DDT. Nuclear fallout. Perhaps the heart attack epidemic was due to Americans being scared to death? Certainly it appeared that there was nowhere to run and no place to hide from the dangers of modern life.

IN AUTUMN 1960, *TIME* MAGAZINE SUMMARIZED THE NATION'S FEARS in a cover story titled "Environment v. Man." Readers learned that every year, more than four hundred new chemicals were unleashed on an unknowing public, substances that wormed their way "into the air people breathe, the water they drink and the food they eat." The "invisible" invaders "damage plants, kill fish, slip undetected through sewage-treatment plants and blanket entire cities with clouds of noxious vapor."[16]

The onslaught also explains the robust sales and gut-punching impact of Rachel Carson's (1907-1964) 1962 book *Silent Spring*. Had it been published in, say, 1952, it's unlikely that it would have had the same reception. Instead, it landed in the hands of a public versed in the dangers of DES, DDT, and Sr-90.[17]

After Carson died in 1964 (cancer), others hoisted the flag, including scientist Barry Commoner (1917-2012). While serving in the Navy during World War II, he directed the construction of a device that enabled aircraft to bombard enemies with DDT, an effort to destroy crops. That experience and the literal and figurative fallout from nuclear weapons taught him to practice science with a conscience.

"Personally, I was not an environmentalist," he said. Rather, he recognized that contemporary life was rife with "hazard[s]" that traveled by "air," and contaminated plants and other living things.[18]

From there, he deduced "ecology": nature as "an integrated whole," and argued that the "separation of the laws of nature among the different sciences is a human conceit." In 1966, he founded the Center for the Biology of Natural Systems at Washington University in St. Louis, Missouri, where he searched for ways to use science in service to that integrated whole.

Carson, Commoner, and other "environmentalists" provided a science-based framework for pondering life, nature, and the planet. In contrast, Ralph Nader (1934-) framed his agenda in terms of consumers' rights, channeling Americans' fears, frustration, and outrage into legal assaults on corporations and governments.[19]

HE BEGAN HIS CAREER IN THE LATE FIFTIES, WHEN "CONSUMERS" were much on the minds of politicians at the highest levels. In 1959, a group of senators introduced a bill to establish a federal Department of Consumers. The sponsors noted that "the Department of Commerce, the Department of the Interior, the Department of Agriculture, and the Department of Labor represent the American people in their capacities as producers. There is no department to represent them in their capacity as consumers."[20]

When John F. Kennedy (1917-63; president 1961-63) campaigned for president, he described "the consumer" as "the only man in our economy without a high-powered lobbyist in Washington. I intend to be that lobbyist." Once elected, he asked Congress for a "Consumer's Bill of Rights" that would protect consumers' "right to safety, the right to be informed, the right to choose, and the right to be heard." All told, in the 1960s Congress passed twenty-eight pieces of "consumer protection" legislation.[21]

Nader threw himself into this effort. He believed that citizens were routinely endangered by the actions of government bureaucrats, elected officials, and profit-driven corporations. (He especially loathed the latter, which he dubbed "private governments.") Against this triad's dominance, Nader argued, consumers were powerless, a point amply demonstrated by the environmental terrors of the 1950s.[22]

Nader's genius lay in his ability to particularize his attacks on corporate power. Consider the seatbelt. His bestselling 1965 book, *Unsafe at Any Speed*, detailed the automobile industry's devotion to profits rather than consumer safety. It's the reason why, in the United States, vehicle seatbelts are required by law.

But it wasn't only seatbelts. It was tainted beef and cranberries and radioactive wastes and a poultry industry that doubled as a salmonella breeding facility. Nader argued that Americans deserved to be safe from dangers they did not cause and over which they had no control.

Exposing those invisible dangers required evidence that could only be found with thousands of hours of dogged research, mostly digging through government documents. Nader solved this problem by organizing his quests into hundreds of project-specific "interest groups," each staffed by eager young "Raiders" devoted to rooting out evil in the name of consumer-citizens. It helped that thanks to postwar expansion in higher education and the arrival in college of the first wave of baby boomers, the supply of "educated young people willing to work for peanuts" was at an all-time high.[23]

"Consumer activism" quickly became both a career and an aggressive segment of a new, non-profit, "public interest" lobbying industry that coalesced in the 1960s and 1970s. Droves of law students and lawyers embraced Nader's crusades, and eschewed conventional careers to work as Nader's Raiders.

In 1969, Nader landed on the cover of *Time* magazine, his face presented as a Warholesque collision of orange and green sliced by a banner announcing "The Consumer Revolt."[24]

"Evidently there's a dearth of causes right now," grumbled a vice president at the Jewel grocery chain. "Consumerism has become like motherhood and the flag, with everybody jumping on the bandwagon." Another critic, a fierce supporter of "free markets," described Nader as "perhaps the single most effective antagonist of American business." Thanks to "the media," he had "become a legend in his own time and an idol of millions of Americans."[25]

According to Ralph, those critics had it backward. "Other issues such as Vietnam and civil rights have divided the country into camps," he argued. Those with something to sell would always be divided from those who wanted to buy. But among *consumers*, there was "no split." Everyone, black or white, young or old, rich or poor, was a consumer. Consumerism was a "people's movement."[26]

By that definition, anything and everything that affected "people" was up for grabs by Nader's Raiders.

IN THE LATE 1960s, FRESH OFF HIS VICTORY OVER DETROIT AND automobile safety standards, Nader launched a crusade to save the hot dog.

At the time, Americans were unnerved by a stream of Keys-inspired reporting about the relationship between fatty diets and disease. Nader used that as a springboard to educate the public about the ways in which corporations sacrificed public health for profits. His decision to use the hot dog as medium and messenger was, yes, a stroke of genius.

For the baby-boom generation, those pinky-brown cylinders of who-knew-what had long ruled as the unofficial king of kid food: hot dog consumption soared 75 percent in the twenty years after the end of World War II. Here was a target that consumers cared about.

Using statistics ferreted from obscure USDA reports, Nader informed Americans that the dog had gone to the dogs. In 1937, he explained, the typical frankfurter contained about 19 percent fat and 20 percent protein. The 1967 model, however, boasted 33 percent fat and less than 12 percent protein. Evidence, surely, of nefarious activity amongst meatpackers and food processors.[27]

In response, the USDA agreed to consider new rules for hot dog fat content, and organized a public hearing so that interested parties could weigh in.

On the appointed day, the meat men argued that 35 percent fat content yielded a juicy, toothsome dog preferred by consumers. More like coronary delights, insisted their foes, and toxic to kids and grownups alike. They demanded that hot dogs contain no more than 25 percent fat.

Virginia Knauer (1915-2011), President Richard Nixon's Director of Consumer Affairs, intervened, announcing a 30 percent content level. The consumerites were delighted; USDA officials and meat industry representatives, flummoxed. Was the White House telling the Department of Agriculture what to do? Yes, Knauer assured them, it was.

Nixon (1913-1994; president 1969-1974) later phoned Knauer to affirm that he backed her "100%" on "the hot dog issue." He was on a low-cholesterol diet himself, he explained, but he identified with the dog because of his "humble origins." "Why, we were raised on hot dogs and hamburgers. We've got to look after the hot dog."[28]

That hearing took place in a stuffy federal building; Nader wanted to reach millions. He passed this particular political hot dog over to his friends at *Consumer Reports* (whose circulation had nearly doubled in recent years). They responded with a splashy, under-the-skin exposé.

"Once upon a time," *CR*'s reporter told readers, the frankfurter had been "a reasonably honest product" composed of meat, a bit of water, a dollop of fat, and plenty of protein.[29]

No more. The 1970s dog contained as much 33 percent fat and, legally, as much as 54 percent water. An "All Meat" dog could, and likely did, contain any number and kind of ingredients: lips and tongues; pork, beef, chicken, mutton, or goat; cereal, dried milk, and soy meal.

Then there was the doghouse, the plastic kennels that secured individual hot dogs en route from processing plant to grocery shelf to grocery cart to ketchup and bun at the table. The package's airtight seal was supposed to prevent bacteria from breeding inside. A safe threshold was 10 million bacteria per gram; forty percent of the magazine's samples surpassed that number. One contained 140 million bacteria per gram.

Add in sodium nitrite — newsworthy at the time because of its allegedly carcinogenic qualities — salt, spice, monosodium glutamate, corn syrup, sodium ascorbate, and/or ascorbic acid, and there it was: the all-American hot dog.

The *CR* report captured the public's attention, and the USDA agreed to reconsider hot dog regulations and labels. Per operating procedure, the department invited the public to weigh in.

The public obliged.

A Maryland schoolgirl took pencil in hand to make a polite but firm request: Please stop adding "pig swill" to hot dogs, she wrote. "We get bad lunches at school as it is and I would hate to have to turn down hot dogs if you put it in. And besides I would starve the whole day!" P.S., she added, "If you really have to put pig snouts in, could you blow their noses first, please??"[30]

The young lady had company. A New Jersey woman complained that it was bad enough that meat makers added "cancer producing" preservatives to their products. But making hot dogs from "the same meat that they now put in dog food" was too much. "How much more does the American consumer have to take?" she asked. "Let us get off the dollar bandwagon and get back to eating pure foods. Our children ask the industries to stop polluting their bodies."

The "wiener is being clobbered," mourned the president of the American Meat Institute as hot dog sales plunged. Oscar Mayer Jr. interpreted the attacks as "personal affronts to him and his meat-packing forebears." The Mayer family had been manufacturing sausages and other pork products since the late nineteenth century. Their hot dog was a long-time bestseller, in part thanks to its memorable advertising ditty: "Oh, I wish I were an Oscar Mayer wiener." Mayer Jr. was "absolutely stunned" by the uproar.[31]

Other meat processors were infuriated. "I have an answer to the stupid jerks in Washington, including Nader," said the president of an Illinois meat-processing company. "I would suggest that all packers stop buying [livestock] for a two-week period to show the American people what these jerks in Washington are doing to the farmer and packer and, in the end, the American consumer. It's time someone tells these jerks where they fit."[32]

The president of another meat company offered a more measured response in a letter to an assistant secretary of agriculture. He suggested that rather than ban protein-rich byproducts like tongue, liver, and lips, the USDA educate the public about their nutritional value.

A ban based on emotion and "aesthetics," he argued, would propel the USDA down a slippery slope. Gelatin, for example, was manufactured from bone. Did the department plan to ban "gelatin desserts" such as Jell-O? Mushrooms were "grown in manure" and typically eaten raw. Would it also ban them?[33]

In the end, both sides got something they wanted as the USDA opted for the middle road rather than the slippery slope. Under new rules, sausages manufactured from just one type of meat would wear a label boasting that fact. Ones made from the dreaded snouts, eyes, and lips contained words like "byproducts" or "variety meats," terminology blessedly vague by processors' standards and appallingly vague by those of consumer advocates.

NADER USED THE SAME GRAB-'EM-BY-THE-GUTS STRATEGY IN A 1967 attack that led to the passage of a new meat inspection law, the Wholesome Meat Act, and inadvertently wiped out many small meatpackers in the process. His inspiration came from two events that had occurred a few years earlier.

The first concerned federal definitions of and standards for "ham." The second involved a New York City meat processor charged with making beef from diseased and dead cows, and selling horse meat as beef. Both cases centered on *intra*state meatpackers, companies that conducted business only within a state's borders. There were thousands such operations. Collectively, they accounted for fifteen percent of the nation's slaughter and twenty-five percent of its meats.

Intrastate packers operated in a different regulatory universe than *inter*state meatpackers such as Monfort, IBP, Swift, and Armour. The interstate giants were subject to a host of regulatory mechanisms, including federal inspection. Intrastate meatpackers, in contrast, operated with relatively little oversight. Federal inspection laws did not apply to them; state laws were few.

The investigations into ham standards and horse meat generated piles of reports that documented a horrific lack of sanitary standards in intrastate packing plants. For various reasons, those documents had been kept private, filed away and identified only as the Clarkson Report.

In the years following, Congress regularly pondered legislation to impose federal inspection standards on all meatpacking plants. As expected, the debates were rancorous: did Americans need yet another federal tentacle in their lives? But the debates were also ill-informed: Congress knew nothing about the hidden Clarkson Report.

In summer 1967, the House Agriculture Committee scheduled hearings for three new intrastate inspection proposals. Ralph Nader was ready and waiting.

An insider had tipped him off to the existence of the Clarkson Report (informants abounded). Once Nader accessed the documents, he dispatched selected extracts to the House Agriculture committee, and published two short essays in the *New Republic*, pithy pieces loaded with gory details. When the hearings began, he set off on a ten-day, cross-country trek to promote the Clarkson Report and encourage Americans to call their representatives.[34]

When President Lyndon B. Johnson (1908-1973, president 1963-1969) signed the Wholesome Meat Act in December 1967, Nader was by his side, invited to the White House for the occasion.

Alas, this good deed provoked painful unintended consequences via its compliance requirements, effectively dooming many intrastate packers. As written, the legislation required states to enforce compliance of the new standards, but gave them zero incentive to do so (or not). If the compliance deadline came and went, federal officials would conduct inspections on the state's behalf — and then hand future inspections back to the state.

Consumer activists warned that inspectors, beholden to neither state nor federal officials, would become pawns of meatpackers, who would encourage them to look the other way when tainted meats passed along the line.

Worse, intrastate packers were the industry's smallest and most vulnerable members; few had the resources to comply with the new requirements.

Such was the case with United Packers in Opelousas, Louisiana. The inspector who visited told the owner that he would need to replace all of the floors, walls, and ceilings. It would cost at least a quarter-million dollars, and even that, the inspector warned, might not be enough to meet compliance.

United's vice president complained that he could understand if such regulations enhanced consumer safety and improved food purity, but as far as he could tell, that was "the furthest from being the situation."

"Is there a conspiracy between big business and USDA to put small independent companies out of business?" he asked. "Needless to say, if the giants in the meat industry are the only ones left in business, then the consumer will certainly suffer and the farmer and rancher . . . will be forced to accept the prices the giants are willing to pay."[35]

Ralph couldn't have said it better himself.

Activists also challenged contemporary agriculture and livestock production. Many were inspired by Barry Commoner, who feared that Americans courted disaster when they ignored the damage inflicted by industrial agriculture's "massive intervention" into nature. He urged Americans to think of agriculture as part of a "larger, over-all system of life[,] . . . the biosphere." Such an "ecosystem cannot be divided into manageable parts."[36]

Much of the heavy lifting was shouldered by new, Nader-like, public-interest nonprofits that specialized in "environmental" issues. Eco-warriors, for example, argued that factory farming was too reliant on nonrenewable resources (a charge that fell flat at a moment when most Americans assumed that cheap energy was infinite). They charged that too many farms had been carved from fragile, unsuitable terrain; that livestock confinement, pesticides, and fertilizers poisoned land, air, and water.

The use of DES and antibiotics in livestock production provided critics with plenty of low-hanging fruit.

The reputation of DES had declined markedly since the early 1950s when Wise Burroughs and Eli Lilly launched Stilbestol. In one case, an employee who handled DES in his job at a pharmaceutical company sued his employer. Despite wearing a respirator and rubber gloves, the DES had "poisoned" him. He'd "suffered effemination," and "been rendered permanently impotent," depriving him of "the rights and benefits of marital relations."[37]

When male employees at another company experienced breast

development and impotence after working with DES, FDA staff urged the owner to hire older workers who might not be as concerned about DES's "devirilizing effect."[38]

Even some packers and feeders questioned the wisdom of adding DES to livestock feed. One packer complained that hormone-fed cattle failed to "cut out a carcass that's as good as they look on the hoof." "The beef we're seeing today," he said in 1955, "doesn't measure up to the old corn-fed beef. It looks plump and good on the outside, but when you cut it open the quality isn't there. The way things are going, corn-fed beef will be a thing of the past in four or five years."[39]

Nonetheless, by the 1960s DES was seemingly everywhere. No one disputed that it was carcinogenic, but doing something about that required breaking an ongoing, bureaucratic stalemate between the USDA and the FDA. It was the latter's responsibility to scrutinize "drugs" and other additives, and the former's job to identify things like DES residues in meat. Two different tasks; two different criteria. Stalemate. And DES continued to be used.

But in 1970, the Associated Press got the public's attention when it reported that some US beef contained DES. Federal inspectors pulled tainted carcasses from meatpackers' lines, and a spokesman for the FDA assured Americans they had nothing to fear. "Most of us can't get too excited about the occasional animal showing up [with] two parts per billion of stilbestrol," he said.[40]

His seeming disregard stemmed less from indifference than from a belief in his own expertise. Unlike average Americans — the ones reading newspapers — he and other experts understood the intricacies of DES, animal nutrition, and physiology, including the fact that bovines' bodies contain natural estrogens. To an expert, minute traces of DES residue were nothing to worry about. A human would have to eat tons (literally) of residues before suffering any damage.

Indeed, the FDA was so confident about the safety of DES that it granted cattle feeders permission to double the amount they could use.[41]

What the public heard, however, was the word "cancer" coupled with an airy dismissal from a bureaucrat indifferent to the public's health. In March 1971, a House committee began hearings to investigate the use of DES and other chemicals in the nation's food supply.

Unbeknownst to the committee, FDA officials had recently learned about the "DES daughters" — young women who had been diagnosed with a rare form of vaginal cancer. Their mothers had all been prescribed DES while pregnant, confirming a link between DES and cancer. During the House hearings, FDA staff who testified concealed the information.

But in April, the report was made public. Soon after, the National Resources Defense Council (NRDC), one of the new environmental public-interest groups, asked a court to ban DES in livestock used for human food. More hearings followed, including one that focused entirely on DES in food. The chair of the hearings was infuriated by the extent to which staff at both the FDA and USDA had lied to Congress in earlier hearings.[42]

In 1973, the FDA banned DES, although the prohibition did not go into effect until 1979, stalled by a series of court challenges. DES left the farm, but livestock producers were still allowed to use non-carcinogenic hormones.

ANTIBIOTICS ALSO CAME UNDER ATTACK, AND FOR GOOD REASON: IN the late 1950s, scientists discovered that bacteria developed immunity to antibiotics, which could be passed on to their offspring, and even to unrelated bacterial species nearby. In 1966, the *New England Journal of Medicine* described the resistance effect as "intellectually fascinating and therapeutically frightening." Unless humans began taking more care with how and when they administered such drugs, physicians treating infectious disease would "find themselves back in the preantibiotic Middle Ages."[43]

An FDA committee subsequently recommended that food manufacturers limit their use of antibiotics to ones not used on humans. The committee explained that without more evidence, it was reluctant to issue a stronger recommendation. It might be true that long-term doses of antibiotics provoked bacterial resistance, but scientists did not understand how or even if those doses affected humans who ate meat from drug-treated livestock. Barring definitive data, the committee found no reason to ban the drugs.

Activists continued to press. In 1972, FDA officials ruled that antibiotic-laced livestock feeds constituted a "potential health hazard." Manufacturers would henceforth be required to demonstrate the "safety and efficacy of their products."[44]

Translation: as long as stock producers followed the rules, antibiotics were safe from the meddling of Nader and his Raiders.

The "bad news," complained the editor of a livestock industry magazine, was that manufacturers would be forced to spend millions on testing, an expense they would pass on to farmers and consumers. There was no "better research" available, fumed an official with the National Livestock Producers Association, "than the 200 million healthy Americans eating 200 pounds of red meat and poultry per capita annually, thanks largely to low-level use of antibiotics. I'd say that ought to be enough research."[45]

It's tempting to conclude that federal officials caved to pressure from lobbying by pharmaceutical manufacturers and meat industry trade groups. But two other factors carried more weight.

First, at the time, none of the available research had produced irrefutable evidence linking antibiotic-laced feeds to human antibiotic resistance. In the words of the FDA's commissioner, the data was "grossly inadequate." No one had died from eating meat from animals raised on antibiotics (or DES), so no one could be certain beyond a doubt that the drugs posed a danger. If 100 percent certainty was the relevant criterion, uncertainty backed the status quo.[46]

Second, the scientific community had more at stake than did farmers, pharmaceutical manufacturers, and political activists: their professional credibility. Imposing a ban based on no evidence was a cure worse than the disease; it undermined the authority of science. In this case, science trumped knee-jerk fear.

ANOTHER ATTACK ON AGRICULTURE WAS ORGANIZED BY THE Agribusiness Accountability Project (AAP), a Nader-sponsored group that dissected relationships between and among farmers, corporations, the USDA, and land grant schools. Best known for a report titled *Hard Times, Hard Tomatoes*, the AAP research group argued that corporate interests had "captured" the USDA and land grant research complex and transformed farms into factories, thereby destroying family farms.[47]

The AAP's work sparked a short-lived attack on "corporate farming." In 1972, for example, activists persuaded a Nebraska state legislator to introduce a bill banning agricultural operations that produced or sold more than $5 million worth of goods (roughly $27 million today). Nebraska was "relatively free of the cancer" of corporate farming; his bill would ensure that it stayed that way.[48]

A more durable result of the Naderist critique of mainstream agriculture can be found in a push for "practical alternatives" to the treadmill of industrial growth agents, assembly-line thinking, and cheap fuel: mixed rather than mono-agriculture; farming with nature rather than chemicals.[49]

The Nebraska-based Center for Rural Affairs (CRA) led the way. Founded in 1973 (and going strong a half century later) CRA promoted agriculture based on "appropriate farm technology and organic methods" as alternatives to expensive, energy-inefficient inputs. This was no hippie-feel-good, Garden-of-Eden project. CRA's leadership relied on science-based information produced by researchers at Barry Commoner's laboratory.[50]

CRA worked with practicing (and practical) farmers on the ground, but urbanites provided much of the fodder for alt-agriculture's popularity. The late sixties and early seventies were permeated with a fondness for what a later generation would dub DIY — do it yourself — in the name of getting back at the Big Corporations. Make your own beer! Bake your own bread! Make your own food.

Central to the construction of that ethos was Stewart Brand's *Whole Earth Catalog* (1968).

Its purpose was straightforward: share knowledge. Offer ordinary people the nuts-and-bolts of the methods and tools with which to build, well, almost anything, and included information on growing and processing one's own food. The catalog may have unintentionally romanticized off-the-grid lifestyles. Fringe farmers — as often as not urbanites looking for a way out of the rat race — devoured the catalog's pages, seeking insight into techniques and technology.[51]

J.I. Rodale (1898-1971) and son Robert (1930-1990) of Pennsylvania also captured the mainstream. For decades, the Rodales had published magazines and books devoted to organic gardening and farming, operating in relative isolation and scorned by most. (The "Don Quixote of the compost heap," wrote one reporter in 1966.) During the sixties and seventies, however, the Rodale reputation and profits attained new heights as a new generation of [urban] farmers embraced compost and hoe.[52]

Another literary sensation prompted consumers to question the wisdom of factory farming and meat consumption. In *Diet for A Small Planet* (1971), California social worker Frances Moore Lappé (1944-) argued that meat production was both inefficient and wasteful. Farmers committed millions of acres to livestock feed rather than human food, and polluted air and water in the process.

IN SUM, A MULTIFARIOUS CRITIQUE OF AMERICAN AGRICULTURE TOOK shape in the 1970s. Thanks to lobbying by an activist alliance, for example, the 1976 farm bill included funding for "farm-to-consumer" projects aimed at creating new markets for small farmers; "farmers' markets" in popular parlance.

In 1979, the USDA sponsored a study of organic agriculture in the United States and Europe. Secretary of Agriculture Bob Bergland explained that "energy shortages, food safety, and environmental concerns have all contributed to the demand for more comprehensive information on organic farming technology." The final report "strongly" recommended that the USDA support (read: finance) research and education to "address the needs and problems of organic farmers." The 1981 farm bill authorized "multidisciplinary organic farming research projects" aimed at implementing the report's ideas and recommendations.[53]

Mainstream agriculture was not amused.

Some of its contempt was prompted by reformers who focused on mystical properties, and framed alt-agriculture as a kind of pastoral utopia. Farmers, wrote one essayist in this vein, must be allowed to seek "voluntary simplicity." Farmers "must derive happiness and humane satisfaction from a life" free of the "consumerism, leisure, and delirious pursuit of novelty that characterizes [sic] our society."[54]

Other critiques turned on more substantive issues. A 1978 "debate" between Earl Butz (1909-2008) and Wendell Berry (1934-) framed the issues at stake.

Berry, a writer, farmer, and political activist, had emerged as the poet laureate, as it were, of alternative agriculture. He owned and operated a small farm in rural Kentucky, and relied primarily on horsepower so as to remain independent of "the oil companies."

Berry opined that "independent" farmers like himself embodied the "traditional values" necessary for a good society: "thrift, stewardship, private property, [and] political liberties." Those values were being eroded by ones rooted in the "urban industrial" worldview.

Butz was an agricultural economist who'd devoted his career to the agricultural complex at land grant schools and the USDA, including a stint as Agriculture Secretary from 1971 to 1976. He dismissed Berry and his ilk as muddle-headed idealists who enjoyed the wherewithal to spin agricultural fantasies thanks to "modern, scientific, technological agriculture." Agriculture was a "machine" designed to make food and fiber, not a romantic retreat for poets and professors. "We can go back to organic agriculture in this country if we must," said Butz, but "someone must decide which 50 million of our people will starve!"[55]

THE MOMENT CAME AT KEN MONFORT HEAD ON. HE DIDN'T HAVE much choice other than to meet it.

In the late sixties, he announced plans to build a 125,000-head feedlot south of town. A group of homeowners near the site said no. The spokesman for "Operation Fresh Air" argued that Monfort's feedlots were a drag on Greeley's economy. "If you were [an employer] and you wanted to come to Colorado and the clean, Western fresh air, would you locate in Greeley between two feed lots?" he asked.

A city councilman agreed. Whenever visitors came to town, he said, "they invariably inquire [about] the strange odor" and ask "how do you stand it?"[56]

But the editor of one local newspaper sided with the Monforts. He noted that in the previous year, the company had purchased $2.5 million worth of feedstuffs from area farmers, and property taxes on the new lot would contribute almost a half-million dollars to local coffers.

Unsure how deep the opposition ran, Ken announced that he would abandon the project. That prompted an outpouring of support in favor of the expansion, and he decided to proceed. As a concession, he closed the family's original feedlot and built a new one farther from town.

Kenny also read *Diet for A Small Planet*, and concluded that Americans must rethink their appetite for meat. "Food is a scarce item," he argued. "It will be scarcer." Humans, he said, "should come first," and livestock "last on the list" of those getting grain.[57]

Ken being Ken, however, he spotted a profit angle. In 1971, he instructed his feedlot employees to isolate a thousand yearlings, feed them diets free of antibiotics and DES, and send them to slaughter minus the chemical dip used to destroy parasites. Monfort distributed "E-Colo-Beef" to health food stores, where it sold for 40 percent more than his conventional meat. (The brand name is not as tone deaf as it seems. In the early 1970s, *E. coli* had not yet achieved bacterial celebrity status.)

The project didn't last long. The cattle needed 10 to 15 percent longer to reach market weight, which meant a higher feed bill. Once slaughtered, the carcasses yielded less meat. Three-quarters of the livers were diseased, and parasite-infected flesh had to be cut away.

"When you start trimming away $2 a pound meat to get rid of grubs it starts getting expensive," admitted one Monfort executive. (Another later described the short-lived project as "a colossal blunder . . . that [would not] happen again.")[58]

But in 1971, Ken had other, more compelling reasons to dump organic for conventional. He and everyone else in the business of making meat were watching the bottom fall out of their lives.

IV: PLENTY: ITS PLEASURES AND ITS PRICE

CHAPTER 11

"THE GREATEST AGE OF AGRICULTURE"

In 1969, two housewives living in Levittown, New York, launched a meat boycott. They were fed up with the high cost of living (by then an American icon, like baseball and apple pie). Soon they and other women were picketing local grocery stores "For Lower Prices," as they called their group.

When the boycott spread to other locations, an angry Iowa farmer delivered a live 400-pound steer to the front door of one of the women, Mickey DeLorenzo. His message to her: "Long Island suburban housewives don't know what it takes . . . to bring a calf from birth to slaughter" or "what [was] going on out [there] in the Corn Belt."[1]

Mickey and her husband took it in stride. They named him Flip after their group (FLP); she described him as a "living symbol of the boycott.[2]

Over the next few years, more boycotts, often directed at meat, broke out. Many were organized by women, and encouraged by politicians and state legislators. "I'll boycott until I grow feathers from eating so much chicken," vowed one woman in 1973. Another told a reporter that her family, including "two men with good appetites," had voted to join the boycott. It "won't be easy," she said.³

A 1973 poster for a meat boycott.

A group of New York City restaurateurs ran newspaper ads with headlines screaming "Don't Eat Beef!" The copy below lured readers to "Join us to fight against those ridiculous beef prices" by offering a 10 percent discount to diners who ordered an alternative.⁴

An infuriated, frustrated Ken Monfort pronounced himself "appalled by how little consumers [knew] about the real world." They paid "$2 a pound for certain fluff like Sara Lee cakes, and argue[d] about paying $1 a pound for chuck roast." Food production was attached to "basic costs," he complained, and "the more they want us to do for them, the less value they're getting."⁵

His "basic costs" had spiraled into the stratosphere. In 1972, he and other Colorado cattle feeders paid $50 for a ton of corn. A year later, the price had more than doubled, and doubled again in 1974, including a 40 percent increase during the summer alone.

"A year ago," Monfort told a reporter in summer 1973, he'd bought cattle that were two-thirds of the way to market weight; he fed the final third. "Today we're buying 58 per cent and adding 42" and paying exorbitant prices to do so. He slashed his cattle numbers by twenty thousand, but it wasn't enough to keep him in black.[6]

"We've taken beatings before," he mused, "but this is the biggest loss in my experience."[7]

By early 1974, he was losing as much as $125 on each animal he sent to the packing plant. Roughly $2 million, and a mere drop compared to the $50 million he'd lost on paper: Monfort Beef's share price had dropped from $16, when Ken took the company public in 1970, to $4 by early 1974.

"It seemed like a good idea at the time," he said. "We're not going to back down now."[8]

MONFORT'S WOES AND THE MEAT BOYCOTTS WERE A RESPONSE TO A series of tectonic events in the American economy that shaped a turning point in US history. The upsets and upheavals were so many, and so simultaneous were they, that it's not easy to construct a straightforward timeline. But the through line could be described as the "unexpected failure of success."[9]

By the 1970s, for example, Americans had booked thirty-some years of managing agricultural surpluses; the paradox appeared to be under control. By then, too, the mostly US-sponsored, postwar "Green Revolution" had taught much of the world how to farm like Americans. In 1970, its godfather, Norman Borlaug was honored with a Nobel Prize for his work in ending world hunger.

Surely famine, an age-old human tragedy, had been conquered for good. Surely thanks to well-managed, global food supplies, no one would starve. US officials "divested" the nation's grain surpluses. Who needed stockpiles? Better to export, they considered, than to store.[10]

Worse timing there never was. Disinvestment coincided with a series of global crop failures, including the Soviet wheat harvest, that collapsed global grain supplies. More than most world leaders, Soviets feared food shortages, remembering that a cabbage scarcity had tipped old Russia into revolution. In July 1972, the Kremlin purchased 433 million bushels of American wheat.

The event came to be known as the Great Grain Robbery.

US wheat prices doubled; food prices rose precipitously. A year later, Americans were paying more for a loaf of bread than their communist counterparts. Taxpayers also shouldered the cost of farm subsidies, which soared from $67 million to $300 million.

In summer 1973, with no grain to spare, the federal government was forced to renege on a shipment it had promised India, where thirty million people were starving. India promptly bought what it needed from the Soviets, who had plenty on hand thanks to the Americans.[11]

Secretary of Treasury George Schultz conceded that the US had been "burned" by the Soviets.[12]

Then there was the oil embargo (October 1973-March 1974), and an ensuing "panic at the pump." In October 1973, a group of Arab states attacked Israel. America's postwar role as a global superpower meant the US aided Israel; the Soviets backed the Arab countries. In retaliation, the Organisation of Arab Petroleum Exporting Countries (OAPEC) embargoed oil shipments to the US.[13]

The impact was immediate, visible, and emotional. As the price of oil and energy rose, so did the price of almost everything else. Americans spent hours in their cars, waiting in long lines of other cars, hoping to snag gasoline before the station ran out. Agriculture, dependent on cheap fuel, was particularly affected, which caused pain at the supermarket.

At the same time, the United States lost its decades-long dominance as manufacturer for the world. US-funded projects to rebuild war-torn Europe and Asia had worked. Suddenly, or so it seemed, new, ultra-high-technology factories around the world were cranking out an array of goods — steel, clothing, radios, toasters, automobiles — that were cheaper than those made in the United States.

The deluge of inexpensive manufactured goods battered American manufacturing. Factories closed their doors. Many who lost their jobs never worked again.

For the first time in eighty years, the United States recorded a trade deficit. The dollar declined. Consumer prices marched up. So did inflation: 11 percent in 1974; six to nine percent the rest of the decade; 13.5 percent in 1980. Unemployment bounced up and down, mostly up.

Housewives picketed grocery stores; butchers blamed high meat prices on packers; packers blamed grocers. Livestock producers like Monfort teetered on the brink. And everyone else was convinced that the culprit was either farmers, Russians, mysterious middlemen, or the equally mysterious "them" in Washington, DC, who seemed not to care about average, hard-working Americans.

"We've got a worldwide food panic on our hands, and unless something is done we're going to have shortages in this country," insisted an executive with a Kansas City grain mill.[14]

But what should that something be?

Should the United States stockpile food to protect Americans from future shortages? Should it do as some poor nations demanded and give it away? Should Congress reduce tariffs on imports? Raise them? And what to do about rising food costs? Impose more price ceilings? Freeze wages? Expand and extend unemployment payouts?

Although the State Department was more accustomed to wielding food aid as a diplomatic cudgel than to giving it away for free, the US could not afford to appear indifferent to global starvation. According to experts, global food supplies were at their lowest levels in twenty years. In late 1974, the United Nations' Food and Agriculture Organization (FAO) hosted a World Food Conference in order to coordinate a response and to ponder "systematic world food security policy."[15]

American officials who attended the gathering, including USDA Secretary Earl Butz, wrestled with thorny questions.

Suppose farmers gassed up their tractors and cranked out huge grain surpluses to meet this global catastrophe — and the predicted demand failed to materialize? Farmers would be furious, and taxpayers stuck with the bill for agricultural subsidies. On the other hand, if the FAO was correct, and farmers failed to keep pace with global demand, domestic food prices would rise anyway. Citizen-consumers would be out for blood, which, of course, they would extract on election day.

At the White House, in Congress, in offices strung along the corridors of the Departments of Agriculture, State, and Treasury, debate raged. "Let's just say we're, well, a little befuddled," an employee at the Treasury Department confided to a reporter.[16]

In the end, President Nixon and his befuddled bureaucrats bet on a hungry planet: the famine was real and action must be taken. And even if it wasn't real, Nixon's recent exercise in Asian diplomacy was expected to generate Chinese orders for US wheat, corn, and hogs. Economists calculated that over the next decade, American farmers needed to increase production of food and fiber by a third.[17]

Butz was not persuaded that the planet's billions would starve to death anytime soon. His opinion carried little weight. Nixon's advisers had concluded that agriculture "had become far too important to be left to the agriculturists."[18]

As long as the crisis persisted, agricultural policy would come not from the USDA but from the White House or State Department. The White House ordered Butz to board the famine express. Grain farmers should produce to the max.

GLOBAL STARVATION WAS GOOD FOR BUSINESS.

"We're on the threshold of the greatest age of agriculture that this country has ever known," crowed the president of the American National Cattlemen's Association in 1973. One analyst described the "farm belt" as the "new IBM." Deep-pocketed investors and corporations, from inside the US and abroad, prowled the countryside looking for land with which to reap the profits of the greatest age.[19]

North Carolina proved attractive thanks to its cheap land, low-wage labor, and temperate climate. Insurance giant John Hancock, for example, bought thousands of acres there, as did investors from Japan, Australia, and Italy.

North Carolina native and multimillionaire (trucking) Malcolm McLean spent $60 million for 375,000 acres of land in eastern

North Carolina. He planned to grow corn and feed a million hogs a year.

"It's a question of supply and demand," explained one of McLean's employees. "People are starving. It's just like the energy crisis except that people are going to find it difficult to wait in line for food."[20]

McLean dubbed his operation First Colony Farm for its proximity to the settlement established by Sir Walter Raleigh nearly four centuries earlier. Perhaps McLean envisioned crossing a new kind of frontier: a journalist reported that the facility bore "the same relation to a farm that a computer does to an abacus."[21]

But if the farm aspired to a futuristic fantasy, the name of the geographic area in which it lay evoked the health and safety concerns of the 1970s. First Colony occupied a significant chunk of Dismal Swamp, an environmentally complex area that lay between the Pamlico and Albemarle Sounds. Environmentalists pounced, and rightly so.

No one in state government was inclined to stop the project.

An official with North Carolina's Department of Natural and Economic Resources explained that "the food crisis is up and coming, and I guess the feeling is that it's just not good to stop and do an environmental study when it will take so long and cost so much."[22]

The belief that the world was about to starve was so widespread, and the potential profits of alleged starvation so immense, that it inspired a modern version of the Marquis de Morès, whom we met in Chapter 3.

In late 1973, one Charles McQuoid showed up in Kahoka, Missouri, a dot of a burg in the northeast corner of the state. He told locals that he planned to spend at least $300 million to build a vertically integrated hog and pork production complex. His would be the largest such facility in the United States. It would occupy nearly seven thousand acres of land, include a slaughterhouse capacity of 2.5 million hogs a year, and employ two thousand people.[23]

McQuoid promised big money all around. An annual donation

to the University of Missouri, half for swine research, half for the football team. A million dollars to the local school district and an area hospital. An eighteen-hole golf course, a swimming pool and country club. An airstrip to accommodate the "foreign dignitaries" who would visit the area.[24]

Local farmers objected, and Missouri Senator Thomas Eagleton persuaded a Senate committee to investigate the project's potential for antitrust violations. But the Missouri commissioner of agriculture approved the project in early 1974. "I don't think, as I view the situation today, that this will be the demise of the small hog farmer," said the commissioner.[25]

Doubters enjoyed the last laugh. McQuoid, a former insurance salesman (and occasional visitor to a Chicago bankruptcy court), was fake from start to finish. His alleged backers were nonexistent, his collateral bogus. After borrowing $155,000 from two local bankers, he skipped town.

McQUOID WAS A FAKE; DON TYSON WAS NOT. TYSON ALREADY owned one of the nation's largest broiler companies, and in the 1970s he added "biggest hog farmer" to his resumé.

Tyson Foods was founded by Don's father, John Tyson (1905-1967), in the early 1930s. John started out, as so many did, by trucking live chickens from northwest Arkansas to Kansas City, Chicago, St. Louis, and other regional cities.

Like Jesse Jewell, John integrated early and often; by the time the World War II broiler boom began, he owned a hatchery, feed mill, and feed dealership. A friend once described John as "a very ambitious man. There is a thin line between ambition and greed. I don't think John ever got over the line, but he was pretty ambitious."[26]

Son Don (1930-2011) made no distinction between greed and ambition; as far as he was concerned, both were essential components of a businessman's briefcase. A "gregarious, voluble fellow," he augmented his ambition with an optimist's outlook, greeting the world with "an easy, cherubic smile" (the resemblance to a cherub enhanced by his bald, billiard-ball-shaped head).[27]

The angelic facade concealed a shrewd entrepreneurial brain. In the time it took an ordinary soul to notice a possible opportunity, Don Tyson had already calculated its risks and profit potential, and devised several possible scenarios in which that potential might play out. He coupled that talent with a ruthless disregard for anything but profit. "If it makes money, we expand it," he said. "If it doesn't, we cut its throat. . . . The 11th Commandment is that you need to make a profit."[28]

In Tyson's world, friends in high places equaled money in the bank. "The business of politics consists of a series of unsentimental transactions between those who need votes and those who have money," he once said, "a world where every quid has its quo."[29]

"[T]here is," said one devotee, "only one Don Tyson. There is no man in the world quite as sharp in the poultry business." A company executive raved that Tyson was "one of those that comes along once in a lifetime." "I have him on a pedestal. He's Superman."[30]

"Don Tyson," said an employee, "is a lying, thieving S.O.B.," a view others shared in large part because Tyson hated unions and worked relentlessly to eradicate their presence among his growers and employees.[31]

One example makes the case: In the spring of 1962, a group of Arkansas broiler growers met to organize, hoping their combined numbers would give them more negotiating clout with Tyson and the region's other broiler producers.

Don Tyson dispatched employees to line the road with company trucks and record attendees' license plate numbers. When the meeting began, the driver of one truck, his vehicle conveniently lacking a muffler, raced his engine to drown out the speakers inside the building.[32]

Don had joined his father's company in the early 1950s. The broiler industry's boomtown turbulence taught him two lessons.

One: safety lay in size and market share. The Tysons must either "expand or expire. There was no middle ground. We had to grow or die." Two: chaos and bad times equal opportunity. The Tysons expanded quickly by buying the plants and equipment of failed broiler makers.³³

In 1963, Don convinced his father to take the company public. Doing so would open their books to scrutiny; shareholders might challenge their steamroller approach. But in Don's mind, the benefits of a Wall Street presence and opportunities for funding, mergers, and acquisitions outweighed the risks.

And Don Tyson wanted it all. "We're not committed to the broiler business as such," he explained in 1964. "We're not overlooking ducks, geese, or anything else that will make us money! . . . We intend to be 'Mr. Poultry' in every sense of the word . . . ." (Turkeys proved the exception. "I've had two turkey plants, and two red-headed women in my lifetime," he said later, "and never done good with any of them.")³⁴

Like Jesse Jewell, Tyson believed that "value added" products served up profits and mitigated the industry's gyrations. Chicken noodle soup and chicken pot pies were central to the transformation of the broiler from basic commodity to retail merchandise. The 1970s offered fertile terrain for that vision.

In the wake of the global famine, foreign governments compensated for protein shortages by snapping up American chicken products. Those were less expensive than beef or pork and, thanks to new freezing technologies, easy to ship. In 1976, the Soviet Union ordered 2,500 tons of frozen chicken from US manufacturers, and the Iraqis 35,000.

As beef-centric restaurants struggled, Tyson also parlayed his long-standing presence in the hotel-restaurant-institution (HRI) sector into profit. High-end restaurateurs added chicken cordon bleu and chicken Kiev to their menus, and fast-food chains, from Long John Silver's to Burger King, supplemented burgers and fried fish with chicken sandwiches.

NOT ENOUGH. DON TYSON WANTED IN ON HOGS, TOO.

Swine appealed to his calculator brain: their birth-to-market cycle was longer than that of chickens, and he could use that to balance the volatility of broiler production. Tyson's existing feed mills would manufacture the necessary rations. By increasing the volume of his purchased raw materials, he would reduce production costs.

In the late 1960s, Don dipped a toe into hogs — and quickly backed off. It was not "easy to grow pigs in confinement like broilers because of the disease problems," he said. "It takes tremendous capital [but] management knowhow [sic], as we know it in the broiler business, is not as available."[35]

A decade later and wiser, he launched hog production "on an integrated basis." He built his first hog facility in Arkansas not far from company headquarters; in 1977 he bought First Colony from Malcolm McLean. A reporter described a ten-thousand-acre facility that included farrowing, breeding, and feeding operations. A half-million porcines lived in a "glimmering row of buildings that . . . seem[ed] to stretch forever," each structure overseen by a professional manager.[36]

"It's got all the advantages of working in a factory right here on the farm," explained one barn manager, the barn in this case being an immense, temperature-and-humidity-controlled structure where odor, waste, disease, and farrowing were managed like so many factors in an equation. "Those aren't just hog buildings up there in those hills," said another employee. "They're Cadillacs."[37]

By 1980, Tyson had expanded to Nebraska. There he built a breeding facility, with plans to sell the piglets to nearby National Farms, Inc. (NFI), owned by the Bass family of Texas (whose immense fortune was dispersed among global corporations, chunks of Fort Worth, horse ranches, apartments, hotels, and oil wells, to name a few).[38]

In the 1970s, NFI farmed forty thousand acres scattered across Texas, Nebraska, and Kansas, raising grain and processing alfalfa-based feeds for its cattle operations. According to NFI president Bill Haw, farmers had "a God-given mission to feed the world."[39]

As part of that mission, Haw built a couple of experimental hog farms to assess the profit potential of converting part of National's corn crop to pork. Satisfied with the results, and with Tyson nearby to provide feeder stock, Haw announced that NFI would join the "leading edge" of modern hog farming. By 1984, employees at National's Nebraska facility were feeding 350,000 pigs a year, an output then worth about $40 million.[40]

The editor of a national farm magazine was blunt about the implications: such moves, he wrote, "ought to scare the hell out of every hog farmer in the country."[41]

"WE THINK THE BASIC FOOD INDUSTRY IS A HELL OF A PLACE TO BE," Mike Harper, the CEO of ConAgra, told a reporter in 1981.[42]

ConAgra began life in 1919 as Nebraska Consolidated Mills Co., a collection of once-independent grain mills that joined forces. Postwar expansion was followed by decline. Rebranding in the early 1970s as ConAgra did not help; the company was adrift, teetering on bankruptcy. The board hoped that Harper, who cut his corporate teeth in the broiler industry, and cut an imposing figure (six foot-six, a "booming voice," and he "looks like a truck coming at you"), could fix an "awful, awful disaster."[43]

Harper decided that integration and diversification offered the clearest path forward. ConAgra's survival depended on control of assets, whether cattle, corn, or chicken Kiev (frozen and ready to eat, of course). To that end, he bought river barges and terminals as well as grain elevators and a grain-processing outfit.

He loaded his shopping cart with food manufacturers, including Chun King and Patio Mexican, often buying at rock-bottom prices because their owners didn't know what to do with them.

That was the case with Banquet Foods, Inc., the nation's largest purveyor of frozen processed foods, and owned by RCA, which specialized in electronics, media equipment, and entertainment. RCA's leaders had no idea how to manage food, frozen or otherwise. ("They were thinking of Skylab when Banquet was talking chicken pot pies," said one amused onlooker.)[44]

Next, Harper set out to buy a meatpacking plant or two. Company-owned facilities would be able to respond efficiently to signals from Banquet or Chun King: more frozen beef stew or Kung

Pao Chicken; fewer tv dinners with beef steak. He had plenty of packers to choose from. The combination of the 1967 Wholesome Meat Act, the decade's economic turmoil, and the rise of IBP-like packers, had pushed dozens of small ones into bankruptcy. Armour, Swift, and Wilson teetered on collapse.

In 1978, Harper went after MBPXL, a beef-packing behemoth born from the merger of two IBP clones whose sales outnumbered ConAgra's by two to one. He shook hands on the deal, but at the last minute, grain giant Cargill snatched MBPXL from his hands and re-named it Excel.

Undaunted, Mike Harper set out to snare Armour. Its owner, Greyhound Corporation, was more accustomed to operating buses than packing plants. Its managers floundered in the turbulence of food making and meatpacking. Greyhound's chairman groused that he never had a chance with Armour, thanks to Monfort and IBP. They were "a bunch of piranhas cutting away at [Armour's] base." Armour, pronounced another observer was "dead in the water."[45]

But like the guy said: Mike Harper "buys things you wouldn't get a wooden nickel for and gets change back." The Armour acquisition included two slaughtering plants, one each for pork and beef, and nineteen facilities that manufactured value-added foods such as hot dogs and frozen entrées. A few weeks later, ConAgra reopened the facilities with new corporate logos and non-union labor.[46]

Four years later, Harper flew to Colorado, and persuaded Ken Monfort to sell him his feedlots, packing plant, and brand.

Monfort needed little convincing. He had never recovered from the bloodbath of the early 1970s, not least because he paid union wages; his production costs were 50 percent higher than those of IBP, which had eliminated union labor.

When he asked his employees for concessions in late 1979, they struck. The confrontation was ugly and painful for both sides.

Monfort argued that union work rules and high wages were driving the company to ruin. Nonsense, replied union leaders. "Monfort wants to return to the industrial dark ages of starvation wages and destructive working conditions," they responded.[47]

The strike ended after seventy-three days. Ken Monfort closed the plant and one of his feedlots, and pared his operations with layoffs and asset dumps. In 1982, he opened a revamped slaughterhouse, minus a union contract, but he never caught up with his competitors. When Mike Harper presented his offer, Ken grabbed the lifeline. Harper, he said, was "the 'big friend' I was looking for."[48]

WHAT GOES UP INEVITABLY COMES DOWN. THE "GREATEST AGE" precipitated another agricultural crisis when the global grain shortage proved short-lived.

Wheat farmers were the first victims of a decade of misery that began in 1977. As requested by the White House, they had produced to the max, typically shouldering more debt to do so. As their land values rose, so did their credit line. During the decade, farm mortgage debt rose a whopping 59 percent, from $71 billion to $113 billion. Experts noted that the last time farmers held so much debt, they were feeding the allies in World War I.[49]

As outsized expectations were replaced by a mountain of surplus grain, commodity prices fell. Debts came due. Anger spread.

In summer 1977, a group of wheat growers in southeastern Colorado organized the American Agriculture Movement (AAM), a loose-knit, militant, neopopulist project whose goal was 100 percent parity for producers. Aside from that, the AAM didn't have much of a formal agenda or organization, but its leaders identified a comfortable enemy and a palatable conspiracy theory: corporations were destroying family farming, and the "government" was letting them get away with it.

Leaders called for a producers' strike, hoping to rile independent farmers in such numbers that Washington, DC, would be forced to pay attention to agriculture's little guys.

The 1979 tractorcade in Washington, DC.

In early 1978, an AAM "tractorcade" descended upon the capitol. President James "Jimmy" Carter (1924-2024, president 1977-81), despite his own farming roots, was not amused. He refused to consider major policy changes. Instead, Congress passed an Emergency Assistance Act (1978) that allowed the USDA to adjust price supports as needed. That was not what protestors wanted. "It was a setup from day one!" claimed one participant.[50]

When the tractorcade returned to DC a year later, it was greeted with boos. Politicians and the public had moved on. AAM membership dwindled, and the group's leadership transitioned from militant protestors to suit-and-tie-wearing interest group. They opened an office in Washington and established a political action committee. (In 1980, the group promoted "gasohol" as a solution to grain surpluses.)

By that time, however, the crisis had migrated from the grain-producing plains, to the corn and hogs of the prairies. In the early 1980s, thousands of Corn Belt farmers faced financial collapse. Rural midwestern communities responded with food banks, penny auctions, foreclosure protests, and suicide hotlines. Funding came from Willie Nelson's Farm Aid concerts and various religious organizations.

Media that had disdained tractorcades fell in love with bankrupt, suicidal farmers. Talk show hosts, broadcast news anchors, and big-city reporters descended on the Midwest. Three actors who had portrayed farm wives in films testified before a congressional task force.

The spotlight proved a mixed blessing. One activist lamented that journalists were often less interested in facts than in finding "a farmer who [would] cry on camera." But by 1984, what had begun in the late seventies as a conspiracy-driven attack on corporate power had turned into a lovefest of strange bedfellows devoted to saving the family farm.[51]

Thanks to them, the crisis came to a head during negotiations for the 1985 farm bill.[52]

EVERY FIVE YEARS (MORE OR LESS), CONGRESS HAMMERS OUT A NEW "farm bill," all of them absurdly complicated variants of the 1933 Agricultural Administration Act, stuffed with programs to support agriculture, nutrition, food safety, and the like.

From the 1930s to the 1960s, farm bills primarily targeted commodities: hogs and cotton, rice and wheat. Negotiations were based on input from three parties: committee members, commodity trade groups and lobbyists, and the USDA. This "iron triangle" promoted, protected, and reinforced legislation that supported the industrial model of agriculture, and the subsidies that guaranteed profits.[53]

But in the 1960s, the triangle fractured. The USDA became increasingly irrelevant to the process. Its power peaked in the 1950s, after which Agriculture served as handmaiden to the White House, to whichever party was in control, and to "the Office of Management and Budget, the United States Trade Representative, and the Council of Economic Advisors, as well as . . . State, Treasury, Defense and, during the 1979 Russian grain embargo, the National Security Council and the Central Intelligence Agency."[54]

Factory farming also split the triangle. The industrial model is predicated on specialization, which seeded special-interest groups — swine breeders and swine feeders, corn growers, broiler makers, cattle grazers, cattle feeders, western feeders, Corn Belt feeders. Each demanded a share of the bill's goodies. Geographic specialization also complicated negotiations. Texas cattle feeders had few commonalities with in/out Corn Belt feeders, and Iowa chicken farmers none at all with Georgia broiler growers.

Urban growth contributed another rupture. As rural populations dwindled, agricultural regions and states lost congressional representation. To get the votes necessary for their agenda, they were forced to make deals with urbanites and "public interest" lobbyists. As a result, by the 1980s, a typical "farm" bill contained input from activists lobbying for "nutrition, welfare, environmentalism, consumerism, animal rights, international trade, international assistance, and rural development."[55]

The "agricultural establishment," moaned one of the old guard, "had lost control of the farm policy agenda."[56]

An economist pronounced it "unthinkable" that farm policy had "tilted towards consumers' interests" and other groups "so completely alien to farmers' thinking and tradition." He grudgingly conceded the need for cooperation, but only because he feared that resistance would lead to "unrest in society."[57]

SUCH WAS THE STATE OF AFFAIRS AS NEGOTIATIONS BEGAN FOR THE 1985 Farm Bill. That year's bill was expected to be historic in every way. This was to be the year that Congress would finally — finally! — alter the decades-old, cobbled-together, Kafkaesque methods of subsidizing agriculture.

Ronald Reagan was in office; trickle-down economics and free markets were all the rage. The White House and Treasury, the nation's "business" community, even the American Farm Bureau, pressured lawmakers to end price supports and controls. Down with price controls! Down with government interference! Let the free market rule!

That did not happen.

Thanks to Willie Nelson, farmer suicides, and protests, elected officials were terrified of the political consequences of turning their backs on the "family farm." As a result the 1985 bill ended up with $10 billion more dollars than anyone had expected.

The windfall included funding for research in and development of "Low-Input Sustainable Agriculture" (LISA) to help "family farms" compete with "agribusiness." The wording was intentional: "low-input" appealed to Republican budget slashers, and "sustainable" was preferable to "organic." "We warned everybody that you don't even use the word organic," explained a lobbyist involved in the negotiations. "If you're asked, you can answer the question, but you don't even mention it when you're up there [on the Hill lobbying]."[58]

Reaction was immediate.

A writer for a mainstream farm magazine described LISA as a foolish desire to "replac[e] the mechanical and scientific advancements of the past 50 years with sweat and a lower standard of living." A ConAgra executive suggested an alternative name for the alternative package: "I'd call it FIDO, fewer inputs, declining outputs. A real dog." Another agribusiness insider was even less kind. "Our worthless opponents are not constrained [by] honesty." Otherwise, "they wouldn't call it LISA, they would call it LILO — Low Input, Low Output."[59]

The critics had a point. Small-scale alt-farming did not have a hope of feeding people on the scale necessary in the late twentieth century; the money and effort invested in it could have been used to better purpose. By the 1980s, livestock pollution, for example, had become a mainstay of agricultural critiques. It would have made more sense to lobby for research devoted to managing and mitigating the impacts of manure on land and water.

Nor did the 1985 farm bill have much impact on the "family farm," other than to imprint another generation of activists with the idea that such a thing once existed and still did or would. Small-scale hog farmers, for example, faced a steep trek toward survival. According to a 1985 USDA report, the food-making infrastructure supported big farmers, not small ones. In hog production (as in the rest of agriculture), life and death depended on "those who provide the capital," and in the 1980s, banks were not willing to fund small ventures.[60]

When the editors of *National Hog Farmer* surveyed readers in 1987, 29 percent of the respondents identified "large corporate hog farms" as their worst enemy. Another 23 percent feared encroachment from vertical integrators who raised hogs for use in their packing plants and food factories. The owner of one of the nation's largest independent hog farms predicted that "within 10 years, [his] operation probably [would] be considered very small." He was careening toward the entrepreneur's fork in the road, when he would have to decide: get big or get out.[61]

THOSE FEARS, AND URBAN SUPPORT FOR FAMILY FARMS, INSPIRED NEW efforts to ban "corporate" farms. Networks of rural activists in Iowa, Minnesota, and Missouri spread the gospel: protect family farms.[62]

In 1983, Nebraskans voted on Initiative 300, a constitutional amendment that would prevent the spread of corporate farms. That initiative was aimed directly at Bill Haw and National Farms, and indirectly at Tyson. NFI had announced plans to expand its Nebraska hog operations; by extension, pig-supplier Tyson would expand, too.

Activists pushed back. If NFI got its way, one group warned, the state's hog prices would drop by a dollar or more per hundredweight, and cost "small" farmers about $2,400 a year in income.

"Do you get the feeling," asked one farmer, "that we small producers — dumbly and blindly, like a sheep being led to slaughter — are being forced out by the greed of those high-rollers?" "Have you stopped to figure out how many 100-sow farm units will be replaced by 24,000 sows?"[63]

A Tyson spokesman had a response. "If the people of Nebraska want Tyson to get the hell out, we will do that."[64]

The people did. Voters approved Initiative 300.

Bill Haw then turned to South Dakota, whose 1974 corporate farm ban exempted livestock feeders. He announced plans to build on a site near Pierre, the state's capital and one of its largest cities (population nine thousand).

Opponents were ready and waiting. The South Dakota Farm Alliance, which included the National Farmers Organization, South Dakota Meat Promoters, and the Catholic Rural Life Conference, persuaded Pierre voters to say no to Haw.

Next, Haw tried the burg of Doland, South Dakota (population 430). That town's council voted unanimously to support Haw's project, a boon for a tiny town in the middle of nowhere. Others were less enamored: a resident told one councilman that if NFI came to town, he would no longer patronize the man's hardware store. (Where the man would then buy his tools and other necessities was not clear; online shopping was years away.)[65]

In late 1988, South Dakota voters banned corporate hog farms.

But the issue was complicated. Anti-corporate laws were primarily the result of urbanites' votes. The people most affected by the laws — the folks "out there" in the boonies — often supported corporate ventures because they offered secure employment.

In Nebraska, for example, National Farms employed 150 full-time people, and more hands during busy seasons. It paid higher-than-average wages, and workers enjoyed health insurance and pension contributions. NFI also bought most of its inputs from local businesses.

Fertilizer was an exception, but that didn't bother the manager of a local fertilizer dealership. "They can get [it] cheaper elsewhere. If I was their size, I'd do it the same way. You have to be good businessmen."[66]

Jobs at NFI offered another benefit: leisure time. One man told a reporter that he had begun farming right out of high school. Over the years, marriage and family fostered resentment toward farming's seven-day-a-week schedule. He signed on with National so he could work regular hours, enjoy more time with his wife and children, and remain in a rural area.[67]

Those who warned of unintended consequences often proved right. In 1990, for example, John Morrell & Co. closed its Kansas packing plant, the state's biggest slaughtering operation; the closure threw some seven hundred people out of work.

Why? Because a 1981 state law banned corporate farms, and the state's "family" farmers couldn't supply enough hogs to keep the plant operating at capacity. Morrell, already struggling to stay afloat, either had to import livestock from other states or close the plant.

Kansas's loss was Colorado's gain. There, Bill Haw had already built a huge hog farm. "We don't need to do business in a populist, antibusiness environment," he said. Colorado wanted his two hundred jobs and $3 million a year. So that's where he went.[68]

Such was livestock production in the US as the twentieth century rolled to a close: a rich mix of economics, politics, technology, and science. And flexible: livestock production had to be flexible because, as the late-century years demonstrated, a confounding mix of consumer desire and demographics kept processors and growers on edge.

CHAPTER 12

MAKE MINE BIODYNAMIC
AND MEDIUM RARE

As the century ended, worrying episodes led many Americans to view beef and pork as public enemies one and two.

In 1977, for example, a Senate committee chaired by Democrat George McGovern of South Dakota recommended that Americans eat more poultry and fish, and reduce their intake of "meat," meaning pork and beef. The staffers who researched and wrote the McGovern Report were Naderites eager to challenge the powerful meat lobby. Their research consisted primarily of newspaper and magazine reports, as well as expertise from a Harvard professor who admired the work of Ancel Keys. "We really were totally naive," one staff member later conceded.[1]

The press conference to announce the findings was a masterpiece of glib assertion. Eat less or no meat, McGovern urged Americans as he summarized the document's largely unsupported claims about the relationship between diet and health. He introduced experts who espoused similar assertions, all of which reporters dutifully recorded and passed on to the public as fact.[2]

The meat industry was not amused. As one participant put it, "hell broke loose." McGovern quickly released a revised version of the document that made no mention of meat.

Several years later, widespread disease outbreaks were linked to beef tainted with *Escherichia coli* O157:H7, a newly discovered and exceptionally virulent form of an otherwise common bacteria. Experts who tracked an outbreak in a South Dakota cattle herd blamed antibiotic resistance. If their analyses were correct, there was no longer any doubt that "antimicrobial-resistant organisms of animal origin cause serious human illness."[3]

A consumer advocacy group petitioned the FDA to ban the use of drug additives in livestock feed, but a hearing on the request ended like every other discussion of the subject: it raised more questions than it answered, and scientists' seemingly irrefutable evidence provided openings for political debate.

BEEF CONSUMPTION PLUNGED, FROM 91 POUNDS PER CAPITA IN 1977 to 76 pounds in 1980.

"A story about the beef industry belongs in the obituary column," mourned Ken Monfort. A Nebraska cattle raiser agreed. "Nobody eats beef anymore," he said. "Sometimes I wonder if I would be better off not getting out of bed in the morning."[4]

"We thought everybody would always eat beef," said the director of the California Cattlemen's Association, "but it turned out not to be true." In desperation, the group petitioned the American National Cattlemen's Association to support a ban on low-level antibiotics. Perhaps eliminating those would bring people back to beef. NCA leadership declined the request.[5]

Texan Paul Engler, at the time the world's largest cattle feeder, announced that he would no longer use two controversial antibiotics. He didn't believe that antibiotic-laced feeds were dangerous, but consumers did. The "inference" of danger was already out there, he argued, so "why jeopardize the demand for your product?" "By dropping antibiotics," added a company vice president, "we are trying to teach the public that beef is healthy."[6]

Cattle feeders pooled their funds to support pro-beef advertising with slogans like "the Mercedes of Meat" and "Somehow, nothing satisfies like beef." Those did little to bolster the deposed king's sagging reputation. A financial analyst warned cattlemen that it was time to accept "the harsh reality that the collapse in consumer taste for beef is permanent." Theirs was a "declining industry," he emphasized, "and the only question is how far it will decline."[7]

Pork producers fought their own battles. According to a 1983 consumer poll, forty-five percent of respondents said they'd cut back on fresh pork for "health reasons." Nearly a quarter had reduced consumption of all pork products, fresh or processed.[8] It contained too much salt, cholesterol, fat, and calories.

Even McDonald's, the wizard of food, struggled to work its magic on pork. In the summer of 1980, the company began testing a "McRib" sandwich, rib-shaped slabs of ground and chopped pork slathered with barbecue sauce. The pork industry salivated at the potential, but the McRib proved a no-go; the company pulled it from the menu in 1983.[9]

Part of the problem was preference: Kansas City-style barbecue sauce leans sweet, North Carolina's leans tart; McDonald's one-taste-suits-all could not overcome such regional differences. The ersatz ribs also made for messy eating, a drawback to Americans accustomed to dining on the run and in their cars.

But McDonald's conceded that consumer resistance to pork killed the McRib: good taste and low price could not overcome pork's bad reputation.

So why, company analysts wondered, was the Egg McMuffin so popular? After all, it contained a slice of ham (or bacon if requested). A bit of market research revealed the answer: Americans would eat pork when it was processed and convenient — whether as bacon, "lean" microwaveable sausages, or Egg McMuffins. McRibs, not so much.

According to the president of the National Livestock and Meat Board (which we first met campaigning for meat back in the 1920s), consumers were in control. "It's the younger, more highly educated, high-income people who are turning away from beef toward more vegetables and white meat in their diet," he explained. "These are the opinion leaders that are . . . influencing the eating habits of our bread and butter customers."[10]

THE BIG WINNER WAS THE BIRD.

Every report that blasted meat, heart disease, fat, and cholesterol touted the virtues of chicken (and, to a lesser extent, fish) as a healthy alternative. In 1960, Americans ate twenty-eight pounds of chicken per capita; in 1970, forty; by 1980, forty-eight pounds. In 1987, poultry toppled King Beef. No wonder hog farmers adopted an ad campaign that described pork as "the other white meat."[11]

Don Tyson relished the moment. He dumped millions into the "precooked frozen" market, moving beyond conventional TV dinners with their tinfoil compartments of sliced chicken and pasty potatoes, into chicken-based hot dogs, corn dogs, and bologna; packaged, pre-sliced chicken; chicken and turkey "ham"; boneless turkey breasts; chicken patties and steaks; frozen, ready-to-cook chicken Kiev and pre-fried chicken that only needed heating before eating.

Tyson hit the broiler jackpot when he won a contract to supply McDonald's with its newest offering: the Chicken McNugget, which consisted of a bit of chicken and batter, and many calories and fat.[12]

McNuggets were an instant success — and drew instant fire from Michael Jacobson (1943-), the most famed Nader acolyte and the brain behind the Center for Science in the Public Interest (CSPI). In a complaint filed with the Federal Trade Commission, CSPI accused the burger chain of false advertising. The company touted McNuggets' contents as "delicious chunks of juicy breast and thigh meat," but Jacobson pointed out that the bites also contained sodium phosphate, chicken skin, and beef fat.[13]

Who cared? Not many. Eating healthy had come to mean eating chicken, even if it was a McNugget: a bit of chicken, a lot of calories and fat.

THE MILLIONS OF CONSUMERS DRIVING THE NUGGETS AND HEAT-AND-eat fried chicken sales did not want what their grandparents ate.

"I think my mother could cook it better," Don confided to a reporter who asked about his freezer-section fried chicken, "but I'm not sure my wife could." Not that it mattered: "People who eat precooked frozen today are not as fussy as the previous generation," he added, and predicted that "succeeding generations" would prove even "less discriminating."[14]

Less discriminating? Or less interested?

There were, after all, an infinity of ways to "spend" time, but only so many hours in which to do so. If work required forty (or more) hours a week, why cook if you don't have to or don't want to?

A record number of late-century households were headed by adults who worked outside the home, including women in their thirties and forties, the core grocery-shopping demographic. Cooking was a low priority for many households (except when it was hip, and necessitated an investment in stainless steel appliances, kitchen islands, and the like).[15]

For many consumers, convenience trumped flavor. Back in the 1920s, shoppers regarded canned soups and boxed biscuit mixes as gifts from the gods of time-saving. Fifty-plus years later, Americans carried convenience to its logical end: they paid someone to fix their food for them, and often paid to have it delivered.

Consider one example: In the mid-1970s, and amid inflation and unemployment, a manufacturer of plastic packaging materials enjoyed robust sales. Delighted but puzzled, the company conducted a study to determine what drove its good fortune.

The answer: supermarkets were installing "deli" departments to meet the demands of "young and leisure-oriented shoppers" (aka young-adult baby boomers), who subsisted on fried chicken, macaroni and cheese, and pre-sliced meats and cheeses, and regarded grocery stores as kitchens. Thus the demand for "to go" packaging.[16]

Conveniences like in-store delis fueled a cycle: the easier it was to put dinner on the table without cooking, the less relevant cooking skills became. Kids who grew up in homes where no one cooked became adults who didn't know how to cook; they relied on manufacturers, grocery stores, and microwave ovens to do it for them.

Indeed, the microwave oven was arguably the most important food preparation technology of the twentieth century. A time-strapped, convenience-crazed nation recognized its value immediately: it enabled them to zap foods to fork-ready condition in minutes, even seconds. It was up to manufacturers to supply zappable foods, from TV dinners to pizza to chicken nuggets.[17]

MOSTLY, HOWEVER, AMERICANS WANTED WHAT THEY WANTED.

By the 1980s, affluence and entitlement had splintered the relatively homogeneous midcentury consumer market into myriad fragments. "Niches" and "segments," industry analysts labeled them, defined by age, income, race, ethnicity, geography, and a mysterious inner drive for self-satisfaction. For example, both consumer desire and in-group identity found popular expression in jeans adorned with "designer" labels, or T-shirts emblazoned with logos or slogans offering clues to the wearer's lifestyle and personality.

Comestibles also conveyed image and status and provided (instant!) gratification.

In the 1980s, for example, "yuppies"("young urban professionals"), a teensy demographic segment, briefly captured outsized attention from economists and the media. Among other accomplishments, yuppies boosted sales of imported beer: in Yuppieville, imports carried more cachet than American brands.

At the same time, an even narrower segment favored "craft" beer for its "artisanal" roots, relative scarcity, and middle finger to "corporate" beer. In the late '90s, "hipsters" scorned imports and craft brews in favor of corporate beers like Pabst Blue Ribbon, which they embraced for its anti-hipness.[18]

Aging baby boomers wanted low-salt foods. Busy parents wanted (cheap) food that could be combined with, say, hamburger or pasta and turned into a meal for four. Even better? A package that contained both burger and pasta.

The diet-conscious demanded low-calorie, fat-free foods. SnackWell's, a line of low-fat crackers and cookies, was one of the biggest food successes of the 1990s because it allowed Americans to eat out of both sides of their mouths, pronouncing themselves "healthy" eaters with one side, while satisfying junk-food desires with the other.

Teenagers and twenty-somethings wanted anything and everything that could be microwaved: teenagers because they were hungry after school or too busy working jobs to eat at home, or because their working parents were too tired to cook; the twenty-somethings because they didn't know how to cook, and didn't realize that cooking from scratch was cheaper than toasting a Pop-Tart.

Restaurateurs scrambled to keep up. Some diners wanted steak. Some wanted chicken. Some wanted chicken grilled with teriyaki sauce, and others wanted it on pizza. The health-conscious demanded salads (perhaps to compensate for indulging in "all-natural" ice cream the night before). The budget-conscious wanted all-you-can-eat buffets, gastronomic free-for-alls that required restaurants to seek rock-bottom prices on everything from lettuce and tomatoes to pickled beets and precooked meats.

The uber-affluent and the fad-chasers demanded culinary exotica and a rarefied dining experience. High-end restaurateurs that catered to these enthusiasts distinguished their offerings not just by price but by the food, which ranged from the esoteric to the weird and often included a backstory.

At Alice Waters's Chez Panisse restaurant in Berkeley, California, for example, meats came from animals that had lived a "wholesome" life or been raised "biodynamically," concepts presumably lost on the hoi polloi at Applebee's. At Nora's in Washington, DC, menus identified the precise origins of items served, including the name of the West Virginia pond that provided its trout.[19]

The chef at the Quilted Giraffe in Manhattan offered his diners grilled "free-range" chicken. The price? A mere $75 (that's a staggering $215 today). "Before they became available," said the chef in 1986, "we never deigned to serve chicken." Only the "cachet" of organic-natural had given him "the nerve to sell chicken at that price."[20]

THE SECRET TO THE CORNUCOPIA WAS LOW PRICES. FROM 1960 TO

1990, the cost of food fell by a third. In the early 1990s, on average, consumers spent 11 percent of their disposable income on food.

Obviously many households spent more: ones earning less than $10,000 a year, for example, devoted about 35 percent of income to food. Incomes of $20,000 to $30,000 spent about 17 percent; the wealthiest spent less than nine.

Those numbers included the pleasure of letting someone else do the cooking. In 1960, Americans spent about 27 percent of their food dollars outside the home. By the early 1990s, that share had risen to nearly 50 percent, about half of which was spent on fast and/or prepared foods.

Cheap food was cheap in part because taxpayers subsidized farmers, and because meatpackers and food processors controlled costs with vertical integration, and relied on contractors to ensure the supplies they needed.

Meat costs remained low because late century "product development," as it was dubbed, began "on the farm," rather than in the processing plant — that is, in the immense feeding and confinement operations owned by food conglomerates. The late-century hogs those facilities produced bore no resemblance to the basic commodities of yesteryear, whose prices depended on supply, demand, and the cost of corn. Those traditional "fuzzy" price signals were gone, replaced by ones based on calorie and cholesterol counts and a product's "convenience" quotient, as two analysts described it.[21]

Put simply, packers and processors no longer wanted hogs. They wanted four-legged sources of specific types of pork: low-fat, low-cholesterol for diet-crazy Americans; fattier cuts for lucrative Asian markets. Packers insisted on "value-added" hogs bred with specific genetic traits, and raised on computer-designed rations and biotechnologies like porcine somatotropin (pST), a drug that increased weight gain per pound of feed and reduced fat accumulation by as much as 80 percent.[22]

IN AN AGE OF AFFLUENCE, FOOD FADS, ESPECIALLY DIETS, ABOUNDED. Most came and went, but the "natural foods" fad was an exception.

The "countercuisine" of the 1970s — think granola, sludgy, whole-bran casseroles, and hippie co-ops — became a full-blown market niche in the 1980s.[23]

Among its early purveyors was the Coleman family, owners of a cattle operation near the south-central Colorado town of Saguache. Their counterculture saga began in the 1970s when the family faced what Mel Coleman, Sr. (1925-2002) described as a "losing battle," thanks to the energy crisis, inflation, and declining demand for meat. All told, they lost nearly a half-million dollars from 1975 to 1978 (that's somewhere between two and five million in today's dollars).[24]

The minutes of a company meeting in the summer of 1976 capture the family's woes in terse terms: "Inflation costs and depressed cattle market have made it impossible for the corporation to continue on as we have." Six months later, Mel, wife Polly, and the rest of the family pondered eleventh-hour options: they could refinance the grazing operation, or sell their cows and acres, or both. "We had to do something — and quickly — or we were going to lose everything," Mel said.[25]

The "something" came from Nancy Coleman, who was married to son Greg. The younger Colemans had recently moved from Saguache to Boulder. Then as now, Boulder was a bastion of hippie entrepreneurism and counterculture lifestyles. (The Naropa Institute and Celestial Seasonings were only two of the town's alternative enterprises.)

Nancy had been raised on good food and sought it out at local "health food stores," as they were called then, of which there were many in and around Boulder. But she couldn't find anything like the beef that she'd grown up eating.

On a trip back to the Coleman ranch, and presumably knowing that the family's cattle operation was in trouble, she suggested that her in-laws change tactics. Instead of selling livestock to conventional meatpackers, why not market their beef as a natural, drug-free product?

Mel said later that a "tingle ran down [his] spine" when he heard her idea. It made sense to him not least because the

Colemans boasted a healthy environmental perspective thanks to firsthand experience. Back in the 1930s, a mining company had dumped residue into a creek near Coleman land, killing the water's fish. Mel remembered the dead fish for the rest of his life. "It will permanently warp you to have to deal with something like that," he said.[26]

Then in the late 1940s, the family dusted cattle with the insecticide DDT. The experience left more bad memories, as a well as a bad taste in Mel's mouth and bad air in his lungs. The chemical soaked his coat so thoroughly that he had trouble breathing, even out in the open air. As for the darling of the 1950s, DES, he wanted none of it. The first time he encountered cattle dosed with it, the animals' strange behavior "made [his] . . . lip curl."[27]

He was equally skeptical about antibiotics. For a brief period in the 1960s, the family dosed calves in order to protect them from pneumonia. A few years later, the herd experienced an outbreak of "scours," a form of dysentery. Coleman's veterinarians dosed calves with antibiotics to no avail. Fifteen percent died. Mel was convinced that his stock "had developed a resistance to antibiotics." That "scared me," he said. "Right there, we stopped using [them]."[28]

IN 1979, THE FAMILY INCORPORATED COLEMAN NATURAL MEATS, headed by the then-fifty-four-year-old Mel, Sr. This was not a 100 percent "natural" operation. The Colemans inoculated newborns. Their cattle ate hay grown with manufactured fertilizers, and protein supplements that contained synthetic materials. But the family's operation was more "natural" than most, a solid selling point to a certain niche of consumers.

In 1980, a slaughterhouse ran the Colemans' first "natural" carcass through its line. Mel was there waiting for it, a new, $300, custom-made, ink roller in hand. The carcass came to a stop. Mel rolled the stamp over its surface. There it was: a side of "Coleman Natural Beef," ready to change the world and fatten the Coleman bank account.

Or not.

The local USDA inspector happened to be on site that day and he ordered Mel to stop. "I don't have papers on that roller," he said. "Do you have permission to roll that carcass?" "Permission?" said Coleman. "This is my roller . . . What more permission do I need?" Much more, explained the inspector, in the form of paperwork and official USDA sanction.[29]

Mel scraped the ink off the carcass and set out to master the byzantine USDA regulatory process. He made an appointment with the department's regional office and explained to the agent that he wanted permission to use the words "natural beef" on his labels. "What the hell are you talking about, Coleman?" she asked. "Cattle are natural — all cattle are natural!"

Mel encountered one dead end after another in Colorado, and eventually took himself to Washington, DC, and the heart of the maze. Two years and a two-foot-thick file of paperwork later, he received permission to use the word natural to describe his products.

Persuading retailers to carry the beef was another struggle. The obvious outlets were natural food stores. But many catered to vegetarians and weren't interested in selling meat, natural or otherwise. Other would-be dealers didn't understand the product.

"If you don't have to buy antibiotics and hormones," one asked Coleman, "shouldn't natural beef cost less?" Queried another: "If I stock your beef and call it 'natural,' what does that say about the rest of my beef?" Would customers assume that "it's bad because it's full of chemicals?"[30]

By 1982, Mel had landed just two accounts — one natural food store and a Denver hospital. He'd also exhausted the possibilities in Colorado. His son persuaded him to try California, arguing that when it came to fads, culinary or otherwise, Californians led rather than followed. Off Coleman went, renting a car (which also served as his hotel) and driving from one retailer to another.

The break came when he visited the headquarters of Mrs. Gooch's Ranch Markets, a small chain of Southern California health food stores. ("Just a bunch of hippies sellin' food," according to Coleman).[31] The owners wanted to carry natural meats but had not been able to find a decent product. One look at Mel Coleman, dressed in his usual Colorado-ranch attire of cowboy hat and jeans, and a company executive knew he'd found the real deal. The Gooch family signed a contract, and spread the word to owners of other health food stores around the country.

Two years later while working their booth at a natural foods trade show, the Colemans met an executive from Grand Union, a major East Coast grocery chain. That encounter led to a contract to deliver five hundred cattle a week. The Colemans could not supply that number as quickly as Grand Union wanted meat in its refrigerators, but many Colorado ranchers were hanging by a financial thread. Grand Union gave Coleman a letter of credit that enabled him to contract with others to raise cattle on his behalf.

Grand Union spared no expense promoting the meat. Coleman Natural hailed from a land where "the mountain air is clear, the water pure, and soil uncontaminated." Polly and Mel flew east to introduce the product, grilling steaks in store parking lots and handing out samples.[32]

Not everyone was impressed. One customer accused Mel of wearing a cowboy hat and boots in order to "look like a real rancher." A shopper who identified himself as a college professor accused Coleman of lying: it was impossible to raise cattle without the use of drugs. "How do you think we did it in the 1930s?" Mel retorted.[33]

But Mel and Polly converted shoppers taste sample by taste sample, one five-hundred-count box of toothpicks a day. The family built a fabricating plant in Denver (they shipped their product as boxed beef). They moved headquarters: from a spare room at the family ranch, to a rented room at a nearby motel, to a building in downtown Saguache, to Denver. Thirty ranchers scattered over two states raised cattle on contract and according to Coleman specifications.

By the end of the eighties, Coleman meats could be found in more than 1,500 retail outlets, and the family was selling $20 million in meat products a year.

When retailers asked for lamb, veal, pork, and rabbit, the Colemans accessed those from other ranchers. They introduced a "starter" meat: Rocky Mountain Pure beef came made from cattle finished on additive-free feed but not necessarily raised on organic grasses or hay. Mel was convinced that if customers tried Rocky Mountain Pure, they would "upgrade" to 100 percent organic beef, which sold for 25 percent more than conventional meats.[34]

"We tell retailers that our product will bring in . . . people who buy dollar-fifty chicken and Häagen-Dazs ice cream," explained the Colemans' marketing consultant. Hooey, scoffed the meat buyer for a major Southern California grocery chain. He pronounced Coleman's meat "overpriced and overbilled," and natural beef a "fad."[35]

MAYBE. MAYBE NOT. IN THE 1980s, CATTLEMEN WERE DESPERATE TO stanch the bleeding in beef consumption. Coleman's beef sold for a 25 percent premium. Who wouldn't want a piece of the action? A 1984 USDA rule eased the way: any meat could be labeled "natural" as long as it contained no artificial ingredients and the carcass had been "minimally processed," a vague stipulation that could include anything and everything.

An alliance of Wyoming ranchers began marketing branded grass-fed beef. A Mennonite cooperative in Kansas launched a beef line marketed as (mostly) free of hormones and other additives.[36]

Northern California cattle ranchers Bill Niman and Orville Schell also produced natural beef, most of which they sold to local restaurants, including Alice Waters's Chez Panisse. Schell, a writer, was known less for cattle and beef than for his attacks on modern agriculture and meat industries' addiction to pharmaceuticals.

"I hope I don't radiate any aura of holier-than-thou," Schell told a reporter in 1986. He and Niman could "charge more" for their product, he explained, because "[f]ood consciousness" in the San Francisco Bay Area had "reached a state of evolution that [was] almost off the charts."

(That prompted an eye-rolling retort from Mel Coleman: "We sold to Los Angeles, Austin, Houston and Boston before Marin and Boulder came around. The Bay Area is really slow in doing this.")[37]

No surprise, fly-by-nights weaseled into the natural niche. A

Colorado grocery chain stopped carrying natural meats because its buyer couldn't distinguish good guys like Coleman from the less-than-honest. "I've got ranchers coming in here every week asking me to buy their natural beef," he said, but he was "skeptical" about their credentials.[38]

Nor was the hype limited to beef. Consider "Rocky the Range" chicken.

The creation of a marketing team, Rocky was peddled as "free-range" and "stress-free," and cost twice as much as conventional broilers. The chickens were raised by a Petaluma grower who fenced some coops and cut doors in the sides so birds could roam in and out. Beyond that, chickens destined for Rockyhood were fed and watered exactly like the rest of the grower's flock; no foraging allowed.

A curious reporter persuaded two Los Angeles chefs to conduct a blind taste test of Rocky and a conventional broiler.

Rocky failed. Chef Wolfgang Puck (among the first to surf the late-century, food-fetish, celebrity-chef wave) was annoyed that he could find no difference between the two birds. "I definitely think we should find out why they charge so much money," he announced.[39]

USDA officials were even less impressed. In 1990, the department told Rocky's owners to cease and desist with its terminology.

"We don't have a working definition for range," explained a department spokesperson. "What is 'range' in the regulatory sense? . . . A horse rounding up chickens on the range?" The department also nixed "stress-free." "We can't be wasting the government's time with words we can't enforce," he said. "I guess a chicken could be stress free, but how could you tell?"[40]

Who could blame the department? In the 1980s, the burgeoning natural foods industry was (and remains) a morass of misinformation, wacky claims, and blatant lies. Who knew if biodynamically raised beef or pork was nutritionally superior to conventional meat? What, precisely, did "free range" mean in practice? Should consumers believe the commercial rabbit grower who claimed that his wooden cages maximized the impact of "beneficial magnetic forces" that improved the quality of the meat?[41]

MEL COLEMAN WAS PREPARED TO STAND HIS GROUND AGAINST frauds, but then came a blow that infuriated him. In 1989, the USDA announced that it would no longer certify beef as hormone-free. A department spokeswoman explained that it lacked the "wherewithal" and expertise to make such a judgment. (To be fair, bovines, like humans, have hormones. Indeed, no meat is hormone-free — only feed.)[42]

Mel denounced the decision as a "great injustice." He was no fan of "government," but at least the USDA had "a little bit of credibility for consumers." Federal labeling was his only defense against fakes, and the federal imprimatur "essential" to his success, he argued. "It's all we are."[43]

Coleman, by then an old hand at schmoozing bureaucrats, politicians, and power players, directed his rage at the 1990 farm bill negotiations. The chair of the Senate agriculture committee, Senator Patrick Leahy, a Vermont Democrat, had long supported alternative agriculture and helped Coleman and others craft a bill that would give producers legal access to the term "organic."

Coleman quickly discovered he'd overestimated the overlords' enthusiasm for change, and perhaps their common sense, too.

A Missouri congressman who opened the hearing complained that organic farming implied that organic crops and meats were "better than food produced by other farming methods."

"I don't, personally, believe that to be the case," he explained. "We have a safe, reliable, and affordable food supply with ample choices for all consumers." "I'm still trying to figure out how you can have an organic cow," he concluded.[44]

Translation: organic foods were not necessary, nor were standards for them.

Texan Eligio "Kika" de la Garza, who chaired the House Agriculture Committee, was even more skeptical. He'd conducted a bit of preliminary, on-the-ground investigating, during which he'd talked to an organic farmer. The congressman asked her where she obtained the fertilizer for her four-acre urban farm.

"I assume you use manure," he'd told her. "No, no, no," she replied. "I use commercial fertilizer." Baffled, the congressman quizzed her further and learned, eventually, that she defined hers as an organic farm simply because she didn't use synthetic pesticides.

"Goodness knows," de la Garza told the audience, "sheep, goat, poultry, cattle — it's all too complicated. If someone uses manure, you have to go back to see that the manure didn't come from cattle that had chemical therapeutic treatment."[45]

The two USDA representatives who attended the hearing were even less enthusiastic. At the time, the Department opposed federal organic meat standards, partly because it was focused on the big picture of keeping shelves stocked, and partly because it was steeped in conventional practices. (To say nothing of the implied insult to the rest of the nation's livestock producers.)

The "greatest" threat to the nation's food supply, one explained, was posed by "microbial contaminations" like salmonella, not "pesticides, animal drugs, or other chemicals." Banning the latter did nothing to address the dangers of the former. The other USDA spokesman was even more dismissive. Livestock was "constantly exposed to parasites, bacteria, and viruses." It was "impossible" to produce cattle, hogs, and chickens without using "synthetic drugs" and "therapeutic doses of antibiotics."[46]

If only we could travel back in time and watch Mel Coleman's reaction. If he wasn't banging his head against the nearest wall, he probably wanted to do so. Making organic meat wasn't impossible; he'd been doing it for years.

A bill finally made its way to House and Senate, but few lawmakers would commit to "organic." (If the content of the legislators' discussions is any indication, it's clear that most were confused about what the word meant.) The inevitable compromise was a bill that established a National Organic Standards Board (NOSB), and charged it with establishing standards.

WHILE THE NEWLY CREATED NOSB HAMMERED OUT DETAILS, A process no one expected to end any time soon, Coleman launched a new marketing campaign that avoided the "o" word and adhered to the law: "What would beef be without hormones, steroids or antibiotics: It would be Coleman."

Coleman's peers decided they'd had enough of him (although perhaps they'd had their fill of alternative agriculturalists and a public that turned up its nose at beef). The Colorado Cattlemen's Association and the National Cattlemen's Association protested Coleman's "negative advertising." By touting his meats as organic and natural, he cast "doubt on the safety and wholesomeness of the generic beef supply."[47]

"Our problem with this campaign is that it clearly implies that Coleman beef is safer to eat than other beef and the scientific facts simply do not support that," they explained. "Isn't there some way to promote your product without kicking undue 'mud' in the face of the rest of the beef industry?" (It was surely no coincidence that Monfort/ConAgra, which processed Coleman's cattle, picked that moment to raise its per-head slaughter fee by $5.)[48]

Coleman refused to back down. "I've paid a lot of dues in this industry and I'm not going to apologize just because we do things differently," he said. "All the ads do is say our animals don't get [chemical additives] and if you're interested in that kind of a product, we've got it."[49]

Because in the US, there was a food for every person, palate, and pocketbook.

CHAPTER 13

FOUR STORIES AND ALTERNATIVE OUTCOMES

AMERICANS WANTED CHEAP, HIGH-QUALITY, LOW-FAT MEAT, AND THEY wanted it from a drive-up window, but there were hidden costs they mostly wanted to ignore.

Four stories from the 1990's highlight Americans' contradictory relationships with their food and their values in the most recent era of the paradox of plenty.

I. *JACK IN THE BOX*

In 1993, scores of people became ill, and some died, from food-poisoning traced to undercooked hamburgers purchased at Jack in the Box, a west coast fast-food chain. The specific culprit was one scientists had linked to bacterial resistance a decade earlier: *E. coli* O157:H7. The tiny organism promptly became a household name, as did Jack in the Box. And the tragedy highlighted the extent to which Americans were playing with fire when it came to food.

In this case, people died because employees failed to cook meat to a required temperature. Cities and states were responsible for ensuring that employees followed the rules, but their food inspection programs suffered from that most common of ailments: lack of funds.

In Kansas, for example, inspectors traveled to and examined thirty-two restaurants during a forty-hour week. Any one inspector might manage a cursory search for, say, cockroaches and overflowing dumpsters, but it's unlikely she'd have time for much more.[1]

In the Jack in the Box case, the meat itself was not to blame, but that didn't stop many from castigating the USDA, which oversaw meat inspection. Certainly the tragedy brought meat inspection to the public's attention; and the public discovered that meat inspection was nothing to brag about.

When federal, interstate meat inspection began in 1906, agents examined livestock before and after slaughter, looking for visual evidence of disease; they also checked packing plants' adherence to official sanitary standards. That system continued for decades, with additions from time to time — for example, rules requiring "humane" slaughtering methods. In 1974, a court ruled that bacteria were not adulterants; inspectors were not required to look for or consider them when giving a carcass the thumbs-up or down.[2]

Alarmed by Jack in the Box and the proliferation of O157:H7, activists demanded an overhaul of federal meat inspection, arguing that strategies that worked when slaughterhouse lines moved at the pace of a single-load rifle were useless on modern kill lines that operated at machine-gun pace.

Speaking for the packers, the American Meat Institute conceded the point, while blaming federal inspectors who resisted change. "They're not microbiologists," argued an AMI spokesman. "They don't know where they'll fit [in a new system]."[3]

Not so, retorted an official with the inspectors' union. His members were "not against technology, and we're not against moving forward." Nonetheless, they opposed proposals to replace conventional inspection with a "science-based system."[4]

II. NORTH CAROLINA

Jack in the Box cast doubt on meat safety and food inspection. In the mid-1990s, North Carolina manure spills cast doubt on livestock production.

In the late twentieth century, no state benefited more from the new geography of hog farming than North Carolina, and no company more than Murphy Farms, in the 1990s one of the nation's biggest hog operations.

Murphy Farms was the brainchild of Wendell Murphy (1938–). After graduating from college in 1960, he taught high school briefly, but like Warren Monfort, another schoolteacher-turned-agricultural-power-player, Murphy wanted a different life.

In the early 1960s, he bought a corn mill, which he operated with his father and brother. From there it was a short leap into feeding hogs. In 1964, the Murphys recruited their first contract growers, modeling their venture after the broiler industry. Over the next twenty years, the Murphys signed more contractors, embraced confinement, and built farrowing operations.

They encountered an entrepreneurial crossroads in the early 1980s. They could make, and were making, more hogs than North Carolina's packers could process. They had a choice: plateau as a company (and probably become an attractive acquisition for someone else), or go big.

Enter Smithfield Foods, a Virginia-based hog-slaughter and pork-processing operation. President Joseph Luter III wanted to expand, but couldn't lay his hands on as many hogs as he needed, thanks to urban sprawl devouring Virginia farms. He'd been trucking a third of his kill from the Midwest, which raised his costs. Luter's woes became the Murphys' opportunity.[5]

In early 1990, Luter announced plans to construct the world's largest hog slaughter facility in Bladen County, North Carolina, the area where hog-farming giants raised millions of animals. When county officials held a hearing on the request, more than a thousand people showed up, many wearing "I support Smithfield" buttons. A "wildly cheering" crowd roared its approval when the state's commissioner of agriculture urged county officials to let Smithfield move forward.⁶

Not everyone was happy. "We are not against the smaller [hog] farmer," explained a spokesman for the Alliance for a Clean Swine Industry, but he and other opponents objected to "the bondage of feces and urine" created by giant corporate hog farms. But what mattered more? Jobs or odor?⁷

The new plant opened in 1992 and ignited North Carolina's already robust hog industry: in 1991, growers turned out 2.8 million hogs; in 1994, the number hit 7 million, nearly all of them in the southeastern corner of the state.

Then came 1995.

In February, the *Raleigh News & Observer* published a series surveying the history and impact of North Carolina's hog industry. The reporting won a 1996 Pulitzer Prize, and captured the complexity, paradox, and unease that was meat in late-twentieth-century America.

State of the art lagoon waste management system for a 900-head hog farm. The facility is completely automated and temperature controlled.

Reporters described the complaints of people who loathed the industry's odors and feared the pollution; detailed the way the legislature had smoothed the path for hog farming and the world's biggest slaughtering house; and noted the gratitude of those who saw impoverished counties gain jobs and income.[8]

One installment featured an unflattering portrayal of state senator Wendell "Boss Hog" Murphy, who had called the legislative shots that built the industry. (Murphy loved the attention. "All of a sudden, I found myself a hero," he said later. "It was like all of a sudden people [were saying]: 'Man, you are really good. We didn't know you were doing all this stuff.'")[9]

And then came the storms.

That summer, torrential, prolonged rainfall inundated parts of North Carolina. When water swamped a dike on an "industrial swine" farm, 30 million gallons of feces and urine poured into the New River. Hog waste stood eight inches deep on a nearby road. Sludge coated crops in the fields.

"Didn't nobody mean for it to happen," said an owner of the company that had built the lagoon. "It just happened."[10]

Maybe, maybe not. It was true that the two-year-old facility had been built according to strict environmental guidelines. But the "environmental Alamo" of 1995 destroyed the illusion that giant hog farms were benign.[11]

The environmental Alamo had siblings: In 1999, Hurricane Floyd struck the North Carolina coast. Four rivers flooded, and thousands of hog carcasses littered the state's countryside. The stench, mess, and detailed reporting about it fueled yet another debate about livestock production and meat.

III. *GUYMON, OKLAHOMA*

By the early 1990s, corporate hog farms had become the norm: operations defined by scale (not hundreds but hundreds of thousands of hogs) and efficiency, thanks to extensive automation, confinement, antibiotics, and other tools.

Among them was Seaboard Corporation, born in 1918 as a

grain milling enterprise. In the early eighties, the company expanded its international portfolio, focusing on grain and foodstuffs, such as chickens and hogs, the latter an effort to conquer Asian markets. (The shift fit Seaboard's then-current mission as an "entrepreneurial organization." "We could produce chairs for conference rooms," a company vice president said, as long as the chairs made money.)[12]

Seaboard built a hog facility in Colorado, already home to Tyson and National Farms, Inc., and scouted locations for a second farm and a slaughterhouse.

The Oklahoma panhandle fit the bill. Tyson operated a breeding facility there, and local farmers raised the piglets on contract. Better yet: Oklahoma welcomed corporate farms.

A 1991 state law allowed corporate farms to vertically integrate via breeding facilities, feed mills, and processing plants, and to provide "technical . . . assistance" to growers — a euphemism for contract farming. In 1993, the governor signed a bill that allowed such farms to operate without a permit. Corporations with permits gained permanent protection from "nuisance" suits.[13]

City leaders and business owners in Guymon (population ten thousand) in Texas County, Oklahoma, wanted in on the action. In recent years, town and county had suffered a string of economic hits, including the 1987 closure of a Swift packing plant. Local movers and shakers hoped to replace lost industries before the local economy spiraled into irrevocable decline. They wooed Seaboard and won, thanks in part to a package of incentives that totaled more than $30 million.

This townspeople-driven project dismayed farmers and residents of nearby rural areas. "Now why do the poor people of Guymon Oklahoma . . . have to subsidize a corporation of that size and magnitude[?]" asked one farmer. Another found the situation both frustrating and comical. "I'm sure those executives were saying — What? They want to do what? Oh, boy. Just so we'll locate there?"[14]

Seaboard's arrival created hundreds of jobs and attracted other hog-related, job-producing companies. The pervasive foul odor that came with them turned neighbor against neighbor.

Locals engaged in that oldest of American activities: defining the distinction between personal liberty and public well-being. "The trouble is that the odor goes across the fence and that doesn't seem right at all," declared a local cattle rancher. "That can ruin somebody's property values and make it so they can't enjoy their own property. It seems like a real infringement to me."[15]

A cattle feeder who'd viewed Seaboard's arrival as an opportunity to diversify into hogs scoffed. The "pigs came and you don't like it," he said. "My attitude is — leave!" As far as he was concerned, "you control your own life, you can live anywhere you want, you can do anything you want. You can use your property in any fashion you feel proper. And the government should stay the hell out of it."[16]

Still others thought this went too far. "I'm an advocate of individual rights, but there's a limit," said an Oklahoma state legislator. "You can't just let mass pollution happen. And in some cases you are going to be stepping on individual rights when you regulate."[17]

IV. *OPRAH*

Oprah Winfrey's journey to a Texas courtroom began in 1996. Winfrey, whose popular talk show reached some 14 million viewers daily, devoted an episode to bovine spongiform encephalopathy (aka mad cow disease), which was ravaging herds in England. Her guest, a former Montana cattle rancher, railed against the dangers of meat in general and diseased meat in particular. According to him, if mad cow struck American herds, the outbreak would make "AIDS look like the common cold."[18]

Winfrey turned to the live audience, and camera, and said, "It has just stopped me cold from eating another burger! I'm stopped!"[19]

Within hours, cattle futures plunged; trading was halted. Millions were lost on paper. A few weeks later, a group of Texas cattle ranchers and feeders sued Winfrey claiming that she had violated the 1995 False Disparagement of Perishable Food Products Act. Such "veggie libel laws" were all the rage in the early 1990s, thanks to a television news program that publicized the dangers of Alar, a coating used by apple growers to protect their fruit.

Oprah's trial, which began in early 1998, didn't last long. The judge ruled that disparagement laws did not apply: the plaintiffs failed to prove intent. She walked out of the Amarillo courtroom cleared of any wrongdoing.

But Oprah Winfrey was Oprah Winfrey, and her fears of mad cow disease and hamburger spawned more consumer doubts about meat, and the farms and factories that produced it.

EVEN AS HOG FACTORIES AND FAST-FOOD CHAINS FLOURISHED, A coalition of activists was attempting to build an alternative food system based on small-scale, traditional crop and livestock production, and small-scale, local marketing venues, such as the "farmer's markets" first funded by Congress in 1976. This group, the Community Food Security Coalition (CFSC), included aging Raiders, urban food security and hunger activists, organic food enthusiasts, environmentalists, and rural reformers.[20]

In their view, the existing American food system was sick. They wanted to heal it. American food, explained some of those involved, came "from a global everywhere" and thus from "nowhere . . . in particular." Most people had no idea "how and by whom what they consume is produced, processed, and transported." Disconnected "from each other and from the land," Americans were "less responsible to each other and to the land." "Where do we go from here? How can we come home again?"[21]

Their answer: alternative agriculture and markets. An alternative food system would renew the nation's soul. Food would unite Americans, and teach them that town and country, farm and city, were parts of a whole, and they themselves citizens of a unified environmental, economic, and social community.

Despite the somewhat fuzzy rhetoric, in the mid-nineties, the CFSC proved surprisingly successful. It added a "Community Food Projects" agenda to the farm bill, which committed USDA resources to alternative food and farming.

The Coalition pushed back, hard, when the National Organic Standards Board (NOSB) finally released a set of organic standards in 1997 (nearly a decade after the Board was chartered). The proposed standards would allow organic foodstuffs to contain or be raised with genetically modified organisms, and would permit the use of irradiation and fertilizers manufactured from sewage sludge.

Thanks to the new-fangled "internet," the CFSC persuaded a quarter million people to comment. Bombarded with objections, the USDA backed down and told the NOSB to start over.[22]

The coalition also proved successful at promoting new markets and farms. Farmers' markets, for example, proliferated "like robins in spring." In 1999, a Massachusetts sustainable agriculture group launched a public relations drive urging consumers to be "Local Heroes" and buy food from local farmers.[23]

Be careful what you wish for.

By the turn of the century, the organic food sector made up just 4 percent of all American food sales, but it was growing about 20 percent a year. Roughly half of all organic food purchases were made in conventional grocery stores, including Costco and other big-box retailers. Every major grocery chain boasted its own private-label brands of organic goods, including meat. Retail behemoth Wal-Mart's decision to expand its organic food offerings translated into pressure on packers and food processors to come up with the specified goods.

The race to supply supermarket chains and big box stores occupied commercial organic farmers' attentions and harvests. Farmers' markets? Not so much. Why bother with a farmers' market when organic "handlers," as they were called, crowded the farmhouse door, begging for supplies that were scarce relative to demand?

Was alternative the new normal?

THE ALT-UNIVERSE PROVED A BOON FOR LIVESTOCK PRODUCERS. Sort of.

In 2002, the NOSB and the USDA issued guidelines for organic meat. Organic beef, pork, and poultry would come from animals raised without hormones or antibiotics, that had been fed organically grown, all-vegetable feedstuffs manufactured in an organic-certified mill.[24]

Producers were required to provide outdoor access for livestock; confinement was allowed under limited conditions and only for brief periods. One of those conditions, however, constituted a significant loophole: producers could confine their livestock if leaving them on pasture posed "a risk to soil or water quality." Finally, the livestock had to be slaughtered and processed in an organic-certified facility.[25]

On one hand, the arrival of standards boosted sales of organic meats, which ratcheted up by about 50 percent a year. True, the $600 million that consumers spent on organic meat was a mere jot of the $158 billion that they spent on all beef, pork, and poultry. But signs pointed toward continued growth.

On the other hand, signs also pointed to big packers and chain supers dominating this new alternative meat industry, not the small-scale farms the CFSC had envisioned.

Exhibit A: Peaceful Pastures in Tennessee, whose owners raised and marketed organic poultry. Tennessee law mandated that all poultry slaughter take place in a USDA-inspected facility. There were plenty of such operations around, but they only handled conventional poultry. The couple considered building a small processing facility on their farm — until they read the fine print in the rules.[26]

"I'd have to build an office for the inspector," said owner Jenny Drake, complete with a separate phone line. The couple would have to pave their parking lot and install handicapped-accessible bathrooms.[27]

"We have to meet the same physical standards as a Tyson's, and we just can't do it," she sighed. "[I'm] so right-wing I make Rush Limbaugh look like a liberal," she added, but as far as she was concerned, big business and the "rich agribusiness lobby" were making her life miserable.[28]

Virginia farmer Joel Salatin agreed. He raised organic hogs, chickens, and cattle, and he, too, tried to build an on-farm slaughter facility. USDA officials directed him to the guidelines, a detailed list of necessities that infuriated Salatin, who saw no need to build employee bathrooms.

"I told them we were 50 feet away from two houses with bathrooms, and besides, we're a family operation: We don't have employees. It didn't matter to them," he complained. "Then they said we had to have twelve changing-lockers for employees — even if we didn't have employees." Salatin denounced the obstacles as "bureaucracy in action," a bureaucracy with but one purpose: to "protect big agribusiness from rural independent competition."[29]

Even those who sold primarily at farmers' markets struggled. A Massachusetts man pondered applying for the organic designation — until he learned that he'd have to "hire someone to do the paperwork, pay twice the price for organic feed, and find a certified slaughterhouse that would take a small amount of animals." His customers, almost entirely face-to-face, were already paying up to $5 a pound for his ground beef. The cost of obtaining and maintaining organic certification would "price [him] out of the ball game."[30]

He abandoned the effort. He'd just tell customers how his meat was made, and hope they believed him.

USDA employees were sympathetic — to a point. The Department agent who dealt with the Tennessee couple understood that these rules favored big operators rather than someone who wanted to slaughter and sell a few hundred chickens a year. But, he asked, "do we want to let people slaughter meat in the backyard and sell it on the sidewalk?" Doing so, he feared, could introduce tainted meats into the nation's food supply.[31]

His argument sounded absurd to those trying to reform Americans' hearts, minds, and diets: one only need consult the daily news to know that whatever else they might be, conventional foods, especially meat, were hardly safe.

RED TAPE NOTWITHSTANDING, ALTERNATIVE LIVESTOCK PRODUCTION attracted conventional cattle and hog farmers looking for something, anything, to lift stagnant sales of beef and pork. That was particularly true of cattle growers, many of whom pinned their hopes on the high end of the market. After all, enthusiasts snapped up certified Angus steaks, highly marbled, flavorful cuts of Wagyu beef, and pricey "lite" beef from livestock bred for lean rather than fat.

In the early years of the new century, the winner of this carnivorous contest was grass-fed beef.

The idea was not new. Since the 1940s, the trade journal *Stockman Grass Farmer* had catered to the interests of a small group of ranchers who specialized in finishing cattle on grass. Grass-fed beef enjoyed a brief moment of glory during the 1970s, when some feeders, including Ken Monfort, sent range cattle directly to slaughter rather than finishing them on high-priced grain. The result was a low-cost beef alternative. In the 1990s, some cattle producers reversed that equation, promoting grass-fed as a premium product and (allegedly) healthier than grain-fed beef.

Texas cattle ranchers Wendy and Jon Taggert began finishing part of their herd on grass, and marketing it as New Image Grass Beef. Jon explained that they wanted "a little bit bigger piece of the pie" to stay on their own plates. Beef "is a very healthy product," Wendy told a reporter by way of elaboration. "We're just making it healthier."[32]

Grass-fed beef enjoyed an expected gift in 2002. Michael Pollan, a journalist, writer, and University of California-Berkeley professor, published a *New York Times Magazine* article in which he claimed that corn-finished beef was bad for cattle and people. Such meat was neither cheap nor healthy, he wrote, not if consumers "add[ed] in the invisible costs: of antibiotic resistance, environmental degradation, heart disease, *E. coli* poisoning, corn subsidies, imported oil and so on."[33]

Grass-fed beef, Pollan told readers, was a superior alternative. It contained less fat overall than corn-fed beef, and more "good" fat, too. "A growing body of research suggests that many of the health problems associated with eating beef are really problems with cornfed beef." Humanity, he wrote, "may not be well adapted to eating grain-fed animals." (He blamed the USDA beef grading system, saying that it "continues to reward marbling.")

Weeks after the article appeared, a group of Northern California ranchers organized the Western Grasslands Beef Alliance, a marketing group devoted to selling grass-fed beef to high-end area restaurants. The product cost twice as much as conventional, but the group found plenty of takers for their product because of its "political and culinary appeal" to upscale buyers.[34]

Pollan's essay convinced Alice Waters, by then a high-powered, "foodie" celebrity, to serve grass-fed beef in her Berkeley restaurant rather than the grain-finished meat she'd been buying from Niman Ranch.

Bill Niman, that company's cofounder, was aghast. He'd been raising organic cattle for years, finishing them on (organic) grains before slaughter. He resented the notion that his beef was unhealthy or ecologically incorrect.

Niman dispatched an e-mail to Pollan. "As you know," he told the writer, "the story is very complicated and the lay public considers all feedlot cattle the same. This is absolutely not true."

The belief that grass-fed beef or other free-range meats could replace conventional was also unrealistic, Niman told a reporter.[35]

"People want to imagine a beautiful vision of a chicken out there eating earwigs and cows roaming free around the pasture," he said. But that vision could not "feed millions of people every day." That was particularly true of grass-fed beef, he explained, which was as seasonal as "a peach or a tomato. Eat it in May or June 'cause that is when it is peaking."[36]

Niman's arguments carried little weight with those eager to claim a share of the exotica niche or to change the world. Inspired by Pollan's article, the Chefs Collaborative, a collection of "prominent" chefs, restaurateurs, and food activists, launched a campaign to persuade restaurant owners to switch to grass-fed beef.[37]

The project raised a few eyebrows.

An executive with a small chain of upscale steakhouses found it "ironic" that the collaborative claimed to have been inspired by the "standard of excellence" found in European meats. Every day, he catered to European tourists searching for quality beef of a sort they could not find at home. A founder of the Center for Consumer

Freedom, a watchdog group opposed to "nanny culture," denounced the collaborative as "a haughty organization with an elitist point of view" and a "let them eat cake" attitude.[38]

"We are an elitist organization," responded collaborative member Eric Schlosser, "but change has to start someplace, and people who have better access to information and spending power can be the start of all sorts of changes."[39]

Alas, the Pollan factor expanded by magnitudes with the 2006 publication of *The Omnivore's Dilemma*. Based on articles Pollan had published in the *New York Times*, the book was an immediate bestseller, and remained one for several years. Its centerpiece and most indelible image was his portrayal of conventional livestock production: thousands of cattle crammed into feedlots, shin-deep in shit, their bodies riddled with bacteria and damaged by a diet of corn.[40]

From an investor's point of view, this grim scenario translated into the hottest ticket to profit since the microwave oven: organic alternatives to conventional beef, pork, and poultry.

The ensuing mad dash to profit altered dynamics in the meat industries. In 2002, investors snapped up both Coleman Natural Meats and Niman Ranch.

Niman lost its independence first. In the thirty-odd years since Bill Niman and Orville Schell had founded their venture, the company had never earned a profit. But when Schell left the partnership in the late 1990s, Niman launched a strategy of aggressive growth.

"I consciously deferred profitability [in order] to expand the brand," he explained.[41]

He added organic pork to his offerings (contracting with a small army of hog producers), and expanded distribution from Northern California to the entire United States.

His ambitions outstripped his funds. In late summer 2002, Chicago-based Natural Food Holdings committed two of its executives and a fistful of cash to the task of saving Niman. In exchange,

Natural commandeered four of the seven seats on the Niman board of directors.

The new investors sold the original feedlot, choosing instead to send cattle to conventional feeders for finishing, and shipping the livestock long distances to slaughter. Those decisions generated profits but infuriated Niman. He resigned when the investors acquired the company outright in 2009, publicly berating the new owners for betraying his mission.

The Coleman family also cashed out in 2002, albeit with considerably less drama. Mel Coleman, Sr. died early in that year. New president Mel Coleman, Jr. sold the family business to Petaluma Holdings, which owned one of the country's largest processors of organic poultry. The new owners planned to sell their natural and organic meats to big chain stores like Costco and Safeway.[42]

DOWN ON THE FARM, THE DISTINCTION BETWEEN ALTERNATIVE AND conventional livestock production was becoming blurry.

The same year Niman and Coleman were acquired, several groups of animal rights activists launched a campaign to end the use of gestation stalls, the narrow metal pens where hog growers confined sows during and after pregnancy. Hogs, especially females, are both territorial and hierarchical. Weak ones, especially females, don't last long in a group. Stalls kept sows safe.

Activists argued that the pens' small size constituted cruelty to animals. The sows had little room to move and could not turn around while in them.

The campaign to end their use began innocuously enough with a letter-writing campaign.

"The Easter holiday celebrates the resurrection of the Prince of Peace," read the text of the form letter that supporters sent to their local newspapers in spring 2002. "Yet some of us still observe this special occasion by serving ham, produced by abusing and killing a sentient, innocent, gentle creature, as the centerpiece of their holiday dinner."[43]

A sow remains in the gestation stall while her newborns feed.

Those letters marked the opening foray of a sophisticated crusade. Over the next few years, animal rights activists released undercover videos shot at hog farms; marshaled scientific research that indicated that stalls cost rather than saved money; and launched ballot initiatives to ban their use.

Livestock producers fought back, with science that proved stalls protected sows, and with arguments that the expense of switching from stalls to large pens or pasture would bankrupt small farmers and enrich Big Ag. They painted their opponents as meddlers who didn't understand animal psychology.

"Nothing [is] more heartbreaking than watching a timid sow cower in the corner, afraid to approach the feed and water until the dominant sow [leaves] the area," one farmer wrote in a newspaper opinion piece. (The anti-stall coalition shrugged off such concerns and urged the livestock industry to breed less aggressive animals.)[44]

The reformers had the upper hand.

Over the next few years, voters in several states endorsed stall bans. Major hog producers, including Smithfield (by then the world's largest), agreed to phase out stalls. So, too, some purveyors, from Costco and Safeway to Cheesecake Factory, Burger King, and McDonald's, agreed to stop buying pork from stall-using producers.

In 2003, McDonald's upped the stakes: after working with an anti-antibiotic coalition, it would no longer buy meat made from animals fed antibiotics that were also used by humans. Presumably McDonald's executives were also inspired by the success of their investment in Chipotle, a small fast-food chain dedicated to serving "food with integrity," including organic and natural meats. Integrity translated into success: 578 Chipotle outlets by 2006 and double-digit growth each year. (From 2008 to 2018, ten food poisoning episodes were traced to Chipotle outlets.)

Emboldened, campaigners expanded their aim. In 2008, Californians approved an initiative sponsored by the Humane Society of the United States (HSUS). It banned gestation stalls, conventional poultry cages (a typical cage has a footprint about the size of a sheet of notebook paper), and the single-animal pens used to confine sheep.

Activists succeeded in part by exploiting a simple fact: twenty-first-century Americans don't live on farms and most have never met a farmer. Where livestock producers saw an ignorant urban population, food reformers saw a populace that believed farms ought to be Elysian idylls like the one operated by Joel Salatin.

That farms like his could not begin to feed the nation was irrelevant to many alt-activists. That disconnect between Americans and their food, between ideal and reality, was reformers' most powerful weapon, one that allowed them to imagine a new future for meat in America.

The "pink slime" uproar of 2012 encapsulated the perplexities and conundrums of Americans' desire to have it all.

In the meat industry, pink slime was known as Lean Finely Textured Beef (LFTB). The concept dated back to the 1970s when inflation, rising fuel costs, and declining demand cut into meatpackers' profits. Scrambling for ways to reduce costs, they came up with "mechanical deboning," which used bladed devices to scrape bits of meat from bone. This technology didn't last long: prodded by consumer advocates, the USDA banned it because of fears that the beef would be laced with bone slivers.

But the idea stuck because it offered a way to get more meat from each carcass. In the early 1980s, entrepreneur Eldon Roth invented an alternative, using centrifuge rather than blades to whip scraps of meat, fat, and gristle into bone-free, lean beef. Roth compacted these beef bits into blocks that he sold to meatpackers and food processors who mixed it with fattier beef to make the lean ground beef that consumers preferred. In the wake of the 1993 Jack in the Box episode, Roth refined his process by subjecting the scraps to a brief blast of ammonia (a natural component of beef) that destroyed *E. coli*.

There was nothing dangerous about LFTB — it was beef. Nor, as some claimed, was LFTB "dog food." Meatpackers had long sold meat scraps to pet food manufacturers, not because the scraps were unfit for human consumption, but because packers had no USDA- or FDA-approved way to salvage those otherwise edible bits. As soon as federal authorities approved Roth's innovation, edible beef scraps that once went into pet food could be used for other purposes.

Bottom line, LFTB helped meatpackers do what they'd always done: earn a profit while giving Americans meat at a price they would pay. Moreover, Eldon Roth and his company, Beef Products Inc., were highly regarded in the meat industry, not just for Roth's considerable inventive prowess and his product, but also for his rigorous attention to sanitation and food safety. Indeed, BPI's stock-in-trade was a commitment to providing packers with a clean product; Roth's facilities were touted as the most sanitary in the country.

In short, the Roth process was simply a high-tech version of what frugal cooks have done since humans stood upright: utilize every available morsel of protein and calories. Only a food-rich society enjoys the luxury of dispensing with frugality.

In spring 2011, Jamie Oliver, a British celebrity chef known to American television audiences, devoted a segment of one of his shows to pink slime. On air, he doused beef with ammonia to make his point about its toxicity as an audience of horrified moms and distressed kids watched. The following year, ABC News ran multiple segments about the evils of pink slime, including the fact that school lunch programs routinely served LFTB in their hamburgers.

A Texas food activist launched an online petition to demand that the department get pink slime out of school kitchens. The USDA agreed to let school districts make their own decisions about its use, and by early summer nearly every state education department had said no to LFTB. (The holdouts were Iowa, Nebraska, and North Dakota.) Within weeks, Roth had shut down three of his four plants.

The din drowned out voices asking important questions:

Were taxpayers prepared to spend more on school lunch programs in order to cover the cost of more expensive meat products?

Were parents prepared to give up their evenings so that they could attend school board meetings and demand that Big Food be evicted from school cafeterias? Were teachers and parents prepared to reduce classroom time devoted to math and reading so that kids could gain an appreciation of good food by planting and weeding schoolyard gardens?

Were those demanding an end to LFTB, cattle feedlots, and antibiotics willing to turn off their laptops and iPads, move to the country, and put in the long days that "natural" farming demands?

IN SHORT, AND LIKE SO MANY OTHER MOMENTS DETAILED IN THIS book, the LFTB episode embodied the messy complexity that is not just meat in America, but Americans themselves.

Not long after Roth turned out the lights in his facilities, another event took place, one that went largely unnoticed. In August 2012, the Community Food Security Coalition announced plans to cease operations. It had so successfully sown seeds that there was no longer enough grant money to go around for the many groups clamoring for it. The CFSC handed its food-reform baton to others who had been inspired by its work.

That's a "clean out your desk" moment we can applaud. Organic foods were supermarket staples; what was once "alternative" was now an expectation; consumers paid high prices for grass-fed beef and organic pork in order to express commitment to a better world. Or — to a high standard of living.

Once again, Americans, the masters of having it all, had it all: convenience, cachet, cheap food, and the feeling of doing good.

AFTERWORD

Here is where I am supposed to offer up an intelligent summary of these many pages. Or at least mention Impossible Burgers.

I'll go with the latter.

"Laboratory" meat arrived in the public consciousness around 2013, just as I published my first book about meat in America. This was the height of the early-century food debate; naturally, the media was agog.

And naturally, nothing has changed since then. Sure, Impossible Burgers are available at Burger King and your local grocery store — but US meat consumption is as high as ever.

If meat's American history tells us anything, it is that we Americans generally get what we want. Meat three times a day? No problem. Meat deboned, precut, and ready to cook? There it is. Organic, grass-fed, local pork and beef? All yours, as long as you don't mind paying the price or taking the time to find it. (A chain supermarket or Big Box will sell you organic, grass-fed meat, but if it's local you're after, you're on your own.)

What we don't want, apparently, is fake meat. Nor is that likely to change soon.

"Cultured meat" options have made little traction in part because they are difficult to scale up. It's one thing to make plant-based burgers by the dozens, and much harder and more costly to make them by the millions. The nation's venture capitalists have demonstrated little interest in pushing forward with such projects (perhaps they're too absorbed with AI). Or perhaps they sense, as do I, that there's not much future for fake meat, at least not in the US anytime soon.[1]

Without or without fake meat, we remain mired in the conundrum that is meat in America.

On one hand, many of us want lots of meat, and we don't care how it's made as long as it doesn't cost much. On the other, some of us want to break the chains that bind livestock production and meatpacking to assembly-line processes. Critics argue that "efficiency" is in the eye of the beholder, and that the environmental costs of conventional livestock production mean that there's nothing efficient about it. Others argue that our ability to make affordable meat, not just for ourselves but for the rest of the world, is worth the price.

Therein lies our American dilemma: whose version of efficiency best serves the needs and wants of the majority? Are we prepared to turn our backs on the practicalities of conventional agriculture in order to make small farms and organic the new normal? Can we have the best of both worlds: a majority urban population and small-scale agriculture, too?

I don't know (although I doubt it).

I do know this: whatever we think of "Boss Hog" Murphy or Eldon Roth on one hand, and Eric Schlosser and Michael Pollan on the other, we are all responsible for what we have wrought. Decade upon decade, Americans have insisted on having it all — cheap food and odor-free air and quality meat and disposable incomes that enable us to buy cell phones.

If the devastation wrought in the rains of North Carolina or the debacle over pink slime teaches us anything, it is that we won't transform our meat culture by taming Big Food or replacing Big Ag with a locavore-centered, alternative food system, but by examining our sense of entitlement and the way it contributes to the high cost of cheap living.

Factory farming freed our grandparents and great-grandparents, and thus us, from the need to grow and process food; freed them, and us, to dream big and think deep. Pollan, Schlosser, and I can write books because we don't have to spend time planting seeds and pulling weeds. Factory farming's biggest crop is intellectual capital.

So, thanks, Big Ag — and the USDA and family and corporate farms — for giving us the cheap food that has nourished an extraordinary abundance of creative energy. Now let's do something with it. Let's decide what kind of society we want — not what kind of farming, not what kind of meat, but what kind of society.

In the United States, deep change happens slowly (or in the case of 2025, all at once). Our political machinery is less well oiled than it is unwieldy and cantankerous, but, like an old Farmall tractor, it will get the job done (or used to; here's hoping it still will).

Two things, however, are certain: We won't move forward until we can talk to rather than at each other about the high price of cheap food. And we won't starve while we try to decide how, if at all, to reinvent the American way of meat, and redefine the meaning of "plenty."

ACKNOWLEDGEMENTS

I finished writing this book during the first six months of trump 2.0. Never have I been so aware of the power and importance of truth and facts, knowledge and scholarship.

Never have I been so aware that scholarly research in general and humanities higher education in particular are being systematically starved to death in the United States.

The Bibliography is my acknowledgement of the works of hundreds of others. My appreciation of and homage to scholarship at a moment when scholarship is under assault.

Flip through the Bibliography and, it's clear that this book's foundations consist in large measure of research and analysis conducted by the USDA over the past 160-plus years. Sadly, much of that Department now lies in disarray (as does most of the rest of the federal government). I hope the powers will not also destroy its extraordinary trove of information.

Flip through the Bib again, and you'll notice it includes dozens of (often dazzling) PhD dissertations. These are the work of apprentices, as it were, junior colleagues starting their journey into the weird realm of the scholar. Their work gave verve and life to mine. I'm grateful to them.

In the current moment, sadly, it's hard to imagine that in, say, twenty years, there will be any history PhDs. Or in any non-STEM field. Or any STEM for that matter. At least not in the US.

I am particularly indebted to: Gergely Baics, Christopher Deutsch, Lawrence B. Glickman, Daniel T. Gresham, Emily Pawley, Ariel Ron, and Joshua Specht. Their work inspired me to re-think — to re-imagine, if you will — my 2013 book about meat.

Parts II and III (Chapters 7-13) are built on a disturbing number of hours and years of research, prowling through niche, obscure, and delightful agricultural trade journals, as well as less obscure national business media and local media where relevant. The numbers of potential anecdotes and quotes came close to, I don't know, a million?

When I finished the manuscript, I decided to gamble and hire an editor. (Only one of my books has been edited by someone other than me, so this was a [pricey] gamble.)

The gamble paid off. Jen B. Robinson brought her considerable brain and eccentric sensibility to a close reading of these pages. It was like taking a writing class. She made me realize how lazy I'd gotten, prose-wise. And she came up with the title. (I would never have been so adventurous.)

Obviously every flaw is mine, and mine alone.

I am deeply grateful to my beloved friend Carrie Kabak, who designed the cover. She's the most talented person I've ever known, and she has a saint's patience.

Many thanks to Tom Streeter, who answered a ridiculous number of stupid questions. And not once was cranky.

Thanks also to the Lunch Ladies, who serve friendship and love.

As always, I am both inspired and supported by my family. I'd be lost without them. Especially the founder of the feast, philosopher and composer William S. Robinson.

NOTES

CHILDREN OF PLENTY

1. Three excellent surveys of beef and pork are J.L. Anderson, *Capitalist Pigs: Pigs, Pork, and Power in America* (West Virginia University Press, 2019); Roger Horowitz, *Putting Meat on the American Table: Taste, Technology, Transformation* (Johns Hopkins University Press, 2006); and Joshua Specht, *Red Meat Republic: A Hoof-to-Table History of How Beef Changed America* (Princeton University Press, 2019). All are steeped in research and written by historians but readily accessible to general audiences (a rarity). I also recommend Wilson J. Warren, *Meat Makes People Powerful: A Global History of the Modern Era* (University of Iowa Press, 2018), especially Chapter 1.
2. Quoted in Virginia DeJohn Anderson, "King Philip's Herds: Indians, Colonists, and the Problem of Livestock in Early New England," *William and Mary Quarterly* 3d series, 51 (October 1994): 604.
3. Quoted in Anderson, "King Philip's Herds," 604.
4. Quoted in James S. Magg, "Cattle Raising in Colonial South Carolina" (Master's thesis, University of Kansas, 1964), 26.
5. Quoted in Lewis Cecil Gray, *History of Agriculture in the Southern United States to 1860* (Carnegie Institution of Washington, 1933), 206.
6. See Henry Michael Miller, "Colonization and Subsistence Change on the 17th Century Chesapeake Frontier" (PhD diss., Michigan State University, 1984), 378.
7. This discussion of the biology, chemistry, and nutrition of meat is based primarily on two sources, both marvels of accessible prose. First, the two editions of Harold McGee's masterwork *On Food and Cooking: The Science and Lore of the Kitchen*. The original edition appeared in 1984 (Collier Books). McGee rewrote nearly every page for the revised, updated version (Scribner 2004). Second, Alan Davidson's *Oxford Companion to Food*, 2d ed. (Oxford University Press, 2006). An excellent general source for information about meat in early human history is Kenneth F. Kiple and Kriemhild Coneè Ornelas, eds., *The Cambridge World History of Food* (Cambridge University Press, 2000).
8. See Dessa E. Lightfoot, "'God Sends Meat and the Devil Sends Cooks': Meat Usage and Cuisine in Eighteenth-Century English Colonial America" (PhD diss., College of William and Mary, 2018). Colonial and preindustrial statistics represent the best estimates compiled by many scholars. I relied on information in Edwin J. Perkins, "Socio-Economic Development of the Colonies," in *A Companion to the American Revolution*, ed. Jack P. Greene and J.R. Pole (Blackwell Publishers, 2000); and Carole Shammas, *The Pre-Industrial Consumer in England and America* (Clarendon Press, 1990).
9. Gottlieb Mittelberger, *Journey to Pennsylvania*, ed. and trans. Oscar Handlin and John Clive (Belknap Press of Harvard University Press, 1960), 49.

10. Quoted in James E. McWilliams, *A Revolution in Eating: How the Quest for Food Shaped America* (Columbia University Press, 2005), 185.
11. "A Mutiny of the Servants," *William and Mary Quarterly* 11 (July 1902): 34–37.
12. Quoted in Magg, "Cattle Raising," 28.
13. Quoted in Magg, "Cattle Raising," 28.
14. William Bradford, *Of Plymouth Plantation, 1620–1647*, ed. Samuel Eliot Morison (Alfred A. Knopf, 1959), 253, 254.
15. Quoted in Virginia DeJohn Anderson, *Creatures of Empire: How Domestic Animals Transformed Early America* (Oxford University Press), 207.
16. Quoted in Anderson, *Creatures of Empire*, 221.
17. Quoted in Anderson, *Creatures of Empire*, 236.
18. See Emma Hart, "From Field to Plate: The Colonial Livestock Trade and the Development of an American Economic Culture," *William and Mary Quarterly* 73, no. 1 (January 2016): 107-40.

CHAPTER 1

1. This chapter was particularly and indelibly inspired and informed by Gergley Baics, *Feeding Gotham: The Political Economy and Geography of Food In New York, 1790-1860* (Princeton University Press, 2016); and Ariel Ron, *Grassroots Leviathan: Agricultural Reform and the Rural North In the Slaveholding Republic* (Johns Hopkins University Press, 2020).
2. On the divergent paths of urban and rural diets, see J.L. Anderson, *Capitalist Pigs: Pigs, Pork, and Power in America* (West Virginia University Press, 2019), especially Chapter 3; and Roger Horowitz, "The Politics of Meat Shopping In Antebellum New York City," in *Meat, Modernity, and the Rise of the Slaughterhouse*, ed. Paula Young Lee (University of New Hampshire Press, 2008),167-77, 279-82.
3. [P.T. Barnum], *The Life of P.T. Barnum Written by Himself* (Redfield, 1855), 26. According to the best calculations, New-Yorkers ate about 150 pounds of fresh beef a year. See Baics, *Feeding Gotham*, Chapter 2.
4. A terrific introduction is Andrew C. Baker, "Cities and Agriculture in America," in *A Companion to American Agricultural History*, ed. R. Douglas Hurt (Wiley Blackwell, 2022), 129-43. Also see Ruth Glasser, "The Farm *in* the City *in* the Recent Past: Thoughts on a More Inclusive Urban History," *Journal of Urban History* 44, no. 3 (2018): 501-18.
5. For meat consumption, see Baics, *Feeding Gotham*, 62; 285n12; and Appendix B.
6. See Baics, *Feeding Gotham*; Hendrik Hartog, *Public Property and Private Power: The Corporation of the City of New York In American Law, 1730-1870* (Cornell University Press, 1983); and William Novak, *The People's Welfare: Law and Regulation in Nineteenth-Century America* (University of North Carolina Press, 1996).
7. For excellent studies of the region's foodshed: Cindy R. Lobel, *Urban Appetites: Food and Culture in Nineteenth-Century New York* (University of Chicago Press, 2014); Marc Linder and Lawrence S. Zacharias, *Of Cabbages and Kings County: Agriculture and the Formation of Modern Brooklyn* (University of Iowa Press, 1999); Louis P. Tremante, III, "Agriculture and Farm Life in the New York City Region, 1820–1870" (PhD diss., Iowa State University, 2000); Louis Tremante, "Agriculture in the Vicinity of Mid-Nineteenth Century New York City: Five Drivers," *New York*

History 97, no. 3/4 (Summer/Fall 2016): 265–92. For a good look at how water transit shaped livestock and meat shipping see Rudolf A. Clemen, "Waterways in Livestock and Meat Trade," *American Economic Review* 16, no. 4 (December 1926): 640-52.

8. The classic contemporary chronicles of New York's butchers are Thomas F. De Voe, *The Market Book: A History of the Public Markets of the City of New York* (1862; rprt. A.M. Kelley, 1970); Thomas F. De Voe, *The Market Assistant, Containing a Brief Description of Every Article of Human Food Sold in the Public Markets of the Cities of New York, Boston, Philadelphia, and Brooklyn; Including the Various Domestic and Wild Animals, Poultry, Game, Fish, Vegetables, Fruits, &c., &c., with Many Curious Incidents and Anecdotes* (Riverside Press for the author, 1867). His papers are held by the New-York Historical Society.
9. An excellent description of a butcher's day and work is Thomas David Beal, "Selling Gotham: The Retail Trade in New York City from the Public Market to Alexander T. Stewart's Marble Palace, 1625-1860" (PhD diss., State University of New York-Stony Brook, 1998), 342-57.
10. Quoted in Helen Tangires, *Public Markets and Civic Culture in Nineteenth-Century America* (Johns Hopkins University Press, 2003), 65. Also see Helen Tangires, "Celebrating Nature's Bounty: Butcher Parades in Nineteenth-Century New York and Philadelphia," in *Food and Celebration: From Fasting to Feasting*, ed. Patricia Lysaght (Zalozba, 2002), 393–400.
11. Quoted in Baics, *Feeding Gotham*, 57.
12. [Charles] H. Haswell, *Reminiscences of an Octagenarian of the City of New York (1816-1860)* (Harper & Brothers Publishers, 1896), 89.
13. Quoted in Beal, "Selling Gotham,", 308.
14. Richard B. Stott, *Workers in the Metropolis: Class, Ethnicity, and Youth in Antebellum New York City* (Cornell University Press, 1990), 180. See Stott's Chapter 6 for a detailed look at the immigrant food experience and consumption in general, in New York City in the early-nineteenth century.
15. Quoted in Stott, *Workers in the Metropolis*, 180.
16. "Cobbett on the Expenses of House-Keeping in America," *American Farmer* 6, no. 16 (July 9, 1824): 123.
17. "Consumption of Meat," *American Farmer and Spirit of the Agricultural Journals of the Day* 3, no. 2 (June 2, 1841): 9.
18. Quoted in Bayrd Still, *Mirror for Gotham: New York as Seen by Contemporaries from Dutch Days to the Present* ([New York] University Press, 1956), 87.
19. Quoted in Still, *Mirror for Gotham*, 112.
20. Quoted in Joanna Cohen, *Luxurious Citizens: The Politics of Consumption in Nineteenth-Century America* (University of Pennsylvania Press, 2017),167.
21. For this episode, and all quotes, see Baics, *Feeding Gotham*, 39-40.
22. For "consumers" in the early republic, see Cohen, *Luxurious Citizens*.
23. Quoted in Baics, *Feeding Gotham*, 42.
24. Quoted in Baics, *Feeding Gotham*, 41.
25. Asa Greene, *A Glance At New York: Embracing the City Government, Theatres, Hotels, Churches, Mobs, Monopolies, Learned Professions, Newspapers, Rogues, Dandies, Fires and Firemen, Water and other Liquids, &C. &C.* (A. Greene, 1837), 109-10, 113-14.
26. Greene, *Glance At New York*, 109-10, 113-14.

27. Quoted in Horowitz, "Politics of Meat Shopping," 175; and in Tangires, *Public Markets*, 78, 79.
28. Quoted in Beal, "Selling Gotham," 336, 337; and Horowitz, "Politics of Meat Shopping," 174.
29. For the home market, especially as it related to agriculture, see Ron, *Grassroots Leviathan*, especially Chapter 3.

    On one point, Ron is adamant: the "spectacular growth" of US manufacturing in the Greater Northeast, "is unintelligible without prosperous nearby farmers to consume the goods."(76) According to Ron, this swath of the electorate created a template for state-funded agriculture without using partisan politics. Instead, they latched on to the general enthusiasm for national development.

    This was a largely white, northern project. The patriarchs who controlled the nation's Slave Region wanted nothing to do with it. Their main focus was cotton as a global export. Ron outlines the ways in which these visions for the future divided the Greater Northeast from the Slave Region, politically, culturally, and economically.

30. The phrase Greater Northeast is courtesy of Ron, *Grassroots Leviathan*. The "home market" idea has been analyzed many times by historians, but for my time and money, Ron's is the best take, in large measure because he focused on the cultural aspects of the effort, rather than the political.
31. Quoted in Ron, *Grassroots Leviathan*, 7.
32. Quoted in Ron, *Grassroots Leviathan*, 114, 146; italics in the original. Livestock was central to this vision, because manure was essential to its success. On the role of manure, see Lobel, *Urban Appetites*, 44-45; and Ron, *Grassroots Leviathan*, 98-103.
33. Quoted in Lobel, *Urban Appetites*, 40; and Horowitz, "Politics of Meat Shopping," 171. Lobel discusses the impact of the canal on the city's food supplies on 40-43.
34. River banks are denoted relative to water flow: traveling downriver, the left bank is on the left; the right, on the right. Traveling upriver, the left bank is still the left bank, and the right, the right.
35. See especially Chapter 13 of Percy Wells Bidwell and John I. Falconer, *History of Agriculture in the Northern United States, 1620-1860* (Carnegie Institution of Washington, 1925); and the relevant sections of USDA, Agricultural History Series. No. 5. *A History of Livestock Raising in the United States, 1607-1860*, by James Westfall Thompson. (1942, reprt. Scholarly Resources, 1973); hereafter Thompson, *History of Livestock Raising*. There are hundreds of other ways to approach the subject but these two are a good place to begin.
36. Quoted in Anderson, *Capitalist Pigs*, 17.
37. Quoted in Anderson, *Capitalist Pigs*, 55.
38. Quoted in Anderson, *Capitalist Pigs*, 17, 108. Anderson's Chapter 2 offers a fascinating on-the-ground look at hog raising and production.
39. The bibles here are the magnificent Margaret Walsh, *The Rise of the Midwestern Packing Industry* (1982; reprt., University Press of Kentucky, 2015); and Mary Yeager, *Competition and Regulation: The Development of Oligopoly in the Meat Packing Industry* (JAI Press, 1981), especially Chapters 1 and 2. Her notes are a masterpiece in their own right.

40. Quoted in Anderson, *Capitalist Pigs*, 72.
41. Bidwell and Falconer, *History of Agriculture*, 391. Also see Paul Wallace Gates, "Cattle Kings in the Prairies," *Mississippi Valley Historical Review* 35, no. 3 (December 1948): 379-412.
42. There was also a lively market of livestock headed to the enslaved region of the deep south. It's worth noting that prior to the nineteenth century, many believed that neither cattle nor hogs could be driven such long distances. By 1815 or so, these long-distance droves had become common. See Thompson, *History of Livestock*, 92, 94, 107, 116-17.
43. Rev. I.F. King, "The Coming and Going of Ohio Droving," *Ohio Archaeological and Historical Society Publications* 17 (1908): 249.
44. The tale is recounted in Thompson, *History of Livestock*, 95.
45. For the steamboat-railroad comparison, see Yeager, *Competition and Regulation*, 27. For a useful look at railroad gestation, see John Lauritz Larson, *The Market Revolution In America: Liberty, Ambition, and the Eclipse of the Common Good* (Cambridge University Press, 2010).

    There are a multitude of railroad histories, but one recent study says what needs to be said: Richard White, *Railroaded: The Transcontinentals and the Making of Modern America* (W.W. Norton, 2011).

    What the railroads gave, they also took away. New transportation logistics wreaked havoc on East Coast farmers, who were all but eliminated from the meatmaking equation. As one man explained, they could not compete with the "great facilities for bringing cattle from the far west at a low price, and in great quantities, at all times of the year."

    So, too, with hogs: "The number of swine raised . . . in New England, is far less than formerly," noted the commissioner of agriculture in 1861. Between the "high price of grain" in New England on one hand, and the speed with which western hogs could be "rushed from the Mississippi to the Atlantic" on the other, eastern hog farming was no longer profitable. Quotes are from Bidwell and Falconer, *History of Agriculture*, 399, 439.
46. There are a zillion studies, but this historian's bible remains William Cronon, *Nature's Metropolis: Chicago and the Great West* (W.W. Norton & Company, 1991), which includes a superb examination of the city's role in making meat.
47. For centuries, Native Americans traveled far and wide across central North America.
48. Quoted in Bidwell and Falconer, *History of Agriculture*, 393.
49. The best discussion of the railroads' early relationship with livestock is Yeager, *Competition and Regulation*, especially Chapters 1 and 2.
50. A good description of Chicago yards prior to 1865 is Jack Wing [John M. Wing], *The Great Union Stock Yards of Chicago* (Religio-Philosophical Publishing Association, 1865).
51. Garet Garrett, "Our Daily Meat," *Collier's* 48 (December 23, 1911): 20.
52. US Senate, Select Committee on Transportation and Sale of Meat Products, *Investigation of Transportation and Sale of Meat Products with Testimony*, 51st Cong., 432; hereafter *Investigation of Transportation and Sale*. The document is often referred to as the Vest Report after committee chair George G. Vest.

    There are few substantive biographies of Armour, but a particularly good source is his entry in *American National Biography*. Perhaps the best way to understand the man is by reading newspaper coverage of his exploits as well as obituaries published at the time of his death in January 1901. I pieced together Armour's early career primarily from Milwaukee newspapers.

Also see Cora Lillian Davenport, "The Rise of the Armours, an American Industrial Family" (Master's thesis, University of Chicago, 1930); Harper Leech and John Charles Carroll, *Armour and His Times* (D. Appleton-Century Company, 1938); and a string of biographical essays prompted by the early-twentieth-century "trust-busting" movement.

53. Like most things economic, cogent explanations of futures trading, corners, and the like are hard to come by. An excellent description and analysis written for the non-economist can be found in Cronon, *Nature's Metropolis*, 127-32.
54. Garrett, "Our Daily Meat," 20.
55. See Horowitz, "Politics of Meat Shopping," 170.
56. See Catherine McNeur, "The 'Swinish Multitude': Controversies Over Hogs in Antebellum New York City," *Journal of Urban History* 37, no. 5 (2011): 639–60.

    I calculated the number based on information in "Beef In the City and in the Country and on the Railroads," *New York Times*, November 15, 1855, 4; the reporter noted that 4500 head of cattle were on hand, "a fair weekly supply for the consumption of the City." 4500 x 52 = 234,000.

    Also see "One Hundred Millions Pounds of Beef," *New York Times*, December 27, 1855, 4. The author assumed average useful beef weight at 650 pounds, or 111 million pounds. At 9.5 cents a pound, citizens spent more than $12 million.
57. "Board of Health," *New York Times*, August 29, 1866, 5.
58. *Sanitary Condition of the City: Report of the Council of Hygiene and Public Health of the Citizens' Association of New York*, 2d ed. (1866; repr., Arno Press, 1970), 168.
59. On this point see Baics, *Feeding Gotham*, Chapter 6.
60. "Butchers and the Wrongs of Cattle," *New York Times*, July 27, 1853, 4.

CHAPTER 2

1. "The Communipaw Abattoir," *New York Times*, November 12, 1868, 8.
2. "Opening of the New Abbattoirs [*sic*] -- Great Celebration at Communipaw," *New York Times*, October 18, 1866, 2.
3. "Report on Slaughtering for Boston Market," *First Annual Report of the State Board of Health of Massachusetts* (Wright & Potter, 1870), 20, 21, 22.
4. City of Boston, *Report on the Sale of Bad Meat in Boston* (n.p., [1871]), 56.
5. "Metropolitan Board of Health," *New York Times*, March 13, 1866, 4; "Local Intelligence," *New York Times*, June 20, 1866, 8.
6. "The City of Chicago *v*. Louis Rumpff. Same *v*. James Turner," 45 Ill. 90 (1862), 97, 99.
7. Ronald M Labbé and Jonathan Lurie, *The Slaughterhouse Cases: Regulation, Reconstruction, and the Fourteenth Amendment* (University Press of Kansas, 2003).
8. "The State of Louisiana, ex re., S. Belden, Attorney General, *v*. Wm Fagan, et al.," 22 La. Ann. 545 (1870), 552.
9. Quoted in Labbé and Lurie, *Slaughterhouse Cases*, 106.
10. "State of Louisiana, ex re.," 555; Labbé and Lurie, *Slaughterhouse Cases*, 133.

11. Labbé and Lurie, *Slaughterhouse Cases*, 133, 208.
12. Ernest Freeberg, *A Traitor to His Species: Henry Bergh and the Birth of the Animal Rights Movement* (Basic Books, 2020).
13. Letter from Henry Bergh to Jackson Schultz, July 16, 1866; Bergh Papers, Buffet vol. 4; American Society for the Prevention of Cruelty to Animals.
14. See Henry Bergh to Messrs. Allerton, Dutcher and Moore, October 26, 1866; Buffett papers, vol. 4, American Society for the Protection of Cruelty to Animals; and "Mr. Bergh's Observations at the Communipaw Abattoir," *New York Times*, December 16, 1868, 2. Also see "The Condition of Cattle On Their Arrival at the New-York Stock-Yards," *New York Times*, August 27, 1870, 2; and annual reports of the ASPCA.
15. USDA, *Report of the Commissioner on Agriculture for the Year 1870*, 10; and "The Market Systems of the Country, Their Usages and Abuses," in same, 251.
16. "Transportation of Fresh Meats to Market," *Scientific American* n.s. 15 (November 10, 1866): 323.
17. City of Boston, *Report on the Sale of Bad Meat*, 11, 12; E.H. Dixon, "The Beef Market," *New-York Tribune*, August 22, 1868, 2.
18. "Frozen Meat," *Prairie Farmer* 42 (July 22, 1871): 228; "Cheaper Beef for the East," *New York Times*, December 8, 1873, 2.
19. Mary Yeager, *Competition and Regulation: The Development of Oligopoly in the Meat Packing Industry* (JAI Press, 1981), 38-39, 55-58.
20. It's unfashionable to focus on the alleged great white man, and here I do not. Rather, I am interested in how families build businesses. That Swift's turned into a behemoth is irrelevant. What matters is that I could trace, albeit obliquely, how the Swift family built that company.

    Having said that, it's important to note that G.F. Swift was white and male, and those were the most valuable currencies in the United States. No others enjoyed such access to the keys to the kingdom.
21. "The Fresh-Beef War," *Boston Herald*, November 14, 1882, 11. Swift is not identified by name in the article, but it's clear from details that the reporter was interviewing Swift and a partner, presumably his brother Edwin.
22. US Senate, Select Committee on Interstate Commerce, *Report of the Senate Select Committee on Interstate Commerce*, 49th Cong. (1886), 661.
23. *Report of the Senate Select Committee*, 661.
24. See Joshua Specht, *Red Meat Republic: A Hoof-to-Table History of How Beef Changed America* (Princeton University Press, 2019), Chapter 3, especially 160-70.
25. New York State Legislature, Special Committee on Railroads, *Proceedings of the Special Committee on Railroads*, 6 vols. (Evening Post Steam Presses, 1879–1880): 4:3317. The document is often referred to as the Hepburn Report, after committee chair A.B. Hepburn.
26. New York State Legislature, *Proceedings of the Special Committee*, 4:3318.
27. New York State Legislature, *Proceedings of the Special Committee*, 2:1727.
28. The classic work on systems is Thomas P. Hughes, *Networks of Power: Electrification in Western Society, 1880-1930* (Johns Hopkins University Press, 1983).

    Swift resembled Thomas Edison and the era's other "system" builders. Consider a decidedly non-meat example: Edison's incandescent light bulb. By itself, it had no worth, other than as a curiosity. The bulb gained value only after Edison and his investors devised an integrated system that included a source of electricity, and a means of transmitting it to individual bulbs in a shop, factory, or home.

The system included poles, wire, generators, transformers, and the like; financing packages and contracts; managerial and engineering skill; the willingness of urban residents to grant permission for the installation of the system's physical components; and the political acumen necessary to persuade them to do so.

29. For the Grand Trunk's role, see Kristin Hoganson, "Meat in the Middle: Converging Borderlands in the U.S. Midwest, 1865-1900," *Journal of American History* 98, no. 4 (March 2012): 1025-51, especially 1038-39; and Specht, *Red Meat Republic*, Chapter 4, especially 191-201.

The episode is a good example of how histories come to be told. Swift's hagiographers claimed that the major railroads refused to deal with him; they feared his dressed beef. Swift, being his heroic self, fought back and the rest, as they say, was history.

Here's a different interpretation: the roads and their partners were committed to shipping live stock rather than dressed beef. But in the late 1870s, they had no compelling reason to see Swift as a threat. After all, others had tried to ship dressed beef and failed.

As important, in the 1870s the railroad industry suffered more than its usual chaos thanks to a series of violent strikes that stopped traffic for weeks. That was on top of the ongoing demands of maintaining tracks, engines, and cars; the burden of managing the largest workforces in the world; and the thousand other problems that plagued the small group of people wrestling with the first grand corporate venture of the modern age.

Swift's failure to arrange shipping contracts with the railroads was less a nefarious plot (although the railroaders were capable of those) than it was his inability to capture the attention of people as distracted as any multitasker in the digital age.

But the Swift mythology also ignores the most crucial fact: the railroad men who allegedly thwarted him were irrelevant to his plans. The railroad/stockyard/slaughterhouse complex focused resources and clout in the New York-Philadelphia-Baltimore metropolitan area, the nation's most densely populated region.

Best of all, the GT's managers delighted in functioning as a boil in the sides of American railroad magnates. Like all railroaders, they enjoyed nothing so much as a splendid little rate war. They agreed to haul Swift's refrigerated cars from Chicago to New England.

30. Louis F. Swift and Arthur Van Vlissingen Jr, *The Yankee of the Yards: The Biography of Gustavus Franklin Swift* (A.W. Shaw Company, 1927), 24, 29-30, 201, 208.
31. Swift and Van Vlissingen, Jr, *Yankee of the Yards*, 208.
32. "Boston Enterprise," *Boston Journal*, July 26, 1879, 3.
33. "The Western Refrigerator Beef," *Trenton State Gazette*, October 23, 1882, 3.
34. The description of the facility here and in the following is from "A Huge Meat Refrigerator," *New York Times*, October 10, 1882, 8.
35. "The Western Refrigerator Beef," 3.
36. "Cheaper Beef," *Harper's Weekly* 26 (October 21, 1882): 663.
37. "Cheaper Beef," 663; "The Western Refrigerator Beef," 3.

38. US Senate, Select Committee on Transportation and Sale of Meat Products, *Investigation of Transportation and Sale of Meat Products with Testimony*. 51st Cong. (1888), 432. Hereafter *Investigation of Transportation and Sale*.
39. "The Pressed Beef Business," [sic] *Springfield Republican (MA)*, February 16, 1883, 2; reprinted from the *Philadelphia Press*.
40. "Dressed Beef," *New York Times*, November 15, 1882, 4.
41. Quotes in "Dressed Beef," *Chicago Tribune*, October 24, 1882, 5; "The Dressed Beef Innovation," *Wheeling Register (WV)*, March 27, 1883, 2.
42. "Dressed Beef," *New York Times*, November 15, 1882, 4.
43. "Dressed Beef and Live Cattle," *New York Times*, November 15, 1882, 5.
44. "Western Dressed Beef," *Boston Globe*, November 23, 1882, 1.
45. The quotations here and following are from "The Fresh-Beef War,: *Boston Herald*, November 14, 1882, 11.
46. Shipping statistics are in USDA, *Third Annual Report of the Bureau of Animal Industry for the Year 1886*, "Dressed-Meat Traffic," by Norman J. Colman, 278. A lower estimate was made in US Treasury Department, *Report on the Internal Commerce of the United States*. 48th Cong. (1886), 264. A good summation of the rapid rise of dressed beef is Specht, *Red Meat Republic*, Chapter 4, especially 201-17
47. "City Article," *Boston Journal*, September 8, 1883, 3.
48. Here I am indebted to the fine work of Lawrence B. Glickman. His *A Living Wage: American Workers and the Making of Consumer Society* (Cornell University Press, 1997) is the bible on this particular subject. (At least for me.)
49. There's a reason that many early-nineteenth-century Black southerners owned slaves. It was the ultimate expression of power in a particular time and place. But this ideal of independence was also the context for relations between Black and white Americans. Slavery was viewed as an insult to free labor. And when that free labor was a wage earner, being treated like a Black person was an insult to all that was American.
50. Jefferson Cowie, *The Great Exception: The New Deal and the Limits of American Politics* (Princeton University Press, 2016), 44.
51. Quoted in Lawrence Glickman, "Workers of the World, Consume: Ira Steward and the Origins of Labor Consumerism," *International Labor and Working-Class History* 52 (Fall 1997): 72-86; quote 81.
52. Quoted in Glickman, "Workers of the World," 77.
53. Quoted in Glickman, "Workers of the World," 81.
54. W.O. Atwater, "Pecuniary Economy of Food: The Chemistry of Foods and Nutrition V.," *Century* 35, no. 3 (January 1888): 443. For a delightful survey of late-century meat/beef culture, see Chapter 5 of Specht, *Red Meat Republic*.
55. *Investigation of Transportation and Sale*, 407.
56. "The Non-Beef-Eating Nations," *Saturday Evening Post*, November 13, 1869, 8. It's impossible to read late-nineteenth-century magazines and newspapers without encountering discussions of the relationships among nation-building, national power, and food. Two good surveys are Warren Belasco, *Meals to Come: A History of the Future of Food* (University of California Press, 2006); and Mark R. Finlay, "Early Marketing of the Theory of Nutrition: The Science and Culture of Liebig's Extract of Meat," in *The Science and Culture of Nutrition, 1840–1940*,

ed. Harmke Kamminga and Andrew Cunningham (Rodopi, 1995), 48–74. Finlay's essay is especially good for the European view.
57. On this point, see Vincent J. Knapp, "The Democratization of Meat and Protein in Late Eighteenth- and Nineteenth-Century Europe," *The Historian* 59, no. 3 (March 1997): 541-51. For a survey of the global nature of supply and demand, see Wilson J. Warren, *Meat Makes People Powerful: A Global History of the Modern Era* (University of Iowa Press, 2018).
58. The prediction is in Belasco, *Meals to Come*, 27.

CHAPTER 3

1. Pike quotes are from Elliott Coues, ed., *The Expeditions of Zebulon Montgomery Pike, To Headwaters of the Mississippi River, Through Louisiana Territory, and in New Spain, During the Years 1805-6-7*, 3 vols. (Francis P. Harper, 1895): 2: 525.
2. William H. Keating, comp., *Narrative of an Expedition to the Source of St. Peter's River, Lake Winnepeek, Lake of the Woods, &c. Performed in the year 1823, by Order of the Hon. J.C. Calhoun, Secretary of War, Under the Command of Stephen H. Long, U.S.T.E.*, 2 vols. (Geo. B. Whittaker, 1825): 2:238, 239.
3. Quoted in Steven Hahn, *A Nation Without Borders: The United States and Its World in an Age of Civil Wars* (Viking/Penguin Random House, 2016), 139.
4. See especially Chapter 3 of Elliott West, *Continental Reckoning: The American West in the Age of Expansion* (University of Nebraska Press, 2023), quote 40.
5. David Igler, *Industrial Cowboys: Miller & Lux and the Transformation of the Far West, 1850-1920* (University of California Press, 2001).
6. Quoted in Igler, *Industrial Cowboys*, 88.
7. Quoted in William Cronon, *Nature's Metropolis: Chicago and the Great West* (W.W. Norton & Company, 1991), 215. For a solid survey, I highly recommend Chapter 2 of Joshua Specht, *Red Meat Republic: A Hoof-to-Table History of How Beef Changed America* (Princeton University Press, 2019).
8. Quoted in Scott Michael Kleeb, "The Atlantic West: Cowboys, Capitalists and the Making of an American Myth" (PhD diss., Yale University, 2006), 88.
9. For a good analysis of this moment, see Specht, *Red Meat Republic*, especially Chapters 1 and 2.
10. USDA, *Report of the Commissioner of Agriculture for the Year 1863*, "Distribution and Movement of Neat Cattle in the United States," by Silas L. Loomis, 248-64, quote 259. Loomis defined "neat cattle" as stock kept to provide "beef, butter, cheese, and milk."
11. Loomis, "Distribution and Movement of Neat Cattle," 259 (emphasis in the original); and USDA, *Report of the Commissioner of Agriculture for the Year 1864*, "Importance of Raising and Feeding More Cattle and Sheep," by Charles W. Taylor, 255.
12. The hot war ended in 1865, but a cold war simmered for a decade as north and south learned how to merge their separate ambitions.

The south yielded nothing. It lost its labor, its crops and livestock, some of its cities, much of its rail infrastructure. But it lost no power in Washington, DC.

Indeed, the white men who populated the federal government recognized that if union were to continue, it must be, as in the first republic, on southern terms. The ensuing compromise shaped the Second Republic, and left millions of Black Americans to fend for themselves in the quasi-constitutional, white, terrorist state of the deep south. That cold war lasted eighty years. Or perhaps it never ended.

See, for example, Heather Cox Richardson, *How the South Won the Civil War: Oligarchy, Democracy, and the Continuing Fight for the Soul of America* (Oxford University Press, 2020).
13. "Driving Cattle from Texas to Iowa, 1866," *Annals of Iowa* 14, no. 4 (April 1924): 252, 253.
14. "Driving Cattle from Texas to Iowa," 252, 253.
15. C.F. Gross to J.B. Edwards, May 4, 1925, J.B. Edwards Collection, microfilm version, Kansas State Historical Society.
16. Joseph G. McCoy, "Historic and Biographic Sketch," *Kansas Magazine* 1 (December 1909): 49. For a marvelous appreciation of McCoy, see Don D. Walker, "History Through a Cow's Horn: Joseph G. McCoy and His Historical Sketches of the Cattle Trade," in *Clio's Cowboys: Studies in the Historiography of the Cattle Trade* (University of Nebraska Press, 1981), 1–24.
17. Joseph G. McCoy, *Historic Sketches of the Cattle Trade of the West and Southwest* (Ramsey, Millett & Hudson, 1874), 44.
18. In the 1860s, theories abounded about the cause of Texas fever, but another quarter-century passed before veterinarians discovered the source of the disease: microscopic organisms that attacked the animals' blood cells. Ticks spread the disease from one animal to another. See Alan L. Olmstead and Paul W. Rhode, *Arresting Contagion: Science, Policy, and Conflicts Over Animal Disease* (Harvard University Press, 2015), Chapter 11. For a take on Longhorns, see Joshua Specht, "The Rise, Fall, and Rebirth of the Texas Longhorn: An Evolutionary History," *Environmental History* 21, no. 2 (2016): 343-63.
19. McCoy, *Historic Sketches*, 96.
20. McCoy, *Historic Sketches*, 57. See Joshua Specht, "'For the Future in the Distance': Cattle Trailing, Social Conflict, and the Development of Ellsworth, Kansas," *Kansas History* 40, no. 2 (2017): 104-19. The would-be trail king earned a bit of a return on his investment by publishing an account of his western adventure, an often hilarious, and always lopsided, view of the West-according-to-McCoy. *Historic Sketches of the Cattle Trade* did as much as anything to seal the image of the Far West as the land of danger and daring, bad guys, good guys, Injuns, saloons, rustlers, and easy women.
21. For superb coverage of this episode, see Specht, *Red Meat Republic*, Chapter 2.
22. Quoted in Kleeb, "The Atlantic West," 57.
23. Quoted in Richard Graham, "The Investment Boom in British-Texan Cattle Companies, 1880–1885," *Business History Review* 34, no. 4 (Winter 1960): 423, 424; James S. Brisbin, *The Beef Bonanza; or, How to Get Rich on the Plains* (1881; repr., University of Oklahoma Press, 1959), 36, 74.
24. Quoted in Ernest Staples Osgood, *The Day of the Cattleman* (1929; repr., University of Chicago Press, 1966), 96, 103.
25. "A Marquis under Arrest," *New York Times*, May 20, 1887, 1. Also see Donald Dresden, *The Marquis de Morès: Emperor of the Bad Lands* (University of Oklahoma Press, 1970); and D. Jerome Tweton, *The Marquis de Morès: Dakota Capitalist, French Nationalist* (North Dakota Institute for Regional Studies, 1972).

26. Quoted in D. Jerome Tweton, "The Marquis De Mores [sic] and His Dakota Venture: A Study in Failure," *Journal of the West* 6, no. 4 (October 1967): 529.
27. "De Mores [sic]," *Brooklyn Eagle*, October 5, 1885, 2; "In the Bad Lands," *Bismarck Tribune*, January 20, 1885, 6.
28. Quoted in Kleeb, "The Atlantic West," 220. An excellent discussion of the bust, to which I am indebted, is Specht, *Red Meat Republic*, Chapter 6, especially 106-18.
29. Quoted in Kleeb, "The Atlantic West," 189, 190.
30. US Senate, Select Committee on Transportation and Sale of Meat Products, *Investigation of Transportation and Sale of Meat Products with Testimony*. 51st Cong. (1888): 4, 5. Hereafter *Investigation of Transportation and Sale*.
31. *Investigation of Transportation and Sale*, 82, 83.
32. "Views of a Ranchman," *New York Times*, November 26, 1886, 6. I intentionally avoided discussion of the "populism" that accompanied such rumors and rage, but see Charles Postel, *The Populist Vision* (Oxford University Press, 2007).
33. "Opposed to the Chicago Men," *New York Times*, February 28, 1886, 2.
34. *Investigation of Transportation and Sale*, 360–61.
35. *Investigation of Transportation and Sale*, 360–61.
36. *Investigation of Transportation and Sale*, 425, 472, 480.
37. "High Prices of Beef," *Washington Post*, September 22, 1895, 1, 11; quote on 11.
38. Quoted in David M. Wrobel, *The End of American Exceptionalism: Frontier Anxiety from the Old West to the New Deal* (University Press of Kansas, 1993), 56. Americans would look abroad to sustain their vitality. As a result of the late-century wave of imperial wars, the US ended up owning several pieces of real estate, most of them in the Pacific.
39. Quoted in Donald J. Pisani, *To Reclaim a Divided West: Water, Law, and Public Policy, 1848-1902* (University of New Mexico Press, 1992), 296.
40. Quoted in Donald J. Pisani, *Water and the American Government: The Reclamation Bureau, National Water Policy, and the West, 1902-1935* (University of California Press, 2003), 3. The commenter was Frederick Haynes Newell, who learned his engineering chops under the tutelage of John Wesley Powell, and served as the first director of the Bureau of Reclamation.
41. Quoted in Pisani, *To Reclaim a Divided West*, 294-95.
42. Quoted in Pisani, *Water and the American Government*, 2, 4.
43. Quoted in Pisani, *Water and the American Government*, 2, 4.
44. For stockmen's associations and organizations, and cattlemen's "rights," see Rodgers Taylor Dennen, "From Common to Private Property: The Enclosure of the Open Range," (PhD diss., University of Washington, 1975), esp. 41-81; and R. Taylor Dennen, "Cattlemen's Associations and Property Rights in the American West," *Explorations in Economic History* 13 (1976): 423-36. Also see Edward Everett Dale, *The Range Cattle Industry: Ranching on the Great Plains from 1865 to 1925* (1930; repr., University of Oklahoma, 1960); Fred A. Shannon, *The Farmer's Last Frontier: Agriculture, 1860-1897* (1945; repr., M.E. Sharpe, 1989), Chapters 9 and 10.
45. For this I am indebted to the fine work of Neal A. Knapp, "Making Machines of Animals: The International Livestock Exposition, 1900-1920" (PhD diss., Boston University, 2019).

46. See Knapp, "Making Machines." The first few pages of Alvin H. Sanders are also useful: *The Story of the International Live Stock Exposition From its Inception in 1900 to the Show of 1941* (International Live Stock Exposition Association, 1942).

CHAPTER 4

1. People tend to think of the moment as either steeped in obscene displays of wealth — a gilded age peopled with fat robber barons — or in equally obscene displays of poverty, with millions crammed into unsanitary urban hovels, dying young after years of sweatshop and factory labor. Both those versions are accurate. But so is the fact that a "consumer" economy only makes sense when there is a critical mass of humanity with the wherewithal to dig into the material feast.
   In this case, the mass was white, and the moment steeped in urgency and violence: whites' determination to maintain supremacy provoked decades of riots and lynchings in both north and south.
2. Mary Hinman Abel, "Safe Foods and How to Get Them," *Delineator* 66 (September 1905): 394.
3. George Buchanan Fife, "The So-Called Beef Trust," *Century* 65 (November 1902): 155. To be clear, there was money in that magic. The more byproducts the greater the cost advantage. That cushioned revenues when beef prices were low.
4. In 1957, consumption finally climbed to 159 pounds. Statistics are from USDA, AMS, "Livestock and Meat Statistics 1957," *Statistical Bulletin*, No. 230, July 1958; USDA, BAI, *Meat Production, Consumption and Foreign Trade of the United States 1900-1927*, comp. John Roberts. [1930].
5. For urban foraging: Katherine Leonard Turner, *How the Other Half Ate: A History of Working-Class Meals at the Turn of the Century* (University of California Press, 2014); and Tracy Deutsch, *Building a Housewife's Paradise: Gender, Politics, and American Grocery Stores in the Twentieth Century* (University of North Carolina Press, 2010), Chapter 1. On high-end dining: Andrew P. Haley, *Turning the Tables: Restaurants and the Rise of the American Middle Class, 1880-1920* (University of North Carolina Press, 2011), Chapter 1.
6. Haley, *Turning Tables*, argues that restaurants served as a useful marker for early-twentieth-century, middle-class identity.
7. See Nicolaas John Mink, "The Restaurant: Food, Power, and Social Change" (PhD diss., University of Wisconsin-Madison, 2010), Chapter 1.
8. For cafeterias, see Mink, "The Restaurant," Chapter 3.
9. See Mink, "The Restaurant," 172-74, for how restaurants rehabilitated the hamburger after its reputation was tarnished during the "embalmed meat" scandal of the late 1890s. See Edward F. Keuchel, "Chemicals and Meat: The Embalmed Beef Scandal of the Spanish-American War," *Bulletin of the History of Medicine* 48 (1974): 249-64.
10. Helen Zoe Veit, *Modern Food, Moral Food: Self-Control, Science, and the Rise of Modern American Eating in the Early Twentieth Century* (University of North Carolina Press, 2013), 39. Her discussion of food fads is a must-read.
11. See particularly Adam D. Shprintzen, *The Vegetarian Crusade: The Rise of an American Reform Movement, 1817-1921* (University of North Carolina Press, 2013);

Karen Iacobbo and Michael Iacobbo, *Vegetarian America: A History* (Greenwood, 2004); and Margaret Puskar-Pasewicz, "'For the Good of the Whole': Vegetarianism in Nineteenth-Century America" (PhD diss., Indiana University, 2004).

12. Quoted in Shprintzen, *The Vegetarian Crusade*, 122, 124. For more on the Kellogg family, see his Chapter 5 and Howard Markel, *The Kelloggs: The Battling Brothers of Battle Creek* (Vintage, 2017).
13. Quoted in Daniel T. Gresham, "Reshaping the U.S. Cattle Industry: Producers and Packers, 1914-1933" (PhD diss., Kansas State University, 2019), 142. Gresham has a good discussion of the meatpackers' attempts to fight back.
14. Prohibition, it's worth noting, was entirely and completely the work of a savvy lobbying group. I regard the Anti-Saloon League as the godfather of modern lobbying. See Maureen Ogle, *Ambitious Brew: A History of American Beer* (Blue Willow Books, 2019), Chapter 4.
15. Quoted in Charles F. McGovern, *Sold American: Consumption and Citizenship, 1890-1945* (University of North Carolina Press, 2006), 137; and Mark Hendrickson, *American Labor and Economic Citizenship: New Capitalism From World War I to the Great Depression* (Cambridge University Press, 2013), 30. Hendrickson's book is invaluable for tracking the idea of the "consumer economy" from WWI to the 1930s. The government official was Secretary of Labor James J. Davies (Davis), who held that office for most of the 1920s. For the theoretical underpinnings, I am indebted to Kathleen G. Donohue, *Freedom from Want: American Liberalism and the Idea of the Consumer* (Johns Hopkins University Press, 2003), especially Chapter 2. Also see McGovern, *Sold American*, especially Chapter 4.
16. For the basics see: USDA, ERS, Centennial Committee, *Century of Service: The First 100 Years of the United States Department of Agriculture*, by Gladys L. Baker, Wayne D. Rasmussen, Vivian Wiser, and Jane M. Porter. 1963. Hereafter Baker, *Century of Service*. Also see Daniel Carpenter, *The Forging of Bureaucratic Autonomy: Reputations, Networks, and Policy Innovation in Executive Agencies, 1862-1928* (Princeton University Press, 2020), especially Chapter 6.
17. Mink, "The Restaurant," Chapters 2 and 3; quote 74.
18. "Beef Trust Squeezes Poor for $100,000,000," *New York Herald*, March 28, 1902, 3. The "Beef Trust" label stuck despite the fact that packers sold as much pork as beef. Nor did the packers ever organize a formal trust.
19. "Beef Trust Now Seeks Corner in Egg Supply," *New York Herald*, April 18, 1902, 3.
20. "Prosperity Causes High Meat Prices," *Duluth News Tribune*, March 30, 1902, 5.
21. "Labor Discusses Boycott On Beef By Abstaining From Meat For Thirty Days," *New York Herald*, April 21, 1902, 4; "Riots In Paterson Due to Beef Trust," *New York Herald*, April 24, 1902, 3.
22. Quoted in Scott D. Seligman, *The Great Kosher Meat War of 1902: Immigrant Housewives and the Riots that Shook New York City* (Potomac Books, 2020), 51, 58.
23. See "Scores Arrested," *Boston Daily Globe*, May 16, 1902, 8.
24. Quoted in Mary Yeager, *Competition and Regulation: The Development of Oligopoly in the Meat Packing Industry* (JAI Press, 1981), 184. Roosevelt also commissioned a report on the Trust. See Department of Commerce and Labor, Bureau of Corporations, *Report of the Commissioner of Corporations on the Beef Industry*, March 3, 1905.

25. An essential source is Deborah Fitzgerald, *Every Farm a Factory: The Industrial Ideal in American Agriculture* (Yale University Press, 2003).
26. Quoted in Earl Pomeroy, *The American Far West in the Twentieth Century* (Yale University Press, 2008), 35.
27. See Fitzgerald, *Every Farm A Factory*, Chapters 2 and 3. Also see Carpenter, *Forging of Bureaucratic Autonomy*.
28. For these ideas and others, see Herbert W. Mumford, *Beef Production* (By the author, 1907), especially 143-57; and Neal A. Knapp, "Making Machines of Animals: The International Livestock Exposition, 1900-1920" (PhD diss., Boston University, 2019), 222-26.
29. See Baker, et al, *Century of Service*, 50-51.
30. USDA, *Yearbook of Agriculture*, 1909, "Prices of Meat. Increase of Retail Price over Wholesale. Special Investigation," 15-34; quote 16. Hereafter "Prices of Meat."
31. "Prices of Meat," 17.
32. "Prices of Meat," 17.
33. "Prices of Meat," 22, 30.
34. "Prices of Meat," 18, 21.
35. "Prices of Meat," 23.
36. "Prices of Meat," 31.
37. Coverage was widespread. See, for example, "Mass Meeting Due Soon At Capital In Boycott On Trusts," *Christian Science Monitor*, January 6, 1910, 10; "Will Cut Food Prices," *Washington Post*, January 7, 1910, 2; "An Anti-Food Trust League Is Formed," *Nashville Tennessean*, January 16, 1910, A2; "Boycott On Meat Proposed in Ohio," *Chicago Daily Tribune*, January 18, 1910, 2; "Meat Boycott Is Spreading," *Nashville American (TN)*, January 22, 1910, 2; "Chicago To Join Boycott," *New York Times*, January 22, 1910, 2; "Quit Eating Meat," *Washington Post*, January 23, 1910, 8.
38. "They Blame The Farmer," *Baltimore Sun*, January 22, 1910, 2.
39. US Senate, *Investigation Relative to Wages and Prices of Commodities . . . Hearings Before Committee and Digest of Evidence*, 4 vols. 61st Cong. (1910-11): 2:190. Hereafter *Wages and Prices*. Also see USDA, *Yearbook of Agriculture*, 1904, "Consumers' Fancies," by George K. Holmes, 417-34.
40. *Wages and Prices*, 2:190.
41. *Wages and Prices*, 2:195, 1:87.
42. All quotes are from Karen R. Merrill, *Public Lands and Political Meaning: Ranchers, the Government, and the Property Between Them* (University of California Press, 2002), 21, 22.
43. ANLSA was born in 1897 at "an old fashioned cattle convention" cooked up as a publicity stunt by the Livestock Committee of the Denver Chamber of Commerce to promote the role that cattle played in Denver's economy.

    During that event, a group of cattle producers discussed organizing a national association. In the current "age of intense competition and clashing of different interests," explained one supporter, success came to those who formally associated. "All that is needed is cooperation, organization, leadership, and attention to details, and the world is ours."

    The Denver-inspired NLSA did not last long: in the name of association and cooperation, the founders opened membership to groups and people with conflicting interests, such as meatpackers, stockyards owners, and railroad companies.

In 1901, a large group of disgruntled, western cattle producers decamped, and organized the American Cattle Growers Association (ACGA), leaving the NLSA on life support. In 1905, its few remaining members merged with the ACGA to become ANLSA.

For the quotes see "Money In Cattle," *Rocky Mountain News (CO)*, August 14, 1897, 7; and quoted in Charles E. Ball, *Building the Beef Industry: A Century of Commitment* (The National Cattlemen's Foundation, 1998), 23. Also see "Thirty Thousand Attend the Barbecue," *Rocky Mountain News (CO)*, January 28, 1898, 1; and Lyle Liggett, *"There is a Time and a Place . . .": The History of the American National Cattlemen's Association* (The Newcomen Society in North America, 1972).

44. Quotes in this and the following paragraph are from [James E. Poole], "Has Free Trade In Live Stock and Meats Affected Prices?" *Proceedings of the Seventeenth Annual Convention of the American National Live Stock Association Held at Denver, Colorado January 20, 21, and 22, 1914*, 35-46, quotes 41, 42.

See USDA, *Yearbook of Agriculture* 1913, "The South American Meat Industry," by A.D. Melvin, 347-64; and USDA, *Yearbook of Agriculture*, 1914, "Meat Production in the Argentine and Its Effect Upon the Industry in the United States," by A.D. Melvin and George M. Rommel, 381-90, and "Meat Production in Australia and New Zealand," by E.C. Joss, 421-38. Also see Arthur Wallace Dunn, "Beef From South America and Australia," *American Review of Reviews* 49 (January 1914): 49-54.

45. [Poole], "Free Trade In Live Stock," 45.
46. [Poole], "Free Trade In Live Stock," 45.
47. [E.L. Burke], "Some Features of Concentration," *Proceedings of the Seventeenth Annual Convention of the American National Live Stock Association Held at Denver, Colorado January 20, 21, and 22, 1914*, 87-93.
48. His peers described Jastro (1848-1924) as "the most prominent and influential livestock man in the United States." He managed two immense, investor-owned cattle companies in California and New Mexico. Ball, *Building the Beef Industry*, 46.
49. For a recap of the outbreak, see USDA, *Yearbook of Agriculture*, 1915, 19-30.
50. Initial reactions from the packing side are instructive. See "War and the Meat Trade," *National Provisioner* 51, no. 6 (August 8, 1914): 19; "A Bad Beef Situation," *National Provisioner* 51, no. 7 (August 15, 1914): 19; "Canned Meats for Armies," *National Provisioner* 51, no. 12 (September 19, 1914): 34.
51. A.E. de Ricqles, "Report of the Committee on Stock Yards and Live Stock Exchanges," *Proceedings of the Eighteenth Annual Convention of the American National Live Stock Association Held at San Francisco, California March 24, 25, and 26*, 1915, 107-10.
52. For coverage, see "Livestock's Trade Boom Is Launched," *Rocky Mountain News (CO)*, May 29, 1; "U.S. Agents Give Advice on Markets," *Rocky Mountain News (CO)*, June 1, 1915, 1; "Federal Experts Give Plans to Aid Cattle Industry," *Rocky Mountain News (CO)*, June 2, 1915, 5; "Carlson Names Committee to Co-operate with Experts," *Rocky Mountain News (CO)*, June 5, 1915, 8.
53. "Stockmen Open Fight on 'Trust'" *Rocky Mountain News (CO)*, July 9, 1915, 1, 7. Also see "Federal Experts Give Plans to Aid Cattle Industry," *Rocky Mountain*

News (CO), June 2, 1915, 5; "Stockmen Will Plan Union Here," *Rocky Mountain News (CO)*, July 7, 1915, 1, 9.
54. See "Stockmen Urge Federal Inquiry," *Rocky Mountain News (CO)*, July 29, 10; "Stockmen Open Fight on 'Trust,'" 1, 7.
55. US House, *Proceedings of the Conference Relative to the Marketing of Live Stock Distribution of Meats and Related Matters*, 64th Cong (1915), 53-58; hereafter *Proceedings of the Conference*, 12.
56. "Address of Mr. A.E. de Ricqles, Delivered at the Conference on 'Marketing of Live Stock,' on July 8, 1915, At the Brown Palace Hotel, Denver, Colo." in *Proceedings of the Conference*, 53-58. de Ricqles made the pitch several times over the months. Here I conflate his many presentations.
57. *Proceedings of the Conference*, 15, 16.
58. "Address of Mr. A.E. de Ricqles," 53-58.
59. *Proceedings of the Conference*, 14, 15.
60. *Proceedings of the Conference*, 127.
61. *Proceedings of the Conference*, 39.
62. *Proceedings of the Conference*, 132.
63. *Proceedings of the Conference*, 81.
64. "Demands Probe Into 'Trust' of Chicago Packers," *Chicago Daily Tribune*, February 2, 1916, 9. The primary record of events is US House, Committee on the Judiciary, *Investigation of Beef Industries. Hearings Before the Committee on the Judiciary*, 2 parts. 64th Cong. (1916). Hereafter *Investigation of Beef Industries*.

Borland's move took the ANLSA by surprise. After the fact, he explained that his action was prompted by the Missouri Cattle, Swine, and Sheep Feeders' Association, which, following the ANLSA's lead, had voted to demand a federal investigation. His office was then bombarded by similar requests from livestock organizations around the country.

Borland's choice of investigative agency was deliberate: unlike most federal departments and agencies, the FTC possessed subpoena power and the necessary staff to undertake such a study. The hearings began with a heated discussion of the FTC's legal authority to undertake such a project.

More to the point, stockmen were not interested in another Justice Department antitrust investigation. Having been there, done that, they had good reason to assume such an effort would deliver zero results.
65. *Investigation of Beef Industries*, 426.
66. *Investigation of Beef Industries*, 474, 475.
67. *Investigation of Beef Industries*, 500.
68. *Investigation of Beef Industries*, 432.
69. See US House, "Federal Trade Commission to Investigate Food Prices," 64th Cong. (1917); "To Probe Living Cost," *Baltimore Sun*, February 11, 1917, 2.

CHAPTER 5

1. The best account of this event is Dana Frank, "Housewives, Socialists, and the Politics of Food: The 1917 New York Cost-of-Living Protests," *Feminist Studies* 11, no. 2 (Summer 1985): 255-85.
2. "Women Cry 'We Are Starving,'" *Boston Daily Globe*, February 21, 1917, 1, 6.

3. Quoted in Frank, "Housewives," 262; "'Feed America First' Slogan of Food Embargo Organization at Work In St. Louis," *New York Times*, February 23, 1917, 3.
4. Quoted in David B. Danbom, *The Resisted Revolution: Urban America and the Industrialization of Agriculture, 1900-1930* (Iowa State University Press, 1979), 102.
5. "Urge Aid for Starving," *Washington Post*, February 23, 1917, 3.
6. "Contrast Food Riots and Revels As Senate Discusses Living Cost; French Revolution is Recalled," *Washington Post*, February 22, 1917, 2. Here a bit of historical irony is worth noting: while Americans rioted over the high cost of potatoes, Russians were replacing their monarchy with Leninist communism. The 1917 Russian Revolution was ignited in part by the high price of cabbage.
7. Quoted in William Frieburger, "War Prosperity and Hunger: The New York Food Riots of 1917." *Labor History* 25, no. 2 (Spring 1984): 217-39, quote 218.
8. The bill was, inevitably, a masterpiece of accommodation and compromise. Most notably, the powerful prohibition movement, well represented in House and Senate, only signed on after Wilson agreed to deny grain to distillers, and to impose a low alcohol content on beer.
9. "Mr. Hoover Appears Before Senate Agriculture Committee — His Statement." *Food Administration Bulletin* No. 1, 16-27.
10. Quoted in George H. Nash, *The Life of Herbert Hoover: Master of Emergencies, 1917-1918* (W.W. Norton & Company, 1996), 22. Hereafter *Master of Emergencies*.
11. Quoted in Nash, *Master of Emergencies*, 154.
12. Quoted in Nash, *Master of Emergencies*, 31.
13. USDA, US Food Administration Women's Committee, Council of National Defense, "Food and the War," by Herbert Hoover, in *The Day's Food in War and Peace* [1918], 11. This publication served as a textbook for Americans learning to restrict their diets without losing flavor or nutritive value.
14. Quoted in Nash, *Master of Emergencies*, 204.
15. Quoted in Nash, *Master of Emergencies*, 315. Also see Robert M. Aduddell and Louis P. Cain, "Public Policy Toward 'The Greatest Trust in the World,'" *Business History Review* 55, no. 2 (Summer 1981): 217-42, especially 233.
16. Quoted in *Master of Emergencies*, 195.
17. See Rudolf Alexander Clemen, *The American Meat and Livestock Industry* (The Ronald Press, 1923), 473-78, 646-59. Clemen was an economist and an editor at *National Provisioner*, the meatpackers' trade mouthpiece. Much of his research was original, but the early sections of the book are taken almost entirely from USDA, Agricultural History Series. No. 5, *A History of Livestock Raising in the United States, 1608-1860*, by James Westfall Thompson, 1942; rprt Scholarly Resources, 1973. Thompson wrote that work in 1917 and 1918, then laid the manuscript aside. The USDA published it in 1942, shortly after Thompson died. Presumably the Department gave Clemen permission to use the material.
18. Quoted in Nash, *Master of Emergencies, 316*.
19. Quoted in Nash, *Master of Emergencies*, 171-72.
20. Quoted in Nash, *Master of Emergencies*, 179.
21. Quoted in Nash, *Master of Emergencies*, 184, 188.
22. Quoted in Nash, *Master of Emergencies*, 300, 301.
23. Quoted in Nash, *Master of Emergencies*, 174, 175.
24. Quoted in Nash, *Master of Emergencies*, 287.

25. A detailed description of the misery is *Master of Emergencies*, Chapter 8. For examples, see "Hoover Assumes Control of Prices," *New York Times*, November 4, 1917, 17; "D.C. Food Prices to Be Set Today," *Washington Post*, January 3, 1918, 7; "Charge Anarchists Plotted Food Riots," *New York Times*, November 29, 1917, 3; "Nation Faces Hunger Peril In 12 Months,'" *Chicago Daily Tribune*, February 15, 1918, 5.
26. US Senate, Committee on Agriculture and Forestry, *Increased Production of Grain and Meat Products: Hearings Before the Committee on Agriculture and Forestry*, 7 parts. 65th Cong. (1918). Hereafter *Increased Production of Grain and Meat Products*.
27. I ran across many mentions of Mr. A. Sykes during my research, and he was always that: A. Sykes. When I tracked down his full name, I understood why. A was an improvement over Arcellus Subowlus Sykes. Yes, these are the kinds of weird rabbit holes into which scholars often descend.
28. *Increased Production of Grain and Meat Products*, 1:3-19.
29. *Increased Production of Grain and Meat Products*, 1:11.
30. *Increased Production of Grain and Meat Products*, 1:20.
31. *Increased Production of Grain and Meat Products*, 1:29.
32. *Increased Production of Grain and Meat Products*, 1:52, 57.
33. *Increased Production of Grain and Meat Products*, 5:284.
34. *Increased Production of Grain and Meat Products*, 5:287.
35. *Increased Production of Grain and Meat Products*, 5:287.
36. *Increased Production of Grain and Meat Products*, 6:409.
37. *Increased Production of Grain and Meat Products*, 5:352.
38. The exchange is in *Increased Production of Grain and Meat Products*, 5:352, 354, 362.
39. Quoted in Nash, *Master of Emergencies*, 296.
40. Quoted in Nash, *Master of Emergencies*, 296. For a detailed look at Hoover's mind in action, Nash's Chapter 10.
41. Quoted in Nash, *Master of Emergencies*, 297.
42. Quoted in Nash, *Master of Emergencies*, 297.
43. Quoted in Nash, *Master of Emergencies*, 297.

CHAPTER 6

1. "How 'Meat for Health Week' Was Put Over," *National Provisioner* 69, no. 2 (July 14, 1923): 23.
2. For this episode, see "Advocate's Fight for Frankfurter Progressing," *Butchers' Advocate and Market Journal* 82, no. 10 (December 15, 1926): 9; "New York School Board Attacks Frankfurters," *Butchers' Advocate and Market Journal* 82, no. 9 (December 8, 1926): 11. Meat people loathed the phrase "hot dog." This particular sausage was a frankfurter.
3. B.F. McCarthy, "Frankfurters as Wholesome Food," *Butchers' Advocate and Market Journal* 82, no. 16 (January 26, 1927): 9.
4. Quoted in Michael Ackerman, "Interpreting the Newer Knowledge of Nutrition: Science, Interests, and Values in the Making of Dietary Advice in the United States, 1915–1965" (PhD diss., University of Virginia, 2005), 59-60; he discusses vitamins in detail on 52-69; hereafter Ackerman, "Newer Knowledge."

   Also see Rima D. Apple, *Vitamania: Vitamins in American Culture* (Rutgers

University Press, 1996); Kimberly Killion, "The Agricultural Chemist at the Table: Land Grant Colleges, Experiment Stations, and the Birth of Nutrition Science in the United States" (PhD diss., University of California-Berkeley, 2022), Chapter 3; Harvey Levenstein, *Revolution at the Table: The Transformation of the American Diet* (University of California Press, 2003), Chapter 12; Alan L. Olmstead and Paul W. Rhode, *Creating Abundance: Biological Innovation and American Agricultural Development* (Cambridge University Press, 2008), 273-74. More generally, see Helen Zoe Veit, *Modern Food, Moral Food: Self-Control, Science, and the Rise of Modern American Eating in the Early Twentieth Century* (University of North Carolina Press, 2013).

5. For "Newer Nutrition," see Levenstein, *Revolution at the Table*, Chapter 12; and Ackerman, "Newer Knowledge."
6. W.A. Freehoff, "Feed Your Body Vitamines," *Illustrated World* 31 (June 1919): 499.
7. The essential text is Helen Tangires, *Movable Markets: Food Wholesaling in the Twentieth-Century City* (Johns Hopkins University Press, 2019).
8. The quoted proportions are from E.A. Duddy, "Distribution of Perishable Commodities in the Chicago Metropolitan Area," *University Journal of Business* 4, no. 2 (April 1926): 151-81, quote 163. Duddy based his calculations on figures in USDA, BAE in cooperation with New York Port Authority, New York City, *Preliminary Report on Terminal Conditions At the Port of New York As They Affect the Cost of Marketing Fruits and Vegetables*, prepared by Walter P. Hedden, March 1923.
9. For the study of and typical comments about inexperienced grocers, see A.H. Fenske, "'Too Many Retailers,'" *National Provisioner* 69, no. 18 (November 2, 1923): 52; Day Monroe and Lenore Monroe Stratton, *Food Buying and Our Markets* (1925; repr., M. Barrows & Company, 1929).
10. For chain stores, see Tracey Deutsch, *Building a Housewife's Paradise: Gender, Politics, and American Grocery Stores in the Twentieth Century* (University of North Carolina Press, 2010); Gene Arlin German, "The Dynamics of Food Retailing, 1900–1975" (PhD diss., Cornell University, 1978); Marc Levinson, *The Great A&P and the Struggle for Small Business in America* (Hill and Wang, 2011); Susan Strasser, *Satisfaction Guaranteed: The Making of the American Mass Market* (Pantheon Books, 1989); Richard S. Tedlow, *New and Improved: The Story of Mass Marketing in America* (Basic Books, 1990); Lisa C. Tolbert, *Beyond Piggly Wiggly: Inventing the American Self-Service Store* (University of Georgia Press, 2023); William I. Walsh, *The Rise and Decline of the Great Atlantic and Pacific Tea Company* (Lyle Stuart, 1986).
11. See Deutsch, *Building a Housewife's Paradise.*

   State and federal officials swooned, especially during the 1930s when some states imposed sales taxes. The chains provided an efficient way to collect those revenues, far easier than collecting from tens of thousands of shop owners, many of whom rarely kept any records (other than what customers owed them).

   The USDA, rest assured, embraced the chains like long-lost children. The losers, Shane Hamilton notes, were distributors, aka middlemen. Chains purchased direct from manufacturers; no middleman needed. See his *Supermarket USA: Food and Power In the Cold War Farms Race* (Yale University Press, 2019.)
12. Howard C. Greer, "Business Mortality Among Retail Meat Stores in Chicago Between 1920 and 1933," *Journal of Business of the University of Chicago* 9, no. 3 (July 1936): 208, 209.

13. USDA, *Methods and Practices of Retailing Meat*, by W.C. Davis, Bulletin No. 1441, November 1926: 14, 17, 22. Also see "Beef Production in U.S. Undergoes Marked Changes," *Meat and Live Stock Digest* 3, no. 5 (December 1922): 4.
14. "Merchandizing Packaged Meats Without Freezing," *National Provisioner* 82, no. 16 (April 19, 1930): 21.
15. Howard C. Pierce, "Looking Forward in Marketing Poultry and Eggs," *United States Egg and Poultry Magazine* 37, no. 3 (March 1931): 67. Pierce made his remarks to a gathering of poultry producers, but his point applied to the chain's policy for all meats.
16. Gove Hambidge, "Meats in Packages," *Ladies' Home Journal* 46 (December 1929): 89.
17. [John H. Cover], *Consumer Attitude Toward Packaging of Meats* (National Provisioner, 1930), 43.
18. The six-volume report offers a remarkable look at how these interstate packers built their collective empire. See US, FTC, *Food Investigation: Report of the Federal Trade Commission on the Meat-Packing Industry*, 6 vols., 1919. For the socialist leanings of FTC staff members, see the memorandum reprinted as Appendix II in David Gordon, "The Beef Trust: Antitrust Policy and the Meat Packing Industry, 1902-1922" (PhD diss., Claremont Graduate School, 1983), 339-40; and Linda J. Bradley and Barbara D. Merino, "Stuart Chase: A Radical CPA and the Meat Packing Investigation, 1917-1918," *Business and Economic History* 23, no. 1 (Fall 1994): 190-200.
19. Robert M. Aduddell and Louis P. Cain argue that many of the FTC's claims collapse under scrutiny. See "Public Policy Toward 'The Greatest Trust in the World,'" *Business History Review* 55, no. 2 (Summer 1981): 217–42.

    For another detailed rebuttal, see Rudolf Alexander Clemen, *The American Livestock and Meat Industry* (The Ronald Press, 1923), Chapter 34.

    See also "Change of Policy By Meat Packers," *Christian Science Monitor*, November 30, 1918, 5; "Packers Outline A New Campaign," *Christian Science Monitor*, December 10, 1918; Roland Marchand, *Creating the Corporate Soul: The Rise of Public Relations and Corporate Imagery in American Big Business* (University of California Press, 1998), 91-97.
20. Quoted in Aduddell and Cain, "Public Policy," 233.
21. See US House, Interstate and Foreign Commerce Committee, *Government Control of Meat-Packing*, 5 parts. 65th Cong. (1918-19); US Senate, Committee on Agriculture and Forestry, *Government Control of the Meat-Packing Industry*. 2 parts. 65th Cong. (1919).
22. "Packer and Producer Must Get Together," *National Provisioner* 60, no. 9 (March 1, 1919):16, 37. Thomas E. Wilson (1868-1958) was a pivotal figure during these years of transition. He'd long been involved in the packing business, initially as an executive at Morris & Company. In 1915, he was appointed president of Wilson & Company, a re-capitalized variant of what had been Sulzberger & Sons. He quickly emerged as meatpacking's leading spokesman, useful because his name was neither Swift nor Armour. Wilson also served as president of the American Meat Packers Association and its successor, the Institute of American Meat Packers. (As part of an unrelated business venture, in the 1920s, Wilson launched Wilson Sporting Goods.)

23. The phrase is courtesy of the excellent James H. Shideler, *Farm Crisis 1919–1923* (University of California Press, 1957). Also see Murray R. Benedict, *Farm Policies of the United States 1790-1950: A Study of Their Origins and Development* (Twentieth Century Fund, 1953), Chapter 9; and Giovanni Federico, "Not Guilty? Agriculture in the 1920s and the Great Depression," *Journal of Economic History* 65, no. 4 (December 2005): 949-76.

24. "Calls for Curb on Meat Prices," *New York Times*, July 5, 1919, 13; "Our Pork Exports Octupled Since 1914," *New York Times*, January 12, 1920, 19.

25. See "Kendrick Opposes Packing Committee," *Rocky Mountain News (CO)*, April 1, 1919, 7; "Packers Confer With Producers," *Christian Science Monitor*, May 17, 1919, 4; "Economy of Meat Urged By Packers," *Rocky Mountain News (CO)*, May 17, 1919, 2; "Packers and Producers Get Together," *National Provisioner* 60, no. 21 (May 24, 1919): 21, 42; "Live Stock Producers' Committee," *Wallace's Farmer* May 23, 1919, 1129.

26. Quoted in Bradley and Merino, "Stuart Chase," 197. For tales well told, see Beverly Gage, *The Day Wall Street Exploded: A Story of America In Its First Age of Terror* (Oxford University Press, 2009); and Adam Hochschild, *American Midnight: The Great War, a Violent Peace, and Democracy's Forgotten Crisis* (Mariner Books, 2022).

27. The five packers were Armour, Cudahy, Morris, Swift, and Wilson. See Clemen, *American Livestock and Meat Industry*, Chapter 35; Robert M. Aduddell and Louis Cain, "The Consent Decree in the Meatpacking Industry, 1920–1956," *Business History Review* 55, no. 3 (Autumn 1981): 359–78; G.O. Virtue, "The Meat-Packing Investigation," *Quarterly Journal of Economics* 34, no. 4 (August 1920): 626-85; N.S.B. Gras and Henrietta M. Larson, *Casebook in American Business History* (F.S. Crofts & Co., 1939), 623-44.

28. Quoted in Shideler, *Farm Crisis*, 26.

29. For this early phase of the bureau's history, see especially Roy V. Scott, *The Reluctant Farmer: The Rise of Agricultural Extension to 1914* (University of Illinois Press, 1970); and Nancy K. Berlage, *Farmers Helping Farmers: The Rise of the Farm and Home Bureaus, 1914-1935* (Louisiana State University Press, 2016), Chapter 1.

30. "Farmers Must Organize to Protect Their Interests,"*Prairie Farmer* 90, no. 25 (December 14, 1918), 6; "Iowa Farmers in New Organization," *Des Moines Register*, December 1, 1918, M-9; "Farm Bureaux Open Drive," *Christian Science Monitor*, December 12, 1918, 5; "The Farm Bureau and the Farmers' Institute," *Prairie Farmer* 90, no. 25 (December 28, 1918), 3; "To Organize Farmers of Country," *National Provisioner* 61, no. 20 (November 15, 1919): 19; "Farm Bureau Federation is Formed," *National Provisioner* 61, no. 21 (November 22, 1919):18; "Mobilizing the Farm Bureaus," *Wallaces' Farmer*, January 3, 1919, 4; "Farmers to Work With Big Business," *Christian Science Monitor*, March 12, 1920, 14.

31. "The American Farm Bureau Federation," *The Producer* 1, no. 7 (December 1919): 16-17.

32. "The American Farm Bureau Federation," 16-17; "Farmers to Work with Big Business," 14; *National Provisioner* (June 12, 1920): 40; "Producer and Packer," *National Provisioner* 62, no. 26 (June 26, 1920): 21.

33. "Farm Production A Problem," *Christian Science Monitor*, August 5, 1920, 4; "Food Shortage Menace," *New York Times*, August 8, 1920, 76.

34. Quoted in Shideler, *Farm Crisis*, 52.

35. Quoted in Shideler, *Farm Crisis*, 54.

36. See "Soviet Buds to Bloom In West Unless U.S. Aids," *Chicago Daily Tribune*, December 3, 1920, 6.
37. Quoted in Shideler, *Farm Crisis*, 152, 153.
38. For the meetings, see Benedict, *Farm Policies*, 181-83.
39. See "Reed Hits Packer Control Measure," *Los Angeles Times*, June 16, 1921, I3.
40. Shideler, *Farm Crisis*, 229, 230.
41. Shideler, *Farm Crisis*, 203; conference details are on 201-02.
42. Quoted in Benedict, *Farm Policies*, 209.
43. See Shidler, *Farm Crisis*, 67.
44. This is a grossly simplified description of the plan, which was so complicated that almost no one understood it or any other plan suggested at the time. I certainly don't.

    See Benedict, *Farm Policies*, Chapter 10; Elisabeth S. Clemens, *The People's Lobby: Organizational Innovation and the Rise of Interest Group Politics in the United States, 1890-1925* (University of Chicago Press, 1997), Chapters 6 and 8; John Mark Hansen, *Gaining Access: Congress and the Farm Lobby, 1919-1981* (University of Chicago Press, 1991), Chapter 2; R. Douglas Hurt, *Problems of Plenty: The American Farmer in the Twentieth Century* (Ivan R. Dee, 2002), Chapter 2; Shideler, *Farm Crisis*, Chapters 6 and 7; Bill Winders, *The Politics of Food Supply: U.S. Agricultural Policy in the World Economy* (Yale University Press, 2009), Chapter 2.
45. A useful look at the long history of "farm subsidies" is Sarah Ludington, "U.S. Farm and Food Subsidies," in *Food Fights: How History Matters to Contemporary Food Debates*, ed. Charles C. Ludington and Matthew Morse Booker (University of North Carolina Press, 2019), 162-85.
46. Deborah Fitzgerald, *Every Farm a Factory: The Industrial Ideal in American Agriculture* (Yale University Press, 2003), 28. Fitzgerald's book is the bible on the subject. What you need to know is in its pages.
47. W.O. Atwater, "The Food-Supply of the Future," *Century* 43, no. 1 (November 1891): 111.
48. Ernest Hamlin Abbott, "Editorial Correspondence from Washington," *The Outlook*, February 8, 1922, 211.
49. Frank App, "The Industrialization of Agriculture," *Annals of the American Academy of Political and Social Science* 142, no. 231 (March 1929): 232. For more on resistance see Fitzgerald, *Every Farm a Factory*, 122-26.

CHAPTER 7

1. John H. Robinson, "Survey of the Present Status of Poultry Culture in America," *Reliable Poultry Journal* 33, no. 10 (December 1926): 621. My account of broiler history is based primarily on poultry and agriculture trade journals, newspapers, and government documents.

    The best history is James Russell Pryor, "Work, Nature, and the American Dinner Plate: Making Chicken in the Twentieth-Century United States" (PhD diss., Carnegie Mellon University), 2013; hereafter Pryor, "Making Chicken."

    Also: Margaret E. Derry, *Art and Science in Breeding: Creating Better Chickens* (University of Toronto Press, 2012); Monica R. Gisolfi, *The Takeover: Chicken Farming and the Roots of American Agribusiness* (University of Georgia Press, 2017); J. Frank

Gordy, "Broilers," in *American Poultry History 1823-1974: An Anthology Overview of 150 Years*, ed. Oscar August Hanke (American Poultry Historical Society, Inc., 1974), 370-432; Roger Horowitz, *Putting Meat On the American Table: Taste, Technology, Transformation* (Johns Hopkins University Press, 2006), Chapter 5; Ashton Wynette Merck, "The Fox Guarding the Henhouse: Coregulation and Consumer Protection in Food Safety, 1946-2002" (PhD diss., Duke University, 2020); Gordon Sawyer, *The Agribusiness Poultry Industry: A History of Its Development* (Exposition Press, 1971).

2. USDA, "Marketing Poultry," *Farmers' Bulletin*, no. 1377 (1924), 24.
3. See Derry, *Art and Science in Breeding*, Chapter 5.
4. A.F. Hunter, "Why Do We Need Yards?" *American Poultry Advocate* 15 (January 1907): 65-67.
5. For the colony systems see John H. Robinson, *Principles and Practice of Poultry Culture* (Ginn and Company, 1912), 35-36.
6. George F. Paul, "Hatching Chickens by Wholesale," *Technical World* 19 (April 1913): 248-49. This general-audience magazine was published by the Armour Institute of Technology. Philip Armour had a long history of encouraging education in general and technical education in particular.
7. Frank Parker Stockbridge, "In A Chicken Factory," *Technical World* 18, no. 2 (October 1912): 217-20; quote 217.
8. [M.K. Boyer], "'Philadelphia' Poultry," *New York Produce Review and American Creamery* 18 (February 19, 1913): 796. For a detailed look at the ins and outs of making chicken see P.T. Woods, "Producing High Quality Chicken Meat," *Reliable Poultry Journal* 7, no. 10 (December 1910): 988-89, 1046-47.
9. For Petaluma, see Phillip R. Naftaly, "Jewish Chicken Farmers in the Egg Basket of the World: The Creation of Cultural Identity in Petaluma, California" (PhD diss., New School for Social Research, 1999); Kyle Mitchell Livie, "Wide Open Spaces: Rural Communities and the Making of Metropolitan California, 1870-1940," PhD diss., University of California-Los Angeles, 2007).
10. See, for example, Edward Brown, *Report on the Poultry Industry in America* (National Poultry Organisation Society, 1906); and "Producing Table Poultry," *New York Produce Review and American Creamery* 33, no. 9 (December 20, 1911): 407-08. A useful look at the state of commercial poultry production is USDA, *Yearbook of Agriculture*, 1912, "The Handling of Dressed Poultry A Thousand Miles from the Market," by M.E. Pennington, 285-92.
11. Franklin Morton, "Feeding Poultry by Machinery," *Technical World* 7, no. 6 (February 1907): 643. A useful summary of other meatpackers' failed forays into poultry is "Chicken Meat in the Diet," *National Provisioner* 30, no. 26 (June 25, 1904): 22.
12. John H. Robinson, *Broilers and Roasters: The Specialties of the Market Poultrymen* (Farm-Poultry Publishing Co., 1905), 6.
13. "Chicken Meat in the Diet," 22. An analyst at the USDA argued that broilers resisted mass production because millions of midwestern farmers were capable of mass production all on their own. Most farmers kept chickens because they required "practically no expense and all of the product is profit." An "ordinary" farm could readily manage flocks of 30-75. Multiply that by millions of farms and the "magnitude of this form of the industry is so great that it interferes

materially with the special poultry farm." See USDA, *Yearbook of Agriculture*, 1908, "Types of Farming in the United States," by W.J. Spillman, 351-366.
14. "Chicken Meat in the Diet," 22.
15. A good look at chickens and genetics is Derry, *Art and Science*, Chapter 3. Also see Barbara Ann Kimmelman, "A Progressive Era Discipline: Genetics at American Agricultural Colleges and Experiment Stations, 1900-1920," (PhD diss., University of Pennsylvania, 1987).
16. William Boyd, "Making Meat: Science, Technology, and American Poultry Production," *Technology and Culture* 42, no. 4 (October 2001): 631-64; and Derry, *Art and Science*, Chapter 6. An exceptional survey of livestock improvement is Alan L. Olmstead and Paul W. Rhode, *Creating Abundance: Biological Innovation and American Agricultural Development* (Cambridge University Press, 2008), Chapters 9 and 10. Also see, for example, F.B. Hutt, "Research with a Hen," *Science* n.s. 78, no. 2029 (November 17, 1933): 449–52.
17. D.C. Kennard, "The Trend Toward Confinement in Poultry Management," *Poultry Science* 8 (October-November 1928): 23. Also see D.C. Kennard and R.M. Betheke, "Keeping Chickens in Confinement," *Report of Proceedings of the 4th World's Poultry Congress* (H.M. Stationer's Office, 1931): 351-57.
18. A useful analysis of the industry's growth is Hermon I. Miller, "Government," in Oscar August Hanke, ed., *American Poultry History 1823-1974: An Anthology Overview of 150 Years* (American Poultry Historical Society, Inc., 1974), 538-66. Miller was director of the Poultry Division of the USDA's Agricultural Marketing Service.
19. See Miller, "Government."
20. In the 1920s and 1930s, trucking and truckers significantly altered the logistics of food distribution. A must-read is Shane Hamilton, *Trucking Country: The Road to America's Wal-Mart Economy* (Princeton University Press, 2008). For cold storage see, for example, John H. Robinson, "The Live Poultry Situation and What is Coming Out of It," *Reliable Poultry Journal* 33, no. 1 (March 1926): 12-13, 76, 78.

    Also useful are four papers in *Report of the Proceedings of the World's Poultry Congress* (n.p., 1927):

    L.B. Kilbourne, "Commercial Marketing of Poultry Products in the United States By Private Interests," 390-92; Charles J. Eldredge, "The Organization of and Operation of Mercantile Exchanges by the Egg and Poultry Trade in the United States," 392-95; Ralph C. Stokell, "Conservation of Food Products in Public Cold Storage Warehouses in the United States," 395-97; Wm. H. Lapp, "Transport of Live Poultry for Market in the United States," 441-43.
21. Statistics are from Gordon Sawyer, *The Agribusiness Poultry Industry: A History of Its Development* (Exposition Press, 1971), 37.
22. See Horowitz, *Putting Meat on the Table*, 109-10, and Pryor, "Making Chicken," 170-77.
23. Two useful introductions to the topic are Gisolfi, *The Takeover*, Chapter 1; and R. Douglas Hurt, *Problems of Plenty: The American Farmer in the Twentieth Century* (Ivan R. Dee, 2002), especially Chapters 2 and 3.
24. Martin V. Calvin, "Agricultural Side Lines in Cotton States," *Cobb County Times (GA)*, March 29, 1921, 1, 5.
25. Arthur Gannon, "Georgia's Broiler Industry," *Georgia Review* 6, no. 3 (October 1952): 306-16, quote 307; "Swift and Company May Erect $50000 Poultry

Killing Plant," *Macon Telegraph (GA)*, June 11, 1922, 4. Also see Gisolfi, *The Takeover*, as well as Pryor, "Making Chicken."
26. "Poultry Raising Rapidly Growing," *Augusta Chronicle (GA)*, March 6, 1924, A7. For the quotes: "Country Industry in Clay County Booms," *Columbus Daily Enquirer (GA)*, March 4, 1922, 2; *Cobb County Times (GA)*, February 7, 1924, 2.
27. Quoted in Hurt, *Problems of Plenty*, 70; see Chapter 3. Millions of words have been written, but Hurt's work is a superb introduction aimed at a general audience.

   Cattle were not included in the original list of commodities, but quickly earned what amounted to special dispensation: in late 1933, the Agriculture Adjustment Administration was given permission to buy 15 million pounds of beef each month, which the Federal Emergency Relief Administration (FERA) distributed to those in need.

   The move was as much political as it was economic: meatpackers and cattle producers both got a cut of the action, and here was clear evidence that when it came to policy and largesse, the USDA, cattle producers, and meatpackers were more or less joined at the hip. See Hurt, *Problems of Plenty*, 77-78.
28. Quoted in Hurt, *Problems of Plenty*, 70.
29. "An Interview with Jesse Jewell," *Broiler Industry* 22, no. 3 (March 1959): 8. I tracked Jewell's life and work primarily through poultry and agriculture trade magazines, but also see Sawyer, *Agribusiness Poultry Industry*, 86–89; Gordy, "Broilers," 382-83; and Homer Myers, *Pass the Chicken Please: The Life and Times of Jesse Jewell* (n.p., 2008).
30. For a concise summary, see Gisolfi, *The Takeover*, 19. Electrification projects were one of the great success stories of President Roosevelt's New Deal, thanks to the Rural Electrification Administration and the Tennessee Valley Authority; the latter organized the construction of dams and hydroelectric plants across a broad swath of the southeastern United States. A recent history is Sandeep Vaheesan, *Democracy In Power: A History of Electrification in the United States* (University of Chicago Press, 2024).
31. Quoted in Gisolfi, *The Takeover*, 21.
32. For a deep dive into "vertical integration" in the broiler industry after the war, see US House, Select Committee on Small Business, *Problems in the Poultry Industry*, 3 vols, 85th Cong. (1957): 2:145-53; quote 2:146.
33. For wartime stipulations, see Gisolfi, *The Takeover*, Chapter 2; and Kimberly R. Sebold, "The Delmarva Broiler Industry and World War II: A Case in Wartime Economy," *Delaware History* 25, no. 3 (Spring/Summer 1993): 200-214.
34. Quoted in Gisifoli, *The Takeover*, 31.
35. Quoted in Gisolfi, *The Takeover*, 27, 34.
36. Statistic from Gisolfi, *The Takeover*, 25; for the war prisoners, see Sebold, "Delmarva Broiler Industry," 209.
37. "The Steer Hangs High," *Time*, February 8, 1943, 17.
38. "The Steer Hangs High," 17.
39. "The Steer Hangs High," 17. $1.95 in 1943 is approximately $36 now.
40. Statistics from Gilbert C. Fite, *American Farmers: The New Minority* (Indiana University Press, 1981), 87. On wartime productivity, see Wayne D. Rasmussen, "The Impact of Technological Change on American Agriculture, 1862-1962," *Journal of Economic History* 22, no. 4 (December 1962): 578-91.

41. "The Glut Will Not Last," *Time*, May 1, 1944.
42. Here I used *Historical Statistics of the United States: Colonial Times to 1970* (Fairfield Publishers [1965]), Series G 552-584, 186.
43. The phrase is from Lizabeth Cohen's must-read, *A Consumers' Republic: The Politics of Mass Consumption in Post-war America* (Vintage Books, 2003). Two other useful works are Gary Cross, *An All-Consuming Century: Why Commercialism Won in Modern America* (Columbia University Press, 2000); and Meg Jacobs, *Pocketbook Politics: Economic Citizenship in Twentieth-Century America* (Princeton University Press, 2005).

CHAPTER 8

1. "Why Pork Is Losing Popularity," *Farm Journal* 80 (December 1956): 123.
2. John A. McWethy, "Canned Meat: Steak, Pigs' Feet and Corned Beef Hash Rush in Tins to the Table," *Wall Street Journal*, April 13, 1953, 8.
3. McWethy, "Canned Meat," 8.
4. Shane Hamilton argues that the shift to factory farming necessitated the supermarket: with high-tech farmers producing tons of goods, retail had to change to accommodate it. Shane Hamilton, *Supermarket USA: Food and Power In the Cold War Farms Race* (Yale University Press, 2019), especially Chapter 1.
5. See Roger Horowitz, *Putting Meat on the American Table: Taste, Technology, Transformation* (Johns Hopkins University Press, 2006), 137-45.
6. Statistics are from "The Franchise Restaurant Boom . . . Big New Market for Beef," *Farm Journal* 93 (October 1969): B10–B11, B13. For McDonald's, see J. Anthony Lukas, "As American as a McDonald's Hamburger on the Fourth of July," *New York Times Magazine*, July 4, 1971, 22. The Mr. Steak example is from "Franchise Restaurant Boom."
7. "How Much Hunger," *Time*, April 29, 1946; Hoover quoted in Allen J. Matusow, *Farm Policies and Politics in the Truman Years* (Harvard University Press, 1967), 5.
8. Quoted in Nick Cullather, "The Foreign Policy of the Calorie," *American Historical Review* 112, no. 2 (April 2007): 363. For a terrific assessment of the long march toward food-based diplomacy, see Chapters 1 and 2 of Cullather's *The Hungry World: America's Cold War Battle Against Poverty in Asia* (Harvard University Press, 2010).
9. The text is at presidency.ucsb.edu
10. This was when the USDA lost its place as and at the right hand of governance. Thanks to the Cold War and the nation's new role as a "superpower," no one in power (or policy) much cared how food got made as long as it got made in large quantities. The department remained a vital government agency, but having built modern agriculture, having demonstrated in two wars that it had created and managed a flexible system of large-scale food production, in some sense its services were no longer needed. After World War II, all that mattered was that Agriculture keep a firm hand on its helm, the better to accommodate directives from State, Pentagon, and White House.
11. The best recent dissection of this moment in agriculture is Hamilton, *Supermarket USA*, especially Chapters 1 and 5.

12. Lauren Soth, "America's No. 1 Farm Problem," *Successful Farming* 49, no. 3 (March 1951): 47, 63.
13. Quoted in Mary Elizabeth Barham, "Sustainable Agriculture in the United States and France: A Polanyian Perspective" (PhD diss., Cornell University, 1999), 153, 154. Years later, the scientist concluded that his arrogance was misplaced. In the 1970s, he began conducting research on sustainable agriculture. By the late 1990s, he occupied an endowed university chair in the subject.

    Also see: Matthew T. Huber, *Lifeblood: Oil, Freedom, and the Forces of Capital* (University of Minnesota Press, 2013); Christopher F. Jones, *Routes of Power: Energy and Modern America* (Harvard University Press, 2014); Andrew Watson, "'The Single Most Important Factor': Fossil Fuel Energy, Groundwater, and Irrigation on the High Plains, 1955-1985," *Agricultural History*, 94, no. 4 (Fall 2020): 629-63; Caleb Wellem, *Energizing Neoliberalism: The 1970s Energy Crisis and the Making of Modern America* (Johns Hopkins University Press, 2023).
14. A useful essay that focuses on how the Republican-versus-Democratic policy debate played out in the 1960s is Sarah T. Phillips, "The Price of Plenty: Getting Farm Policy Right in the 1960s," *Journal of American History* 109, no. 3 (December 2022): 596-620. I found this article about three days after I settled on a title for the book. I was searching for works titled *The Price of Plenty*, and came up with Phillips's article, which is first rate, as is her book *This Land, This Nation: Conservation, Rural America, and the New Deal* (Cambridge University Press, 2007).
15. Noble Clark, "The Responsibility of Research Workers in Livestock Production in the War Program," *Journal of Animal Science* 2 (1943): 85.
16. Quoted in Nicolas Rasmussen, "Plant Hormones in War and Peace: Science, Industry, and Government in the Development of Herbicides in 1940s America," *Isis* 92, no. 2 (June 2001): 295.
17. "Some Results of Colchicine Injections," *Science* 92 (July 26, 1940): 80. Also see William L. Laurence, "Finds Twin Stars Change in Circling," *New York Times*, December 31, 1940, 17; and "Drug Speeds Chicken's Growth," *Science Digest* 12, no. 1 (July 1942): 72.
18. For the anemia research, see Edward L. Rickes et al., "Crystalline Vitamin B12," *Science* 107 (April 16, 1948): 396; and "New Vitamin from Liver," *Science News Letter* 53, no. 17 (April 24, 1948): 259.
19. The best history of this event is Maryn McKenna, *Plucked: Chicken, Antibiotics, and How Big Business Changed the Way the World Eats* (National Geographic, 2019), especially Chapter 2.
20. "They've Doubled Gains with New Drugs," *Successful Farming* 48, no. 6 (June 1950): 45.
21. "They've Doubled Gains with New Drugs," 44; "Antibiotics Now Proved in Hog and Poultry Ratios, They're the Biggest Feeding News in 40 Years!" *Successful Farming* 49, no. 3 (March 1951): 33. Other useful accounts are "Drug Promotes Growth," *Science News Letter* 57 (April 22, 1950): 243; and "New Vitamin from Liver."

    The B_{12} news overshadowed another announcement made almost simultaneously. A scientist working at a corporate laboratory in Indiana had isolated what he believed to be APF. The man's employer manufactured animal feed that contained soybean plants and dried brewery wastes. When hens ate the stuff, they laid healthier eggs, and their chicks flourished and "grew rapidly." The scientist speculated that the brewery waste contained a microorganism that facilitated growth.

See the reports in William L. Laurence, "New Vitamin Aids Battle on Anemia," *New York Times*, August 26, 1948, 23; William L. Laurence, "Discoveries Concerning Vitamin B-12 Open New Fields in the Science of Nutrition," *New York Times*, December 5, 1948, E9; and Waldemar Kaempffert, "Clinical Advances That Aid Medicine Are Brought to Light by the Chemists," *New York Times*, September 25, 1949, E9.

22. "Chemists in Convention," *Time*, September 20, 1943.
23. This section is indebted to Nancy Langston, *Toxic Bodies: Hormone Disruptors and the Legacy of DES* (Yale University Press, 2020); and Alan I Marcus [sic], *Cancer From Beef: DES, Federal Food Regulation, and Consumer Confidence* (Johns Hopkins University Press, 1994.)
24. After a local newspaper touted Chris's unusual contribution to science, a representative from the Society for the Prevention of Cruelty to Animals descended on the lab. He concluded that Chris was in neither danger nor pain and unlikely to become a "charcoal-broiled steak" anytime soon. Over the next few years, bovine nutritionists exchanged flank holes for artificial rumens. See Fred Knoop, "No Privacy in the Rumen," *Farm Quarterly* 3, no. 4 (Winter 1948): 40, 42.
25. The notion of "dynamic" feed rations as a way to maximize growth is explored in Alan I Marcus [sic], "The Newest Knowledge of Nutrition: Wise Burroughs, DES, and Modern Meat," *Agricultural History* 67, no. 3 (Summer 1993): 66–85; details of Burroughs's research are on 71-72.
26. Garst's experiments were reported in a number of farm journals. See, for example, Knoop, "No Privacy."
27. Chester Charles, "Stilbestrol," *Farm Quarterly* 10, no. 1 (Spring 1955): 49.
28. John A. Rohlf, "Two Million Head on Stilbestrol!" *Farm Journal* 79 (March 1955): 38.
29. Cameron Hervey, "Barnyards Without Mud," *Farm Journal* 73 (March 1949): 20.
30. Hervey, "Barnyards Without Mud." Also see "Mechanical Pastures," *Farm Quarterly* 10, no. 2 (Summer 1955): 104; and Dick Braun, "Pasture or Drylot: Which Is Cheaper?" *Farm Journal* 79 (June 1955): 32, 118.
31. The dysentery example is from J.L. Anderson, *Industrializing the Corn Belt: Agriculture, Technology, and Environment, 1945–1972* (Northern Illinois University Press, 2009), 94.
32. "Half the Work Twice the Hogs," *Farm Journal* 87 (June 1963): 50F. The connection between his sons' plans and the switch is implied in the text.
33. Frederick G. Brownell, "Super Cows and Chickens," *American Magazine* 141 (June 1946): 110. For the statistics, calculated by the USDA, see "Improvement in Meat Chicken Astonishes Even the Experts," *American Egg and Poultry Review* 12 (April 1951): 36.
34. Claude W. Gifford, "Are 'Chains' Dictating Your Prices?" *Farm Journal* 83 (June 1959): 33; and Howard H. Fogel, "What Retailers Say About Broilers," *Broiler Industry* 27, no. 1 (January 1964): 19, 20.
35. For a deep dive into postwar integration in the broiler industry, see US House, Select Committee on Small Business, *Problems in the Poultry Industry*, 3 vols. 85th Cong., (1957), esp. vol. 2. Hereafter *Problems in the Poultry Industry*. Media coverage was extensive. See, for example, a four-part series on "vertical coordi-

nation" in *National Hog Farmer* 16, nos. 6-9, 1971. The best analysis of the hearings is McKenna, *Plucked*, Chapter 3.
36. See *Problems in the Poultry Industry*, 1:232.
37. Quoted in Grant Cannon, "Vertical Integration," *Farm Quarterly* 12, no. 4 (Winter 1958): 90; quoted in Bernard F. Tobin and Henry B. Arthur, *Dynamics of Adjustment in the Broiler Industry* (Division of Research, Graduate School of Business Administration, Harvard University, 1964), 77.
38. Jewell's testimony is in *Problems in the Poultry Industry*, 1:216-41.
39. "Contract Farming: Brings Higher Income, Lower Prices," *Time*, February 3, 1958; and quoted in Cannon, "Vertical Integration," 96.
40. For Davis, see Alan E. Fusonie, "John H. Davis: His Contributions to Agricultural Education and Productivity," *Agricultural History* 60, no. 2 (Spring 1986): 97-110; Alan E. Fusonie, "John H. Davis: Architect of the Agribusiness Concept Revisited," *Agricultural History* 69, no. 2 (Spring 1995): 326-48; Shane Hamilton, "Agribusiness, the Family Farm, and the Politics of Technological Determinism in the Post-World War II United States," *Technology and Culture* 55, no. 3 (July 2014): 560-90.
41. All quotes are from John H. Davis and Ray A. Goldberg, *A Concept of Agribusiness* (Harvard University, 1957). Davis and Goldberg spread the blame for this shortsightedness, but they were particularly critical of the American Farm Bureau. Its leaders, the two argued, insisted on treating agriculture as an independent economic sector rather than as part of a larger whole. In 1957, Davis and co-author Kenneth Hinshaw published *Farmer In A Business Suit* (Simon and Schuster), an homage to the necessity and significance of modern agribusiness.

CHAPTER 9

1. Pella and C.K. went to Colorado sometime in 1906 or 1907; he had relatives there. That initial trek didn't go well. Pella missed her family and friends, and Warren had stayed behind to attend Illinois State Normal University (for "normal" read: teaching). Sometime in 1907, the couple returned to Illinois. The following year, all three moved to Weld County.

   From various tidbits of information, it appears that C.K. himself was less a farmer than an enthusiast; perhaps even a hobbyist. (Leghorn chickens were his thing.)

   I traced the Monforts primarily through newspapers and farm magazines. A big assist came from Walt Barnhart, *Kenny's Shoes: A Walk Through the Storied Life of the Remarkable Kenneth W. Monfort* (Infinity Publishing, 2008). Barnhart relied in part on an unpublished 1971 document written by William Hartman. I was not able to obtain a copy of it.
2. For the region and its agricultural histories, see John F. Freeman with Mark E. Uchanski, *Adapting to the Land: A History of Agriculture in Colorado* (University Press of Colorado, 2022); and the fine work of Michael Weeks, *Cattle Beet Capital: Making Industrial Agriculture in Northern Colorado* (University of Nebraska Press, 2022.)
3. "Prominent Weld County Farmers," *Greeley Daily Tribune (CO)*, January 8/9, 1930, 1, 7.

4. *Tribune-Republican (Greeley CO)*, June 30, 1916, 10; *Greeley Daily Tribune (CO)*, May 5, 1917, 12; "Teachers in Sterling School Are Married in Boulder," *Boulder Daily Camera (CO)*, March 17, 1919, 2; "182 Enlisted in Army During Day in Rush to Join Before Saturday," *Rocky Mountain News (CO)*, December 13, 1917, 4.
5. At one point, someone constructed a portable model of the Monfort ranch that could be toted to county fairs, exhibitions, club meetings, and the like.
6. For a description of the farm, see "Prominent Weld County Farmers." For beet pulp research, see, for example, Colorado State College, Colorado Experiment Station, *Colorado Fattening Rations for Cattle*, by H.B. Osland, E.J. Maynard, and George E. Morton, Bulletin 422, February 1936. Also see Weeks, *Cattle Beet Capital*. For potatoes, see "Seed Guide Given by County Agent," *Greeley Daily Tribune (CO)*, November 16, 1929, 2. For the truck: "A Light Truck Equipment for Hauling Beets," *Grand Junction Daily Sentinel (CO)*, August 30, 1926, 6.
7. "12 Tons per Acre Necessary to Pay Beet Costs, Monfort Asserts in Magazine Article," *Greeley Tribune-Republican (CO)*, November 26, 1929, 8; and quoted in Barnhart, *Kenny's Shoes*, 18. The Monforts grew sugar beets at a time when Cuban competition posed a serious threat to US sugar industries. In northeast Colorado, market jitters were exacerbated by chronic labor problems. During and after World War I, Mexican field hands had become the region's primary source of seasonal labor. That did not sit well with Warren; nor did the fierce competition with Cuba. In the late twenties, Warren urged members of the Mountain States Beet Growers Association to automate and mechanize. A machine, he argued, would provided better work than "is done by foreign labor." "Greeley Beet Growers Favor Cut In Bonus," *Greeley Tribune-Republican (CO)*, February 1, 1930, 1, 12.
8. For a useful look at Weld County's agriculture and the role of cattle in it the 1920s, see Colorado Agricultural Extension Service, *An Agricultural Program for the Irrigated Region of Northern Colorado* ([1930]).
9. Corn was always a sure bet because of its utility: it could be converted into beef and pork, of course, but also oil and flour. Brewers and distillers used corn; so did cereal manufacturers.
10. For information on the early years, see "Industrial Methods As Used On Warren Monfort 'Beef Factory,'" *Greeley Daily Tribune (CO)*, September 14, 1940, 3; "Monfort Will Get National Skelly Award," *Greeley Daily Tribune (CO)*, January 26, 1944, 1, 4; Lynn Heinze, "Monfort Sees Cattle as World Food Buffer — Although Less Beef Consumption Likely, Cattle Have Future," *Greeley Tribune (CO)*, March 9, 1976, B-23.
11. William M. Blair, "Packers Battle Chain Stores in Marketing 'Revolution,'" *New York Times*, March 24, 1958, 42. For California, see any western agricultural media, and urban newspapers, too. This is a grand research opportunity for an historian in search of a project: early twentieth-century, Pacific-coast livestock production and meatpacking.
12. See *An Agricultural Program*, 19-20. "Feeders Urged to Form Organization," *Tribune-Republican (Greeley CO)*, February 19, 1930, 9. Also see "Committees on Northern Colo. Farm Economic Sessions Here Feb. 13 and 14 Are Appointed," *Greeley Republican (CO)*, February 8, 1930, 1, 11.
13. Bruce Wilkinson, "Warren and Ken Monfort Commercial Feeders of the Year," *Feedlot Management* 16, no. 2 (February 1974): 16.

14. See, for example, "Monfort Gets New Top for Fat Carload," *Greeley Daily Tribune (CO)*, April 26, 1935, 8. "Denver Cattle Sales," *Fort Collins Express-Courier (CO)*, December 29, 1936, 9. Also see "Denver Cattle Sales," *Fort Collins Express-Courier (CO)*, January 3, 1937, 15.
15. "Meeker Student Outbids Elders at Denver Show," *Greeley Daily Tribune (CO)*, January 23, 1936, 1. See also "Cattle Feeding is Subject of Pleasant Valley 4H Meet," *Greeley Daily Tribune (CO)*, June 4/5, 1936, 4; "Grand Champion Steer and Owner," *Greeley Daily Tribune (CO)*, August 14, 1936, 9; "North Colorado Stock Takes High Awards at Pueblo," *Greeley Daily Tribune (CO)*, August 26, 1936, 1; "Monfort Herefords Score at Denver," *Greeley Daily Tribune (CO)*, January 20, 1937, 12. See also "Monfort Steers Made Big Gains," *Greeley Daily Tribune (CO)*, January 21, 1937, 12; "Young Monfort Is Now Feeding Angus Steers," *Greeley Daily Tribune (CO)*, May 5, 1938, 14; "4-H Club Folk Are Invited to Steer Feeding Meeting," *Greeley Daily Tribune (CO)*, April 12, 1940, 6.
16. "Championships At Junior Fair Are Announced," *Greeley Daily Tribune (CO)*, August 15, 1940, 16; "Proud of Grand Champion," *Greeley Daily Tribune (CO)*, August 15, 1940, 1; "5,000 See Greatest Livestock Parade in Junior Fair History With 100 Herefords Featured," *Greeley Daily Tribune (CO)*, August 15, 1940, 1, 2.
17. "Ken Monfort Steer Denver Grand Champ," *Greeley Daily Tribune (CO)*, January 13, 1941, 1. Also "Ken Monfort Get [sic] $1,055 For Slit Ear," *Greeley Daily Tribune (CO)*, January 15, 1941, 1; "$1,055 Worth of Beef," *Greeley Daily Tribune (CO)*, January 16, 1941, 5; "The Finish of Slit Ear," *Greeley Daily Tribune (CO)*, January 24, 1941, 10; "Wrist Watch Presented to Ken Monfort," *Greeley Daily Tribune (CO)*, March 11, 1941, 1.
18. "Truck Group Here Headed by Monfort," *Greeley Daily Tribune (CO)*, August 8, 1942, 1; "Applications for Trucks Must Be In By September 23rd," *Greeley Daily Tribune (CO)*, September 21, 1942, 1.
19. "Monfort Will Get National Skelly Award," *Greeley Daily Tribune (CO)*, January 26, 1944, 1; "Monfort Gets Skelly Honor at Breakfast," *Greeley Daily Tribune (CO)*, January 29, 1944, 1,4.
20. "Dick Monfort Is Missing," *Greeley Daily Tribune (CO)*, February 14, 1944, 1. Also see "Miss Swanson Will Wed Greeley Cadet," *Fort Collins Express-Courier (CO)*, January 4, 1942, 3; "In Armed Services," *Greeley Daily Colorado (CO)*, February 13, 1943, 2.
21. "Wife is Told Lt. Monfort Died in Action," *Greeley Daily Tribune (CO)*, April 26, 1944, 1.
22. "OPA Suits Filed," *Fort Collins Coloradoan*, October 8, 1945, 6; "Chain Store Buys Cattle At Greeley," *Fort Collins Coloradoan*, September 11, 1946, 2.
23. "Chain Store Buys Cattle At Greeley." At the time, Monfort explained that the deal was good only for the duration of OPA.
24. See "Monfort-McMillen Engagement Revealed," *Fort Collins Coloradoan*, September 27, 1949, 6; "Kenneth Monfort Weds of Greeley," *Fort Collins Coloradoan*, November 23, 1949, 7.
25. Quoted in "Neighborhood Bully?" *Feedlot Management* 16, no. 2 (February 1974): 27. The description is based on information in Barnhart, *Kenny's Shoes*.
26. Two good summaries of changing range use are USDA, ARS, *Major Uses of Land in the United States: Summary for 1954*, Agriculture Information Bulletin no. 168,

January 1957; and USDA, *Federal and State Rural Lands, 1950, with Special Reference to Grazing*, by R.D. Davidson, Circular 909, May 1952.

In the 1940s, ranchers' frustrations spawned a series of lengthy, well-publicized congressional hearings into the use (or, as many argued, abuse) of the range. For the first time, millions of Americans learned that much of the west belonged to them. Conservationists complained that freeloading ranchers had so abused the range that parts of it could no longer support grazing.

Bernard DeVoto, a Utah native and well-known writer devoted to both conservation and the West, charged that ranchers' "lust" for land could "bring the United States to the verge of [environmental] catastrophe in a single generation." See Karen R. Merrill, *Public Lands and Political Meaning: Ranchers, the Government, and the Property Between Them* (University of California Press, 2002), 178–204. Quote is Bernard DeVoto, "Sacred Cows and Public Lands," *Harper's Magazine* 197 (July 1948): 55. Bernard and Avis DeVoto were a fascinating couple. See Nate Schweber, *This America of Ours: Bernard and Avis DeVoto and the Forgotten Fight to Save the Wild* (Mariner Books, 2022).

27. "Falling Market Hits Colorado's Steak Raisers," *Springfield Union (MA)*, April 15, 1952, 20.

Many sources document the transformation from range to feedlot, but useful summaries are in the aforementioned USDA, *Major Uses of Land*; and USDA, *Federal and State Rural Lands, 1950, with Special Reference to Grazing*, by R.D. Davidson, Circular 909, May 1952; USDA, ESS, *Structural Change in Agriculture: The Experience for Broilers, Fed Cattle, and Processing Vegetables*, by Donn A. Reimund, J. Rod Martin, and Charles V. Moore, Technical Bulletin no. 1648, April 1981, 15-29; and USDA, ESCS, "Beef," by J. Rod Martin in *Another Revolution in U.S. Farming?* by Lyle P. Schertz et al., Agricultural Economic Report no. 441, December 1979, 85-118.

For fed-beef statistics, see Table 43, 88, in USDA, ERS, *Cattle Feeding in the United States*, by Ronald A. Gustafson and Roy N. Van Arsdall, Economic Report no. 186, October 1970; and Table 1, 2, including the note for that table, in USDA, ERS, *Cattle Feeding, 1962-89*, by Kenneth R. Krause, Agricultural Economic Report no. 642, April 1991.

28. "Monfort Builds 400,000-Bushel Elevator at Cozad," *Greeley Daily Tribune (CO)*, February 8, 1951, 1.

29. "Monfort Builds 400,000-Bushel Elevator at Cozad."

30. "Monfort Tells Kiwanis About Agribusiness," *Greeley Daily Tribune (CO)*," April 11, 1958, 4. Perhaps Warren had forgotten his own father's early foray into agriculture as "big business." C.K. prided himself on being a "large-scale" poultry and egg producer.

The Monforts' operation was one of many built in the western plains at midcentury (although few were as large). In 1962, commercial feeders — defined by the USDA as feeding a thousand or more head of cattle — accounted for just a third of the fed cattle sent to slaughter. Eleven years later, two-thirds of the nation's fed cattle came from such lots, and 1 percent of feedlots put out nearly half the nation's fed cattle. Texans in particular embraced feeding. In 1950, they fed a quarter million cattle; twenty years later, they turned out 3 million.

See Orville Howard, "Feeder Cattle Eat Way to $250-Million Industry,"

Amarillo Globe-Times (TX), November 28, 1962, 2; and Jack Hanicke, "Range Change: Ranchers Fatten More Cattle at Home, Using Cheap Grain Sorghums," *Wall Street Journal*, February 13, 1959, 1.
31. US House, Committee on Agriculture, *Prohibit Feeding of Livestock by Certain Packers: Hearings Before the Subcommittee on Livestock and Feed Grains of the Committee on Agriculture*, 89th Cong. (1966), 229. Hereafter *Prohibit Feeding of Livestock*.
32. Lynn Heinze, "Monfort Sees Cattle as World Food Buffer — Although Less Beef Consumption Likely, Cattle Have Future," *Greeley Tribune (CO)*, March 9, 1976, B-23.
33. "Light Is Built into Colorado On-Line Beef Plant," *National Provisioner* 143, no. 1 (July 2, 1960): 17, 19.
34. Jim Hitch, "Monfort Pack, Union Reach Agreement," *Greeley Tribune*, February 23, 1965, 18.

Shortly after the plant opened, the union came calling. Monfort's employees voted to join the Amalgamated Meat Cutters and Butcher Workmen of America. Ken accepted the vote, but persuaded them to eschew the master contract that governed other unionized packing plants. Instead, the parties signed a contract that included cost-of-living increases as well as a profit-sharing plan designed to fund the employees' retirements.

It's unlikely anyone complained: the Monforts paid the highest wages in Greeley.
35. John A. McWethy, "Meat & Synthetics: The Rise of Man-Made Materials Hurts Packers' By-Products Business," *Wall Street Journal*, January 3, 1953, 1, 3.
36. *Prohibit Feeding of Livestock*, 229.
37. For a good analysis, see Roger Horowitz, *Putting Meat on the American Table: Taste, Technology, Transformation* (Johns Hopkins University Press, 2006), Chapter 5.
38. For the study, see A.T. Kearney & Company, *The Search for a Thousand Million Dollars: Cost Reduction Opportunities in the Transportation and Distribution of Grocery Products* (National Association of Food Chains, 1966). A summary of the meat-related contents is "Food Distribution Survey Proposes Cutback in Beef Handling Steps," *National Provisioner* 155, no. 19 (November 5, 1966): 18-20.
39. "Packing Industry Lags Behind Other Foods in Many of Its Market Concepts," *National Provisioner* 151, no. 15 (October 10, 1964): 56.
40. William M. Blair, "Broad Changes Sweep the Cattle Industry," *New York Times*, April 30, 1966, 12. For a detailed description of the operation, see "Feeding Cattle on a Grand Scale," *National Provisioner* 154, no. 8 (February 18, 1966): 20-21.
41. "Cattle Feeding, Slaughtering Makes Future Bright," *Greeley Tribune (CO)*, April 3, 1970, 32.
42. "Where Packing Takes On a New Dimension," *National Provisioner* 156, no. 5 (February 4, 1967): 16-17.
43. "Standardization Comes to the Farm," *Business Week*, March 21, 1959, 167. I kept the citations to a minimum. For every source I cite, there are dozens more. Media coverage ranged from mainstream publications to industry-specific ones.
44. For an incisive look at the many ways in which Corn Belt farmers competed, see J.L. Anderson, *Industrializing the Corn Belt: Agriculture, Technology, and the Environment, 1945-1972* (Northern Illinois University Press, 2009.)

NOTES   327

45. William M. Blair, "Hog Raisers Eye a Contract Plan," *New York Times*, March 2, 1958, 1, 69. Also see Ovid Bay, "Now They're Leasing Hog Breeding Herds," *Farm Journal* 82 (March 1958): 39, 72; "Contract Farming: Brings Higher Income, Lower Prices," *Time*, February 3, 1958; "Is the Hog Business Headed for a Shake-up?" *Farm Journal* 81 (April 1957): 30-31, 186, 190; "Hog Contracts: How Near Your Door?" *Farm Journal* 82 (February 1958): 35, 132.
46. "Contract Farming"; Blair, "Hog Raisers Eye a Contract Plan," 1, 69.
47. Jack Hanicke, "Range Change: Ranchers Fatten More Cattle At Home, Using Cheap Grain Sorghums," *Wall Street Journal*, February 13, 1959, 1.
48. *Prohibit Feeding of Livestock*, 232.
49. "Look What's Happening to Cattle Feeding!" *Farm Journal* 79 (October 1955): 38.
50. Dick Braun, "Pasture or Drylot: Which Is Cheaper?" *Farm Journal* 79 (June 1955): 33.
51. Iowa Development Commission, Agricultural Division, *Beef Confinement Can Pay In Iowa*, 1974, 18.
52. "Cost-Conscious Feedlot," *Farm Quarterly* 15, no. 3 (Autumn 1960): 62–63, 128-29, 130.
53. George A. Montgomery, "Weather Can't Hurt This Feeder," *Farm Journal* 84 (October 1960): 38, 40.
54. Montgomery, "Weather Can't Hurt This Feeder."
55. "Automation of a Hog Farm," *Farm Quarterly* 14, no. 4 (Winter 1960): 79.
56. "Automation of a Hog Farm." For other examples see "Pig Hatcheries," *Farm Quarterly* 6, no. 2 (Summer 1951): 28-29, 94, 96, 98; Dayle Wahlert, "'I'll Raise the Hogs' — 'I'll Raise the Corn,'" *Successful Farming* 56, no. 4 (April 1958): 50-51, 110-12; Dick Seim, "One Way for Family Farms to Stay in Hogs," *Farm Journal* 85 (November 1961): 34-35, 67-68; John F. Hughes, "Does Multiple Farrowing Pay?" *Farm Quarterly* 12, no. 1 (Spring 1957): 44-45, 99-102.
57. John Harvey, "What Farmers Like and Don't Like About Confinement Hog Setups," *Successful Farming* 64 (July 1966): 41.
58. *Beef Confinement Can Pay In Iowa*, 1974, 5.
59. Dick Braun, "Clean Hog Lots with a Pump," *Farm Journal* 82 (December 1958): 34.
60. Braun, "Clean Hog Lots with a Pump, 34.
61. Ray Dankenbring and Ovid Bay, "Lagoons — Everybody's Building 'Em!" *Farm Journal* 84 (November 1960): 38.
62. See the letter from B.E. Burger in *Farm Journal* 85 (March 1961): 20.
63. "Lagoons Aren't Magic but They Can Save You Work," *Farm Quarterly* 18, no. 3 (Fall 1963): 48.
64. "Lagoons Aren't Magic," 48. The calculations are from "The Big Fuss Over Lagoons," *Farm Journal* 88 (April 1964): 57.
65. John Russell, "Manure Odors Can Land You in Court!" *Farm Journal* 89 (August 1965): 19.
66. Russell, "Manure Odors Can Land You in Court!"
67. Ralph Sanders, "Animal Wastes — Pollution — Your Problem, Too," *Successful Farming* 68, no. 11 (October 1970): 34. For a useful look at how this played out, see Jacob A. Blackwell, "An Uncommon Nuisance: Cattle Feeding, Nuisance Complaints, and Legal Remedies on the Southern Plains," in *The Greater Plains:*

Rethinking a Region's Environmental Histories, edited by Kathleen A. Brosnan and Brian Frehner, 156-74 (University of Nebraska Press, 2021).

68. Ralph E. Winter, "Antipollution Laws Force Livestock Men to Devise Ways to Collect, Use Manure," *Wall Street Journal*, March 5, 1974, 38. For a useful look at how the Clean Water Act affected livestock operations, see John H. Martin Jr, "The Clean Water Act and Animal Agriculture," *Journal of Environmental Quality* 26 (1997): 1198–1203.

69. By the early 1970s, 95 of the nation's 141 biggest hog operations lay outside the Corn Belt. See USDA, ERSA, *Cattle Feeding in the United States*, by Ronald A. Gustafson and Roy N. Van Arsdall, Economic Report no. 186, October 1970; USDA, ERS, *Cattle Feeding, 1962–89*, by Kenneth R. Krause, Agricultural Economic Report no. 642, April 1991; USDA, ESS, *Structural Change in Agriculture: The Experience for Broilers, Fed Cattle, and Processing Vegetables*, by Donn A. Reimund, J. Rod Martin, and Charles V. Moore, Technical Bulletin no. 1648, April 1981, 15-29; and USDA, ESCS, "Beef," by J. Rod Martin, in *Another Revolution in U.S. Farming?* by Lyle P. Schertz et al., Agricultural Economic Report no. 441, December 1979, 85-118.

70. Peter H. Prugh, "Beefing Up Profit," *Wall Street Journal*, May 4, 1966, 1, 22.

71. *Wall Street Journal*, April 9, 1956, 9. See Keith Orejel, "The Origins of the Iowa Development Commission: Agricultural Transformation and Industrial Development in Mid-Twentieth-Century Iowa," *Annals of Iowa* 76, no. 1 (Winter 2017): 47-70.

72. "Good Investment," *Denison Bulletin (IA)*, March 25, 1960, 2B. A fascinating look at towns behind the scenes is Keith Orejel, "Factories in the Fallows: The Political Economy of America's Rural Heartland, 1945-1980," (PhD diss., Columbia University, 2015).

73. Prugh, "Beefing Up Profit," *Wall Street Journal*, 1, 22.

Anderson and company hated unions. During the CCPC's first year of operation, for example, a field representative with the United Packinghouse Workers of America told IBP's unskilled employees that they deserved the same wages paid at big-city packing plants. By a one-vote margin, the employees voted to unionize.

Negotiations were ugly when their contract came up for renewal in the summer 1959. Work stoppages plagued the plant for weeks. In early 1960, employees filed papers to establish their own union. A few days later, Andy Anderson resigned and began laying the groundwork for IBP.

My take is that this anti-unionism was a product of region. Unions were not (and are not) part of the culture in the US west and south.

74. Prugh, "Beefing Up Profit," 1, 22; Margaret D. Pacey, "Everything but the Moo," *Barron's National Business and Financial Weekly* 40 (July 22, 1968): 3; and Kenneth C. Crowe and Michael Under, "Iowa Beef's Money Motto Out; but Message Remains," *Des Moines Register (IA)*, April 22, 1973, 6B. The latter article originally appeared in *Newsday*.

75. For announcements of these efforts and company progress, see "Over 200 Stockholders Hear of IBP Progress Monday," *Denison Bulletin (IA)*, December 22, 1961, 1; "IBP Killing 120 per Hour," *Denison Bulletin (IA)*, September 1, 1961, 1; and Ed Heins, "Big Union Gaining at Meat Plants," *Des Moines Register (IA)*, August 10, 1964, 3.

76. Arlo Jacobson, "IBP Tells Grocers: Beef Carcasses 'Old-Fashioned,'" *Des Moines Sunday Register (IA)*, December 5, 1971, 1F.
77. Seth S. King, "Union Unrest Splits Plains Town," *New York Times*, December 17, 1969, 45; Jonathan Kwitny, "Troubled Packer: Iowa Beef's History of Shady Characters Far Outruns '74 Case," *Wall Street Journal*, December 17, 1976, 1.

    Currier Holman came to personify IBP's evils, but he is frustratingly difficult to wrestle into the company's history. I pieced together what I know from various newspapers and from Jonathan Kwitny, *Vicious Circles: The Mafia in the Workplace* (W.W. Norton & Company, 1979).

    Holman grew up in Sioux City, where he worked for a time in a Swift packing plant, first on the floor hauling sheep guts, and then in the office. In the 1950s, he set up shop as an independent cattle buyer.

    He met Anderson in Sioux City in the 1950s, before Anderson moved to Denison. Holman told Kwitny, a *Wall Street Journal* reporter, that the two men often discussed the idea of building a revolutionary new meatpacking plant. (As near as I can tell, Kwitny did not verify that information with Anderson.) When Anderson was laying plans and raising money for IBP in May 1960, Holman was living in Sioux City.

    In the late 1960s and early 1970s, Holman identified himself as an IBP cofounder. In the mid- to late 1970s, he described himself as its founder. He claimed that he designed the company's plants. He claimed he'd played for Knute Rockne at Notre Dame.

    As near as can be determined, he attended but did not graduate from Notre Dame. He tried out for the school's football team but never played in a game. There is ample evidence that Andy Anderson designed IBP's plants.

    As to Holman's claim that he cofounded the company, there is no evidence. Holman is not mentioned in any local news coverage of IBP's early days in Denison. Executive officers, managers, foremen: many are mentioned, but not Currier Holman.

    In December 1961, a local paper described him as a member of the board of directors and plant manager, a step up from his first job at the company: head cattle buyer.

    According to Kwitny, Holman was annoyed by the way union recalcitrance drained the profits out of meatpacking. He was determined to build a modern, and presumably nonunion, plant.
78. "Rough Riders," *Forbes* 113 (June 1974): 66.
79. "Iowa Beef and Its Cochairman Convicted for Plotting to Bribe Union and Retailers," *Wall Street Journal*, October 8, 1974, 4. Holman's saga, at times tragic, at others comical, was detailed in newspaper and meat industry trade journals and in Kwitny, *Vicious Circles*. According to Kwitny, IBP continued to make payments to union officials on the East Coast, payments that the company made no attempt to conceal.
80. *Prohibit Feeding of Livestock*, 229.
81. See for example, Kwitny, *Vicious Circles*, 282; Jerrold Lanes, "Meat-Packing Progress," *Barron's National Business and Financial Weekly* 42, no. 7 (February 12, 1962): 18.
82. Dana L. Thomas, "More Meat on the Bones: The Lean Years May Be Over for

the Nation's Packers," *Barron's National Business and Financial Weekly* 39, no. 30 (July 27, 1959): 15.
83. Richard F. Janssen, "Packers on the Move: Meat Concerns Step Up Outlays on New Plants. Aim to Fatten Profits," *Wall Street Journal*, July 5, 1961, 1. Useful information is in [Arval L. Erikson], "Change Has Been Key Word in Industry Except for Consistently Low Earnings," *National Provisioner* 147, no. 14 (October 6, 1962): 52-54.
84. Harold B. Meyers, "For the Old Meatpackers, Things Are Tough All Over," *Fortune* 79 (February 1969): 92.
85. Paul Ingrassia, "Repackaged Packer: As Fresh-Meat Business Grows Leaner, Swift Samples Other Fare," *Wall Street Journal*, August 10, 1978, 29.
86. Richard Elliott Jr, "Sow's Ear or Silk Purse?" *Barron's National Business and Financial Weekly* 47, no. 15 (April 10, 1967): 14.
87. "Meatpackers Beef It Up," *Business Week*, August 30, 1969, 83, 84.

CHAPTER 10

1. On these episodes and scientists' reactions, see Michael Egan, *Barry Commoner and the Science of Survival: The Remaking of American Environmentalism* (MIT Press, 2007), especially Chapter 2.
2. Mark Ryan Janzen, "The Cranberry Scare of 1959: The Beginning of the End of the Delaney Clause," (PhD diss., Texas A&M University, 2010).
3. Quoted in Richard D. Lyons, "Salmonella Rise Disturbs Experts," *New York Times*, April 9, 1967, 47.
4. John E. McCroan, et al, "Five Salmonellosis Outbreaks Related to Poultry Products," *Public Health Reports* 78, no. 12 (December 1963): 1073-80. For an excellent look at the problems of the broiler makers, see Ashton Wynette Merck, "The Fox Guarding the Henhouse: Coregulation and Consumer Protection in Food Safety, 1946-2002" (PhD diss., Duke University, 2020), especially Chapters 1 and 2. For broilers and antibiotics, see Maryn McKenna, *Plucked: Chicken, Antibiotics, and How Big Business Changed the Way the World Eats* (National Geographic, 2019).
5. See Mildred M. Galton, "Salmonellosis in Livestock," *Public Health Reports* 78, no. 12 (December 1963): 1066-71; USDA, ARS, "Salmonellosis in Cattle," by R.V. Lewis, in *Proceedings of the Salmonella Seminar* ARS 91-50, December 1964, 11-18.
6. See Janzen, "Cranberry Scare." He argues that thanks to Delaney, "an inflexible legislative standard" trumped "scientific discretion."
7. Christopher Deutsch, "Forging A National Diet: Beef and the Political Economy of Plenty in Postwar America" (PhD diss., University of Missouri-Columbia, 2018), 126-29. I am grateful to him for giving me a copy of his dissertation. As I write this, he is working on a book about the topic.
8. Quoted in Deutsch, "Forging a National Diet," 127, 128. According to Deutsch, the "related materials" were chlorinated hydrocarbons. "These chemical compounds have broad powers to disrupt regular biological processes[,] and also bio accumulate, meaning they concentrate, within animals' fat cells after being consumed." Deutsch, 127.

9. Quoted in Deutsch, "Forging a National Diet," 127, 129.
10. On postwar anxiety from a consumer perspective, see Thomas Jundt, *Greening the Red, White, and Blue: The Bomb, Big Business, and Consumer Resistance in Postwar America* (Oxford University Press, 2014). Also see Janzen, "Cranberry Scare of 1959," Chapter 4, for a good discussion of food fears in particular.
11. My take on the history of the heart disease epidemic is informed by Gary Taubes, *Good Calories, Bad Calories: Challenging the Conventional Wisdom on Diet, Weight Control, and Disease* (Alfred A. Knopf, 2007); and Todd Michael Olszewski, "Cholesterol: A Scientific, Medical and Social History, 1908-1962" (PhD diss., Yale University, 2008).
12. This leap into cause and effect rested on virtually no research, and none that controlled for other factors, such as whether postwar Europeans walked more than Americans or engaged in more physical labor.

    In 1948, Congress responded to the fear-mongering by establishing the National Heart Institute and the National Heart Council. Established but did not fund. Advocates for the new agencies launched public relations campaigns warning of the dangers of heart disease, hoping to persuade senators and representatives to part with the public's money. The American Heart Association (AHA), a decades-old but moribund organization of physicians interested in (medical) matters of the heart hired a public relations firm that transformed the AHA into a fundraising powerhouse.

    The ensuing publicity generated research proposals from scientists looking for a share of public and private money. Thus began the search for facts with which to flesh out the phantom epidemic. See Taubes, *Good Calories, Bad Calories*.
13. His claims were both simplistic and incorrect. Fat is essential to human well-being, and the body contains plenty of it in the form of cholesterol, which it uses to manufacture hormones, among other things. Over time, cholesterol can build up in arteries and cause them to "harden."

    Saturated fats, which come primarily from animal products, can also deposit fat in arteries. Eating excessive amounts of that class of fats can contribute to atherosclerosis. But not all fats come from animals; plants contain fat, too, and some fats are unsaturated, even in animal-based foods. Half the fat in beef is saturated, for example, and half unsaturated.

    But Keys was an intellectual bully and a relentless self-promoter of the World According to Keys. Having decided that his view was correct, he promoted it, facts be damned.
14. Quoted in Janzen, "Cranberry Scare of 1959," 55. Also see Mark H. Lytle, *The All-Consuming Nation: Chasing the American Dream Since World War II* (Oxford University Press, 2021), 89-92.
15. Quoted in Janzen, "Cranberry Scare of 1959," 55. The statistic is from "Environment v. Man," *Time*, September 26, 1960. Accessed online.
16. "Environment v. Man."
17. Carson's work has been credited with inspiring the modern environmental movement, but a more accurate assessment is that the book was less a launching pad than a tipping point: Carson articulated fears already shared by many Americans. It helped that, even before *Silent Spring*, Carson was one of the best-known writers in America, thanks to two earlier, best-selling, prize-winning books about nature and science.

18. Quoted in Egan, *Barry Commoner*, 80.
19. See especially Paul Sabin, *Public Citizens: The Attack on Big Government and the Remaking of American Liberalism* (W.W. Norton & Company, 2021). Also see Jonathan Levy, "From Fiscal Triangle to Passing Through: Rise of the Nonprofit Corporation," in *Corporations and American Democracy*, ed. Naomi R. Lamoreaux and William J. Novak, 213-44 (Harvard University Press, 2017).
20. Quoted in Lawrence B. Glickman, *Buying Power: A History of Consumer Activism in America* (University of Chicago Press, 2009), 281. For a guide to such legislation over many decades, see Richard J. Leighton, "Consumer Protection Agency Proposals: The Origin of the Species," *Administrative Law Review* 25, no. 3 (Summer 1973): 269-312.
21. Quoted in Leighton, "Consumer Protection Agency Proposals," 294; and Emily E. LB. Twarog, *Politics of the Pantry: Housewives, Food, and Consumer Protest in Twentieth-Century America* (Oxford University Press, 2017), 67. On this point, and especially the doomed efforts to establish a Consumer Protection Agency, see Glickman, *Buying Power*, Chapter 9. Shortly before his death in late 1963, JFK launched the lengthy procedure necessary to appoint Esther Petersen (1906-1997) as Special Assistant for Consumer Affairs. Kennedy's successor, Lyndon B. Johnson (1908-1973; president 1963-1969), completed the process.
22. Patrick Anderson, "Ralph Nader, Crusader; or, The Rise of a Self-Appointed Lobbyist," *New York Times Magazine*, October 29, 1967, 25. Nader's phrase echoes Upton Sinclair, who regarded early-twentieth-century corporations as "invisible governments."
23. Fred L. Zimmerman, "Auto Critic Shift Gears: Ralph Nader Plans to Expand His Crusades By Opening Firm to Lobby for the Public," *Wall Street Journal*, October 31, 1967, 34. For a detailed look, see Chapter 3 of Sabin, *Public Citizens*.
24. "The U.S.'s Toughest Customer," *Time*, December 12, 1969.
25. Quotes in Lucia Mouat, "Will the Real Bargain Stand Up?" *Christian Science Monitor*, February 2, 1970, 9; and Glickman, *Buying Power*, 287. For a superb look at the backlash to Nader's crusades, see chapter 9 of Glickman, *Buying Power*; and Lawrence B. Glickman, *Free Enterprise: An American History* (Yale University Press, 2019).
26. Lucia Mouat, "The Consumer Fights Back," *Christian Science Monitor*, January 26, 1970, 9.
27. For typical media coverage at the time of the pure meat crusade, see, for example, "Meet Ralph Nader: Everyman's Lobbyist and His Consumer Crusade," *Newsweek*, January 22, 1968, 65-67, 70, 73; and Anderson, "Ralph Nader, Crusader."
28. The Nixon quotes are from "The Administration: Looking After the Hotdog," *Time*, June 27, 1969; and "Mrs. Knauer Says Nixon Opposes Fat Hot Dogs," *New York Times*, July 13, 1969, 22.
29. "Frankfurters," *Consumer Reports* 37, no. 2 (February 1972): 73.
30. Quotes in this and the following paragraph are from "P.S. on Pig Snouts," *National Provisioner* 168, no. 5 (February 3, 1973): 30, 32, 34.
31. Joseph M. Winski, "Makers of Hog Dogs, Speaking Frankly, Say Sales Aren't So Hot," *Wall Street Journal*, May 29, 1973, 1.
32. "'Egghead' Proposals Make Reader Sizzle," *National Provisioner* 166, no. 11 (March 11, 1972): 19.

33. "Aesthetics No Basis for Byproducts Ban," *National Provisioner* 168, no. 2 (January 13, 1973): 15-16. A summary of the new rules: "U.S. Sets New Rules for Processed Meat," *New York Times*, June 2, 1973, 16.
34. Ralph Nader, "Watch that Hamburger," *New Republic* 157 (August 19, 1967): 15-16; Ralph Nader, "We're Still in the Jungle," *New Republic* 157 (July 1967): 11-12. For the road trips, see, for example, James MacNees, "Agriculture United Assailed," *Baltimore Sun*, August 12, 1967, A8; "Meet Ralph Nader: Everyman's Lobbyist and His Consumer Crusade," *Newsweek*, January 22, 1968, 65-67, 70, 73. Nader's letter and the report extracts are on 238-51 of US House, Committee on Agriculture, Subcommittee on Livestock and Grains, *Amend the Meat Inspection Act. Hearings Before the Subcommittee on Livestock and Grains of the Committee on Agriculture House of Representatives*. 90th Cong. (1967).
35. "Why United Packers Has Closed Its Doors," *National Provisioner* 167, no. 26 (December 23, 1972): 18.
36. Quoted in Randal S. Beeman and James A. Pritchard, *A Green and Permanent Land: Ecology and Agriculture in the Twentieth Century* (University Press of Kansas, 2001), 93, 94. The second half of their book is a solid introduction to postwar environmentalism and agriculture.
37. "Effemination," *Time*, April 16, 1951. A New Jersey court ruled that the man, John Stepnowski, was eligible for workers' compensation, but for no other damages. A summary of that ruling and a related appeal is Stepnowski v. Specific Pharmaceuticals, Inc., 18 N.J. Super. 495 (1952). See also the superb work of Nancy Langston, *Toxic Bodies: Hormone Disruptors and the Legacy of DES* (Yale University Press, 2010).
38. Langston, *Toxic Bodies*, 69. The owner of Arapahoe Chemicals, Inc., of Colorado told the Food and Drug Administration (FDA) about his fears. An FDA official responded by saying, in effect, that the agency knew nothing and could do nothing, and suggested that the owner contact the United States Public Health Service. It's not clear how the situation ended.
39. "Stilbestrol-Fed Cattle: How They're Selling Now," *Farm Journal* 79 (August 1955): 16.
40. John S. Lang, "Cancer-Inciting Hormone Found in U.S. Beef Supply," *Des Moines Register (IA)*, June 24, 1970, 1. This Associated Press piece appeared in newspapers nationwide. For a useful look at the politics of DES regulation (and to a lesser extent antibiotics), also see US House, *Regulation of Diethylstilbestrol (DES) and Other Drugs Used in Food Producing Animals*, 93d Cong. (1972).

    Two general sources of information about the DES-in-beef controversy are Harrison Wellford, *Sowing the Wind: A Report from Ralph Nader's Center for the Study of Responsive Law on Food Safety and the Chemical Harvest* (Grossman Publishers, 1972); and Alan I Marcus [sic], *Cancer from Beef: DES, Federal Food Regulation, and Consumer Confidence* (Johns Hopkins University Press, 1994).

    Marcus views the DES battle as an exemplar of a mid-century fracturing of scientific authority. Wellford, a Nader colleague, examined the politics of the regulatory mechanisms. His take on DES also appeared as Harrison Wellford, "Behind the Meat Counter: The Fight Over DES," *Atlantic* 230 (October 1972): 86–90.
41. For uncertainty and the politics and ethics of science during the sixties and

seventies, see Egan, *Barry Commoner*; Langston, *Toxic Bodies*; and Marcus, *Cancer From Beef*.

42. For this episode, see Langston, *Toxic Bodies*, especially Chapter 5. The livestock-specific hearings are US House, Committee on Government Operations, Subcommittee on Intergovernmental Regulations, *Regulation of Diethylstilbestrol (DES): Its Use as a Drug for Humans and in Animal Feeds (Part 1)*, 92nd Cong. (1971).

43. Walter Sullivan, "Bacteria Passing On Resistance to Drugs," *New York Times*, August 9, 1966, 1, 31. The editorial appeared in the *New England Journal of Medicine* on August 4, 1966. See especially McKenna, *Plucked*. For scientists' and veterinarians' take in the mid-1960s, see the essays in *Use of Drugs in Animal Feeds: Proceedings of a Symposium*, Publication 1679 (National Academy of Sciences, 1969).

    The British were not as reticent as Americans. In 1969, the authors of a Parliament-sponsored investigation announced that they rejected the belief that "20 years of experience goes to show that there are no serious ill-effects from giving antibiotics to animals." They argued that Parliament should ban human-use antibiotics in animal feeds. "In the long term," the committee wrote, "we believe it will be more rewarding to study and improve the methods of animal husbandry than to feed diets containing antibiotics." Alvin Shuster, "Britain to Curb Antibiotic Feed," *New York Times*, November 21, 1969, 17.

44. Harold M. Schmeck Jr, "Limitation on Antibiotics in Feed for Livestock Urged by F.D.A.," *New York Times*, February 1, 1972, 19.

45. Neal Black, "FDA Antibiotic Order Not as Bad as Feared," *National Hog Farmer* 18, no. 7 (July 19, 1973): 4; George Getschow, "Meat Producers Fear FDA Will Curb Use of Antibiotics, Thus Reducing Supplies," *Wall Street Journal*, January 6, 1975, 18.

46. Rex Wilmore, "They Want to Ban Antibiotics from Feed," *Farm Journal* 96 (March 1972): 23.

47. Jim Hightower, *Hard Times, Hard Tomatoes; A Report of the Agribusiness Accountability Project on the Failure of America's Land Grant College Complex* (Agribusiness Accountability Project. Task Force on the Land Grant College Complex, 1973). The report received media attention, but its biggest impact may have been in academia. Activist idealism and the AAP's report transformed the field of rural sociology. Scholars increasingly questioned the social and economic consequences of industrial agriculture. Americans prided themselves on feeding the world, these critics argued, but the costs included family farmers run off the land; rural main streets lined with empty shops; and environmental damage. Many sociologists framed their work around a holistic perspective. Farmer and field could not be isolated from the "natural" environment or from communities near, dependent on, and catering to agriculture.

48. "Bill Would Ban Large Corporate Farms," *Omaha World-Herald*, January 6, 1972, 6. For the "technology treadmill" theory see Willard W. Cochrane, *The Development of American Agriculture: A Historical Analysis*, 2d ed. University of Minnesota Press, 1993), Chapter 20.

49. Quoted in Suzanne Peters, "The Land in Trust: A Social History of the Organic Farming Movement," (PhD diss., McGill University, 1979), 283.

50. Quoted in Peters, "Land in Trust," 287. Also see Don Ralston and Marty Strange, "The Center for Rural Affairs: The First 20 Years," *American Journal of*

Economics and Sociology 75, no. 3 (May 2016): 809-37; and Marty Strange, *Family Farming: A New Economic Vision* (University of Nebraska Press, 1988).
51. See Andrew G. Kirk, *Counterculture Green: The Whole Earth Catalog and American Environmentalism* (University Press of Kansas, 2007). Brand's work also inspired dozens of "alternative technology centers" in North America. Many of those included a gardening or farming component; more than a few were attached to universities and colleges.

    Brand is a prolific author. A biography is John Markoff, *Whole Earth: The Many Lives of Stewart Brand* (Penguin Press, 2022).
52. Quoted in Peters, "Land in Trust," 221. For the Rodale empire, see Andrew N. Case, *The Organic Profit: Rodale and the Making of Marketplace Environmentalism* (University of Washington Press, 2018).
53. USDA, *Study Team on Organic Farming, Report and Recommendations on Organic Farming*, July 1980, iii, iv.
54. Curtis E. Beus and Riley E. Dunlap, "Conventional Versus Alternative Agriculture: The Paradigmatic Roots of the Debate," *Rural Sociology* 55, no. 4 (Winter 1990): 608-9.
55. "Earl Butz Versus Wendell Berry," *CoEvolution Quarterly* 17 (Spring 1978): 51, 55, 57; and Beus and Dunlap, "Conventional Versus Alternative," 606, 609.
56. Marc Newton, "Feed Lot Park Proposed," *Greeley Tribune (CO)*, May 10, 1969, 1.
57. Marian Burros, "A Maverick's Views," *Washington Post*, January 8, 1976.
58. Jessica Frazier, "Monfort of Colorado Markets Organic Beef," *Greeley Tribune (CO)*, December 26, 1971, 18; and George Getschow, "Meat Producers Fear FDA Will Curb Use of Antibiotics, Thus Reducing Supplies," *Wall Street Journal*, January 6, 1975, 18.

    University economists confirmed the gap between idea and profit. One study predicted that in the short-term, putting beef cattle back on pasture would result in a 50 percent drop in beef; livestock producers would earn higher profits.

    But over long haul, they concluded, eliminating antibiotics and hormones would drive up farmers' production costs and lead to higher meat prices for consumers who would likely respond by reducing their consumption. (Economists did not calculate an important intangible — how consumers would respond to the taste of grass-fed beef — nor did they factor in rising land prices.)

    As for hogs, analysts predicted that returning to pasture and natural breeding schedules would prevent meatpackers from running their plants at capacity year-round, so they'd charge more for their products.

    A good summary of the "what if" studies is "Antibiotics" in *Animal Feeds: A Report Prepared by the Committee on Animal Health and the Committee on Animal Nutrition [and] Board on Agriculture and Renewable Resources* (National Academy of Sciences, 1979). Also: Texas Agricultural Experiment Station and Department of Agricultural Economics and Sociology, "Economic Consequences of Banning the Use of Antibiotics at Subtherapeutic Levels in Livestock Production," by Henry C. Gilliam, et al., Departmental Technical Report no. 73–2, 1973; and Henry C. Gilliam Jr. and J. Rod Martin, "Economic Importance of Antibiotics in Feeds to Producers and Consumers of Pork, Beef and Veal," *Journal of Animal Science* 40, no. 6 (1975): 1241–55.

CHAPTER 11

1. Quoted in Emily E. LB. Twarog, *Politics of the Pantry: Housewives, Food, and Consumer Protest in Twentieth-Century America* (Oxford University Press, 2017), 85.
2. Twarog, *Politics of the Pantry*, 85.
3. "Rising Clamor for Tough Price Controls," *Time*, April 16, 1973; and "The Great Meat Furor," *Newsweek*, April 9, 1973, 19. Also see US House, Committee on Agriculture, *Rising Cost of Meat. Hearings before the Subcommittee on Domestic Marketing and Consumer Relations*. 93rd Cong. 1974.
4. See the ad in John Russell, "What the Producers Should Learn from . . . the Meat Price Uproar," *Farm Journal* 97 (May 1973): 15.
5. Marian Burros, "A Maverick's Views," *Washington Post*, January 8, 1976, D8.
6. "Doubts Voiced in Bigger Cattle Push," *Aberdeen American News (SD)*, July 17, 1973, 6.
7. Bill Hosokawa, "In Colorado, Bad Days for a Cattleman," *New York Times*, May 31, 1974, 33.
8. "Taking a Bath in Beef," *Forbes* 113, no. 9 (May 1, 1974): 18.
9. A first-rate, accessible take on the food aspect of the "crisis" is Bryan McDonald, *Food Power: The Rise and Fall of the Postwar American Food System* (Oxford University Press, 2017), especially Chapter 6. I thank editor Jen B. Robinson for "unexpected failure of success."
10. The term "disinvest" is from McDonald, *Food Power*.
11. For a useful take on this particular food crisis, see John L. Shover, *First Majority-Last Minority: The Transforming of Rural Life in America* (Northern Illinois University Press, 1976), Chapter 8.
12. Quoted in McDonald, *Food Power*, 170.
13. See Meg Jacobs, *Panic at the Pump: The Energy Crisis and the Transformation of American Politics in the 1970s* (Hill and Wang, 2016). On the role of cheap energy, see especially Caleb Wellem, *Energizing Neoliberalism: The 1970s Energy Crisis and the Making of Modern America* (Johns Hopkins University Press, 2023).
14. Norman H. Fischer and John A. Prestbo, "Cost of Eating: Soaring Grain Prices Seen Braking Output of Meat, Milk, Bread," *Wall Street Journal*, June 11, 1973, 1.

    Mine is a simplified version of an immensely complicated decade and period of economic turmoil. If the 70s were pivotal, it's because in many ways it marked the beginning of the end of American centrality. I'm not sure our psyches have recovered. Certainly, Americans then made little effort to adjust to new global realities — eg, significant shifts in China and the USSR, the collapse of a large segment of the American industrial economy, and no systematic effort to replace it. We've been riding on reputation since the seventies.
15. Howard R. Cottam, "Toward a World Food System," in US Senate, Committee on Agriculture and Forestry, Subcommittee on Agricultural Production, Marketing, and Stabilization of Prices, *U.S. and World Food Security*, 93d Cong. (1974), 71. For a brief but useful summary of the politics of post-war hunger, see A.H. Boerma, "The Thirty Years War Against World Hunger," *Proceedings of the Nutrition Society* 34, no. 3 (1975): 146–57.

    The FAO was a direct response to the food havoc that followed in the immediate wake of World War II. Its task was to monitor and manage the world's food supplies precisely so as to stave off the calamity of the early 1970s.

One oddball result of the 1970s moment? Farmers' markets.

Experts and activists pondered the nation's food security and arrived at a surprising conclusion:

Despite an abundance of cheap food and a hyper-efficient production and distribution system, the United States was food insecure. The majority of Americans lived in cities and relied on food supplies trucked in from other parts of the country. An average supermarket held only about two days' worth of food for the people it regularly served. A powerful storm, a railroad strike, or a military-related event could wipe shelves clean.

This finding resulted in the 1976 Farmer-to-Consumer Direct Marketing Act. It authorized $1.5 million for projects that would forge connections "between the urban consumer and the small farmer," aka farmers' markets. The two quotes are from Cottam, "Toward a World Food System," 34, 71. For more, see Chapter 13.

16. Mitchell C. Lynch, "Land of Plenty: For the Government, the Farm Boom Means Worry and Confusion," *Wall Street Journal*, October 31, 1973, 21.
17. For the economists' claims, see, for example, Norman H. Fischer, "Land of Plenty: Growing Enough Food for the Future May Tax U.S. Farms' Capacity," *Wall Street Journal*, November 19, 1973, 1.
18. Lynch, "Land of Plenty."
19. John A. Prestbo, "Land of Plenty: The Quick Turnaround in Agriculture Picture Brought Joys, Woes," *Wall Street Journal*, October 9, 1973, 41; Joseph Winski, "Land of Plenty: For Agribusiness Firms, the Farm Boom Means a Return to Riches," *Wall Street Journal*, October 15, 1973, 1.
20. Robert B. Cullen, "McLean Stakes $60 Million on Giant Farming Venture," *Lamberton Robesonian (NC)*, November 10, 1974, 4C. In 2024 dollars, $60 million is equal to about $371 million.
21. Cullen, "McLean Stakes $60 Million," 4C. In 2024 dollars, $60 million is equal to about $371 million.
22. Nash Henderson, "N.C. Corporate Farming — I: Companies Escaping Ecology Laws Requirements," *High Point Enterprise (NC)*, October 30, 1974, 13A. This series on the environmental and political impact of corporate farms first appeared in the *Winston-Salem Sentinel* and was reprinted by the Associated Press.
23. McQuoid's escapade was covered by trade journals and Missouri newspapers, but the most accessible accounts, and ones that ponder the implications of large-scale farming for rural America, are Calvin Trillin, "U.S. Journal: Kahoka, Missouri," *New Yorker*, May 6, 1974, 88, 90, 92-94, 96-97; and Gene A. Meyer, "If Proposed Corporate Hog Farm Succeeds, Future of Small Producer May Be in Doubt," *Wall Street Journal*, February 19, 1974, 34.
24. "Pigs in the Sky," *National Provisioner* 169, no. 25 (December 22, 1973): 23.
25. "Work Expected to Begin in March on Large Hog Plant," *Joplin Globe (MO)*, February 17, 1974, 3D.
26. Quoted in Brent E. Riffel, "The Feathered Kingdom: Tyson Foods and the Transformation of American Land, Labor, and Law" (PhD diss., University of Arkansas, 2008), 148.

27. Paul Duke Jr and Rick Christie, "Don Tyson Marshals His Flock to Fight," *Wall Street Journal*, October 13, 1988; and Kim Clark and Melanie Warner, "Tough Times for the Chicken King," *Fortune* 134, no. 8 (October 28, 1996).
28. Clark and Warner, "Tough Times."
29. Quoted in Riffel, "Feathered Kingdom," 231.
30. Quoted in Riffel, "Feathered Kingdom," 201; Clark and Warner, "Tough Times."
31. Clark and Warner, "Tough Times."
32. The example is in Riffel, "Feathered Kingdom," 121.
33. Quoted in Marvin Schwartz, *Tyson from Farm to Market* (University of Arkansas Press, 1991), 12.
34. "Tyson's Foods Looks at Future," *Broiler Industry* 27, no. 3 (March 1964): 12, 14; and Riffel, "Feathered Kingdom," 156n20.
35. "Don Tyson Suggests a Better 'Game Plan,'" *Broiler Industry* 37, no. 6 (June 1974): 34.
36. "Don Tyson Suggests a Better 'Game Plan,'" 3; and photo caption in Dean Houghton, "An Exclusive Look at Tyson, the Nation's Largest Hog Farm," *Successful Farming* 77 (August 1979): 29.
37. "Don Tyson Suggests a Better 'Game Plan,'" 30.
38. On the Bass family holdings, see Ann Crittendon, "Even for Texans, the Basses Are Rich," *New York Times*, December 13, 1981, F1, F17.
39. Robert Dorr, "Center-Pivot Irrigation Boom Slows to Trickle," *Omaha World-Herald*, December 16, 1984; accessed online.
40. "Here Comes the Corporate Sow," *Farm Journal* 108 (October 1984): 15; "The $50 Million Hog Farm," *Farm Journal* 108 (October 1984): 13. Haw did not mention another factor that surely informed his decision: thanks to a 1981 change in the federal tax code, the company's investment in the necessary buildings would earn tax credits and qualify National for accelerated depreciation.
41. Dick Hanson, "Across the Editor's Desk," *Successful Farming* 77 (August 1979): 3.
42. "Conagra [sic] Positioning for Future," *New York Times*, January 31, 1981, 31.
43. Sue Shellenbarger, "ConAgra Grows Rapidly Despite Missteps by Shrewdly Acquiring and Reviving Firms," *Wall Street Journal*, December 7, 1982, 35; Joseph Winski, "The Grand and Daring Strategy of ConAgra," *Chicago Tribune*, October 18, 1978, C10.
44. David P. Garino, "New Owner Rejuvenates Banquet Foods," *Wall Street Journal*, February 8, 1982, 29.
45. Betsy Morris and Roy J. Harris Jr, "ConAgra to Buy Greyhound Unit for $166 Million," *Wall Street Journal*, June 30, 1983, 8; and in Alexander Stuart, "Meatpackers in Stampede," *Fortune* 103 (June 29, 1981): 71. See, too, "The Old-Line Meatpackers Struggle to Survive," *Business Week*, November 13, 1978, 78, 80.
46. Bill Saporito, "ConAgra's Performance," *Fortune* 114, no. 9 (October 27, 1986): 70.
47. Quoted in Walt Barnhart, *Kenny's Shoes: A Walk Through the Storied Life of the Remarkable Kenneth W. Monfort* (Infinity Published, 2008), 208.
48. "How ConAgra Grew Big — and Now, Beefy," *Business Week*, May 18, 1987, 87.
49. See Barry J. Barnett, "The U.S. Farm Financial Crisis of the 1980s," *Agricultural History* 74, no. 2 (Spring 2000): 366-80; William P. Browne and John Dinse, "The Emergence of the American Agricultural Movement, 1977-1979," *Great*

Plains Quarterly 5, no. 4 (Fall 1985): 221-35; William P. Browne, "Challenging Industrialization: The Rekindling of Agrarian Protests in a Modern Agriculture, 1988-1987," *Studies in American Political Development* 7 (Spring 1993): 1-34.
50. Browne and Dinse, "Emergence," 226.
51. Quoted in William P. Browne, *Private Interests, Public Policy, and American Agriculture* (University Press of Kansas, 1988), 88. For this phase of the crisis, see especially Pamela Riney-Kehrberg, *When A Dream Dies: Agriculture, Iowa, and the Farm Crisis of the 1980s* (University Press of Kansas, 2022).
52. One consequence of the disarray: the more, and more diverse, the players involved, the more difficult it was to accomplish anything beyond the basics, in this case support for commodities.

    None of the players had any interest in "agriculture" as a whole or in its relation to the totality of American society. All any one player could hope was that he/she/it would manage to forge an alliance with other players in an effort to insert his/her/its agenda into the bill.

    A trio of political scientists who watched this process unfold over the years argued that fundamental agricultural "reform" "fails not because agricultural policy making is closed to" everyone but "agribusiness," a "bit of conventional wisdom [that] is badly out of date," but because "there are too many players, each seeking something from decision processes."

    See James T. Bonnen, William P. Browne, and David B. Schweikhardt, "Further Observations on the Changing Nature of National Agricultural Policy Decision Processes, 1946-1995," *Agricultural History* 70, no. 2 (Spring 1996): 130-52, quotes 151.
53. On the iron triangle, see, for example, Adam Sheingate, "Bending the 'Iron Triangle': Power, Politics, and Policy," *Agricultural History* 98, no. 3 (2024): 436-43. Also see James L. Novak, Larry D. Sanders, and Amy D. Hagerman. *Agricultural Policy in the United States: Evolution and Economics*, 2d. ed. (Routledge, 2022), Chapter 3.
54. Bonnen, Browne, and Schweikhardt, "Further Observations," 142. Also see James T. Bonnen, "Observations on the Changing Nature of National Agricultural Policy Decision Processes, 1946-1976," in *Farmers, Bureaucrats, and Middlemen: Historical Perspectives on American Agriculture*, ed. Trudy Huskamp Peterson, 309-29 (Howard University Press, 1980).
55. Browne, "Challenging Industrialization," 19. For a fascinating look at the ways in which "rural" states used apportionment to hold power, see Ryan Stockwell, "The Family Farm in the Post-World War II Era: Industrialization, the Cold War and Political Symbol," (PhD diss., University of Missouri-Columbia, 2008).
56. Don Paarlberg, "Agriculture Loses Its Uniqueness," *American Journal of Agricultural Economics* 60, no. 5 (December 1978): 772.

    Paarlberg served on the faculty at Purdue University, helped launch the Food for Peace program in the 1950s, and worked in high positions under three USDA secretaries. This 1978 publication is based on a speech he gave in 1975 at the National Public Policy Conference. For that, see Garth Youngberg, "Alternative Agriculturalists: Ideology, Politics, and Prospects," in *New Politics of Food*, ed. Don F. Hadwiger and William P. Browne (D.C. Heath and Company, 1978), 242-43.

    For one of Paarlberg's more blunt assessments see "The Farm Policy Agen-

da," *Increasing Understanding of Public Problems and Policies, 1975* (Farm Foundation, 1975), 95-102. He elaborates in *Farm and Food Policy: Issues of the 1980s* (University of Nebraska Press, 1980).
57. Luther Tweeten, "Domestic Food and Farm Policy Issues and Alternatives," *Increasing Understanding of Public Problems and Policies*, 1975 (Farm Foundation, 1975), 103, 104, 111.
58. Quoted in Mary Elizabeth Barham, "Sustainable Agriculture in the United States and France: A Polanyian Perspective," (PhD diss., Cornell University, 1999), 161. Also see Mary Summers, "From the Heartland to Seattle: The Family Farm Movement of the 1980s and the Legacy of Agrarian State Building," ed. Catherine McNicol Stock and Robert D. Johnston, *The Countryside in the Age of the Modern State: Political Histories of Rural America*, 303-25 (Cornell University Press, 2001).

By 1987, lobbyists had pried loose $4 million. By the early 1990s, LISA's 183 projects had received $39 million. A useful account of the late-century effort to "mainstream" sustainable agriculture is J. Patrick Madden, *The Early Years: The LISA, SARE, and ACE Programs* (Western SARE, n.d.).

Also see US General Accounting Office, Report to Congressional Requesters, *Sustainable Agriculture: Program Management, Accomplishments, and Opportunities*, GAO/RCED-92-233, September 1992; Andrew Marshall, "Sustaining Sustainable Agriculture: The Rise and Fall of the Fund for Rural America," *Agriculture and Human Values* 17, no. 3 (September 2000): 267-77.
59. Curtis E. Beus, and Riley E. Dunlap. "Conventional Versus Alternative Agriculture: The Paradigmatic Roots of the Debate." *Rural Sociology* 55, no. 4 (Winter 1990): 610.
60. USDA, ERS, "Economies of Size in Hog Production," by Roy Van Arsdall and Kenneth E. Nelson, *Technical Bulletin* no. 1712, December 1985, 39, 41.
61. For the survey, see Bill Fleming, "Opinion Page," *National Hog Farmer* 32, no. 11 (November 15, 1987): 9. The respondents were prosperous, business-oriented producers of means, involved in the market and concerned about their family futures. The second quote is from Bill Fleming, "Opinion Page," *National Hog Farmer* 31, no. 5 (May 15, 1986): 10.
62. See Jon Lauck, "The Corporate Farming Debate in the Post-World War II Midwest," *Great Plains Quarterly* 18, no. 2 (Spring 1998): 139-53; Jon Lauck, *American Agriculture and the Problem of Monopoly: The Political Economy of Grain Belt Farming, 1953-1980* (University of Nebraska Press, 2000), especially Chapter 2; Don Ralston and Marty Strange, "The Center for Rural Affairs: The First 20 Years," *American Journal of Economics and Sociology* 75, no. 3 (May 2016): 809-37, esp. 814-17, 825-28; Philip Raup, "Corporate Farming in the United States," *Journal of Economic History* 33, no. 1 (March 1973): 274-90.
63. Letter to the editor, Larry G. Hauer, "Small Producers Being Forced Out," *National Hog Farmer* 28, no. 10 (October 1983): 29.
64. C. David Kotok, "Stock Feeder: Initiative 300 Could Cripple the Industry," *Omaha World-Herald*, June 22, 1983, 2.
65. Russ Keen, "Hog-Farm Opinions Split Doland Folk," *Aberdeen American News (SD)*, February 21, 1988, 1B.
66. Kent Warneke, "Local Farmers, Businesses Supportive — Atkinson Farm Corporation Not Seen as Villain," *Omaha World-Herald*, December 30, 1984.

67. Example is from Warneke, "Local Farmers, Businesses Supportive."
68. "Missouri Gains Hog Farm that Iowa Turned Away," *St. Louis Post-Dispatch*, May 7, 1989, 8E.

CHAPTER 12

1. Quoted in Gary Taubes, *Good Calories, Bad Calories: Challenging the Conventional Wisdom on Diet, Weight Control, and Disease* (Alfred A. Knopf, 2007), 45. For the report, see US Senate, Select Committee on Nutrition and Human Needs, *Dietary Goals for the United States*, 95th Cong. (1977). (The second, revised edition appeared in December 1977.)
2. Opposition came from more than just the meat industry. In 1980, for example, the National Academy of Sciences published a study that challenged the heart-healthy mantra.
    Consumer advocates denounced the academy's findings as biased because one of the report's authors had once worked as a consultant for the egg industry. The author pointed out the lunacy of that criticism: during his career he'd received a quarter-million dollars in grants from industry sources, but $10 million from government agencies. How could he be a corporate patsy because of $250,000, but not a government stooge thanks to $10 million?
    It's worth mentioning that the Harvard scholar who tutored McGovern's staff in the "correct" view, devoted his later career to research funded in part by Frito-Lay. The example of the egg industry consultant is in Taubes, *Good Calories, Bad Calories*, 51; the Frito-Lay connection, 53.
3. Quoted in "Poisoning Linked to Cattle Germs," *New York Times*, September 6, 1984, A20. A fascinating profile of the investigation is Marjorie Sun, "In Search of Salmonella's Smoking Gun," *Science* 226, no. 4670 (October 5, 1984): 30–32.
4. Terri Minsky, "Bleak Pastures: Cattlemen Lose Money as Prices Fail to Rise with Production Costs," *Wall Street Journal*, May 8, 1981, 1.
5. Robert Reinhold, "Beef Industry Reduces Use of Disputed Drugs in Feed," *New York Times*, February 16, 1985, 8.
6. Terri Minsky, "Beef Industry Turning to Ads to Change Meat's Reputation," *Wall Street Journal*, April 1, 1982, 29.
7. Minsky, "Beef Industry Turning to Ads"; and Marj Charlier, "State of the Steak: Beef's Drop in Appeal Pushes Some Packers to Try New Products," *Wall Street Journal*, August 28, 1985, 1.
8. Quoted in Taubes, *Good Calories, Bad Calories*, 47; Bill Fleming, "Survey Confirms: Pork Still Has Image Problem!" *National Hog Farmer* 28, no. 12 (December 15, 1983): 6.
9. On the McRib, see, for example, Dean Houghton, "Pork's Fast-Food Foothold," *Successful Farming* 79 (September 1981): H6, H8; and Debra Switzky, "McRib's Future Uncertain," *National Hog Farmer* 28, no. 9 (September 15, 1983): 48.
10. Bill Eftink, "Chickens Are Stampeding Our Beef Customers," *Successful Farming* 79 (May 1981): 23.
11. Consumption statistics are in USDA, ERS, "Economics of the U.S. Meat Industry," by Richard J. Crom, Agriculture Information Bulletin no. 545, November 1988, Table 4, 7; and USDA, ERS, "Food Consumption, Prices, and Expendi-

tures, 1970–97," by Judith Jones Putnam and Jane E. Allshouse, Statistical Bulletin no. 965, April 1999, Table 4.

12. For a fascinating look at the science and technology of the nugget see Patrick Dixon, *Nuggets of Gold: Further Processed Chicken and the Making of the American Diet* (University of Georgia Press, 2024).

13. "Just What Is a Chicken McNugget," *Wall Street Journal*, October 3, 1985, 33.

14. "Don Tyson Tells How He Hopes to Earn 20% Net," *Broiler Industry* 40, no. 2 (February 1977): 27.

15. For discussions of these changes, see Walter Kiechel III, "The Food Giants Struggle to Stay in Step with Consumers," *Fortune* 98, no. 5 (September 11, 1978): 50-56; Walter Kiechel III, "Two-Income Families Will Reshape the Consumer Markets," *Fortune* 101, no. 5 (March 10, 1980): 110-14, 117, 119-20; Jean Kinsey, "Changes in Food Consumption from Mass Market to Niche Markets," in *Food and Agricultural Markets: The Quiet Revolution*, ed. Lyle P. Schertz and Lynn M. Daft, NPA Report no. 270 (National Planning Association, 1994), 19-43; Jean Kinsey and Ben Senauer, "Consumer Trends and Changing Food Retailing Formats," *American Journal of Agricultural Economics* 78, no. 5, Proceedings Issue (December 1996): 1187-91; and Alan Barkema, Mark Drabenstott, and Kelly Welch, "The Quiet Revolution in the U.S. Food Market," *Economic Review* 76, no. 3 (May/June 1991): 25-41.

16. W.G. Vander Ploeg, "Packers Are Still Facing Effects of 'Deli Revolution,'" *National Provisioner* 171, no. 19 (November 9, 1974): 174.

17. For an interesting look at the connections between food and corporations, see Ken Cooper, "Microlessons: Toward a History Information-Age Cuisine," *Technology & Culture* 56, no. 3 (July 2015): 576-609.

18. For the low-down, see Maureen Ogle, *Ambitious Brew: A History of American Beer* (Blue Willow Books, 2019), 205-30; and Don Russell, "Retro Beer," *All About Beer Magazine* 29, no. 4 (September 1, 2008) at allaboutbeer.com

19. Jane Mayer, "Now You Can Dine Knowing the Entree Lived a Happy Life," *Wall Street Journal*, April 6, 1989, 1; and Sonia L. Nazario, "Are Organic Foods Spiritual Enough? Not for Everyone," *Wall Street Journal*, July 21, 1989, A1.

20. Kathleen A. Hughes, "If Fitness Matters, Shouldn't a Chicken Do a Workout Too?" *Wall Street Journal*, July 16, 1986, 1.

21. For signals, see Alan Barkema and Michael L. Cook, "The Changing U.S. Pork Industry: A Dilemma for Public Policy," *Economic Review* 78, no. 2 (Second Quarter 1993): 49-65.

On quality control as a transaction cost, see V. James Rhodes, "The Industrialization of Hog Production," *Review of Agricultural Economics* 17, no. 2 (May 1995): 112-13.

Rhodes's work is crucial for understanding late-twentieth-century changes in hog farming. He conducted much of his research in agricultural economics at the University of Missouri–Columbia in partnership with Glenn Grimes. For decades, they analyzed hog production; their work provides the most complete set of statistical analyses of changes in the industry.

22. For a useful survey, see Margaret Mellon, "Savior or Monster? The Truth About Genetically Engineered Agriculture," in *Food Fights: How History Matters to Contemporary Food Debates*, ed. Charles C. Ludington and Matthew Morse Booker (University of North Carolina Press, 2019), 15-35.

23. The delightful term is from Warren Belasco, *Appetite for Change: How the Counterculture Took On the Food Industry*, 2d ed. (Cornell University Press, 2007).
24. Quoted in Stephen M. Voynick, *Riding the Higher Range: The Story of Colorado's Coleman Ranch and Coleman Natural Beef* (Glenn Melvin Coleman, 1998), 139.
25. Quoted in Voynick, *Riding the Higher Range*, 145, 149.
26. Quoted in Voynick, *Riding the Higher Range*, 152; Lynn Bronikowski, "Mel Coleman: A Trailblazer Naturally," *Rocky Mountain News*, April 22, 1990.
27. Quoted in Voynick, *Riding the Higher Range*, 119.
28. Quoted in Voynick, *Riding the Higher Range*, 143.
29. The exchanges between Coleman and the inspectors are recounted in Voynick, *Riding the Higher Range*, 156.
30. Voynick, *Riding the Higher Range*, 166.
31. Clay Evans, "Rancher Becomes 'Natural Beef' Guru," *Juneau Empire (AK)*, June 21, 1998, accessed online. The article originally appeared in the *Boulder Daily Camera (CO)*.
32. Quoted in Voynick, *Riding the Higher Range*, 179.
33. Quoted in Voynick, *Riding the Higher Range*, 179-80.
34. Michelle M. Mahoney, "Coleman Launches a Branded Beef Line," *Adweek's Marketing Week*, November 6, 1989.
35. Martin Everett, "How Coleman Sells the Sizzle," *Sales & Marketing Management* 139 (August 1, 1987).
36. For the Wyoming and Kansas examples, see Steve Painter, "Producers of 'Natural' Meat Claim Growing Market Share," *Lexington Herald-Leader (KY)*, May 4, 1986.
37. Katy Butler, "'Natural' Beef Is Big Business," *San Francisco Chronicle*, February 19, 1986.

    In the late 1990s, Schell took a position at the University of California–Berkeley as dean of the School of Journalism. Several years later, he helped recruit a new faculty member: Michael Pollan. The influence of the older man on the younger can be seen by reading just a few pages of Schell's *Modern Meat* and Pollan's *Omnivore's Dilemma*.
38. Keith Schneider, "The Profitable Road to Natural Beef," *New York Times*, September 5, 1986, A10.
39. Hughes, "If Fitness Matters," 17.
40. Carrie Dolan, "Federal Agents Lay Down the Law to Some Chicken-Livered Rangers," *Wall Street Journal*, January 29, 1990, B1.
41. Sonia L. Nazario, "Are Organic Foods Spiritual Enough? Not for Everyone," *Wall Street Journal*, July 21, 1989, A1.
42. Judith Blake, "'Hormone-Free' Label Raises Questions," *Seattle Times*, March 1, 1989. The story was a bit more complicated than that. The European Community had recently voted to ban imports of U.S. beef from cattle raised on synthetic hormones. That prompted a trade war, and one way to end the dispute was by eliminating any chance that some beef was hormone-free and some wasn't.
43. Judith Blake, "Federal 'Natural Beef' Program's Future Concerns Participants," *Seattle Times*, March 8, 1989; Marj Charlier, "Raisers of 'Natural' Cattle Fear Losing Market Niche," *Wall Street Journal*, May 17, 1989.

44. US House, Committee on Agriculture, *Proposed Organic Certification Program*, 101st Cong. (1990), 11, 49. See Samantha L. Mosier, *Creating Organic Standards in U.S. States: The Diffusion of State Organic Food and Agriculture Legislation, 1976-2010* (Lexington Books, 2017).
45. *Proposed Organic Certification Program*, 22.
46. *Proposed Organic Certification Program*, 18, 26.
47. Michelle Mahoney, "Discouraging Words Heard over Ads for Natural Beef," *Denver Post*, March 29, 1991, accessed online.
48. Mahoney, "Discouraging Words."
49. Mahoney, "Discouraging Words."

CHAPTER 13

1. Mike McGraw and Mike Hendricks, "Consumers Can't Depend on USDA for Meat Safety; Inspectors Seldom Test for Pathogens That Must Be Killed in Cooking," *Kansas City Star*, January 31, 1993.
2. After the fact, researchers speculated that *E. coli* was on the move precisely because ranchers and feeders had reduced or eliminated vaccinations. See Tom Paulson, "Risky Food — Why Now? — 10 Years After First Appearance, Tiny Bug Is Still Baffling Experts," *Seattle Post-Intelligencer*, February 22, 1993.
3. Carole Sugarman, "U.S. Meat Inspections Come Under Scrutiny," *Washington Post*, February 9, 1993. Also see Christopher Hanson, "Roadblocks to Reform — U.S. Inspectors Know Trouble but Action Slow," *Seattle Post-Intelligencer*, February 23, 1993.
4. Sugarman, "U.S. Meat Inspections."
5. Bettie Fennell, "Success Keeps Murphy Farms High on the Hog," *Wilmington Star-News (NC)*, January 18, 1987, 1E. For brief histories of Smithfield, see Mitchell Gordon, "High on the Hog," *Barron's National Business and Financial Weekly* 65, no. 47 (November 25, 1985), accessed online; and Sharon Reier, "High on the Hog," *Financial World* 157, no. 14 (June 28, 1988), accessed online.
6. Martha Quillin, "Bladen Divided Over Plant — Slaughterhouse's Jobs Wanted, Not Its Waste," *Raleigh News & Observer (NC)*, March 7, 1991.
7. Quoted in Stuart Leavenworth, "250 Debate Animal-Waste Issue at Public Hearing," *Raleigh News & Observer (NC)*, June 24, 1992.
8. The series is online at pulitzer.org/winners.
9. Quoted in Greg Barnes, "Factory Farms Take Hold," *Fayetteville Observer (NC)*, December 16, 2003.
10. Joby Warrick, "Hog-Waste Spill Fouls Land, River in Onslow," *Raleigh News & Observer*, June 23, 1995. A solid account of the North Carolina spills as well as other conflicts over industrial farms in the 1990s is David Kirby, *Animal Factory: The Looming Threat of Industrial Pig, Dairy, and Poultry Farms to Humans and the Environment* (St. Martin's Press, 2010).
11. Joby Warrick, "Hog Spills Change Lawmakers' Views," *Raleigh News & Observer*, August 6, 1995.
12. Quoted in Chris Mayda, "Passion on the Plains: Pigs on the Panhandle," (PhD diss., University of Southern California, 1998), 162.

13. "Clause in 1991 Bill Opened Gates for Corporate Hog Farms," *Daily Oklahoman*, May 18, 1997. For the Tyson operations, see Michael McNutt, "Swing Operation Prompts Watchdog Group — Strict Regulations Sought to Guard Environment," *Daily Oklahoman*, March 2, 1994. Also see Jim Stafford, "Cattle Industry in Oklahoma Faces Challenging Future," *Daily Oklahoman*, April 25, 1993. Also see Richard Lowitt, "From Petroleum to Pigs: The Oklahoma Panhandle in the Last Half of the Twentieth Century," *Chronicles of Oklahoma* 80, no. 3 (September 2002): 260-83.
14. Both quoted in Mayda, "Passion on the Plains," 176. On the area's economic woes, see Ann DeFrange, "Rural Revival — State Towns Taking Charge of Their Economic Future," *Daily Oklahoman*, October 2, 1994; and Michael McNutt, "Guymon's Economy Booming," *Daily Oklahoman*, December 11, 1994.
15. Quoted in Mayda, "Passion on the Plains," 212.
16. Quoted in Mayda, "Passion on the Plains," 212.
17. Quoted in Mayda, "Passion on the Plains," 213.
18. Sam Howe Verhovek, "Talk of the Town: Burgers v. Oprah," *New York Times*, January 21, 1998, A10. Also see Callie F. Kostelich and Heidi Hakimi-Hood. "'You Are What You Eat': Oprah, Amarillo, and Food Politics," in *Veg(etari)an Arguments in Culture, History, and Practice: The V Word*, ed. Cristina Hanganu-Bresch and Kristin Kondrlik (Springer International Publishing, 2021), 171-94; and Jennifer Jeanne Richardson, "Cowboys and Celebrities: Reading Rhetorics at the Texas Beef *v.* Oprah Winfrey Trial" (PhD diss., Washington State University, 2003).
19. Verhovek, "Burgers v. Oprah," A10.
20. I pieced this story together for the first version of this book, *In Meat We Trust: An Unexpected History of Carnivore America* (Houghton Mifflin Harcourt, 2013). All of the sources I used are in the bibliography for this book. See sections Agriculture: Alternative/Organic/Sustainable, and Foodways: Countercuisine & Food Activists.
21. Jack Kloppenburg Jr., John Hendrickson, and G. W. Stevenson, "Coming in to the Foodshed," *Agriculture and Human Values* 13, no. 3 (Summer 1996): 34, 36, 38. For a good summary of the community food security idea and the problems of putting it into practice, see Molly D. Anderson and John T. Cook, "Community Food Security: Practice in Need of Theory?" *Agriculture and Human Values* 16, no. 2 (June 1999): 141–50.

    Kloppenburg, Hendrickson, and Stevenson argued for "withdrawing from" the global and national food economy in order to build an alternative food system rooted in regional and local food sheds; systems that would link town and country, city dweller and farmer.

    Only then could Americans "reassemble" their "fragmented identities, reestablish community, and become native not only to a place but to each other." Food linked everyone, regardless of class, geography, race, or income. Urban gardens, family farms, or farmers' markets encouraged Americans to shoulder greater responsibility for their air, water, soil, and neighbors.

    Environmental degradation and economic injustice could be alleviated, and spiritual awakening nurtured, one farmer, one garden, one market, one meal at a time.

22. A useful account of the battle for standards is in Samuel Fromartz, *Organic, Inc.: Natural Foods and How They Grew* (Harcourt, 2006), Chapter 6.
23. C. Clare Hinrichs and Patricia Allen, "Selective Patronage and Social Justice: Local Food Consumer Campaigns in Historical Context," *Journal of Agricultural and Environmental Ethics* 21 (2008): 330.
24. For a summary of the rules, see USDA, ERS, Market and Trade Economics Division and Resource Economics Division, *Recent Growth Patterns in the U.S. Organic Foods Market*, by Carolyn Dimitri and Catherine Greene, Information Bulletin no. 777, September 2002, 19.
25. On the complications of making meat, see Chelsea Bardot Lewis and Christian J. Peters, "A Capacity Assessment of New England's Large Animal Slaughter Facilities as Relative to Meat Production for the Regional Food System," *Renewable Agriculture and Food Systems* 27, no. 3 (September 2012): 192-99; Lauren Elizabeth Gwin, "New Pastures, New Food: Building Viable Alternatives to Conventional Beef" (PhD diss., University of California-Berkeley, 2006); and Lauren Gwin, "Scaling-up Sustainable Livestock Production: Innovation and Challenges for Grass-Fed Beef in the U.S.," *Journal of Sustainable Agriculture* 33 (2009): 189-209.

    The point about lack of livestock farmers is made in C. Clare Hinrichs and Rick Welsh, "The Effects of the Industrialization of US Livestock Agriculture on Promoting Sustainable Production Practices," *Agriculture and Human Values* 20, no. 2 (Summer 2003): 125-41.
26. Rod Dreher, "USDA-Disapproved: Small Farmers and Big Government," *National Review* 27 (January 2003). Accessed online. The owners eventually found USDA-sanctioned slaughtering facilities.
27. Dreher, "USDA-Disapproved."
28. Dreher, "USDA-Disapproved."
29. Dreher, "USDA-Disapproved."
30. The Massachusetts man's problem is detailed in Molly Colin, "Elite Meat: Shoppers Sold on Organic Produce Find Its Main-Course Counterpart — Certified Beef, Poultry, and Pork — to Be Elusive," *Christian Science Monitor*, July 14, 2003.
31. Dreher, "USDA-Disapproved."
32. Worth Wren Jr, "Beefing Up Bottom Line — Cattle Industry Using Range of Marketing Initiatives," *Fort Worth Star-Telegram*, May 7, 2000. Also see John Lozier, Edward Rayburn, and Jane Shaw, "Growing and Selling Pasture-Finished Beef: Results of a Nationwide Survey," *Journal of Sustainable Agriculture* 25, no. 2 (2004): 93-112.
33. Michael Pollan, "Power Steer," *New York Times Magazine*, March 31, 2002.
34. Kim Severson, "Grass Roots Revolution — Will New Beef Put Corn-Raised Cattle Out to Pasture?" *San Francisco Chronicle*, June 19, 2002.
35. Kim Severson, "High Stakes — Bay Area at the Forefront of the Big-Bucks Battle Between Proponents of Grass-Fed Beef and Traditional Cattlemen," *San Francisco Chronicle*, June 19, 2002.
36. Severson, "High Stakes."
37. Milford Prewitt, "Chefs Challenge Peers to Serve Grass-Fed Beef," *Nation's Restaurant News*, May 20, 2002, 3.
38. Prewitt, "Chefs Challenge Peers."

39. Prewitt, "Chefs Challenge Peers." Schlosser noted that many historically significant movements, including abolition and women's suffrage, had been "led by educated, middle- and upper-income people." The crusade for a more sustainable food system, he believed, was similar. He was the author of *Fast Food Nation*, a 2001 exposé of the fast-food industry in general and fast-food meat in particular. Prewitt, "Chefs Challenge Peers."
40. *Omnivore's Dilemma* (Penguin Books, 2006), like *The Jungle* and *Silent Spring*, was less launching pad than tipping point. It resonated with a public accustomed to asserting its consumer rights and to the allure of alternative foods, whether meat or arugula. Certainly the book energized a new generation of food activists, and converted millions of otherwise indifferent consumers into organic aficionados.
41. Stacy Finz, "Founder Says New Owners Changing Product Protocol," *San Francisco Chronicle*, February 22, 2009.
42. Petaluma Holdings also owned Swift & Company, the most recent name of what had been ConAgra Beef, the Greeley outfit that began life as Monfort Beef. Over the next few years, PH merged with what had been Natural Food Holdings and then with a third investment firm, KDSB Holdings. In 2006, this new entity incorporated Coleman Natural Foods as the parent company for its alternative meat brands and companies, which by then included Rocky the Range Chicken, Rocky Jr., and Rosie the Organic Chicken. I pieced this together via various business media.
43. See "Letters," *Lancaster Intelligencer Journal (PA)*, March 28, 2002. I found many examples of these form letters, including ones sent on the occasion of World Farm Animals Day, October 2 (also the birthday of Mahatma Gandhi).
44. Steve Moest, "Why Pork Producers Do What They Do," *Freeport Journal-Standard (IL)*, May 6, 2012.

AFTERWORD

1. I highly recommend the excellent reporting from Michael Grunwald, *We Are Eating the Earth: The Race to Fix Our Food System and Save Our Climate* (Simon & Schuster, 2025).

BIBLIOGRAPHY

THE BIBLIOGRAPHY IS ORGANIZED BY TOPIC

1890s Depression **350**
Agricultural Crisis 1980s **350**
Agricultural Inputs: mid-20th c. **351**
Agriculture: Alternative/Organic/Sustainable **352**
Agriculture: In the Field, On the Ground **354**
Agriculture: Policy/Policymaking **358**
American Farm Bureau Federation **361**
Animal Welfare **361**
Antitrust/Monopoly/Corporations **362**
Background/Context: 20th & 21st c. **362**
Background/Context: Colonial-19th c. **364**
Boycotts/Protests **366**
Chickens/Broiler Industry **366**
Cities: Sanitation & Reform **369**
Cities: Urban History **370**
Colorado **371**
Consumers/Consumption **371**
Environment: History/Issues **373**
Environment: Threats/Responses **374**
Family Farm **376**
Food: Prices/High Cost of Living **376**
Food: Retail/Distribution/Grocers **377**
Foodways **378**
Foodways: Countercuisine/Food Activism **383**
Livestock: Cattle & Hogs **384**
Meatpacking/Packers **390**
Native Americans/"Indian Removal" **393**
New York City **394**
Race **394**
Railroads **396**
Slaughterhouse Cases **396**
USDA **397**
Western US: Background/Context **398**
Western US: 19th c. Investors **399**
Western US: Irrigation/Reclamation **401**
World War I **401**
World War II **402**
Databases/Catalogs/Periodicals/Newspapers **403**

1890S/DEPRESSION

Carlson, Mark. "Causes of Bank Suspensions in the Panic of 1893." *Explorations in Economic History* 42 (January 2005): 56-80.

Carter, Susan B., Richard Sutch, and Stanley Lebergott. "The Great Depression of the 1890s: New Suggestive Estimates of the Unemployment Rate, 1890-1905." *Research in Economic History* 14 (1992): 47-76.

Dupont, Brandon R. "Panic in the Plains: Agricultural Markets and the Panic of 1893." *Cliometrica* 3 (2009): 27-54.

Hoffmann, Charles. "The Depression of the Nineties." *Journal of Economic History* 16 (June 1956): 137-64.

Rezneck, Samuel. "Unemployment, Unrest, and Relief in the United States During the Depression of 1893-97." *Journal of Political Economy* 61, no. 4 (August 1953): 324-45.

Steeples, Douglas, and David O. Whitten. *Democracy in Desperation: The Depression of 1893*. Greenwood Press, 1998.

AGRICULTURAL CRISIS 1970S/1980S

Anderson, Wayne. "'A Moral Duty to Uphold the Family Farm': The Religious Response to the 1980s Farm Crisis." *Agricultural History* 96, no. 4 (November 2022): 531-52.

Barnett, Barry J. "The U.S. Farm Financial Crisis of the 1980s." *Agricultural History* 74, no. 2 (Spring 2000): 366-80.

Bovee, David. "The Church and the Land: The National Catholic Rural Life Conference and American Society, 1923-1985." PhD diss., University of Chicago, 1986.

Browne, William P. "Challenging Industrialization: The Rekindling of Agrarian Protests in a Modern Agriculture, 1977-1987." *Studies in American Political Development* 7 (Spring 1993): 1-34.

Browne, William P. "Lobbyists, Private Interests and the 1985 Farm Bill." [1986]. ageconsearch.umn.edu

Browne, William P. "Mobilizing and Activating Group Demands: The American Agriculture Movement." *Social Science Quarterly* 64, no. 1 (March 1983): 19-34.

Browne, William P., and John Dinse. "The Emergence of the American Agriculture Movement, 1977-1979." *Great Plains Quarterly* 5, no. 4 (Fall 1985): 221-35.

Center for Rural Affairs. *Who Will Sit Up with the Corporate Sow?* [Center for Rural Affairs, 1974].

Dudley, Kathryn Marie. *Debt and Dispossession: Farm Loss in America's Heartland*. University of Chicago Press, 2000.

Foley, Michael Stewart. "'Everyone Was Pounding on Us': Front Porch Politics and the American Farm Crisis of the 1970s and 1980s." *Journal of Historical Sociology* 28, no. 1 (March 2015): 104-24.

Lauck, Jon. "The Corporate Farming Debate in the Post-World War II Midwest." *Great Plains Quarterly* 18, no. 2 (Spring 1998): 139-53.

Leiker, James N. "Rage of the Rural Minority: The High Plains Farm Crisis and

Farmer Activism in Colorado and Kansas." *Great Plains Quarterly* 39, no. 3 (Summer 2019): 265-89.
Mooney, Patrick H. *Farmers' and Farm Workers' Movements: Social Protest in American Agriculture*. Twayne Publishers, 1995.
Ralston, Don, and Marty Strange. "The Center for Rural Affairs: The First 20 Years." *American Journal of Economics & Sociology* 75, no. 3 (May 2016): 809-37.
Riney-Kehrberg, Pamela. *When a Dream Dies: Agriculture, Iowa, and the Farm Crisis of the 1980s*. University Press of Kansas, 2022.
Schlatter, Evelyn A. *Aryan Cowboys: White Supremacists and the Search for A New Frontier, 1970-2000*. University of Texas Press, 2006.

AGRICULTURAL INPUTS: MID-20TH CENTURY

Buchanan, Nicholas. "The Atomic Meal: The Cold War and Irradiated Foods, 1945-1963." *History and Technology* 21, no. 2 (June 2005): 211-49.
Daemmrich, Arthur. "Synthesis by Microbes or Chemists? Pharmaceutical Research and Manufacturing in the Antibiotic Era." *History and Technology* 25, no. 3 (September 2009): 237-56.
Finlay, Mark. "Hogs, Antibiotics, and the Industrial Environments of Postwar Agriculture." In *Industrializing Organisms: Introducing Evolutionary History*, edited by Susan R. Schrepfer and Philip Scranton, 237-60. Routledge, 2004.
Gardner, Martha N. "Battling Insects and Infection: American Chemical and Pharmaceutical Expansion During World War II." In *Nature At War: American Environments and World War II*, ed. Thomas Robertson, Richard P. Tucker, Nicholas B. Breyfogle, and Peter Mansoor, 275-97. Cambridge University Press, 2020.
Kirchhelle, Claas. *Pyrrhic Progress The History of Antibiotics in Anglo-American Food Production*. Rutgers University Press, 2020.
Kirchhelle, Claas. "Swann Song: Antibiotic Regulation in British Livestock Production (1953–2006)." *Bulletin of the History of Medicine* 92, no. 2 (Summer 2018): 317-50.
Langston, Nancy. *Toxic Bodies: Hormone Disruptors and the Legacy of DES*. Yale University Press, 2010.
Perkins, John E. "Reshaping Technology in Wartime: The Effect of Military Goals on Entomological Research and Insect-Control Practices." *Technology and Culture* 19, no. 2 (April 1978): 169-86.
Perkins, John H. *Geopolitics and the Green Revolution: Wheat, Genes, and the Cold War*. Oxford University Press, 1997.
Perkins, John H. "Insects, Food, and Hunger: The Paradox of Plenty for U.S. Entomology, 1920-1970." *Environmental Review* 7, no. 1 (Spring 1983): 71-96.
Podolsky, Scott H. *The Antibiotic Era: Reform, Resistance, and the Pursuit of a Rational Therapeutics*. Johns Hopkins University Press, 2015.
Rasmussen, Nicolas. "The Forgotten Promise of Thiamin: Merck, Caltech Biologists, and Plant Hormones in a 1930s Biotechnology Project." *Journal of the History of Biology* 32, no. 2 (Autumn 1999): 245-61.
Rasmussen, Nicolas. "Plant Hormones in War and Peace: Science, Industry, and

Government in the Development of Herbicides in 1940s America." *Isis* 92, no. 2 (June 2001): 291-316.

Rasmussen, Nicolas. "Steroids in Arms: Science, Government, Industry, and the Hormones of the Adrenal Cortex in the United States, 1930-1950." *Medical History* 46 (2002): 299-324.

Summons, Terry G. "Animal Feed Additives, 1940-1966." *Agricultural History* 42, no. 4 (October 1968): 305-13.

US Congress, Joint Committee on Atomic Energy. *"Radiation Processing of Foods: Hearings Before the Subcommittee on Research, Development, and Radiation.* 89th Cong. (1965).

AGRICULTURE: ALTERNATIVE/ORGANIC/SUSTAINABLE

Barham, Mary Elizabeth. "Sustainable Agriculture in the United States and France: A Polanyian Perspective." PhD diss., Cornell University, 1999.

Belden, Joe, Gibby Edwards, Cynthia Guyer, and Lee Webb. *New Directions in Farm, Land and Food Policies: A Time for State and Local Action.* Conference on Alternative State and Local Policies, Agriculture Project, [1979].

Belden, Joe, and Gregg Forte. *Toward a National Food Policy.* Exploratory Project for Economic Alternatives, 1976.

Beus, Curtis E., and Riley E. Dunlap. "Conventional Versus Alternative Agriculture: The Paradigmatic Roots of the Debate." *Rural Sociology* 55, no. 4 (Winter 1990): 590-616.

Buttel, Frederick H. "Ever Since Hightower: The Politics of Agricultural Research Activism in the Molecular Age." *Agriculture and Human Values* 22, no. 3 (2005): 275-83.

Buttel, Frederick H. "The Sociology of Agricultural Sustainability: Some Observations on the Future of Sustainable Agriculture." *Agriculture, Ecosystems and Environment* 46 (1993): 175-86.

Clancy, Katherine L. "Sustainable Agriculture and Domestic Hunger: Rethinking a Link Between Production and Consumption." In *Food for the Future: Conditions and Contradictions of Sustainability*, edited by Patricia Allen, 251-93. John Wiley & Sons, 1993.

Guthman, Julie. *Agrarian Dreams: The Paradox of Organic Farming in California.* University of California Press, 2004.

Guthman, Julie, Amy W. Morris, and Patricia Allen. "Squaring Farm Security and Food Security in Two Types of Alternative Food Institutions." *Rural Sociology* 71, no. 4 (2006): 662-84.

Gwin, Lauren. "Scaling-up Sustainable Livestock Production: Innovation and Challenges for Grass-Fed Beef in the U.S." *Journal of Sustainable Agriculture* 33 (2009): 189-209.

Hinrichs, C. Clare, and Rick Welsh. "The Effects of the Industrialization of US Livestock Agriculture on Promoting Sustainable Production Practices." *Agriculture and Human Values* 20, no. 2 (Summer 2003): 125-41.

Lockeretz, William. "Sustaining Agriculture Near Cities: An Introduction." In

Sustaining Agriculture Near Cities, edited by William Lockeretz, xv-xxii. Soil and Water Conservation Society, 1987.

Lyson, Thomas A., G.W. Stevenson, and Rick Welsh, eds. *Food and the Mid-Level Farm: Renewing an Agriculture of the Middle*. MIT Press, 2008.

Madden, J. Patrick. *The Early Years: The LISA, SARE, and ACE Programs* (Western SARE, n.d.). Accessed online.

Marshall, Andrew. "Sustaining Sustainable Agriculture: The Rise and Fall of the Fund for Rural America." *Agriculture and Human Values* 17, no. 3 (September 2000): 267-77.

Mosier, Samantha L. *Creating Organic Standards in U.S. States: The Diffusion of State Organic Food and Agriculture Legislation, 1976-2010*. Lexington Books, 2017.

National Research Council, Board on Agriculture. Committee on the Role of Alternative Farming Methods in Modern Agriculture. *Alternative Agriculture*. National Academy Press, 1989.

Obach, Brian K. *Organic Struggle: The Movement for Sustainable Agriculture in the United States*. MIT Press, 2015.

Peters, Suzanne. "The Land in Trust: A Social History of the Organic Farming Movement." PhD diss., McGill University, 1979.

Ruben, Barbara. "Common Ground." *Environmental Action* 27, no. 2 (Summer 1995). Accessed online.

Schnell, Steven N. "Food with a Farmer's Face: Community-Supported Agriculture in the United States." *Geographical Review* 97, no. 4 (October 2007): 550-64.

USDA, Study Team on Organic Farming. *Report and Recommendations on Organic Farming*. July 1980.

US General Accounting Office. *Direct Farmer-to-Consumer Marketing Program Should Be Continued and Improved*. CED-80-65. July 9, 1980.

US General Accounting Office. *Report to Congressional Requesters. Sustainable Agriculture: Program Management, Accomplishments, and Opportunities*, GAO/RCED-92-233, September 1992.

US House, Committee on Agriculture. *Proposed Organic Certification Program*. 101st Cong. (June 19, 1990).

Vail, David D. "A Countercultural Agriculture: Organic Farming in a Commercial Age." In *A Companion to American Agriculture History*, edited by R. Douglas Hurt, 188-99. John Wiley & Sons, Incorporated, 2022.

Voynick, Stephen M. *Riding the Higher Range: The Story of Colorado's Coleman Ranch and Coleman Natural Beef*. Glenn Melvin Coleman, 1998.

Wilder, Julia R. "An Upbeat Look at Government Policies and Proposals Involving Cattle and Sustainable Agriculture." *Journal of Sustainable Agriculture* 4, no. 2 (1993): 81-98.

Wimberley, Ronald C., Craig K. Harris, Joseph J. Molnar, and Terry J. Tomazic, eds. *The Social Risks of Agriculture: Americans Speak Out on Food, Farming, and the Environment*. Praeger Publishers, 2002.

Youngberg, Garth. "Alternative Agriculturalists: Ideology, Politics, and Prospects." In *The New Politics of Food*, edited by Don F. Hadwiger and William P. Browne, 227-46. D.C. Heath and Company, 1978.

Youngberg, Garth, Neill Schaller, and Kathleen Merrigan. "The Sustainable

Agricultural Policy Agenda in the United States: Politics and Prospects." In *Food for the Future: Conditions and Contradictions of Sustainability*, edited by Patricia Allen, 295-318. John Wiley & Sons, 1993.

Youngberg, Garth, and Suzanne P. DeMuth. "Organic Agriculture in the United States: A 30-Year Retrospective." *Renewable Agriculture and Food Systems* 28, no. 4 (2013): 294-328.

AGRICULTURE: IN THE FIELD, ON THE GROUND

Anderson, J.L. *Industrializing the Corn Belt: Agriculture, Technology, and Environment, 1945-1972*. Northern Illinois University Press, 2009.

Appleby, Joyce. "Commercial Farming and the 'Agrarian Myth' in the Early Republic." *Journal of American History* 68 (March 1982): 833-49.

Baker, Andrew H., and Holly Izard Paterson. "Farmers' Adaptations to Market in Early-Nineteenth-Century Massachusetts." In *The Farm: The Dublin Seminar for New England Folklife: Annual Proceedings 1986*, edited by Peter Benes, Jane Montague Benes, and Ross W. Beales. Boston University, 1988.

Baker, Andrew H., and Holly V. Izard. "New England Farmers and the Marketplace, 1780-1865: A Case Study." *Agricultural History* 65 (Summer 1991): 29-52.

Baker, O.E. "Changes In Production and Consumption of Our Farm Products and the Trend in Population." *Annals of the American Academy of Political and Social Science* 142 (March 1929): 97-146.

Baltensperger, Bradley H. "Larger and Fewer Farms: Patterns and Causes of Farm Enlargement on the Central Great Plains, 1930-1978." *Journal of Historical Geography* 19, no. 3 (1993): 299-313.

Barron, Hal S. *Mixed Harvest: The Second Great Transformation in the Rural North, 1870-1930*. University of North Carolina Press, 1997.

Bidwell, Percy Wells, and John I. Falconer. *History of Agriculture in the Northern United States, 1620-1860*. Carnegie Institution of Washington, 1925.

Bogue, Allan G. *From Prairie to Corn Belt: Farming on the Illinois and Iowa Prairies in the Nineteenth Century*. University of Chicago Press, 1963.

Bonanno, Alessandro, and Douglas H. Constance. "Corporations and the State in the Global Era: The Case of Seaboard Farms and Texas." *Rural Sociology* 71, no. 1 (2006): 59-84.

[Bradley, Cyrus P.] "Journal of Cyrus P. Bradley." *Ohio Archaeological and Historical Publications* 15 (1906): 207-70.

Brinkman, Joshua T. *American Farming and the History of Technology*. Routledge, 2024.

Bushman, Richard L. *The American Farmer in the Eighteenth Century: A Social and Cultural History*. Yale University Press, 2018.

Cannon, Brian Q. *Reopening the Frontier: Homesteading in the Modern West*. University Press of Kansas, 2009.

Carr, Lois Green, Russell R. Menard, and Lorena S. Walsh. *Robert Cole's World: Agriculture and Society in Early Maryland*. University of North Carolina Press, 1991.

Clapp, Jennifer. *Titans of Industrial Agriculture: How A Few Giant Corporations Came to Dominate the Farm Sector*. MIT Press, 2025.

Cochrane, Willard W. *The Development of American Agriculture: A Historical Analysis*. 2d ed. University of Minnesota Press, 1993.
Coclanis, Peter A. "Born in the U.S.A.: The Americanness of Industrial Agriculture." In *Food Fights: How History Matters to Contemporary Food Debates*, edited by Charles C. Ludington and Matthew Morse Booker, 36-60. University of North Carolina Press, 2019.
Cohen, Benjamin R. *Notes from the Ground Science, Soil, and Society in the American Countryside*. Yale University Press, 2009.
Conkin, Paul K. *A Revolution Down on the Farm: The Transformation of American Agriculture Since 1929*. University Press of Kentucky, 2008.
Danbom, David B. *The Resisted Revolution: Urban America and the Industrialization of Agriculture, 1900-1930*. Iowa State University Press, 1979.
Danhof, Clarence H. *Change in Agriculture: The Northern United States, 1820-1870*. Harvard University Press, 1969.
Drabenstott, Mark. "Industrialization: Steady Current or Tidal Wave?" *Choices: The Magazine of Food, Farm & Resource Issues* 9, no. 4 (4th Quarter 1994). Accessed online.
Drabenstott, Mark. "This Little Piggy Went to Market: Will the New Pork Industry Call the Heartland Home?" *Economic Review* 83, no. 3 (1998): 79-97.
Fite, Gilbert C. *American Farmers: The New Minority*. Indiana University Press, 1981.
Fitzgerald, Deborah Kay. *Every Farm a Factory: The Industrial Ideal in American Agriculture*. Yale University Press, 2003.
Frederico, Giovanni. "Not Guilty? Agriculture in the 1920s and the Great Depression." *Journal of Economic History* 65, no. 4 (December 2005): 949-76.
Gardner, Bruce L. *American Agriculture in the Twentieth Century: How It Flourished and What It Cost*. Harvard University Press, 2002.
Gates, Paul W. *The Farmer's Age: Agriculture 1815-1860*. Harper Torchbooks, 1960.
Gates, Paul W. "Homesteading in the High Plains." *Agricultural History* 51, no. 1 (January 1977): 109-33.
Genoways, Ted. *The Chain: Farm, Factory, and the Fate of Our Food*. Harper, 2014.
Graves, Russell. "Garden City: The Development of an Agricultural Community on the Great Plains." PhD diss., University of Wisconsin-Madison, 2004.
Hart, John Fraser. *The Changing Scale of American Agriculture*. University of Virginia Press, 2003.
Henke, Christopher. *Cultivating Science, Harvesting Power: Science and Industrial Agriculture in California*. MIT Press, 2008.
Herrington, Philip Mills. "The Exceptional Plantation: Slavery, Agricultural Reform, and the Creation of an American Landscape." PhD diss., University of Virginia, 2012.
Hirsh, Richard. "Shedding New Light on Rural Electrification: The Neglected Story of Successful Efforts to Power Up Farms in the 1920s and 1930s." *Agricultural History* 92, no. 3 (Summer 2018): 296-327.
Hopkins, Cyril G. *Soil Fertility and Permanent Agriculture*. Ginn and Company, 1910.
Hudson, John C. *Making the Corn Belt: A Geographical History of Middle-Western Agriculture*. Indiana University Press, 1994.
Hudson, Michael A., Bruce J. Sherrick, and Michael A. Mazzocco. "A Changing

Food and Agribusiness Sector: Its Impacts on Farm Structure." In *Size, Structure, and the Changing Face of American Agriculture*, edited by Arne Hallam, 412-43. Westview Press, 1993.

Hurt, R. Douglas. *American Agriculture: A Brief History*. Revised ed. Purdue University Press, 2002.

Hurt, R. Douglas, ed. *A Companion to American Agricultural History*. John Wiley & Sons, Incorporated, 2022.

Hurt, R. Douglas. *Food and Agriculture During the Civil War*. Praeger, 2016.

Hurt, R. Douglas. *Problems of Plenty: The American Farmer in the Twentieth Century*. Ivan R. Dee, 2002.

Huston, James L. *The British Gentry, the Southern Planter, and the Northern Family Farmer*. Louisiana State University Press, 2015.

Huston, James L. "Northern US Agriculture, the Distribution of Income, and the Economic Growth of the United States in the Nineteenth Century." *Agricultural History* 95, no. 2 (Spring 2021): 212-44.

Johnson, Timothy. "Growth Industry: The Political Economy of Fertilizer in America, 1865-1947." PhD diss., University of Georgia, 2016.

Johnson, Timothy. "Nitrogen Nation: The Legacy of World War I and the Politics of Chemical Agriculture in the United States, 1916-1933." *Agricultural History* 90, no. 2 (Spring 2016): 209-29.

Kloppenburg, Jack Ralph, Jr. *First the Seed: The Political Economy of Plant Biotechnology*. 2d ed. University of Wisconsin Press, 2004.

Krause, Kenneth R., and Leonard R. Kyle. "Economic Factors Underlying the Incidence of Large Farming Units: The Current Situation and Probable Trends." *American Journal of Agricultural Economics* 52, no. 5 (December 1970): 748-61.

Kulikoff, Allan. *From British Peasants to Colonial American Farmers*. University of North Carolina Press, 2000.

Lee, Elizabeth Oliver. "'Potomac's Valley Shall Become a Domain We Create': Commercialism and the South Branch Valley, 1750-1800." PhD diss., West Virginia University, 2008.

Maddox, James G. "Private and Social Costs of the Movement of People Out of Agriculture." *American Economic Review* 50, no. 2 (May 1960): 392-402.

Marcus, Alan I. *Agricultural Science and the Quest for Legitimacy: Farmers, Agricultural Colleges, and Experiment Stations, 1870-1890*. Iowa State University Press, 1985.

McClelland, Peter D. *Sowing Modernity: America's First Agricultural Revolution*. Cornell University Press, 1997.

McConnell, Grant. *The Decline of Agrarian Democracy*. University of California Press, 1953.

Mellon, Margaret. "Savior or Monster? The Truth About Genetically Engineered Agriculture." In *Food Fights: How History Matters to Contemporary Food Debates*, edited by Charles C. Ludington and Matthew Morse Booker, 15-35. University of North Carolina Press, 2019.

Milov, Sarah. "Promoting Agriculture: Farmers, the State, and Checkoff Marketing, 1935-2005." *Business History Review* 90, no. 3 (September 2016): 505-36.

Neth, Mary. *Preserving the Family Farm: Women, Community and the Foundations of Agribusiness in the Midwest, 1900-1940*. Johns Hopkins University Press, 1995.

Nordin, Dennis S., and Roy V. Scott. *From Prairie Farmer to Entrepreneur: The Transformation of Midwestern Agriculture*. Indiana University Press, 2005.

Olmstead, Alan L., and Paul W. Rhode. *Creating Abundance: Biological Innovation and American Agricultural Development*. Cambridge University Press, 2008.

Orejel, Keith. "The Origins of the Iowa Development Commission: Agricultural Transformation and Industrial Development in Mid-Twentieth-Century Iowa." *Annals of Iowa* 76, no. 1 (Winter 2017): 47-70.

Pawley, Emily. *The Nature of the Future: Agriculture, Science, and Capitalism in the Antebellum North*. University of Chicago Press, 2020.

Raup, Philip M. "Corporate Farming in the United States." *Journal of Economic History* 33, no. 1 (March 1973): 274-90.

Rasmussen, Wayne D. "The Impact of Technological Change on American Agriculture, 1862-1962." *Journal of Economic History* 22, no. 4 (December 1962): 578-91.

Rick, James Jonathan. "Machines on the Farm: Capitalism and Technology in Midwestern Agriculture, 1845-1900." PhD diss., College of William and Mary, 2022.

Ron, Ariel. "Farmers, Capitalism, and Government in the Late Nineteenth Century." *Journal of the Gilded Age and Progressive Era* 15 (2016): 294-309.

Ron, Ariel. *Grassroots Leviathan: Agricultural Reform and the Rural North In the Slaveholding Republic*. Johns Hopkins University Press, 2020.

Rothstein, Morton. "The Big Farm: Abundance and Scale in American Agriculture." *Agricultural History* 49, no. 4 (October 1975): 583-97.

Saloutos, Theodore, and John D. Hicks. *Agricultural Discontent in the Middle West 1900-1939*. University of Wisconsin Press, 1951.

Shannon, Fred A. *The Farmer's Last Frontier: Agriculture 1860-1897*. M.E. Sharpe, Inc., 1945.

Shover, John L. *First Majority-Last Minority: The Transformation of Rural Life in America*. Northern Illinois University Press, 1976.

Smith-Howard, Kendra. "Ecology, Economy, Labor: The Midwestern Farm Landscape Since 1945." In *The Rural Midwest Since World War II*, edited by J.L. Anderson, 44-71. Cornell University Press, 2014.

Stoll, Steven. *The Fruits of Natural Advantage: Making the Industrial Countryside in California*. University of California Press, 1998.

Stoll, Steven. *Larding the Lean Earth: Soil and Society in Nineteenth-Century America*. Hill and Wang, 2002.

US Senate, Committee on Agriculture, Nutrition, and Forestry. *Farm Structure: A Historical Perspective on Changes in the Number and Size of Farms*. 96th Cong. (1980).

Vaught, David. *Cultivating California: Growers, Specialty Crops, and Labor, 1875-1920*. Johns Hopkins University Press, 1999.

Watson, Andrew. "'The Single Most Important Factor': Fossil Fuel Energy, Groundwater, and Irrigation on the High Plains, 1955-1985." *Agricultural History* 94, no. 4 (Fall 2020): 629-63.

Weber, Margaret. "The American Way of Farming: Pioneer Hi-Bred and Power in Postwar America." *Agricultural History* 92, no. 3 (Summer 2018): 380-403.

Weber, Margaret. "Manufacturing the American Way of Farming: Agriculture,

Agribusiness, and Marketing in the Postwar Period." PhD diss., Iowa State University, 2018.

Wetherington, Mark V. *American Agriculture: From Farm Families to Agribusiness*. Rowman & Littlefield Publishers, 2021.

Winberry, John J. "The Sorghum Industry, 1854-1975." *Agricultural History* 54, no. 2 (Spring 1980): 343-52.

Wuthnow, Robert. *In the Blood: Understanding America's Farm Families*. Princeton University Press, 2015.

AGRICULTURE: POLICY/POLICYMAKING

Berry, Jeffrey M. *Lobbying for the People: The Political Behavior of Public Interest Groups*. Princeton University Press, 1977.

Benedict, Murray R. *Farm Policies of the United States 1790-1950: A Study of Their Origins and Development*. Twentieth Century Fund, 1953.

Branyan, Robert L. *The Paradox of Plenty: Readings on the Agricultural Surplus Since World War I*. W.C. Brown Book Co., 1968.

Burnett, Paul. "The Visible Land: Agricultural Economics, US Export Agriculture, and International Development, 1918-65." PhD diss., University of Pennsylvania, 2008.

Christensen, Alice M. "Agricultural Pressure and Governmental Response in the United States, 1919-1929." *Agricultural History* 11, no. 1 (January 1937): 33-42.

Christensen, Alice Margaret. "Agricultural Pressure and Government Response in the United States: 1919-1929." PhD diss., University of California-Berkeley, 1936.

Clarke, Sally H. *Regulation and the Revolution in United States Farm Productivity*. Cambridge University Press, 1994.

Clemens, Elisabeth S. *The People's Lobby: Organizational Innovation and the Rise of Interest Group Politics in the United States, 1890-1925*. University of Chicago Press, 1997.

Cochrane, Willard W. *Farm Prices: Myth and Reality*. University of Minnesota Press, 1958.

Coppess, Jonathan. *The Fault Lines of Farm Policy: A Legislative and Political History of the Farm Bill*. University of Nebraska Press, 2018.

Cullather, Nick. "The Foreign Policy of the Calorie." *American Historical Review* 112, no. 2 (April 2007): 337-64.

Cullather, Nick. *The Hungry World: America's Cold War Battle Against Poverty in Asia*. Harvard University Press, 2010.

Davis, John H., and Ray A. Goldberg. *A Concept of Agribusiness*. Division of Research. Graduate School of Business Administration. Harvard University, 1957.

Dean, Virgil W. *An Opportunity Lost: The Truman Administration and the Farm Policy Debate*. University of Missouri Press, 2006.

Deutsch, Christopher. "Forging A National Diet: Beef and the Political Economy of Plenty in Postwar America." PhD diss., University of Missouri-Columbia, 2018.

Freeman, Andrea. *Ruin Their Crops on the Ground: The Politics of Food in the United States, from the Trail of Tears to School Lunch*. Metropolitan Books, 2024.

Fusonie, Alan E. "John H. Davis: Architect of the Agribusiness Concept Revisited." *Agricultural History* 69, no. 2 (Spring 1995): 326-48.
Galston, William A. *A Tough Row to Hoe: The 1985 Farm Bill & Beyond*. Hamilton Press, 1985.
Gilbert, Jess. *Planning Democracy: Agrarian Intellectuals and the Intended New Deal*. Yale University Press, 2015.
Guither, Harold D. *The Food Lobbyists: Behind the Scenes of Food and Agri-Politics*. D.C. Heath and Company, 1980.
Guth, James L. "The National Board of Farm Organizations: Experiment in Political Cooperation." *Agricultural History* 48, no. 3 (July 1974): 418-40.
Hadwiger, Don F. *The Politics of Agricultural Research*. University of Nebraska Press, 1982.
Hadwiger, Don F., and William P. Browne, eds. *The New Politics of Food*. D.C. Heath and Company, 1978.
Hamilton, David E. *From New Day to New Deal: American Farm Policy from Hoover to Roosevelt, 1928-1933*. University of North Carolina Press, 1991.
Hamilton, Shane. "Agribusiness, the Family Farm, and the Politics of Technological Determinism in the Post-World War II United States." *Technology and Culture* 55, no. 3 (2014): 560-90.
Hamilton, Shane. "Revisiting the History of Agribusiness." *Business History Review* 90, no. 3 (2016): 541-45.
Hamilton, Shane. *Supermarket USA: Food and Power in the Cold War Farms Race*. Yale University Press, 2008.
Hansen, John Mark. *Gaining Access: Congress and the Farm Lobby, 1919-1981*. University of Chicago Press, 1991.
Hathaway, Dale E. "Migration From Agriculture: The Historical Record and Its Meaning." *American Economic Review* 50, no. 2 (May 1960): 379-91.
Johnson, H. Thomas. *Agricultural Depression in the 1920s: Economic Fact or Statistical Artifact?* Garland Publishing, 1985.
Lauck, Jon. *American Agriculture and the Problem of Monopoly: The Political Economy of Grain Belt Farming, 1953-1980*. University of Nebraska Press, 2000.
Lichtenstein, Nelson. "Two Cheers for Vertical Integration: Corporate Governance In A World of Global Supply Chains." In *Corporations and American Democracy*, edited by Naomi R. Lamoreaux and William J. Novak, 329-58. Harvard University Press, 2017.
Maddox, James G. "Private and Social Costs of the Movement of People Out of Agriculture." *American Economic Review* 50, no. 2 (May 1960): 392-402.
Matusow, Allen J. *Farm Policies and Politics in the Truman Years*. Harvard University Press, 1967.
McDonald, Bryan. *Food Power: The Rise and Fall of the Postwar American Food System*. Oxford University Press, 2017.
McGlade, Jacqueline. "More a Plowshare Than a Sword: The Legacy of US Cold War Agricultural Diplomacy." *Agricultural History* 83, no. 1 (Winter 2009): 79-102.
Mercier, Stephanie A., and Steve A. Halbrook. *Agricultural Policy of the United States: Historic Foundations and 21st Century Issues*. Springer, 2020.

Nestle, Marion. *Food Politics: How the Food Industry Influences Health and Nutrition.* University of California Press, 2002.
Novak, James L., Larry D. Sanders, and Amy D. Hagerman. *Agricultural Policy in the United States: Evolution and Economics.* 2d. ed. Routledge, 2022.
Paarlberg, Don. "Agriculture Loses Its Uniqueness." *American Journal of Agricultural Economics* 60, no. 5 (December 1978): 769-76.
Paarlberg, Don. *Farm and Food Policy: Issues of the 1980s.* University of Nebraska Press, 1980.
Paarlberg, Robert. *Food Politics: What Everyone Needs to Know.* Oxford University Press, 2010.
Paarlberg, Robert, and Don Paarlberg. "Agricultural Policy in the Twentieth Century." *Agricultural History* 74, no. 2 (Spring 2000): 136-61.
Phillips, Sarah T. "The Price of Plenty: Getting Farm Policy Right in the 1960s." *Journal of American History* 109, no. 3 (December 2022): 596-620.
Phillips, Sarah T. *This Land, This Nation: Conservation, Rural America, and the New Deal.* Cambridge University Press, 2007.
Riley, Barry. *The Political History of American Food Aid: An Uneasy Benevolence.* Oxford University Press, 2017.
Rothstein, Morton. "The Big Farm: Abundance and Scale in American Agriculture." *Agricultural History* 49, no. 4 (October 1975): 583-97.
Schertz, Lyle P. *The Making of the 1996 Farm Act.* Iowa State University Press, 1999.
Shideler, James H. *Farm Crisis, 1919-1923.* University of California Press, 1957.
Shideler, James H. "Herbert Hoover and the Federal Farm Board Project, 1921-1925." *Mississippi Valley Historical Review* 42, no. 4 (March 1956): 710-29.
Tweeten, Luther. "Domestic Food and Farm Policy Issues and Alternatives." *Increasing Understanding of Public Problems and Policies, 1975,* 103-11. Farm Foundation, 1975.
US Congress, Joint Economic Committee. *Policy for Commercial Agriculture: Its Relation to Economic Growth and Stability.* 85th Cong. (1958).
US Congress, Temporary National Economic Committee. *Investigation of Concentration of Economic Power. Large-Scale Organization in the Food Industries.* Monograph no. 35. 1940.
USDA, ARS, *Major Uses of Land in the United States: Summary for 1954.* Agriculture Information Bulletin No. 168. January 1957.
USDA, BAE. *Changing Technology and Employment in Agriculture,* by John A. Hopkins. May 1941. Also published as Works Projects Administration. *National Research Project on Reemployment Opportunities and Recent Changes in Industrial Techniques.*
USDA, BAE. "Kinds of Agricultural Surpluses," by Mordecai Ezekiel. 1927.
USDA, ERS. *The 20th Century Transformation of U.S. Agriculture and Farm Policy,* Economic Information Bulletin, edited by Carolyn Dimitri, Anne Effland, and Neilson C. Conklin. 2005.
USDA, ESC. *Another Revolution in U.S. Farming? Agricultural Economic Report No. 441,* by Lyle P. Schertz et al. December 1979.
US House. *Investigation of Concentration of Economic Power. Final Report and Recommendations of the Temporary National Economic Committee.* 77th Cong. (1941).
US House. *Proceedings of the Conference Relative to the Marketing of Live Stock Distribution of Meats and Related Matters, Held by the Direction of the Hon. David Franklin Houston,* . . .

Conducted by the Office of Markets and Rural Organization. H.Doc. No. 855. 64th Cong. (1915).
US Senate. *Disposal of Agricultural Surpluses — General in Hearings Before a Subcommittee of the Committee on Agriculture and Forestry.* 2 parts. 84th Cong. (1955).
US Senate, Committee on Agriculture and Forestry. *American Foreign Food Assistance: Public Law 480 and Related Materials.* 94th Cong. (1976).
US Senate, Committee on Agriculture, Nutrition, and Forestry. *Farm Structure: A Historical Perspective on Changes in the Number and Size of Farms.* 96th Cong. (1980).
Vogel, David. "The Public-Interest Movement and the American Reform Tradition." *Political Science Quarterly* 95, no. 4 (1980): 607-27.
Wilde, Parke. *Food Policy in the United States: An Introduction.* Routledge, 2013.
Wilson, M.L. "Problem of Poverty in Agriculture." *Journal of Farm Economics* 22, no. 1 (February 1940): 10-29.
Winders, Bill. *The Politics of Food Supply: U.S. Agricultural Policy in the World Economy.* Yale University Press, 2009.
Woeste, Victoria Saker. *Farmer's Benevolent Trust: Law and Agricultural Cooperation in Industrial America, 1865-1945.* University of North Carolina Press, 1998.

AMERICAN FARM BUREAU FEDERATION

Baker, Gladys. *The County Agent.* University of Chicago Press, 1939.
Bay, Edwin. *The History of the National Association of County Agricultural Agents.* National Association of County Agricultural Agents, 1961.
Berger, Samuel R. *Dollar Harvest: The Story of the Farm Bureau.* Heath Lexington Books, 1971.
Berlage, Nancy K. *Farmers Helping Farmers: The Rise of the Farm and Home Bureaus, 1914-1935.* Louisiana State University Press, 2016.
Burritt, M.C. *The County Agent and the Farm Bureau.* Harcourt, Brace and Company, 1922.
Kile, Orville Merton. *The Farm Bureau Movement.* MacMillan Company, 1921.
Scott, Roy V. *The Reluctant Farmer: The Rise of Agricultural Extension to 1914.* University of Illinois Press, 1970.
Porter, Kimberly K. "Embracing the Pluralist Perspective: The Iowa Farm Bureau Federation and the McNary-Haugen Movement." *Agricultural History* 74, no. 2 (Spring 2000): 381-92.

ANIMAL WELFARE

Beers, Diane L. *For the Prevention of Cruelty: The History and Legacy of Animal Rights Activism in the United States.* Swallow Press/Ohio University Press, 2006.
Davis, Janet M. *The Gospel of Kindness: Animal Welfare and the Making of Modern America.* Oxford University Press, 2016.
Freeberg, Ernest. *A Traitor to His Species: Henry Bergh and the Birth of the Animal Rights Movement.* Basic Books, 2020.
Grier, Katherine C. "'The Eden of Home': Changing Understandings of Cruelty and Kindness to Animals in Middle-Class American Households, 1820-1900." In

Animals in Human Histories: The Mirror of Nature and Culture, edited by Mary J. Henninger-Voss, 316-62. University of Rochester Press, 2002.

Harlow, Alvin F. *Henry Bergh: Founder of the A.S.P.C.A.* Julian Messner, Inc., 1957.

Ingram, Darcy. "'It Even Makes the Animals Laugh': Contesting Henry Bergh and the Animal Protection Movement in Nineteenth-Century New York." *Moving the Social* 68 (2022): 5-31.

Steele, Zulma. *Angel in Top Hat*. Harper & Brothers, 1942.

ANTITRUST/MONOPOLY/CORPORATIONS

Gordon, Sanford D. "Attitudes Toward the Trusts Before the Sherman Act." *Southern Economic Journal* 30, no. 2 (October 1963): 156-67.

Hawley, Ellis Wayne. *The New Deal and the Problem of Monopoly*. 1966. Reprint, Princeton University Press, 2015.

Hennessey, Jessica L. and John Joseph Wallis. "Corporations and Organizations in the United States After 1840." In *Corporations and American Democracy*, edited by Naomi R. Lamoreaux and William J. Novak, 74-105. Harvard University Press, 2017.

Hilt, Eric. "Early American Corporations and the State." In *Corporations and American Democracy*, edited by Naomi R. Lamoreaux and William J. Novak, 37-73. Harvard University Press, 2017

Hofstader, Richard. "What Happened to the Antitrust Movement? Notes on the Evolution of an American Creed." In *Antitrust and Business Regulation in the Post War Era, 1946-1964*, edited by Robert F. Himmelberg, 71-151. 1964. Reprint, Garland Publishing, 1994.

Lamoreaux, Naomi R. *The Great Merger Movement in American Business, 1894-1904*. Cambridge University Press, 1985.

Lamoreaux, Naomi R., and William J. Novak, eds. *Corporations and American Democracy*. Harvard University Press, 2017.

Levy, Jonathan. "From Fiscal Triangle to Passing Through: Rise of the Nonprofit Corporation." In *Corporations and American Democracy*, edited by Naomi R. Lamoreaux and William J. Novak, 213-44. Harvard University Press, 2017.

Marchand, Roland. *Creating the Corporate Soul: The Rise of Public Relations and Corporate Imagery in American Big Business*. University of California Press, 1998.

Martin, Albro. "The Troubled Subject of Railroad Regulation in the Gilded Age — A Reappraisal." *Journal of American History* 61, no. 2 (September 1974): 339-71.

Thorelli, Hans B. *The Federal Antitrust Policy: Origination of An American Tradition*. Johns Hopkins University Press, 1955.

Wright, Robert E. *Corporation Nation*. University of Pennsylvania Press, 2014.

BACKGROUND/CONTEXT: 20TH & 21ST CENTURIES

Anderson, J.L., ed. *The Rural Midwest Since World War II*. Northern Illinois University Press, 2014.

Balogh, Brian. *The Associational State: American Governance in the Twentieth Century*. University of Pennsylvania Press, 2015.

Berkowitz, Edward D. *Something Happened: A Political and Cultural Overview of the Seventies*. Columbia University Press, 2006.

Binkley, Sam. *Getting Loose: Lifestyle Consumption in the 1970s*. Duke University Press, 2007.

Cohen, Lizabeth. *Making A New Deal: Industrial Workers in Chicago, 1919-1939*. Cambridge University Press, 1990.

Collins, Robert M. *More: The Politics of Economic Growth in Postwar America*. Oxford University Press, 2000.

Conn, Steven. *The Lies of the Land: Seeing Rural America for What It Is — and Isn't*. University of Chicago Press, 2023.

Cowie, Jefferson. *The Great Exception: The New Deal & the Limits of American Politics*. Princeton University Press, 2016.

Cowie, Jefferson. *Stayin' Alive: The 1970s and the Last Days of the Working Class*. New Press, 2010.

Delton, Jennifer A. *The Industrialists: How the National Association of Manufacturers Shaped American Capitalism*. Princeton University Press, 2020.

Field, Bruce E. *Harvest of Dissent: The National Farmers Union and the Early Cold War*. University Press of Kansas, 1998.

Frank, Thomas. *The Conquest of Cool: Business Culture, Counterculture, and the Rise of Hip Consumerism*. University of Chicago Press, 1997.

Freeman, Joshua B. *American Empire: The Rise of a Global Power, the Democratic Revolution at Home 1945-2000*. Viking, 2012.

Gage, Beverly. *The Day Wall Street Exploded: A Story of America In Its First Age of Terror*. Oxford University Press, 2009.

Glickman, Lawrence B. *Free Enterprise: An American History*. Yale University Press, 2019.

Hendrickson, Mark. *American Labor and Economic Citizenship: New Capitalism From World War I to the Great Depression*. Cambridge University Press, 2013.

Hochschild, Adam. *American Midnight: The Great War, a Violent Peace, and Democracy's Forgotten Crisis*. Mariner Books, 2022.

Hoganson, Kristin L. *The Heartland: An American History*. Penguin Books, 2019.

Huber, Matthew T. *Lifeblood: Oil, Freedom, and the Forces of Capital*. University of Minnesota Press, 2013.

Jacobs, Meg. *Panic at the Pump: The Energy Crisis and the Transformation of American Politics in the 1970s*. Hill and Wang, 2016.

John, Richard R., and Kim Phillips-Fein, eds. *Capital Gains: Business and Politics in Twentieth-Century America*. University of Pennsylvania Press, 2016.

Jones, Christopher F. *Routes of Power: Energy and Modern America*. Harvard University Press, 2014.

Kennedy, David. *Freedom from Fear: The American People in Depression and War, 1929–1945*. Oxford University Press, 1999.

Klein, Maury. *The Genesis of Industrial America, 1870-1920*. Cambridge University Press, 2007.

Kwitny, Jonathan. *Vicious Circles: The Mafia in the Marketplace*. W.W. Norton & Company, 1979.

Lichtenstein, Nelson. *The Retail Revolution: How Wal-Mart Created a Brave New World of Business*. Metropolitan Books, 2009.

Ludington, Charles, and Matthew Morse Booker, eds. *Food Fights: How History Matters to Contemporary Food Debates*. University of North Carolina Press, 2019.

McGerr, Michael. *A Fierce Discontent: The Rise and Fall of the Progressive Movement in America*. Oxford University Press, 2003.

McGirr, Lisa. *Suburban Warriors: The Origins of the New American Right*. Updated edition. Princeton University Press, 2015.

Novak, William J. *New Democracy: The Creation of the Modern American State*. Harvard University Press, 2022.

Orejel, Keith. "Factories in the Fallows: The Political Economy of America's Rural Heartland, 1945-1980." PhD diss., Columbia University, 2015.

Patterson, James T. *Grand Expectations: The United States, 1945-1974*. Oxford University Press, 1996.

Patterson, James T. *Restless Giant: The United States from Watergate to Bush v. Gore*. Oxford University Press, 2005.

Phillips-Fein, Kim, and Julian E. Zelizer, eds. *What's Good for Business: Business and American Politics Since World War II*. Oxford University Press, 2012.

Rauchway, Eric. *The Great Depression & the New Deal: A Very Short Introduction*. Oxford University Press, 2008.

Richardson, Heather Cox. *How the South Won the Civil War: Oligarchy, Democracy, and the Continuing Fight for the Soul of America*. Oxford University Press, 2020.

Rodgers, Daniel T. *Atlantic Crossings: Social Politics In A Progressive Age*. Harvard University Press, 1998.

Shover, John L. *First Majority — Last Minority: The Transforming of Rural Life in America*. Northern Illinois University Press, 1976.

Steger, Manfred B. *Globalization: A Very Short Introduction*. Oxford University Press, 2009.

Stein, Judith. *Pivotal Decade: How the United States Traded Factories for Finance in the Seventies*. Yale University Press, 2010.

Szasz, Andrew. *Shopping Our Way to Safety: How We Changed from Protecting the Environment to Protecting Ourselves*. University of Minnesota Press, 2009.

Warren, Wilson J. *Meat Makes People Powerful: A Global History of the Modern Era*. University of Iowa Press, 2018.

Wellum, Caleb. *Energizing Neoliberalism: The 1970s Energy Crisis and the Making of Modern America*. Johns Hopkins University Press, 2023.

BACKGROUND/CONTEXT: COLONIAL-19TH CENTURY

Anderson, Benedict R. O'G. *Imagined Communities: Reflections on the Origin and Spread of Nationalism*. Revised ed. Verso, 2016.

Balogh, Brian. *A Government Out of Sight: The Mystery of National Authority in Nineteenth-Century America*. Cambridge University Press, 2009.

Belich, James. *Replenishing the Earth: The Settler Revolution and the Rise of the Anglo-World, 1783-1939*. Oxford University Press, 2009.

Bermann, William H. *The American National States and the Early West.* Cambridge University Press, 2012.
Calloway, Colin G. *New Worlds for All: Indian, Europeans, and the Remaking of Early America.* 2d ed. Johns Hopkins University Press, 2013.
Danbom, David B. *Born in the Country: A History of Rural America.* 2d ed. Johns Hopkins University Press, 2006.
Engerman, Stanley L., and Robert E. Gallman, eds. *The Long Nineteenth Century.* Cambridge Economic History of the United States. vol. 2. Cambridge University Press, 2000.
Federico, Giovanni. *Feeding the World: An Economic History of Agriculture, 1800-2000.* Princeton University Press, 2010.
Fink, Leon. *The Long Gilded Age: American Capitalism and the Lessons of a New World Order.* University of Pennsylvania Press, 2015.
Gerstle, Gary. *Liberty and Coercion: The Paradox of American Government from the Founding to the Present.* Princeton University Press, 2015.
Guarneri, Julia. *Newsprint Metropolis: City Papers and the Making of Modern Americans.* University of Chicago Press, 2017.
Hahn, Steven. *A Nation without Borders: The United States and Its World in an Age of Civil Wars, 1830-1910.* Viking, 2016.
Hughes, Thomas P. *Networks of Power: Electrification in Western Society, 1880-1930.* Johns Hopkins University Press, 1983.
John, Richard R. *Network Nation: Inventing American Telecommunications.* Belknap Press of Harvard University, 2010.
Jones, Christopher F. *Routes of Power: Energy and Modern America.* Harvard University Press, 2014.
Larson, John Lauritz. *The Market Revolution In America: Liberty, Ambition, and the Eclipse of the Common Good.* Cambridge University Press, 2010.
Levy, Jonathan. *Ages of American Capitalism: A History of the United States.* Random House, 2021.
Levy, Jonathan. *Freaks of Fortune: The Emerging World of Capitalism and Risk in America.* Harvard University Press, 2012.
Lindert, Peter H. *Unequal Gains: American Growth and Inequality Since 1700.* Princeton University Press, 2016.
Lindert, Peter H., and Jeffrey G. Williamson. "American Colonial Incomes, 1650-1774." *Economic History Review* 69, no. 1 (February 2016): 54-77.
Meyer, David R. *The Roots of American Industrialization.* Johns Hopkins University Press, 2003.
Misa, Thomas J. *A Nation of Steel: The Making of Modern America, 1865-1925.* Johns Hopkins University Press, 1995.
Morris, Charles R. *The Dawn of Innovation: The First American Industrial Revolution.* Public Affairs, 2012.
Nelson, Scott Reynolds. *Oceans of Grain: How American Wheat Remade the World.* Basic Books, 2022.
Novak, William J. *The People's Welfare: Law and Regulation in Nineteenth-Century America.* University of North Carolina Press, 1996.

Peskin, Lawrence A. *Manufacturing Revolution: The Intellectual Origins of Early American Industry*. Johns Hopkins University Press, 2007.

Porter, Glenn, and Harold C. Livesay. *Merchants and Manufacturers: Studies in the Changing Structure of Nineteenth-Century Marketing*. Johns Hopkins University Press, 1971.

Riney-Kehrberg, Pamela, ed. *The Routledge History of Rural America*. Routledge Taylor & Francis Group, 2016.

Saler, Bethel. *The Settlers' Empire: Colonialism and State Formation in America's Old Northwest*. University of Pennsylvania Press, 2015.

Taylor, Alan. *American Civil Wars: A Continental History, 1850-1873*. W.W. Norton & Company, 2024.

Taylor, Alan. *American Republics: A Continental History of the United States, 1783-1850*. W.W. Norton & Company, 2021.

Wrobel, David M. *The End of American Exceptionalism: Frontier Anxiety from the Old West to the New Deal*. University Press of Kansas, 1993.

Zakim, Michael, and Gary J. Kornblith, eds. *Capitalism Takes Command: The Social Transformation of Nineteenth-Century America*. University of Chicago Press, 2011.

BOYCOTTS/PROTESTS

Béja, Alice. "The Political Uses of Food Protests: Analyzing the 1910 Meat Boycott." *Journal of American Studies* 57, no. 2 (2023): 178-96.

Frank, Dana. "Housewives, Socialists, and the Politics of Food: The 1917 New York Cost-of-Living Protests." *Feminist Studies* 11, no. 2 (Summer 1985): 255-85.

Frieburger, William. "War Prosperity and Hunger: The New York Food Riots of 1917." *Labor History* 25, no. 2 (Spring 1984): 217-39.

Hyman, Paula E. "Immigrant Women and Consumer Protests: The New York City Kosher Meat Boycott of 1902." *American Jewish History* 70, no. 1 (September 1980): 91-105.

Lynn, Denise. "'United We Spend': Communist Women and the 1935 Meat Boycott." *American Communist History* 10, no. 1 (April 2011): 35-52.

Nusco, Kimberly. "The South Providence Kosher Meat Boycott of 1910." *Rhode Island Jewish Historical Notes* 14, no. 1 (November 2003): 96-126.

Nusco, Kimberly Susan. "The South Providence Kosher Meat Boycott of 1910: A Study of Jewish Women's Consumer Activism." Master's thesis, University of Rhode Island, 2003.

Seligman, Scott D. *The Great Kosher Meat War of 1902: Immigrant Housewives and the Riots That Shook New York City*. Potomac Books, 2020.

Twarog, Emily E. LB. *Politics of the Pantry: Housewives, Food, and Consumer Protest in Twentieth-Century America*. Oxford University Press, 2017.

CHICKENS/BROILER INDUSTRY

Arkansas Agricultural Experiment Station. *From Hills and Hollers: Rise of the Poultry Industry in Arkansas*, by Stephen F. Strausberg. Special Report 170. [1995].

Boyd, William. "Making Meat: Science, Technology, and American Poultry Production." *Technology and Culture* 42, no. 4 (October 2001): 631-64.

Boyd, William, and Michael Watts. "Agro-Industrial Just-in-Time: The Chicken Industry and Postwar American Capitalism." In *Globalising Food: Agrarian Questions and Global Restructuring*, edited by David Goodman and Michael Watts, 192-225. Routledge, 1997.

Bugos, Glenn E. "Intellectual Property Protection in the American Chicken-Breeding Industry." *Business History Review* 66, no. 1 (Spring 1992): 127-68.

Cooke, Kathy J. "From Science to Practice, or Practice to Science? Chickens and Eggs in Raymond Pearl's Agricultural Breeding Research, 1907-1916." *Isis* 88, no. 1 (March 1997): 62-86.

Curran, Arthur Ranger. "The Georgia Broiler Industry 1959-69: A Case Study of Evolving Industrial Patterns In An Industry Over a Decade." PhD diss., University of Georgia, 1970.

Derry, Margaret E. *Art and Science in Breeding: Creating Better Chickens*. University of Toronto Press, 2012.

Dixon, Patrick. *Nuggets of Gold: Further Processed Chicken and the Making of the American Diet*. University of Georgia Press, 2024.

Dixon, Patrick M. "The Hamlet Factory Fire and the Political Economy of Poultry in the Twentieth Century." PhD diss., Georgetown University, 2015.

Dowdy, Nancy Patrice. "J.K. Southerland: From Check-R-Mix to Fancy Pack, Pioneering the Poultry Industry in North Central Arkansas." PhD diss., Arkansas State University, 2015.

Gisolfi, Monica R. "The Southern History of the Chicken McNugget: The Georgia Poultry Industry and the Rise of Fast Food, 1929 to 1983." *Southern Studies* 25, no. 2 (Fall/Winter 2018): 19-31.

Gisolfi, Monica R. *The Takeover: Chicken Farming and the Roots of American Agribusiness*. University of Georgia Press, 2017.

Gisolfi, Monica Richmond. "From Cotton Farmers to Poultry Growers: The Rise of Industrial Agriculture in Upcountry Georgia, 1914–1960." PhD diss., Columbia University, 2007.

Gordy, J. Frank. "Broilers." In *American Poultry History 1823-1974: An Anthology Overview of 150 Years*, edited by Oscar August Hanke, 370-432. American Poultry Historical Society, Inc., 1974.

Hahn, Steven. *The Roots of Southern Populism: Yeoman Farmers and the Transformation of the Georgia Upcountry, 1850-1890*. Oxford University Press, 1983.

Hanke, Oscar August, ed. *American Poultry History 1823-1974: An Anthology Overview of 150 Years*. American Poultry Historical Society, Inc., 1974.

Horowitz, Roger. "'Be Loyal to Your Industry': J. Frank Gordy, Jr., the Cooperative Extension Service, and the Making of a Business Community in the Delmarva Poultry Industry, 1945–1970." *Delaware History* 27, no. 1/2 (Spring 1996): 3-18.

Horowitz, Roger. "Making the Chicken of Tomorrow: Reworking Poultry As Commodities, 1945-1990." In *Industrializing Organisms: Introducing Evolutionary History*, edited by Susan R. Schrepfer and Philip Scranton, 215-35. Routledge, 2004.

Horowitz, Roger. *Putting Meat On the American Table: Taste, Technology, Transformation.* Johns Hopkins University Press, 2006.

Jones, Lu Ann. *Mama Learned Us To Work: Farm Women in the New South.* University of North Carolina Press, 2002.

Josephson, Paul R. *Chicken: A History from Farmyard to Factory.* Polity Press, 2020.

Kim, Chul-Kyoo and James Curry. "Fordism, Flexible Specialization and Agri-Industrial Restructuring: The Case of the U.S. Broiler Industry." *Sociologia Ruralis* 33, no. 1 (1993): 61-80.

Kimmelman, Barbara Ann. "A Progressive Era Discipline: Genetics at American Agricultural Colleges and Experiment Stations, 1900-1920." PhD diss., University of Pennsylvania, 1987.

McKenna, Maryn. *Big Chicken: The Incredible Story of How Antibiotics Created Modern Agriculture and Changed the Way the World Eats.* National Geographic Partners, 2017.

Merck, Ashton W. "The Fox Guarding the Henhouse: Coregulation and Consumer Protection in Food Safety, 1946-2002." *Enterprise and Society* 22, no. 4 (December 2021): 921-29.

Merck, Ashton Wynette. "The Fox Guarding the Henhouse: Coregulation and Consumer Protection in Food Safety, 1946-2002." PhD diss., Duke University, 2020.

Milgrim, Herbert Joseph. "Productivity and Growth of the Broiler Chicken Industry." PhD diss., New York University, 1968.

Miller, Hermon I. "Government." In *American Poultry History 1823-1974: An Anthology Overview of 150 Years*, edited by Oscar August Hanke, 538-66. American Poultry Historical Society, Inc., 1974.

Myers, Homer. *Pass the Chicken Please: The Life and Times of Jesse Jewell.* CreateSpace Independent Publishing Platform, 2017.

Naftaly, Phillip R. "Jewish Chicken Farmers in the Egg Basket of the World: The Creation of Cultural Identity in Petaluma, California." PhD diss., New School for Social Research, 1999.

Omo-Osagie, Solomon Iyobosa, II. "Commercial Poultry Production on Maryland's Lower Eastern Shore and the Involvement of African Americans, 1930s to 1990s." PhD diss., Morgan State University, 2007.

Pryor, James Russell. "Work, Nature, and the American Dinner Plate: Making Chicken in the Twentieth-Century United States." PhD diss., Carnegie Mellon University, 2013.

Riffel, Brent E. "The Feathered Kingdom: Tyson Foods and the Transformation of American Land, Labor, and Law, 1930-2005." PhD diss., University of Arkansas, 2008.

Sawyer, Gordon. *The Agribusiness Poultry Industry: A History of Its Development.* Exposition Press, 1971.

Schwartz, Marvin. *Tyson: From Farm to Market.* University of Arkansas Press, 2015.

Sebold, Kimberly R. "The Delmarva Broiler Industry and World War II: A Case in Wartime Economy." *Delaware History* 25, no. 3 (Spring/Summer 1993): 200-214.

Skinner, John L., ed. *American Poultry History, 1974-1993. Vol. II: An Anthology of the Next 20 Years: People-Places-Progress.* Watt Pub., 1996.

Smith, Page, and Charles Daniel. *The Chicken Book.* North Point Press, 1982.

Soule, George. *Vertical Integration in the Broiler Industry on the Delmarva Peninsula and Its Effect on Small Business.* n.p., 1960.
Striffler, Steve. *Chicken: The Dangerous Transformation of America's Favorite Food.* Yale University Press, 2005.
Tobin, Bernard F., and Henry B. Arthur. *Dynamics of Adjustment in the Broiler Industry.* Harvard University, 1964.
University of Delaware, Agricultural Experiment Station. *A Short History of the Broiler Industry in Delaware,* by M.M. Daugherty. No. 15. 1944.
University of Maryland, Agricultural Experiment Station. *The Delmarva Broiler Industry,* by James M. Gwin. Bulletin A-57. 1950.
USDA, Agricultural Adjustment Administration. *An Economic Survey of the Commercial Broiler Industry,* by W.D. Termohlen, J.W. Kinghorne, E.L. Warren, and J.H. Radabaugh. 1936.
USDA, ESC. "Poultry and Eggs," by George B. Rogers. In *Another Revolution in U.S. Farming?,* by Lyle P. Schertz et al., 148-89. Agricultural Economic Report No. 441. December 1979.
USDA, ESC. *Structural Change in Agriculture: The Experience for Broilers, Fed Cattle, and Processing Vegetables,* by Donn A. Reimund, J. Rod Martin, and Charles V. Moore. Technical Bulletin No. 1648. April 1981.
Welt, Aaron. "Butchers, Bakers, and Jewish Strong-Arm Men: Organized Crime in the Kosher Food Trades During the Age of Mass Jewish Migration, 1900-1917." *Journal of American Ethnic History* 40, no. 2 (Winter 2021): 92-118.
Williams-Forson, Psyche A. *Building Houses Out of Chicken Legs: Black Women, Food, and Power.* University of North Carolina Press, 2006.

CITIES: SANITATION AND REFORM

Brinkley, Catherine, and Domenic Vitiello. "From Farm to Nuisance: Animal Agriculture and the Rise of Planning Regulation." *Journal of Planning History* 13, no. 2 (May 2014): 113-35.
Duffy, John. *The Sanitarians: A History of American Public Health.* University of Illinois Press, 1990.
Griscom, John Hoskins. *The Sanitary Conditions of the Laboring Population of New York: With Suggestions for Improvements.* Harper, 1845.
Grob, Gerald N. *The Deadly Truth: A History of Disease in America.* Harvard University Press, 2002.
Kiechle, Melanie A. *Smell Detectives: An Olfactory History of Nineteenth-Century Urban America.* University of Washington Press, 2017.
McNeur, Catherine. "The 'Swinish Multitude': Controversies Over Hogs in Antebellum New York City." *Journal of Urban History* 37, no. 5 (2011): 639-60.
McNeur, Catherine. *Taming Manhattan: Environmental Battles in the Antebellum City.* Harvard University Press, 2014.
McShane, Clay, and Joel Tarr. *The Horse in the City: Living Machines in the Nineteenth Century.* Johns Hopkins University Press, 2007.
Melosi, Martin V., ed. *Pollution and Reform in American Cities, 1870-1930.* University of Texas Press, 1980.

Melosi, Martin V. *The Sanitary City: Urban Infrastructure in America from Colonial Times to the Present*. Johns Hopkins University Press, 2000.

New York City. *Sanitary Condition of the City: Report of the Council of Hygiene and Public Health of the Citizens' Association of New York*. 2d ed. 1866. Reprint, Arno Press, 1970.

Robichaud, Andrew A. *Animal City: The Domestication of America*. Harvard University Press, 2019.

Rosen, Christine Meisner. "Businessmen Against Pollution in Late Nineteenth Century Chicago." *Business History Review* 69 (Autumn 1995): 351-97.

Rosen, Christine Meisner. "Costs and Benefits of Pollution Control in Pennsylvania, New York, and New Jersey, 1840-1906." *Geographical Review* 88, no. 2 (April 1998): 219-40.

Rosen, Christine Meisner. "Differing Perceptions of the Value of Pollution Abatement Across Time and Place: Balancing Doctrine in Pollution Nuisance Law, 1840-1906." *Law and History Review* 11, no. 2 (Autumn 1993): 303-81.

Rosen, Christine Meisner. "'Knowing' Industrial Pollution: Nuisance Law and the Power of Tradition in a Time of Rapid Economic Change, 1840-1864." *Environmental History* 8 (October 2003): 563-95.

Rosen, Christine Meisner. "Noisome, Noxious, and Offensive Vapors: Fumes and Stenches in American Towns and Cities, 1840-1865." *Historical Geography* 25 (1997): 49-82.

Rosen, Christine Meisner. "The Role of Pollution Regulation and Litigation in the Development of the U.S. Meatpacking Industry, 1865-1880." *Enterprise & Society* 8 (June 2007): 297-347.

Rosenberg, Charles E. *The Cholera Years: The United States in 1832, 1849, and 1866*. 1962. Reprint, University of Chicago Press, 1987.

CITIES: URBAN HISTORY

Baker, Andrew C. "Cities and Agriculture in America." In *A Companion to American Agricultural History*, edited by R. Douglas Hurt, 129-43. Wiley Blackwell, 2022.

Blumin, Stuart M. *The Emergence of the Middle Class: Social Experience in the American City, 1760-1900*. Cambridge University Press, 1989.

Boehm, Lisa Krissoff, and Steven H. Corey. *America's Urban History*. Routledge, Taylor & Francis Group, 2015.

Carp, Benjamin L. *Rebels Rising: Cities and the American Revolution*. Oxford University Press, 2007.

Cronon, William. *Nature's Metropolis: Chicago and the Great West*. Rev. ed. W.W. Norton & Company, 2009.

Duis, Perry R. *Challenging Chicago: Coping With Everyday Life, 1837-1920*. University of Illinois Press, 1998.

Glasser, Ruth. "The Farm *in* the City *in* the Recent Past: Thoughts On A More Inclusive Urban History." *Journal of Urban History* 44, no. 3 (2018): 501-18.

Jackson, Kenneth T. *Crabgrass Frontier: The Suburbanization of the United States*. Oxford University Press, 1985.

McDonald, John F. *Urban America: Growth, Crisis, and Rebirth*. M.E. Sharpe, 2008.

Monkkonen, Eric H. *America Becomes Urban: The Development of U.S. Cities & Towns, 1780-1980*. University of California Press, 1988.
Otterstrom, Samuel. *A Geographical History of United States City-Systems: From the Frontier to the Urban Transformation*. Edwin Mellen Press, 2004.
Pred, Allan R. *Urban Growth and the Circulation of Information: The United States System of Cities, 1790-1840*. 1973. Reprint, Harvard University Press, 2015.
Schultz, Stanley K. *Constructing Urban Culture: American Cities and City Planning, 1800-1920*. Temple University Press, 1989.
Upton, Dell. *Another City: Urban Life and Urban Spaces in the New American Republic*. Yale University Press, 2008.
Warner, Sam Bass, Jr. *The Urban Wilderness: A History of the American City*. Harper & Row, 1972.

COLORADO

Abbott, Carl, Stephen J. Leonard, and Thomas J. Noel. *Colorado: A History of the Centennial State*. 5th ed. University Press of Colorado, 2013.
Andreas, Carol. *Meat Packers and Beef Barons: A Company Town in a Global Economy*. University of Colorado Press, 1994.
Arrington, Leonard J. "Science, Government, and Enterprise in Economic Development: The Western Beet Sugar Industry." *Agricultural History* 41, no. 1 (January 1967): 1-18.
Barnhart, Walt. *Kenny's Shoes: A Walk Through the Storied Life of the Remarkable Kenneth W. Monfort*. Infinity Publishing, 2008.
Colorado State Agricultural College, Agricultural Experiment Station. *Cattle Feeding in Colorado*, by Wells W. Cooke. Bulletin No. 34. 1896.
Colorado Agricultural College, Extension Service. *Colorado's Agriculture*, by Roud McCann and Thos. H. Summers, [1924].
Freeman, John F. with Mark E. Uchanski. *Adapting to the Land: A History of Agriculture in Colorado*. University Press of Colorado, 2022.
Henderson, David Allen. *The Beef Cattle Industry of Colorado*. PhD diss., University of Colorado, 1951.
May, William John, Jr. *The Great Western Sugarlands: The History of the Great Western Sugar Company and the Economic Development of the Great Plains*. Garland, 1989.
Sheflin, Douglas. "The New Deal Personified: A. J. Hamman and the Cooperative Extension Service in Colorado." *Agricultural History* 90, no. 3 (Summer 2016): 356-78.
Tyler, Daniel. *WD Farr: Cowboy in the Boardroom*. University of Oklahoma Press, 2011.
Weeks, Michael. *Cattle Beet Capital: Making Industrial Agriculture in Northern Colorado*. University of Nebraska Press, 2022.

CONSUMERS/CONSUMPTION

Blanke, David. *Sowing the American Dream: How Consumer Culture Took Root in the Rural Midwest*. Ohio University Press, 2000.

Blaszczyk, Regina Lee. *American Consumer Society, 1865-2005: From Hearth to HDTV*. Harlan Davidson, Inc., 2009.

Breen, T.H. *The Marketplace of Revolution: How Consumer Politics Shaped American Independence*. Oxford University Press, 2004.

Calder, Lendol Glen. *Financing the American Dream: A Cultural History of Consumer Credit*. Princeton University Press, 1999.

Carson, Cary. *Face Value: The Consumer Revolution and the Colonizing of America*. University of Virginia Press, 2017.

Cohen, Joanna. *Luxurious Citizens: The Politics of Consumption in Nineteenth-Century America*. University of Pennsylvania Press, 2017.

Cohen, Lizabeth. *A Consumers' Republic: The Politics of Mass Consumption in Postwar America*. Vintage Books, 2003.

Currarino, Rosanne. "The Politics of 'More': The Labor Question and the Idea of Economic Liberty in Industrial America." *Journal of American History* 93, no. (June 2006): 17-36.

Donohue, Kathleen G. *Freedom from Want: American Liberalism and the Idea of the Consumer*. Johns Hopkins University Press, 2003.

Ewen, Stuart. *Captains of Consciousness: Advertising and the Social Roots of the Consumer Culture*. BasicBooks, 2001.

Fox, Richard Wightman, and T.J. Jackson Lears. *The Culture of Consumption: Critical Essays in American History, 1880-1980*. Pantheon Books, 1983.

Gallman, Robert E. and John Joseph Wallis, eds. *American Economic Growth and Standard of Living Before the Civil War*. University of Chicago Press, 1992.

Glickman, Lawrence. "Workers of the World, Consume: Ira Steward and the Origins of Labor Consumerism," *International Labor and Working-Class History* 52 (Fall 1997): 72-86.

Glickman, Lawrence B. *Buying Power: A History of Consumer Activism in America*. University of Chicago Press, 2009.

Glickman, Lawrence B., ed. *Consumer Society in American History: A Reader*. Cornell University Press, 1999.

Glickman, Lawrence B. *A Living Wage: American Workers and the Making of Consumer Society*. Cornell University Press, 1999.

Goldstein, Carolyn M. *Creating Consumers: Home Economists in Twentieth-Century America*. University of North Carolina Press, 2012.

Hodge, Christina J. *Consumerism and the Emergence of the Middle Class in Colonial America: The Genteel Revolution*. Cambridge University Press, 2014.

Hoganson, Kristin L. *Consumers' Imperium: The Global Production of American Domesticity, 1865-1920*. University of North Carolina Press, 2007.

Horowitz, Daniel. *The Morality of Spending: Attitudes Toward Consumer Society in America, 1875-1940*. Johns Hopkins University Press, 1985.

Igo, Sarah. *The Averaged American: Surveys, Citizens, and the Making of a Mass Public*. Harvard University Press, 2007.

Jacobs, Meg. *Pocketbook Politics: Economic Citizenship in Twentieth-Century America*. Princeton University Press, 2005.

Jundt, Thomas. *Greening the Red, White, and Blue: The Bomb, Big Business, and Consumer Resistance in Postwar America*. Oxford University Press, 2014.

Kline, Ronald R. *Consumers in the Country: Technology and Social Change in Rural America*. Johns Hopkins University Press, 2000.
Laird, Pamela Walker. *Advertising Progress: American Business and the Rise of Consumer Marketing*. 1998. Johns Hopkins University Press, 2019.
Leach, William. *Land of Desire: Merchants, Power, and the Rise of A New American Culture*. Pantheon Books, 1993.
Lebergott, Stanley. *Pursuing Happiness: American Consumers in the Twentieth Century*. Princeton University Press, 2014.
Lytle, Mark H. *The All-Consuming Nation: Chasing the American Dream Since World War II*. Oxford University Press, 2021.
Marchand, Roland. *Advertising the American Dream: Making Way for Modernity 1920-1940*. University of California Press, 1985.
Martin, Ann Smart. *Buying Into the World of Goods: Early Consumers in Backcountry Virginia*. Johns Hopkins University Press, 2010.
Martin, Edgar R. *The Standard of Living in 1860: American Consumption Levels on the Eve of the Civil War*. University of Chicago Press, 1942.
McGovern, Charles F. *Sold American: Consumption and Citizenship, 1890-1945*. University of North Carolina Press, 2006.
Moskowitz, Marina. *Standard of Living: The Measure of the Middle Class in Modern America*. Johns Hopkins University Press, 2004.
Olegario, Rowena. *The Engine of Enterprise: Credit in America*. Harvard University Press, 2016.
Samson, Peter Edward. "The Emergence of A Consumer Interest in America 1870-1930." PhD diss., University of Chicago, 1980.
Shammas, Carole. *The Pre-Industrial Consumer in England and America*. Clarendon Press, 1990.
Silla, Cesare. *The Rise of Consumer Capitalism in America, 1880-1930*. Routledge, 2018.
Sullivan, Bob. *Legislative Foundations of American Consumer Society: Regulation, Deregulation and Their Impacts from the 1930s to Today*. McFarland & Company, Inc., 2021.
Tedlow, Richard S. *New and Improved: The Story of Mass Marketing in America*. Basic Books, 1990.

ENVIRONMENT: HISTORY & ISSUES

Andrews, Richard N.L. *Managing the Environment, Managing Ourselves: A History of American Environmental Policy*. 3d ed. Yale University Press, 2020.
Beeman, Randall S., and James A. Pritchard. *A Green and Permanent Land: Ecology and Agriculture in the Twentieth Century*. University Press of Kansas, 2001.
Case, Andrew N. *The Organic Profit: Rodale and the Making of Marketplace Environmentalism*. University of Washington Press, 2018.
Daloz, Kate. *We Are as Gods: Back to the Land in the 1970s on the Quest for a New America*. PublicAffairs, 2016.
Egan, Michael. *Barry Commoner and the Science of Survival: The Remaking of American Environmentalism*. MIT Press, 2007.
Gottlieb, Robert. *Environmentalism Unbound: Exploring New Pathways for Change*. MIT Press, 2001.

Hays, Samuel P. *Beauty, Health, and Permanence: Environmental Politics in the United States, 1955-1985*. Cambridge University Press, 1987.

Kirk, Andrew G. *Counterculture Green: The Whole Earth Catalog and American Environmentalism*. University Press of Kansas, 2007.

Lytle, Mark H. *The Gentle Subversive: Rachel Carson, Silent Spring, and the Rise of the Environmental Movement*. Oxford University Press, 2007.

Rome, Adam. *The Bulldozer in the Countryside: Suburban Sprawl and the Rise of American Environmentalism*. Cambridge University Press, 2001.

Rothman, Hal. *Saving the Planet: The American Response to the Environment in the Twentieth Century*. Ivan R. Dee, 2000.

Rothman, Hal K. *The Greening of a Nation? Environmentalism in the United States Since 1945*. Harcourt Brace College Publishers, 1998.

Sellers, Christopher C. *Crabgrass Crucible: Suburban Nature and the Rise of Environmentalism in Twentieth-Century America*. University of North Carolina Press, 2012.

Worster, Donald. *Nature's Economy: A History of Ecological Ideas*. 2d ed. Cambridge University Press, 1994.

Zimring, Carl A. *Clean and White: A History of Environmental Racism in the United States*. New York University Press, 2015.

ENVIRONMENT: THREATS/RESPONSES

Blackwell, Jacob A. "An Uncommon Nuisance: Cattle Feeding, Nuisance Complaints, and Legal Remedies on the Southern Plains." In *The Greater Plains: Rethinking a Region's Environmental Histories*, edited by Kathleen A. Brosnan and Brian Frehner, 156-74. University of Nebraska Press, 2021.

Bosso, Christopher J. *Pesticides and Politics: The Life Cycle of a Public Issue*. University of Pittsburgh Press, 1987.

Capper, J.L. "The Environmental Impact of Beef Production in the United States: 1977 Compared with 2007." *Journal of Animal Science* 89, no. 12 (2011): 4249-61.

Davis, Frederick Rowe. *Banned: A History of Pesticides and the Science of Toxicology*. Yale University Press, 2014.

Dewey, Scott Hamilton. *Don't Breathe the Air: Air Pollution and U.S. Environmental Politics, 1945-1970*. Texas A&M University Press, 2000.

Dunlap, Thomas R. *DDT: Scientists, Citizens, and Public Policy*. Princeton University Press, 1981.

Durning, Alan B., and Holly B. Brough. *Taking Stock: Animal Farming and the Environment*. Worldwatch Paper 103. Worldwatch Institute, July 1991.

Finlay, Mark R. and Alan I [sic] Marcus. "'Consumerist Terrorists': Battles Over Agricultural Antibiotics in the United States and Western Europe." *Agricultural History* 90, no. 2 (Spring 2016): 146-72.

Halvorson, Charles. *Valuing Clean Air: The EPA and the Economics of Environmental Protection*. Oxford University Press, 2021.

Janzen, Mark Ryan. "The Cranberry Scare of 1959: The Beginning of the End of the Delaney Clause." PhD diss., Texas A&M University, 2010.

Johnsen, Carolyn. *Raising a Stink: The Struggle Over Factory Farms in Nebraska*. University of Nebraska Press, 2003.

Kinkela, David. *DDT and the American Century: Global Health, Environmental Politics, and the Pesticide That Changed the World.* University of North Carolina Press, 2011.

Kirby, David. *Animal Factory: The Looming Threat of Industrial Pig, Dairy, and Poultry Farms to Humans and the Environment.* St. Martin's Griffin, 2010.

Lavin, Chad. "Factory Farms in a Consumer Society." *American Studies* 50, no. 1/2 (Spring/Summer 2009): 71-92.

Mallin, Michael A. "Impacts of Industrial Animal Production on Rivers and Estuaries." *American Scientist* 88, no. 1 (January-February 2000): 26-37.

Marcus, Alan I. *Cancer from Beef: DES, Federal Food Regulation, and Consumer Confidence.* Johns Hopkins University Press, 1994.

Marcus, Alan I. "The Newest Knowledge of Nutrition: Wise Burroughs, DES, and Modern Meat." *Agricultural History* 67, no. 3 (Summer 1993): 66-85.

Mart, Michelle. *Pesticides, a Love Story: America's Enduring Embrace of Dangerous Chemicals.* University Press of Kansas, 2015.

Martin, John H., Jr. "The Clean Water Act and Animal Agriculture." *Journal of Environmental Quality* 26, no. 5 (September-October 1997): 1198-1203.

Meyers, Keith. "In the Shadow of the Mushroom Cloud: Nuclear Testing, Radioactive Fallout, and Damage to U.S. Agriculture, 1945 to 1970." *Journal of Economic History* 79, no. 1 (March 2019): 244-74.

National Research Council. *Use of Drugs in Animal Feeds: Proceedings of a Symposium.* Publication 1679. National Academy of Sciences, 1969.

National Research Council. Board on Agriculture. Committee on Technological Options to Improve the Nutritional Attributes of Animal Products. *Designing Foods: Animal Product Options in the Marketplace.* National Academy Press, 1988.

National Research Council. Committee on Animal Health. *Antibiotics in Animal Feeds: A Report Prepared by the Committee on Animal Health and the Committee on Animal Nutrition [and] Board on Agriculture and Renewable Resources, National Research Council.* National Academy of Sciences, 1979.

Otter, Chris. "Toxic Foodways: Agro-Food Systems, Emerging Foodborne Pathogens, and Evolutionary History." *Environmental History* 20, no. 4 (October 2015): 751-64.

Peterson, Everett B., Paul V. Preckel, Thomas W. Hertel, and Anya M. McGuirk. "Impacts of Stimulants in the Domestic Livestock Sector." *Agribusiness* 8, no. 4 (July 1992): 287-307.

Spiller, James. "Radiant Cuisine: The Commercial Fate of Food Irradiation in the United States." *Technology and Culture* 45, no. 4 (October 2004): 740-63.

Tesh, Sylvia Noble. *Uncertain Hazards: Environmental Activists and Scientific Proof.* Cornell University Press, 2018.

Texas Agricultural Experiment Station and Department of Agricultural Economics and Sociology. "Economic Consequences of Banning the Use of Antibiotics at Subtherapeutic Levels in Livestock Production," by Henry C. Gilliam, J. Rod Martin, William G. Bursch, and Richard B. Smith. Departmental Technical Report Number 73-2, 1973.

US General Accounting Office. *Animal Agriculture: Information on Waste Management and Water Quality Issues.* GAO/RCED-95-200BR. June 1995.

US House, Committee on Energy and Commerce. *Antibiotic Resistance and the Use of Antibiotics in Animal Agriculture, Hearing Before the Subcommittee on Health . . . Serial No.*

111-144. 111th Cong. (2010).

US House, Committee on Government Operations. *Regulation of Diethylstilbestrol (DES) and Other Drugs Used in Food Producing Animals H.R. 93-708.* 93 Cong. (1973).

US House, Committee on Government Regulations. *Regulation of Food Additives — Nitrites and Nitrates. H.R. 92-1338.* 92d Cong. (1972).

US Office of Technology Assessment. *Drugs in Livestock Feed.* June 1979.

US Office of Technology Assessment. *Impacts of Antibiotic-Resistant Bacteria.* OTA-H-629. September 1995.

Winders, Bill, and Elizabeth Ransom, eds. *Global Meat: The Social and Environmental Consequences of the Expanding Meat Industry.* MIT Press, 2019.

FAMILY FARM

Effland, Anne. "Small Farms/Family Farms: Tracing a History of Definitions and Meaning." *Agricultural History* 95, no. 2 (Spring 2021): 313-30.

"Forum: Ideology of the Small Family Farm and Its Influence on US Public Policy." *Agricultural History* 95, no. 2 (Spring 2021).

Levins, Richard A. *Willard Cochrane and the American Family Farm.* University of Nebraska Press, 2000.

Stockwell, Ryan. "The Family Farm in the Post-World War II Era: Industrialization, The Cold War and Political Symbol." PhD diss., University of Missouri-Columbia, 2008.

Stockwell, Ryan J. "Growing A Modern Agrarian Myth: The American Agriculture Movement, Identity, and the Call to Save the Family Farm." Master's thesis, Miami University, 2003.

Strange, Marty. *Family Farming: A New Economic Vision.* University of Nebraska Press, 1988.

Summer, Mary. "From the Heartland to Seattle: The Family Farm Movement of the 1980s and the Legacy of Agrarian State Building." In *The Countryside in the Age of the Modern State: Political Histories of Rural America,* edited by Catherine McNicol Stock and Robert D. Johnston, 303-25. Cornell University Press, 2001.

Vogeler, Ingolf. *The Myth of the Family Farm: Agribusiness Dominance of U.S. Agriculture.* Westview Press, 1981.

FOOD: PRICES/HIGH COST OF LIVING

Gordon, Robert J. *The Rise and Fall of American Growth: The U.S. Standard of Living Since the Civil War.* Princeton University Press, 2017.

Hall, Tom G. "Wilson and the Food Crisis: Agricultural Price Control During World War I." *Agricultural History* 47, no. 1 (January 1973): 25-46.

Macleod, David I. "Food Prices, Politics, and Policy in the Progressive Era." *Journal of the Gilded Age and Progressive Era* 8, no. 3 (July 2009): 365-406.

Pope, Daniel. "American Economists and the High Cost of Living: The Late Progressive Era." *Journal of the History of Behavioral Sciences* 17 (Winter 1981): 75-87.

Rauchway, Eric. "The High Cost of Living in the Progressives' Economy." *Journal of American History* 88, no. 3 (December 2001): 898-924.
Stapleford, Thomas A. *The Cost of Living in America: A Political History of Economic Statistics, 1880-2000*. Cambridge University Press, 2009.
US Department of Labor, BLS. *Wholesale Prices 1890-1914*. Bulletin of the United States Bureau of Labor Statistics 181. 1915.
US Senate. *Investigation Relative to Wages and Prices of Commodities . . . Hearings Before Committee and Digest of Evidence*. 4 vols. 61st Cong. (1911).
US Senate. *Report of the Select Committee on Wages and Prices of Commodities, Part 1*. 61st Cong. (1910).

FOOD: RETAIL/DISTRIBUTION/GROCERS

Basker, Emek, Chris Vickers, and Nicolas L. Ziebarth. "Competition, Productivity, and Survival of Grocery Stores in the Great Depression." *International Journal of Industrial Organization* 59 (2018): 282-315.
Deutsch, Tracey. *Building a Housewife's Paradise: Gender, Politics, and American Grocery Stores in the Twentieth Century*. University of North Carolina Press, 2010.
German, Gene Arlin. "The Dynamics of Food Retailing, 1900-1975." PhD diss., Cornell University, 1978.
Hamilton, Shane. "Analyzing Commodity Chains: Linkages or Restraints?" In *Food Chains: From Farmyard to Shopping Cart*, edited by Warren Belasco and Roger Horowitz, 16-25. University of Pennsylvania Press, 2009.
Hamilton, Shane. "The Economies and Conveniences of Modern-Day Living: Frozen Foods and Mass Marketing, 1945-1965." *Business History Review* 77, no. 1 (Spring 2003): 33-60.
Hamilton, Shane. *Trucking Country: The Road to America's Wal-Mart Economy*. Princeton University Press, 2008.
Kinsey, Jean, and Ben Senauer. "Consumer Trends and Changing Food Retailing Formats." *American Journal of Agricultural Economics* 78, no. 5, Proceedings Issue (December 1996): 1187-91.
Levinson, Marc. *The Great A&P and the Struggle for Small Business in America*. Hill and Wang, 2011.
Mack, Adam. "'Good Things to Eat In Suburbia': Supermarkets and American Consumer Cultures, 1930-1970." PhD diss., University of South Carolina, 2006.
Morton, Alan Q. "Packaging History: The Emergence of the Uniform Product Code (UPC) in the United States, 1970-75." *History and Technology* 11, no. 1 (1991): 101-11.
Spellman, Susan V. *Cornering the Market: Independent Grocers and Innovation in American Small Business*. Oxford University Press, 2016.
Tangires, Helen. *Movable Markets: Food Wholesaling in the Twentieth-Century City*. Johns Hopkins University Press, 2019.
Tolbert, Lisa C. "The Aristocracy of the Market Basket: Self-Service Food Shopping in the New South." In *Food Chains: From Farmyard to Shopping Cart*, edited by Warren Belasco and Roger Horowitz, 179-95. University of Pennsylvania Press, 2009.

Tolbert, Lisa C. *Beyond Piggly Wiggly: Inventing the American Self-Service Store*. University of Georgia Press, 2023.
USDA. *Rearranging the Economic Landscape: The Food Marketing Revolution, 1950-91*, by Alden C. Manchester. Agricultural Economic Report No. 660. September 1992.
Vitiello, Domenic, and Catherine Brinkley. "The Hidden History of Food System Planning." *Journal of Planning History* 13, no. 2 (2014): 91-112.
Walsh, William I. *The Rise and Decline of the Great Atlantic and Pacific Tea Company*. Lyle Stuart, 1986.

FOODWAYS

Ackerman, Michael. "Interpreting the Newer Knowledge of Nutrition: Science, Interests, and Values in the Making of Dietary Advice in the United States, 1915-1965." PhD diss., University of Virginia, 2005.
Anderson, Jay Allan. "'A Solid Sufficiency': An Ethnography of Yeoman Foodways in Stuart England." PhD diss., University of Pennsylvania, 1971.
Apple, Rima D. *Vitamania: Vitamins in American Culture*. Rutgers University Press, 1996.
Aronson, Naomi. "Fuel for the Human Machine: The Industrialization of Eating in America." PhD diss., Brandeis University, 1978.
Aronson, Naomi. "Social Definitions of Entitlement: Food Needs, 1885-1920." *Media, Culture and Society* 4 (1982): 51-61.
Barkema, Alan, Mark Drabenstott, and Kelly Welch. "The Quiet Revolution in the U.S. Food Market." *Economic Review* 76, no. 3 (May/June 1991): 25-41.
Barnett, L. Margaret. "'Every Man His Own Physician': Dietetic Fads, 1890-1914." In *The Science and Culture of Nutrition, 1840-1940*, edited by Harmke Kamminga and Andrew Cunningham, 155-78. Rodopi, 1995.
Belasco, Warren. *Meals to Come: A History of the Future of Food*. University of California Press, 2006.
Berson, Josh. *The Meat Question: Animals, Humans, and the Deep History of Food*. MIT Press, 2019.
Bowen, Joanne. "A Study of Seasonality and Subsistence: Eighteenth-Century Suffield, Connecticut." PhD diss., Brown University, 1990.
Carolan, Michael. *The Real Cost of Cheap Food*. Earthscan, 2011.
Connor, John M., and William A. Schiek. *Food Processing: An Industrial Powerhouse in Transition*. 2d ed. John Wiley & Sons, 1997.
Craig, Lee A., Barry Goodwin, and Thomas Grennes. "The Effect of Mechanical Refrigeration on Nutrition in the United States." *Social Science History* 28, no. 2 (Summer 2004): 325-36.
Davidson, Alan, ed. *The Oxford Companion to Food*. 2d ed. Oxford University Press, 2006.
Dickau, Joel. "Inventing Texture: Food Science and Culinary Culture in Postwar America." PhD diss., University of Toronto, 2023.
Duran, Nancy. "Dietary Intake: Changes Related to Seasonal Hunger and Economic Class at the Beginning of the Twentieth Century." *Food, Culture & Society* 9, no. 1 (2006): 41-48.
Fiddes, Nick. *Meat: A Natural Symbol*. Routledge, 1991.

Finlay, Mark R. "Early Marketing of the Theory of Nutrition: The Science and Culture of Liebig's Extract of Meat." In *The Science and Culture of Nutrition, 1840-1940*, edited by Harmke Kamminga and Andrew Cunningham, 48-74. Rodopi, 1995.

Freidberg, Susanne. *Fresh: A Perishable History*. Belknap Press of Harvard University Press, 2009.

Friedman, Karen J. "Victualling Colonial Boston." *Agricultural History* 47 (July 1973): 189-205.

Gabaccia, Donna R. *We Are What We Eat: Ethnic Food and the Making of Americans*. Harvard University Press, 1988.

Goodwin, Barry K., Thomas J. Grennes, and Lee A. Craig. "Mechanical Refrigeration and the Integration of Perishable Commodity Markets." *Explorations in Economic History* 39 (2002): 154-82.

Goodwin, Lorine Swainston. *The Pure Food, Drink, and Drug Crusaders, 1879-1914*. McFarland & Company, 1999.

Haley, Andrew P. *Turning the Tables: Restaurants and the Rise of the American Middle Class, 1880-1920*. University of North Carolina Press, 2011.

Haushofer, Lisa. *Wonder Foods: The Science and Commerce of Nutrition*. University of California Press, 2022.

Hilliard, Sam Bowers. *Hog Meat and Hoecake: Food Supply in the Old South, 1840-1860*. Southern Illinois University Press, 1972.

Horowitz, Roger. *Putting Meat On the American Table: Taste, Technology, Transformation*. Johns Hopkins University Press, 2006.

Horowitz, Roger, Jeffrey M. Pilcher, and Sydney Watts. "Meat for the Multitudes: Market Culture in Paris, New York City, and Mexico City over the Long Nineteenth Century." *American Historical Review* 109, no. 4 (October 2004): 1054-83.

Hurt, R. Douglas. *Food and Agriculture During the Civil War*. Praeger, 2016.

Iacobbo, Karen, and Michael Iacobbo. *Vegetarian America: A History*. Greenwood, 2004.

Iowa State College of Agriculture and Mechanic Arts, Agricultural Experiment Station. *Changes in the Demand for Meat and Dairy Products in the United States Since 1910*, by Geoffrey Shepherd. Research Bulletin 368. November 1949.

Kamminga, Harmke, and Andrew Cunningham. "Introduction: The Science and Culture of Nutrition, 1840-1890." In *The Science and Culture of Nutrition, 1840-1940*, edited by Harmke Kamminga and Andrew Cunningham, 1-14. Rodopi, 1995.

Kellogg, J.H. *The Battle Creek Sanitarium System: History, Organization, Methods*. n.p., 1908.

Kideckel, Michael S. "Fresh From the Factory: Breakfast Cereal, Natural Food, and the Marketing of Reform, 1890-1920." PhD diss., Columbia University, 2018.

Killion, Kimberly. "The Agricultural Chemist at the Table: Land Grant Colleges, Experiment Stations, and the Birth of Nutrition Science in the United States, 1887-1930." PhD diss., University of California-Berkeley, 2022.

Kiple, Kenneth F., and Kriemhild Coneè Ornelas, eds. *The Cambridge World History of Food*. Cambridge University Press, 2000.

Landon, David B. "Feeding Colonial Boston: A Zooarchaeological Study." *Historical Archaeology* 30, no. 1 (1996): 1-153.

Laudan, Rachel. "A Plea for Culinary Modernism: Why We Should Love Fast, Modern, Processed Food (With a New Postscript). In *Food Fights: How History Matters to Contemporary Food Debates*, edited by Charles C. Ludington and Matthew Morse Booker, 262-84. University of North Carolina Press, 2019.

Levenstein, Harvey. *Fear of Food: A History of Why We Worry About What We Eat*. University of Chicago Press, 2012.

Levenstein, Harvey. *Revolution at the Table: The Transformation of the American Diet*. University of California Press, 2003.

Levenstein, Harvey A. *Paradox of Plenty: A Social History of Eating in Modern America*. Revised ed. Oxford University Press, 1993.

Lightfoot, Dessa E. "'God Sends Meat and the Devil Sends Cooks': Meat Usage and Cuisine in Eighteenth-Century English Colonial America." PhD diss., College of William and Mary, 2018.

McCorkle, Chester O., Jr, ed. *Economics of Food Processing in the United States*. Academic Press, 1988.

McGee, Harold. *On Food and Cooking: The Science and Lore of the Kitchen*. Collier Books, 1984.

McGee, Harold. *On Food and Cooking: The Science and Lore of the Kitchen*. Revised ed. Scribner, 2004.

McMahon, Sarah F. "'A Comfortable Subsistence': A History of Diet in New England, 1630-1850." PhD diss., Brandeis University, 1981.

McMahon, Sarah F. "'A Comfortable Subsistence': The Changing Composition of Diet in Rural New England, 1620-1840." *William and Mary Quarterly* 42 (January 1985): 26-65.

McWilliams, James. *A Revolution in Eating: How the Quest for Food Shaped America*. Columbia University Press, 2005.

Miller, Henry M. "An Archaeological Perspective on the Evolution of Diet in the Colonial Chesapeake, 1620-1745." In *Colonial Chesapeake Society*, edited by Lois Green Carr, Philip D. Morgan, and Jean B. Russo, 176-99. University of North Carolina Press, 1988.

Miller, Henry M. "Colonization and Subsistence Change on the 17th Century Chesapeake Frontier." PhD diss., Michigan State University, 1984.

Mink, Nicolaas John. "The Restaurant: Food, Power, and Social Change." PhD diss., University of Wisconsin-Madison, 2010.

Mudry, Jessica. "Quantifying an American Eater: Early USDA Food Guidance, and a Language of Numbers." *Food, Culture & Society* 9, no. 1 (2006): 44-67.

National Planning Association. "Changes in Food Consumption from Mass Market to Niche Markets," by Jean Kinsey. In Lyle P. Schertz and Lynn M. Daft, *Food and Agricultural Markets: The Quiet Revolution*, 19-43. NPA Report No. 270. National Planning Association, 1994.

National Planning Association. *Food and Agricultural Markets: The Quiet Revolution*, by Lyle P. Schertz and Lynn M. Daft. NPA Report No. 270. National Planning Association, 1994.

Nissenbaum, Stephen. *Sex, Diet, and Debility in Jacksonian America: Sylvester Graham and Health Reform*. Greenwood Press, 1980.

Okun, Mitchell. *Fair Play in the Marketplace: The First Battle for Pure Food and Drugs*. Northern Illinois University Press, 1986.

Olszewski, Todd Michael. "Cholesterol: A Scientific, Medical, and Social History, 1908-1962." PhD diss., Yale University, 2008.

Petrick, Gabriella M. "The Arbiters of Taste: Producers, Consumers and the Industrialization of Taste in America, 1900-1960." PhD diss., University of Delaware, 2006.

Petrick, Gabriella M. "Feeding the Masses: H.J. Heinz and the Creation of Industrial Food." *Endeavour* 33, no. 1 (2008): 29-34.

Pollan, Michael. *The Omnivore's Dilemma: A Natural History of Four Meals*. Penguin Press, 2006.

Puskar-Pasewicz, Margaret. "'For the Good of the Whole': Vegetarianism in Nineteenth-Century America." PhD diss., Indiana University, 2004.

Rees, Jonathan. *The Chemistry of Fear: Harvey Wiley's Fight for Pure Food*. Johns Hopkins University Press, 2021.

Rees, Jonathan. *Refrigeration Nation: A History of Ice, Appliances, and Enterprise in America*. Johns Hopkins University Press, 2013.

Ross, Drew Eliot. "Topography of Taste: Globalization, Cultural Politics, and the Making of California Cuisine." PhD diss., University of Wisconsin-Madison, 1999.

Sartorius, Lester Clayton. "A Statistical Analysis of Eating Places As Marketers of Food Products in Minneapolis and Fairmont, Minnesota, and in the United States." PhD diss., University of Minnesota, 1951.

Schlosser, Eric. *Fast Food Nation: The Dark Side of the All-American Meal*. Houghton Mifflin, 2001.

Senauer, Ben, Elaine Asp, and Jean Kinsey. *Food Trends and the Changing Consumer*. Eagan Press, 1991.

Shapiro, Laura. *Perfection Salad: Women and Cooking at the Turn of the Century*. Henry Holt and Company, 1986.

Shephard, Sue. *Pickled, Potted, and Canned: How the Art and Science of Food Preserving Changed the World*. Simon & Schuster, 2000.

Shprintzen, Adam D. *The Vegetarian Crusade: The Rise of an American Reform Movement, 1817-1921*. University of North Carolina Press, 2013.

Smil, Vaclav. *Should We Eat Meat? Evolution and Consequences of Modern Carnivory*. Wiley-Blackwell, 2013.

Spellman, Susan V. *Cornering the Market: Independent Grocers and Innovation in American Small Business*. Oxford University Press, 2016.

Stanford, Craig B., and Henry T. Bunn. *Meat-Eating & Human Evolution*. Oxford University Press, 2001.

Strasser, Susan. *Satisfaction Guaranteed: The Making of the American Mass Market*. Pantheon Books, 1989.

Tangires, Helen. *Public Market and Civic Culture in Nineteenth-Century America*. Johns Hopkins University Press, 2003.

Taubes, Gary. *Good Calories, Bad Calories: Challenging the Conventional Wisdom on Diet, Weight Control, and Disease*. Alfred A. Knopf, 2007.
Turner, Katherine Leonard. *How the Other Half Ate: A History of Working-Class Meals at the Turn of the Century*. University of California Press, 2014.
Turner, Katherine Leonard, and Helen Zoe Veit. *Food in the American Gilded Age*. Michigan State University Press, 2017.
USDA, BAE and Division of Agricultural Economics, and University of Minnesota. *Eating Places as Marketers of Food Products: A Research and Marketing Act Contract Report*, by Lester Clayton Sartorius and Marguerite C. Burk. Marketing Research Report No. 3. 1952.
USDA, ERS. "Expenditures for Food Away From Home," by Corrine Le Bovit in *Annual Agricultural Outlook Conference, Washington, D.C., November 13-16, 1967*. ageconsearch.umn.edu
USDA, ERS. "Food Consumption, Prices, and Expenditures, 1970-97," by Judith Jones Putnam and Jane E. Allshouse. Statistical Bulletin No. 965. April 1999.
USDA, ERS. *Types of Food Service Offered and Number of Outlets in the Food Service Industry: A Preliminary Report*. ERS-359 [1972]. ageconsearch.umn.edu
USDA, ERS. Food and Rural Economics Division. *America's Eating Habits: Changes and Consequences*, by Elizabeth Frazão. Agriculture Information Bulletin No. 750. April 1999.
US Senate, Select Committee on Nutrition and Human Needs. *Dietary Goals for the United States*, 95th Cong. (Feb. 1977). (The second, revised, edition appeared in December 1977.)
Veit, Helen Zoe. *Modern Food, Moral Food: Self-Control, Science, and the Rise of Modern American Eating in the Early Twentieth Century*. University of North Carolina Press, 2013.
Vileisis, Ann. *Kitchen Literacy: How We Lost Knowledge of Where Food Comes From and Why We Need to Get It Back*. Island Press, 2008.
Walsh, Lorena S. "Consumer Behavior, Diet, and the Standard of Living in Late Colonial and Early Antebellum America, 1770-1840." In *American Economic Growth and Standard of Living Before the Civil War*, edited by Robert E. Gallman and John Joseph Wallis, 217-61. University of Chicago Press, 1992.
Walsh, Lorena S. "Feeding the Eighteenth-Century Town Fork, or, Whence the Beef?" *Agricultural History* 73, no. 3 (Summer 1999): 267-80.
Wilde, Mark William. "Industrialization of Food Processing in the United States, 1860-1960." PhD diss., University of Delaware, 1988.
Young, James Harvey. *Pure Food: Securing the Federal Food and Drugs Act of 1906*. Princeton University Press, 1989.
Zeide, Anna. *Canned: The Rise and Fall of Consumer Confidence in the American Food Industry*. University of California Press, 2018.
Ziegleman, Jane. *97 Orchard Street: An Edible History of Five Immigrant Families in One New York Tenement*. Harper, 2010.

FOODWAYS: COUNTERCUISINE/FOOD ACTIVISM

Allen, Patricia, ed. *Food for the Future: Conditions and Contradictions of Sustainability*. John Wiley & Sons, 1993.
Allen, Patricia. "Reweaving the Food Security Safety Net: Mediating Entitlement and Entrepreneurship." *Agriculture and Human Values* 16, no. 2 (June 1999): 117-29.
Allen, Patricia. *Together at the Table: Sustainability and Sustenance in the American Agrifood System*. Pennsylvania State University Press, 2004.
Belasco, Warren J. *Appetite for Change: How the Counterculture Took On the Food Industry*. 2d ed. Cornell University Press, 2007.
Busch, Lawrence, and William B. Lacy, eds. *Food Security in the United States*. Westview Press, 1984.
Buttel, Frederick H. "Ever Since Hightower: The Politics of Agricultural Research Activism in the Molecular Age." *Agriculture and Human Values* 22, no. 3 (2005): 275-83.
Case, Andrew N. *The Organic Profit: Rodale and the Making of Marketplace Environmentalism*. University of Washington Press, 2018.
Clark, Lisa F. "Organic Limited: The Corporate Rise and Spectacular Change in the Canadian and American Organic Food Sectors." PhD diss., Simon Fraser University, 2007.
Clendenning, Jessica, Wolfram H. Dressler, and Carol Richards. "Food Justice or Food Sovereignty? Understanding the Rise of Urban Food Movements in the USA." *Agriculture and Human Values* 33, no. 1 (March 2016): 165-77.
Cohen, Barbara E., and Martha R. Burt. *Eliminating Hunger: Food Security Policy for the 1990s*. The Urban Institute, 1989.
Dahlberg, Kenneth A. "Regenerative Food Systems: Broadening the Scope and Agenda of Sustainability." In *Food for the Future: Conditions and Contradictions of Sustainability*, edited by Patricia Allen, 75-102. John Wiley & Sons, 1993.
Feenstra, Gail W. "Local Food Systems and Sustainable Communities." *American Journal of Alternative Agriculture* 12, no. 1 (1997): 28-36.
Finn, S. Margot. *Discriminating Taste: How Class Anxiety Created the American Food Revolution*. Rutgers University Press, 2017.
Fisher, Andrew, and Robert Gottlieb. "Community Food Security: Policies for a More Sustainable Food System in the Context of the 1995 Farm Bill and Beyond." The Ralph and Goldy Lewis Center for Regional Policy Studies, School of Public Policy and Social Research, University of California–Los Angeles. Working Paper No. 13. March 1995.
Friedmann, Harriet. "After Midas's Feast: Alternative Food Regimes for the Future." In *Food for the Future: Conditions and Contradictions of Sustainability*, edited by Patricia Allen, 213-33. John Wiley & Sons, 1993.
Fromartz, Samuel. *Organic, Inc.: Natural Foods and How They Grew*. Harcourt, 2006.
Gottlieb, Robert, and Anupama Joshi. *Food Justice*. MIT Press, 2010.
Guthman, Julie. *Agrarian Dreams: The Paradox of Organic Farming in California*. University of California Press, 2004.
Halweil, Brian. *Home Grown: The Case for Local Food in a Global Market*. Worldwatch Paper 163. Worldwatch Institute, November 2002.

Hinrichs, C. Clare, and Patricia Allen. "Selective Patronage and Social Justice: Local Food Consumer Campaigns in Historical Context." *Journal of Agricultural and Environmental Ethics* 21 (2008): 329-52.

Hinrichs, C. Clare, and Thomas A. Lyson, eds. *Remaking the North American Food System: Strategies for Sustainability*. University of Nebraska Press, 2007.

Kauffman, Jonathan. *Hippie Food: How Back-to-the-Landers, Longhairs, and Revolutionaries Changed the Way We Eat*. William Morris, 2018.

Kleiman, Jordan. "Local Food and the Problem of Public Authority." *Technology and Culture* 50 (April 2009): 399-417.

Klonsky, Karen. "Forces Impacting the Production of Organic Foods." *Agriculture and Human Values* 17, no. 3 (September 2000): 233-43.

Kloppenburg, Jack. Jr, John Hendrickson, and G.W. Stevenson. "Coming in to the Foodshed." *Agriculture and Human Values* 13, no. 3 (Summer 1996): 33-42.

Lerza, Catherine, and Michael Jacobson, eds. *Food for People, Not for Profit: A Sourcebook on the Food Crisis*. Ballantine Books, 1975.

Marcello, Patricia Cronin. *Ralph Nader: A Biography*. Greenwood Press, 2004.

Martin, Justin. *Nader: Crusader, Spoiler, Icon*. Perseus Publishing, 2002.

McCarry, Charles. *Citizen Nader*. Saturday Review Press, 1972.

McGrath, Maria. *Food for Dissent: Natural Foods and the Consumer Counterculture Since the 1960s*. University of Massachusetts Press, 2019.

McWilliams, James. *Just Food: Where Locavores Get It Wrong and How We Can Truly Eat Responsibly*. Little, Brown and Company, 2009.

Miller, Laura J. *Building Nature's Market: The Business and Politics of Natural Foods*. University of Chicago Press, 2017.

Mosier, Samantha L. *Creating Organic Standards in U.S. States: The Diffusion of State Organic Food and Agriculture Legislation, 1976-2010*. Lexington Books, 2017.

O'Sullivan, Robin. *American Organic: A Cultural History of Farming, Gardening, Shopping, and Eating*. University Press of Kansas, 2015.

Ruben, Barbara. "Common Ground." *Environmental Action* 27, no. 2 (Summer 1995). Accessed online.

Sabin, Paul. *Public Citizens: The Attack on Big Government and the Remaking of American Liberalism*. W.W. Norton & Company, 2021.

Schell, Orville. *Modern Meat: Antibiotics, Hormones, and the Pharmaceutical Farm*. Random House, 1984.

USDA, ERS. Market and Trade Economics Division and Resource Economics Division. *Recent Growth Patterns in the U.S. Organic Foods Market*, by Carolyn Dimitri and Catherine Greene. Information Bulletin No. 777. September 2002.

Wellford, Harrison. *Sowing the Wind: A Report from Ralph Nader's Center for the Study of Responsive Law on Food Safety and the Chemical Harvest*. Grossman Publishers, 1972.

Winne, Mark. *Closing the Food Gap: Resetting the Table in the Land of Plenty*. Beacon Press, 2008.

LIVESTOCK: CATTLE AND HOGS

Anderson, J.L. *Capitalist Pigs: Pigs, Pork, and Power in America*. West Virginia University Press, 2019.

Anderson, Virginia DeJohn. *Creatures of Empire: How Domestic Animals Transformed Early America*. Oxford University Press, 2004.

Ball, Charles E. *Building the Beef Industry: A Century of Commitment*. The National Cattlemen's Foundation, 1998.

Barkema, Alan, and Michael L. Cook. "The Changing U.S. Pork Industry: A Dilemma for Public Policy." *Economic Review* 78, no. 2 (Second Quarter 1993): 49-65.

Benjamin, Gary L. "Industrialization in Hog Production: Implications for Midwest Agriculture." *Economic Perspectives* 21, no. 1 (January/February 1997): 2-13.

Berry, Michelle K. *Cow Talk: Work, Ecology, and Range Cattle Ranchers in the Postwar Mountain West*. University of Oklahoma Press, 2023.

Bonanno, Alessandro, and Douglas H. Constance. "Mega Hog Farms in the Texas Panhandle Region: Corporate Actions and Local Resistance." *Research in Social Movements, Conflicts and Change* 22 (2000): 83-110.

Bowen, Joanne. "A Comparative Analysis of the New England and Chesapeake Herding Systems." In *Historical Archaeology of the Chesapeake*, edited by Paul A. Shackel and Barbara J. Little, 155-67. Smithsonian Institution Press, 1994.

Brooks, Richard David. "Cattle Ranching in Colonial South Carolina: A Case Study in History and Archaeology of the Lazarus/Catherina Cowpen." Master's thesis, University of South Carolina, 1988.

Burmeister, Charles A. "Six Decades of Rugged Individualism: The American National Cattlemen's Association, 1898-1955." *Agricultural History* 30, no. 4 (October 1956): 143-50.

Clawson, Marion. *The Western Range Livestock Industry*. McGraw-Hill Book Company, 1950.

Coppin, Dawn Michelle. "Capitalist Pigs: Large-Scale Swine Facilities and the Mutual Construction of Nature and Society." PhD diss., University of Illinois-Urbana-Champaign, 2002.

Dale, Edward Everett. *The Range Cattle Industry: Ranching on the Great Plains from 1865 to 1925*. 1930. Reprint, University of Oklahoma Press, 1960.

Dennen, R. Taylor. "Cattlemen's Associations and Property Rights in the American West." *Explorations in Economic History* 13 (1976): 423-36.

Dennen, Rodgers Taylor. "From Common to Private Property: The Enclosure of the Open Range." PhD diss., University of Washington, 1975.

Drabenstott, Mark. "Industrialization: Steady Current or Tidal Wave?" *Choices: The Magazine of Food, Farm & Resource Issues* 9, no. 4 (4th Quarter 1994). Accessed online.

Drabenstott, Mark. "This Little Piggy Went to Market: Will the New Pork Industry Call the Heartland Home?" *Economic Review* [Federal Reserve Bank of Kansas City] 83, no. 3 (1998): 79-97.

Duddy, Edward, and David A. Revzan. "The Changing Importance of the Central Livestock Market." *Journal of Business of the University of Chicago* 11, no. 2, pt. 2 (July 1938). Also published as *Studies in Business Administration* 8, no. 4 (1938): 1-122.

Dunbar, Gary S. "Colonial Carolina Cowpens." *Agricultural History* 35 (July 1961): 125-30.

Frink, Maurice, W. Turrentine Jackson, and Agnes Wright Spring. *When Grass Was King: Contributions to the Western Range Cattle Industry Study*. University of Colorado Press, 1956.

Furuseth, Owen J. "Restructuring of Hog Farming in North Carolina: Explosion and Implosion." *Professional Geographer* 49, no. 4 (1997): 391-403.

Garrison, J. Ritchie. "Farm Dynamics and Regional Exchange: The Connecticut Valley Beef Trade, 1670-1850." *Agricultural History* 61, no. 3 (Summer 1987): 1-17.

Graves, Russell. "Garden City: The Development of an Agricultural Community on the Great Plains." PhD diss., University of Wisconsin–Madison, 2004.

Gresham, Daniel T. "Reshaping the U.S. Cattle Industry: Producers and Packers, 1914-1933." PhD diss., Kansas State University, 2019.

Grey, Mark A. "Those Bastards Can Go to Hell! Small-Farmer Resistance to Vertical Integration and Concentration in the Pork Industry." *Human Organization* 59, no. 2 (Summer 2000).

Hart, Emma. "From Field to Plate: The Colonial Livestock Trade and the Development of an American Economic Culture." *William and Mary Quarterly* 73, no. 1 (January 2016): 107-40.

Henlein, Paul C. *Cattle Kingdom in the Ohio Valley, 1783-1860*. University of Kentucky Press, 1959.

Henlein, Paul C., ed. "Journal of F. and W. Renick on an Exploring Tour of the Mississippi and Missouri Rivers in the Year 1819." *Agricultural History* 30 (October 1956): 174-86.

Hoganson, Kristin. "Meat in the Middle: Converging Borderlands in the U.S. Midwest, 1865-1900." *Journal of American History* 98, no. 4 (March 2012): 1025-51.

Hopkins, John A. *Economic History of the Production of Beef Cattle in Iowa*. State Historical Society of Iowa, 1928.

Idaho Agricultural Experiment Station. "The Western Cattle Feeding Industry: Structural and Marketing Changes, 1952-1962," by Gerald E. Marousek. *Bulletin* 481. July 1967.

Igler, David. *Industrial Cowboys: Miller & Lux and the Transformation of the Far West, 1850–1920*. University of California Press, 2001.

Jordan, Terry G. *North American Cattle-Ranching Frontiers: Origins, Diffusion, and Differentiation*. University of New Mexico Press, 1993.

Knapp, Neal A. "Making Machines of Animals: The International Livestock Exposition, 1900-1920." PhD diss., Boston University, 2019.

Laing, Wesley Newton. "Cattle in Early Virginia." PhD diss., University of Virginia, 1952.

Lee, Elizabeth Oliver. "'Potomac's Valley Shall Become a Domain We Create': Commercialism and the South Branch Valley, 1750-1800." PhD diss., West Virginia University, 2008.

Libecap, Gary D. "Bureaucratic Opposition to the Assignment of Property Rights: Overgrazing on the Western Range." *Journal of Economic History* 41, no. 1 (March 1981): 151-58.

Liggett, Lyle. *"There is a Time and a Place . . .": The History of the American National Cattlemen's Association*. The Newcomen Society In North America, 1972.

Lowitt, Richard. "From Petroleum to Pigs: The Oklahoma Panhandle in the Last

Half of the Twentieth Century." *Chronicles of Oklahoma* 80, no. 3 (September 2002): 260-83.
Maag, James S. "Cattle Raising in Colonial South Carolina." Master's thesis, University of Kansas, 1964.
MacMaster, Richard K. "The Cattle Trade in Western Virginia, 1760-1830." In *Appalachian Frontiers: Settlement, Society, & Development in the Preindustrial Era*, edited by Robert D. Mitchell, 127-49, 314-18. University Press of Kentucky, 1991.
Martin, Laura. "Pork . . . The Other White Meat? An Analysis of Vertical Coordination in the North Carolina Pork Industry." PhD diss., North Carolina State University, 1994.
Mayda, Chris. "Passion on the Plains: Pigs on the Panhandle." PhD diss., University of Southern California, 1998.
McFerrin, Randy and Douglas Wills. "Searching for the Big Die-Off: An Event Study of 19th Century Cattle Markets." *Essays in Economic & Business History* 31 (2013): 33-52.
McGinity, Richard Charles. "Technological Change and Agribusiness Structure: The Beef System." PhD diss., Harvard University, 1980.
Meisner, Joseph Charles. "Investor Capital, Taxes and the Structure of Cattle Feeding." PhD diss., University of Missouri-Columbia, 1974.
Meisner, Joseph C., and V. James Rhodes. *The Changing Structure of U.S. Cattle Feeding*. Special Report 167. University of Missouri-Columbia. November 1974.
Merrill, Karen R. *Public Lands and Political Meaning: Ranchers, the Government, and the Property Between Them*. University of California Press, 2002.
Metcalfe, Robyn S. "American Livestock Improvers and Urban Markets During the Nineteenth Century." *Journal of the Historical Society* 7, no. 4 (December 2007): 475-92.
Norwood, F. Bailey, and Jayson Lusk. *Compassion, By the Pound: The Economics of Farm Animal Welfare*. Oxford University Press, 2011.
Olmstead, Alan L., and Paul W. Rhode. *Arresting Contagion: Science, Policy, and Conflicts Over Animal Disease*. Harvard University Press, 2015.
Orland, Barbara. "Turbo-Cows: Producing a Competitive Animal in the Nineteenth and Early Twentieth Centuries." In *Industrializing Organisms: Introducing Evolutionary History*, edited by Susan R. Schrepfer and Philip Scranton, 167-89. Routledge, 2004.
Osgood, Ernest Staples. *The Day of the Cattleman*. 1929. Reprint, University of Chicago Press, 1957.
Otto, John Solomon. "Livestock-Raising in Early South Carolina, 1670-1700: Prelude to the Rice Plantation Economy." *Agricultural History* 61 (Fall 1987): 13-24.
Percy, David O. "Of Fast Horses, Black Cattle, Woods Hogs, and Rat-Tailed Sheep: Animal Husbandry Along the Colonial Potomac." *The National Colonial Farm Research Report* No. 4. 1979.
Peterson, Everett B., Paul V. Preckel, Thomas W. Hertel, and Anya M. McGuirk. "Impacts of Stimulants in the Domestic Livestock Sector." *Agribusiness* 8, no. 4 (July 1992): 287-307.

Rhodes, V. James. "The Industrialization of Hog Production." *Review of Agricultural Economics* 17, no. 2 (May 1995): 107-18.
Sayre, Nathan F. "Corn and the Range: Rethinking Ranching, Agriculture and the Feedlot." *Journal of Peasant Studies* 51, no. 4 (2024): 1208-29.
Sayre, Nathan F. *The Politics of Scale: A History of Rangeland Science*. University of Chicago Press, 2017.
Schlebecker, John T. *Cattle Raising on the Plains, 1900-1961*. University of Nebraska Press, 1963.
Schneidau, Robert E., and Lawrence A. Duwer. *Symposium: Vertical Coordination in the Pork Industry*. AVI Publishing Company for the Purdue Research Foundation, 1972.
Skaggs, Jimmy M. *The Cattle-Trailing Industry: Between Supply and Demand, 1866-1890*. 1973. Reprint, University of Oklahoma Press, 1991.
Skaggs, Jimmy M. *Prime Cut: Livestock Raising and Meatpacking in the United States, 1607-1983*. Texas A&M University Press, 1986.
Specht, Joshua. "'For the Future in the Distance': Cattle Trailing, Social Conflict, and the Development of Ellsworth, Kansas." *Kansas History* 40 (Summer 2017): 104-19.
Specht, Joshua. *Red Meat Republic: A Hoof-to-Table History of How Beef Changed America*. Princeton University Press, 2019.
Specht, Joshua. "The Rise, Fall, and Rebirth of the Texas Longhorn: An Evolutionary History." *Environmental History* 21, no. 2 (2016): 343-63.
Starrs, Paul F. *Let the Cowboy Ride: Cattle Ranching in the American West*. Johns Hopkins University Press, 1998.
Stewart, Mart A. "'Whether Wast, Deodand, or Stray': Cattle, Culture, and the Environment in Early Georgia." *Agricultural History* 65, no. 3 (Summer 1991): 1-28.
Thompson, Michael D. "High on the Hog: Swine as Culture and Commodity in Eastern North Carolina." PhD diss., Miami University, 2000.
Thompson, Michael D. "This Little Piggy Went to Market: The Commercialization of Hog Production in Eastern North Carolina from William Shay to Wendell Murphy." *Agricultural History* 74, no. 2 (Spring 2000): 569-84.
Thu, Kendall M., and E. Paul Durrenberger, eds. *Pigs, Profits, and Rural Communities*. State University of New York Press, 1998.
University of Missouri-Columbia, Extension Division. *A 1974 Survey of Large-Scale Hog Production in the U.S.*, by V. James Rhodes, Robert M. Finley, and Glenn Grimes. Special Report No. 165. September 1974.
USDA. *Economics of the U.S. Meat Industry*, by Richard J. Crom. Agriculture Information Bulletin No. 545. November 1988.
USDA. *Federal and State Rural Lands, 1950, with Special Reference to Grazing*, by R.D. Davidson. Circular 909. May 1952
USDA. *Yearbook of Agriculture* 1916. "The Function of Live Stock in Agriculture," by George M. Rommel, 467-75.
USDA, Agricultural History Series. No. 5. *A History of Livestock Raising in the United States, 1607-1860*, by James Westfall Thompson. 1942. Reprint, Scholarly Resources, 1973.

USDA, ARS, *Major Uses of Land in the United States: Summary for 1954.* Agriculture Information Bulletin No. 168, January 1957.
USDA, ERS. *The Beef Cow-Calf Industry, 1964-87*, by Kenneth R. Krause. Agricultural Economic Report No. 659. June 1992.
USDA, ERS. *Cattle Feeding, 1962-89*, by Kenneth R. Krause. Agricultural Economic Report No. 642. April 1991.
USDA, ERS, *Cattle Feeding in the United States*, by Ronald A. Gustafson and Roy N. Van Arsdall. Agricultural Economic Report No. 186. October 1970.
USDA, ERS. *Cattle Raising in the United States*, by Roy N. Van Arsdall and Melvin D. Skold. Economic Report No. 235. January 1973.
USDA, ERS. *Decentralization in the Livestock and Slaughter Industry*, by W.E. Anthony and K.E. Egerston. Supplemental Agricultural Economics Report No. 83. 1966.
USDA, ERS. *Economies of Size in Hog Production*, by Roy Van Arsdall and Kenneth E. Nelson. Technical Bulletin No. 1712. December 1985.
USDA, ESC. *Another Revolution in U.S. Farming?*, by Lyle P. Schertz et al. Agricultural Economic Report No. 441. December 1979.
USDA, ESC. "Beef," by Rod J. Martin. *In Another Revolution in U.S. Farming?*, by Lyle P. Schertz et al., 85-118. Agricultural Economic Report No. 441. December 1979.
USDA, ESS. *Structural Change in Agriculture: The Experience for Broilers, Fed Cattle, and Processing Vegetables*, by Donn A. Reimund, J. Rod Martin, and Charles V. Moore. Technical Bulletin No. 1648. April 1981.
USDA, PSD. Consumer and Marketing Service. *Packer Feeding of Cattle: Its Volume and Significance.* Marketing Research Report No. 776. November 1966.
US House, Committee on Agriculture. *Prohibit Feeding of Livestock by Certain Packers: Hearings Before the Subcommittee on Livestock and Feed Grains of the Committee on Agriculture.* 89th Cong. (1966).
US House. Committee on the Judiciary. *Investigation of Beef Industries. Hearings Before the Committee on the Judiciary . . . on H.Res.* 148 Serial 43, Parts 1 and 2. 64th Cong. (1916).
US House. *Proceedings of the Conference Relative to the Marketing of Live Stock Distribution of Meats and Related Matters, Held by the Direction of the Hon. David Franklin Houston, . . . Conducted by the Office of Markets and Rural Organization.* H.Doc. No. 855. 64th Cong. (1915).
US Senate, Committee on Agriculture, Nutrition, and Forestry. "The Changing Structure of the Hog Industry," by V. James Rhodes and Glenn Grimes. In *Farm Structure: A Historical Perspective on Changes in the Number and Size of Farms*, 185-95. 96th Cong. (1980).
US Treasury, Bureau of Statistics. *Report in Regard to Range and Ranch Cattle Business of U.S. Treasury Department Document No. 690*, by Joseph Nimmo. 1885. Also published as part of Treasury Department, *Report on the Internal Commerce of the United States*, 48th Cong. (1885).
Whitaker, James. *Feedlot Empire: Beef Cattle Feeding in Illinois and Iowa, 1840–1900.* Iowa State University Press, 1975.
Wood, Charles L. *The Kansas Beef Industry.* 1980. Reprint, University Press of Kansas, 2020.

MEATPACKING/PACKERS

Aduddell, Robert. "Location and Collusion in the Meat Packing Industry." In *Business Enterprise and Economic Change: Essays in Honor of Harold F. Williamson*, edited by Louis P. Cain and Paul J. Uselding, 85-117. Kent State University Press, 1973.

Aduddell, Robert M., and Louis Cain. "The Consent Decree in the Meatpacking Industry, 1920-1956." *Business History Review* 55, no. 3 (Autumn 1981): 359-78.

Aduddell, Robert M., and Louis P. Cain. "A Strange Sense of Deja Vu: The Packers and the Feds, 1915-82." *Business and Economic History* 11 (1982): 49-60.

Arnould, Richard J. "Changing Patterns of Concentration in American Meat Packing, 1880-1963." *Business History Review* 45, no. 1 (Spring 1971): 18-34.

Atkinson, Eva Lash. "Kansas City's Livestock Trade and Packing Industry, 1870-1914: A Study in Regional Growth." PhD diss., University of Kansas, 1971.

Blum, Joseph A. "South San Francisco: The Making of an Industrial City." *California History* 63 (Spring 1984): 114-34.

Bradley, Linda J., and Barbara D. Merino. "Stuart Chase: A Radical CPA and the Meat Packing Investigation, 1917-1918." *Business and Economic History* 23, no. 1 (Fall 1994): 190-200.

Brinkley, Catherine, and Domenic Vitiello. "From Farm to Nuisance: Animal Agriculture and the Rise of Planning Regulation." *Journal of Planning History* 13, no. 2 (2014): 113-35.

Broadway, Michael J., and Donald D. Stull. "'I'll Do Whatever You Want, But It Hurts': Worker Safety and Community Health in Modern Meatpacking." *Labor: Studies in Working-Class History of the Americas* 5, no. 2 (2008): 27-37.

Broadway, Michael J. and Donald D. Stull. "The Wages of Food Factories." *Food & Foodways* 18, no. 1/2 (2010): 43-65.

Butz, Dale E., and George L. Baker. *The Changing Structure of the Meat Economy*. Harvard University, Graduate School of Business Administration, Division of Research, 1960.

Clemen, Rudolf Alexander. *The American Livestock and Meat Industry*. The Ronald Press, 1923.

Davenport, Cora Lillian. "The Rise of the Armours, An American Industrial Family." Master's thesis, University of Chicago, 1930.

Deutsch, Christopher. "'We Dislike to See Suffering': The Fight for Humane Slaughter in the United States in the 1950s." *History of Retailing and Consumption* 5, no. 1 (2019): 8-28.

Dougherty, Richard. *In Quest of Quality: Hormel's First 75 Years*. Geo. A. Hormel & Co., 1966.

Doyle, William Michael. "The Evolution of Financial Practices and Financial Structures Among American Manufacturers, 1875-1905: Case Studies of the Sugar Refining and Meat Packing Industries." PhD diss., University of Tennessee, 1991.

[Fink, Albert]. *Report upon the Relative Cost of Transporting Live Stock and Dressed Beef*. Russell Brothers, 1883.

Geib, Paul E. "'Everything but the Squeal': The Milwaukee Stockyards and Meat-

Packing Industry, 1840-1930." *Wisconsin Magazine of History* 78, no. 1 (Autumn 1994): 3-23.

Gordon, David. "The Beef Trust: Antitrust Policy and the Meat Packing Industry, 1902-1922." PhD diss., Claremont Graduate School, 1983.

Gordon, Stephen Canning. "The City as 'Porkopolis': Some Factors in the Rise of the Meat Packing Industry in Cincinnati, 1825-1861." Master's thesis, Miami University, 1981.

Gordon, Stephen Canning. "From Slaughterhouse to Soap-Boiler: Cincinnati's Meat Packing Industry, Changing Technologies, and the Rise of Mass Production, 1825-1870." *IA* 16 (1990): 55–67.

Gras, N.S.B., and Henrietta M. Larson. *Casebook in American Business History*. F.S. Crofts & Co., 1939.

Harley, C. Knick. "Steers Afloat: The North Atlantic Meat Trade, Liner Predominance, and Freight Rates, 1870-1913." *Journal of Economic History* 68, no. 4 (December 2008): 1028-58.

Hazlett, O. James. "Chaos and Conspiracy: The Kansas City Livestock Trade, 1886-1892." *Kansas History* 15, no. 2 (Summer 1992): 126-44.

Homenuck, Henry Peter Michael. "Historical Geography of the Cincinnati Pork Industry: 1810-1883." Master's thesis, University of Cincinnati, 1965.

Horowitz, Roger. *Putting Meat On the American Table: Taste, Technology, Transformation*. Johns Hopkins University Press, 2006.

Hurt, R. Douglas. "Pork and Porkopolis." *Cincinnati Historical Society Bulletin* 40 (1982): 191-215.

[Institute of American Meat Packers]. *The Packing Industry*. University of Chicago Press, 1924.

Johnson, Arthur M. "Theodore Roosevelt and the Bureau of Corporations." *Mississippi Valley Historical Review* 45, no. 4 (March 1959): 571-90.

Keuchel, Edward F. "Chemicals and Meat: The Embalmed Beef Scandal of the Spanish-American War." *Bulletin of the History of Medicine* 48 (1974): 249-64.

Knapp, Joseph G. "A Review of Chicago Stock Yards History." *The University Journal of Business* 2 (June 1924): 331-46.

Knapp, Vincent J. "The Democratization of Meat and Protein in Late Eighteenth- and Nineteenth-Century Europe." *The Historian* 59, no. 3 (March 1997): 541-51.

Leavitt, Charles Townsend. "Some Aspects of the Western Meatpacking Industry, 1830-60." *Journal of Business of the University of Chicago* 4 (January 1931): 68-90.

Leech, Harper, and John Charles Carroll. *Armour and His Times*. D. Appleton-Century Company, 1938.

Leonard, Christopher. *The Meat Racket: The Secret Takeover of America's Food Business*. Simon & Schuster, 2014.

Libecap, Gary D. "The Rise of the Chicago Packers and the Origins of Meat Inspection and Antitrust." *Economic Inquiry* 30 (April 1992): 242-62.

McCarty, H.H., and C.W. Thompson. "Meat Packing in Iowa." *Iowa Studies in Business* 12 (1933).

Pachirat, Timothy. *Every Twelve Seconds: Industrialized Slaughter and the Politics of Sight*. Yale University Press, 2011.

Pacyga, Dominic A. *Slaughterhouse: Chicago's Union Stock Yard and the World It Made*. University of Chicago Press, 2015.

Perren, Richard. *The Meat Trade in Britain*. Routledge & Kegan Paul, 1978.

Perren, Richard. "The North American Beef and Cattle Trade with Great Britain, 1870-1914." *Economic History Review* n.s. 24, no. 3 (August 1971): 430-44.

Perren, Richard. *Taste, Trade and Technology: The Development of the International Meat Industry Since 1840*. Ashgate, 2006.

Piott, Steven L. "Missouri and the Beef Trust: Consumer Action and Investigation, 1902." *Missouri Historical Review* 76, no. 1 (October 1981): 31-52.

Rees, Jonathan. *Refrigeration Nation: A History of Ice, Appliances, and Enterprise in America*. Johns Hopkins University Press, 2013.

Renner, G.K. "The Kansas City Meat Packing Industry Before 1900." *Missouri Historical Review* 55 (October 1960): 18-29.

Stanley, Kathleen. "Industrial and Labor Market Transformation in the U.S. Meatpacking Industry." In *The Global Restructuring of Agro-food Systems*, edited by Philip McMichael, 129-44. Cornell University Press, 1994.

Stull, Donald D., and Michael J. Broadway. *Slaughterhouse Blues: The Meat and Poultry Industry in North America*. Thomson/Wadsworth, 2004.

Swift, Louis F., and Arthur Van Vlissingen Jr. *The Yankee of the Yards: The Biography of Gustavus Franklin Swift*. A.W. Shaw Company, 1927.

Thiboumery, Arion Jean. "Small Meat Processors Working Group: Managing Knowledge in a New Era of Agriculture." PhD diss., Iowa State University, 2009.

Ufkes-Daniels, Frances M. "Agrarian Ideology, Market Structure and the Reproduction of Consent: Producer-Packer Relations in an Era of U.S. Meat Industry Restructuring." PhD diss., University of Iowa, 1995.

US Census, 12th Census. Part 3: Manufacturing. *Slaughtering and Meat Packing*, by Harry C. McCarty.

USDA. *Economics of the U.S. Meat Industry*, by Richard J. Crom. Agriculture Information Bulletin No. 545. November 1988.

USDA, BAI. "Dressed-Meat Traffic," by Norman J. Colman in *Third Annual Report of the Bureau of Animal Industry for the Year 1886*.

USDA, BAI. *Meat Production, Consumption and Foreign Trade of the United States 1900-1927*, compiled by John Roberts. [1930].

USDA, ERS. "Economics of the U.S. Meat Industry," by Richard J. Crom. *Agriculture Information Bulletin* No. 545. November 1988.

USDA, PSD. Consumer and Marketing Service. *Packer Feeding of Cattle: Its Volume and Significance*. Marketing Research Report No. 776. November 1966.

US Federal Trade Commission. *Food Investigation: Report of the Federal Trade Commission on the Meat-Packing Industry*. 6 vols. 1919.

US House, Committee on Agriculture. *Amend the Meat Inspection Act. Hearings Before the Subcommittee on Livestock and Grains*. 90th Cong. (1967).

US House, Committee on Agriculture. *Prohibit Feeding of Livestock by Certain Packers: Hearings Before the Subcommittee on Livestock and Feed Grains of the Committee on Agriculture*. 89th Cong., 1966.

US House. Committee on Interstate and Foreign Commerce. *Government Control of Meat-Packing Industry. Hearings Before the Committee on Interstate and Foreign Commerce . . . on H.R. 13324.* 5 parts. 65th Cong. (1918-19).

US House, Committee on the Judiciary. *Investigation of Beef Industries. Hearings Before the Committee on the Judiciary . . . on H.Res. 148 Serial 43, Parts 1 and 2.* 64th Cong. (1916).

US Senate. *Government Control of the Meat Packing Industry. Hearings Before the Committee on Agriculture and Forestry . . . on S.5305 A Bill to Stimulate the Production, Sale, and Distribution of Live Stock and Live-Stock Products, and for Other Purposes.* 2 parts. 65th Cong. (1918).

US Senate, Select Committee on Transportation and Sale of Meat Products. *Investigation of Transportation and Sale of Meat Products with Testimony, S. Rpt. 829.* 51st Cong. (1888).

Virtue, G.O. "The Meat-Packing Investigation." *Quarterly Journal of Economics* 34, no. 4 (August 1920): 626-85.

Wade, Louise Carroll. *Chicago's Pride: The Stockyards, Packingtown, and Environs in the Nineteenth Century.* University of Illinois Press, 1987.

Warren, Wilson J. *Tied to the Great Packing Machine: The Midwest and Meatpacking.* University of Iowa Press, 2007.

Winans, Charles. *The Evolution of a Vast Industry: Being the Reprint of An Article . . . in Harper's Weekly in Ten Consecutive Issues.* 2d edition. [Harper & Brothers], 1908.

Yeager, Mary. *Competition and Regulation: The Development of Oligopoly in the Meat Packing Industry.* JAI Press, 1981.

NATIVE AMERICANS/"INDIAN REMOVAL"

Blackhawk, Ned. *The Rediscovery of America: Native Peoples and the Unmaking of U.S. History.* Yale University Press, 2023.

Frymer, Paul. *Building an American Empire: The Era of Territorial and Political Expansion.* Princeton University Press, 2017.

Hämäläinen, Pekka. *Indigenous Continent: The Epic Contest for North America.* Liveright Publishing Corporation, 2022.

Hämäläinen, Pekka. *Lakota America: A New History of Indigenous Power.* Yale University Press, 2019.

Ostler, Jeffrey. *Surviving Genocide: Native Nations and the United States From the American Revolution to Bleeding Kansas.* Yale University Press, 2019.

Saunt, Claudio. *Unworthy Republic: The Dispossession of Native Americans and the Road to Indian Territory.* W.W. Norton & Company, 2020.

White, Richard. *The Middle Ground: Indians, Empires, and Republics in the Great Lakes Region, 1650-1815.* Twentieth Anniversary Edition. Cambridge University Press, 2011.

Wilson, James. *The Earth Shall Weep: A History of Native America.* Grove Press, 1998.

Witgen, Michael. *An Infinity of Nations: How the Native New World Shaped Early North America.* University of Pennsylvania Press, 2012.

Witgen, Michael John. *Seeing Red: Indigenous Land, American Expansion, and the Political*

Economy of Plunder in North America. Omohundro Institute of Early American History and Culture, 2022.

NEW YORK CITY

Albion, Robert G. *The Rise of New York Port, 1815-1860.* C. Scribner's Sons, 1939.

Baics, Gergely. *Feeding Gotham: The Political Economy and Geography of Food in New York, 1790-1860.* Princeton University Press, 2016.

Beal, Thomas David. "Selling Gotham: The Retail Trade in New York City from the Public Market to Alexander T. Stewart's Marble Palace, 1625-1860." PhD diss., State University of New York-Stony Brook, 1998.

Burrows, Edwin G. *Gotham: A History of New York City to 1898.* Oxford University Press, 1999.

Day, Jared N. "Butchers, Tanners, and Tallow Chandlers: The Geography of Slaughtering in Early-nineteenth-century New York City." In *Meat, Modernity, and the Rise of the Slaughterhouse*, edited by Paula Young Lee, 178-97, 282-84. University of New Hampshire Press, 2008.

Fullilove, Courtney. "The Price of Bread: The New York City Flour Riot and the Paradox of Capitalist Food Systems." *Radical History Review* 118 (Winter 2014): 15-41.

Hartog, Hendrik. *Public Property and Private Power: The Corporation of the City of New York in American Law, 1730-1870.* University of North Carolina Press, 1983.

Horowitz, Roger. "The Politics of Meat Shopping In Antebellum New York City." In *Meat, Modernity, and the Rise of the Slaughterhouse*, edited by Paula Young Lee, 167-77, 279-82. University of New Hampshire Press, 2008.

Jackson, Kenneth T. *The Encyclopedia of New York City.* Yale University Press and New-York Historical Society, 2010.

Linder, Marc. *Of Cabbages and Kings County: Agriculture and the Formation of Modern Brooklyn.* University of Iowa Press, 1999.

Lobel, Cindy R. *Urban Appetites: Food and Culture in Nineteenth-Century New York.* University of Chicago Press, 2014.

Rock, Howard B. *Artisans of the New Republic: The Tradesmen of New York City in the Age of Jefferson.* New York University Press, 1984.

Still, Bayrd. *Mirror for Gotham: New York as Seen by Contemporaries from Dutch Days to the Present.* University Press, 1956.

Stott, Richard B. *Workers in the Metropolis: Class, Ethnicity, and Youth in Antebellum New York City.* Cornell University Press, 1990.

Tremante, Louis. "Agriculture in the Vicinity of Mid-Nineteenth Century New York City: Five Drivers." *New York History* 97, no. 3/4 (Summer/Fall 2016): 265-92.

Tremante, Louis P. III. "Agriculture and Farm Life in the New York City Region, 1820-1870." PhD diss., Iowa State University, 2000.

RACE

See also Native Americans/"Indian Removal"

BIBLIOGRAPHY

Aarim-Heriot, Najia. *Chinese Immigrants, African Americans, and Racial Anxiety in the United States, 1848-82*. University of Illinois Press, 2003.

Collins, Ann V. *All Hell Broke Loose: American Race Riots from the Progressive Era through World War II*. Praeger, 2012.

Evans, William McKee. *Open Wound: The Long View of Race in America*. University of Illinois Press, 2009.

Foner, Eric. *The Second Founding: How the Civil War and Reconstruction Remade the Constitution*. W.W. Norton & Company, 2019.

Franklin, John Hope. *From Slavery to Freedom: A History of African Americans*. 9th ed. McGraw-Hill, 2011.

Guyatt, Nicholas. *Bind Us Apart: How Enlightened Americans Invented Racial Segregation*. Basic Books, 2016.

Hahn, Steven. *A Nation Under Our Feet: Black Political Struggles in the Rural South, from Slavery to the Great Migration*. Belknap Press of Harvard University Press, 2003.

Holloway, Jonathan Scott. *The Cause of Freedom: A Concise History of African Americans*. Oxford University Press, 2021.

Holt, Thomas C. *Children of Fire: A History of African Americans*. Hill and Wang, 2010.

Holt, Thomas C. *The Movement: The African American Struggle for Civil Rights*. Oxford University Press, 2021.

Irons, Peter. *White Men's Law: The Roots of Systemic Racism*. Oxford University Press, 2022.

Jacobson, Matthew Frye. *Barbarian Virtues: The United States Encounters Foreign Peoples at Home and Abroad, 1876-1917*. Hill and Wang, 2000.

Jacobson, Matthew Frye. *The Rise and Fall of the White Republic: Class Politics and Mass Culture in Nineteenth-Century America*. Harvard University Press, 1990.

Jacobson, Matthew Frye. *Whiteness of a Different Color: European Immigrants and the Alchemy of Race*. Harvard University Press, 1998.

Johnson, Walter. *River of Dark Dreams: Slavery and Empire in the Cotton Kingdom*. Belknap Press of Harvard University Press, 2013.

Jones, Martha S. *Birthright Citizens: A History of Race and Rights in Antebellum America*. Cambridge University Press, 2018.

Jones, Reece. *White Borders: The History of Race and Immigration in the United States from Chinese Exclusion to the Border Wall*. Beacon Press, 2021.

Karp, Matthew. *This Vast Southern Empire: Slaveholders at the Helm of American Foreign Policy*. Harvard University Press, 2016.

Larson, Edward J. *American Inheritance: Liberty and Slavery in the Birth of A Nation, 1765-1795*. W.W. Norton & Company, 2023.

Painter, Nell Irvin. *Creating Black Americans: African-American History and Its Meanings, 1619 to the Present*. Oxford University Press, 2007.

Roediger, David R. "The Pursuit of Whiteness: Property, Terror, and Expansion, 1790-1860." *Journal of the Early Republic* 19, no. 4 (1999): 579-600.

Roediger, David R. *The Wages of Whiteness: Race and the Making of the American Working Class*. Revised ed. Verso, 2007.

Saxton, Alexander. *The Rise and Fall of the White Republic: Class Politics and Mass Culture in Nineteenth-Century America*. Verso, 1990.

Seeley, Samantha. *Race, Removal, and the Right to Remain: Migration and the Making of the United States*. Omohundro Institute of Early American History and Culture, 2021.

Takaki, Ronald T. *Iron Cages: Race and Culture in 19th-Century America*. Revised ed. Oxford University Press, 2000.

Tischauser, Leslie Vincent. *Race Relations in the United States, 1920-1940*. Greenwood Press, 2008.

RAILROADS

Cochran, Thomas C. *Railroad Leaders, 1845-1890: The Business Mind in Action*. Harvard University Press, 1953.

Gordon, Sarah. *Passage to Union: How the Railroads Transformed American Life, 1829-1929*. Ivan R. Dee, 1996.

Grant, H. Roger. *Railroads and the American People*. Indiana University Press, 2012.

Hiltzik, Michael A. *Iron Empires: Robber Barons, Railroads, and the Making of Modern America*. Houghton Mifflin Harcourt, 2020.

Martin, Albro. *Railroads Triumphant: The Growth, Rejection, and Rebirth of a Vital American Force*. Oxford University Press, 1992.

Miner, H. Craig. *A Most Magnificent Machine: America Adopts the Railroad, 1825-1862*. University Press of Kansas, 2010.

New York State Legislature, Special Committee On Railroads. *Proceedings of the Special Committee on Railroads Appointed under a Resolution of the Assembly to Investigate Alleged Abuses in the Management of Railroads Chartered by the State of New York*, vols. 1-6. Evening Post Steam Presses, 1879.

Stilgoe, John R. *Train Time: Railroads and the Imminent Reshaping of the United States Landscape*. University of Virginia Press, 2007.

Stover, John F. *American Railroads*. 2nd ed. University of Chicago Press, 1997.

Thomas, William G. *The Iron Way: Railroads, the Civil War, and the Making of Modern America*. Yale University Press, 2011.

US Senate, Senate Select Committee on Interstate Commerce. *Report of the Senate Select Committee on Interstate Commerce*. 49th Cong. (1886).

Ward, James Arthur. *Railroads and the Character of America, 1820-1887*. University of Tennessee Press, 1986.

White, John H. *The Great Yellow Fleet: A History of American Railroad Refrigerator Cars*. Golden West Books, 1986.

White, John H., Jr. "Riding in Style: Palace Cars for the Cattle Trade." *Technology and Culture* 31, no. 2 (April 1990): 265-70.

White, Richard. *Railroaded: The Transcontinentals and the Making of Modern America*. W.W. Norton, 2011.

SLAUGHTERHOUSE CASES

Barnett, Randy E. "The Three Narratives of the *Slaughter-House Cases*." *Journal of Supreme Court History* 41, no. 3 (2016): 295-309.

Johnson, Lindgren. "To 'Admit All Cattle Without Distinction': Reconstructing Slaughter in the Slaughterhouse Cases and the New Orleans Crescent City

Slaughterhouse." In *Meat, Modernity, and the Rise of the Slaughterhouse*, edited by Paula Young Lee, 198-215. University of New Hampshire Press, 2008.

Labbé, Ronald M., and Jonathan Lurie. *The Slaughterhouse Cases: Regulation, Reconstruction, and the Fourteenth Amendment*. University Press of Kansas, 2003.

Parmet, Wendy E. "From Slaughter-House to Lochner: The Rise and Fall of the Constitutionalization of Public Health." *American Journal of Legal History* 40 (1996): 476-505.

Ross, Michael A. "Justice Miller's Reconstruction: The Slaughter-Houses Cases, Health Codes, and Civil Rights in New Orleans, 1861-1873." *Journal of Southern History* 64, no. 4 (November 1998): 649-76.

USDA

Carlson, Laurie M. *William J. Spillman and the Birth of Agricultural Economics*. University of Missouri Press, 2005.

Carpenter, Daniel. *The Forging of Bureaucratic Autonomy: Reputations, Networks, and Policy Innovation in Executive Agencies, 1862-1928*. Princeton University Press, 2020.

Ferleger, Louis A. *Planting the Seeds of Research: How America's Ultimate Investment Transformed Agriculture*. Anthem Press, 2020.

Ferleger, Louis, and William Lazonick. "The Managerial Revolution and the Developmental States: The Case of U.S. Agriculture." *Business and Economic History* 22, no. 2 (Winter 1993): 67-98.

Fitzgerald, Deborah. *Every Farm A Factory: The Industrial Ideal in American Agriculture*. Yale University Press, 2003.

Harding, T. Swann. *Two Blades of Grass: A History of Scientific Development in the U.S. Department of Agriculture*. University of Oklahoma Press, 1947.

Hoing, Willard Lee. "James Wilson as Secretary of Agriculture, 1897-1913." PhD diss., University of Wisconsin, 1964.

Marcus, Alan I [sic], ed. *Science As Service: Establishing and Reformulating Land-Grant Universities, 1865-1930*. University of Alabama Press, 2015.

Marcus, Alan I [sic], and Richard Lowitt. *The United States Department of Agriculture in Historical Perspective*. Agricultural History Society, 1991.

McDean, Harry C. "Professionalism, Policy, and Farm Economists in the Early Bureau of Agricultural Economics." *Agricultural History* 57, no. 1 (January 1983): 64-82.

Moss, Jeffrey W., and Cynthia B. Lass. "A History of Farmers' Institutes." *Agricultural History* 62, no. 2 (Spring 1988): 150-63.

Rasmussen, Wayne D., and Gladys L. Baker. *The Department of Agriculture*. Praeger Publishers, 1972.

Ron, Ariel. *Grassroots Leviathan: Agricultural Reform and the Rural North In the Slaveholding Republic*. Johns Hopkins University Press, 2020.

Ross, Earle D. "The United States Department of Agriculture During the Commissionership: A Study in Politics, Administration, and Technology, 1862-1889." *Agricultural History* 20, no. 3 (July 1946): 129-43.

Tyler, Hannah. "In Numbers We Trust? A History of the US Department of Agriculture and Its Agricultural Surveys during the 1920s." *Histoire & Mesure* 38,

no. 1 (2023): 39-64.
USDA. *A History of Agricultural Experimentation and Research in the United States 1607-1925 Including a History of the United States Department of Agriculture, Miscellaneous Publication No. 251*, by Alfred Charles True. 1937.
USDA. *Century of Service: The First 100 Years of the United States Department of Agriculture*, by Gladys L. Baker, Wayne D. Rasmussen, Vivian Wiser, and Jane M. Porter. 1963.
USDA. *Farmers, Cooperatives, and USDA: A History of Agricultural Cooperative Service*, by Wayne D. Rasmussen. 1991.
Wik, Reynold M. "The USDA and the Development of Radio in Rural America." *Agricultural History* 62, no. 2 (Spring 1988): 177-88.
Wilcox, Earley Vernon. *Tama Jim*. The Stratford Company, 1930.
Wiser, Vivian. "Public Policy and USDA Science, 1897-1913." *Agricultural History* 64, no. 2 (Spring 1990): 24-30.

WESTERN US: BACKGROUND/CONTEXT

Abbott, Carl. *The Metropolitan Frontier: Cities in the Modern American West*. University of Arizona Press, 1993.
Aron, Stephen. *The American West: A Very Short Introduction*. Oxford University Press, 2015.
Bergmann, William H. *The American National State and the Early West*. Cambridge University Press, 2012.
Bernstein, David. *How the West Was Drawn: Mapping, Indians, and the Construction of the Trans-Mississippi West*. University of Nebraska Press, 2018.
Brown, Dee. *The American West*. Scribner, 1994.
Bryan, Jimmy L., Jr. "'Our Eyes Ached with the Very Vastness': Reimagining the Great American Desert as the Great American Prairie." *Great Plains Quarterly* 39, no. 3 (Summer 2019): 243-63.
Cunfer, Geoff. *On the Great Plains: Agriculture and Environment*. Texas A&M University Press, 2005.
Cunfer, Geoff. "Social Fertility On An Agricultural Frontier: The US Great Plains, 1880-2000." *Social Science History* 45, no. 4 (Winter 2001): 733-62.
Cunfer, Geoff, and Bill Waiser, eds. *Bison and People on the North American Great Plains: A Deep Environmental History*. Texas A&M University Press, 2016.
Deutsch, Sarah. *Making A Modern West: The Contested Terrain of A Region and Its Borders, 1898-1940*. University of Nebraska Press, 2022.
Deverell, William, ed. *A Companion to the American West*. Blackwell Publishing Ltd., 2004.
Dillon, Richard H. "Stephen Long's Great American Desert." *Proceedings of the American Philosophical Society* 111, no. 2 (April 14, 1967): 93-108.
Dykstra, Robert R. *The Cattle Towns*. Alfred A. Knopf, 1968.
Edwards, Richard, Jacob I. Friefeld, and Rebecca S. Wingo. *Homesteading the Plains: Toward A New History*. University of Nebraska Press, 2017.
Etulain, Richard W., and Michael P. Malone. *The American West: A Modern History, 1900 to the Present*. 2d. ed. University of Nebraska Press, 2007.

Hurt, R. Douglas. *The Big Empty: The Great Plains in the Twentieth Century*. University of Arizona Press, 2011.

Isenberg, Andrew C. *The Destruction of the Bison: An Environmental History, 1750-1920*. Cambridge University Press, 2000.

Kleeb, Scott Michael. "The Atlantic West: Cowboys, Capitalists and the Making of an American Myth." PhD diss., Yale University, 2006.

Knowlton, Christopher. *Cattle Kingdom: The Hidden History of the Cowboy West*. Houghton Mifflin Harcourt, 2017.

Larsen, Lawrence H. *The Urban West At the End of the Frontier*. 1978. Reprint, University Press of Kansas, 2023.

Limerick, Patricia Nelson. *The Legacy of Conquest: The Unbroken Past of the American West*. W.W. Norton, 2006.

Milner, Clyde A., II, Carol A. O'Connor, and Martha A. Sandweiss, eds. *The Oxford History of the American West*. Oxford University Press, 1994.

Nash, Gerald D. *The American West in the Twentieth Century: A Short History of an Urban Oasis*. University of New Mexico Press, 1985.

Nash, Gerald D. *The Federal Landscape: An Economic History of the Twentieth-Century West*. University of Arizona Press, 1999.

O'Brien, Dan. *Great Plains Bison*. University of Nebraska Press, 2017.

Pomeroy, Earl. *The American Far West in the Twentieth Century*. Yale University Press, 2008.

Robbins, William, G. *Colony and Empire: The Capitalist Transformation of the American West*. University Press of Kansas, 1994.

Van Nuys, Frank. *Americanizing the West: Race, Immigrants, and Citizenship, 1890-1930*. University Press of Kansas, 2002.

Webb, Walter Prescott. *The Great Plains*. 2d ed. University of Nebraska Press, 2022.

West, Elliott. *Continental Reckoning: The American West in the Age of Expansion*. University of Nebraska Press, 2023.

White, Richard. "Animals and Enterprise." In *The Oxford History of the American West*, edited by Clyde A. Milner II, Carol A. O'Connor, and Martha A. Sandweiss, 237-73. Oxford University Press, 1994.

White, Richard. *"It's Your Misfortune and None of My Own": A New History of the American West*. University of Oklahoma Press, 1991.

Wright, Gavin. "World War II, The Cold War, and the Knowledge Economies of the Pacific Coast." In *World War II and the West It Wrought*, edited by Mark Brilliant and David M. Kennedy, 74-99, 202-07. Stanford University Press, 2020.

Wrobel, David M. *America's West: A History, 1890-1950*. Cambridge University Press, 2017.

WESTERN US: 19TH C. INVESTORS

Bieber, Ralph P. "Introduction." In *Historic Sketches of the Cattle Trade of the West and Southwest*, by Joseph G. McCoy and edited by Ralph P. Bieber, 17-68. Arthur H. Clark Company, 1940.

Billiot, Mary Jo, Randy McFerrin, and Douglas Wills. "Returns in the Western Cattle

Industry: Reconstructing the Financial History of the Matador Land and Cattle Company, 1883-1920." *Essays in Economic & Business History* 35, no. 2 (2017): 1-25.

Brayer, H.O. "The Influence of British Capital on the Western Range-Cattle Industry." *Journal of Economic History* 9 (1965): 85-98.

Clements, Roger V. "British Investment and American Legislative Restrictions in the Trans-Mississippi West, 1880-1890." *Mississippi Valley Historical Review* 42, no. 2 (September 1955): 207-28.

Graham, Richard. "The Investment Boom in British-Texan Cattle Companies 1880-1885." *Business History Review* 34, no. 4 (Winter 1960): 421-45.

Gressley, Gene M. *Bankers and Cattlemen*. Alfred A. Knopf, 1966.

MacDonald, James. *Food from the Far West; or, American Agriculture with Special Reference to the Beef Production and Importation of Dead Meat from America to Great Britain*. W.P. Nimmo, 1878.

Maggor, Noam. *Brahmin Capitalism: Frontiers of Wealth and Populism in America's First Gilded Age*. Harvard University Press, 2017.

Maggor, Noam. "To Coddle and Caress These Great Capitalists: Eastern Money, Frontier Populism, and the Politics of Market-Making in the American West." *American Historical Review* 122, no. 1 (February 2017): 55-84.

McCoy, Joseph G. *Historic Sketches of the Cattle Trade of the West and Southwest*, edited by Ralph P. Bieber. 1874. Arthur H. Clark Company, 1940.

McFarlane, Larry A. "Nativism or Not? Perceptions of British Investment in Kansas, 1881-1901." *Great Plains Quarterly* 7, no. 4 (1987): 232-43.

McFarlane, Larry A. "Opposition to British Agricultural Investment in the Northern Plains States, 1884-1900." *Nebraska History* 67, no. 2 (1986): 115-33.

Mothershed, Harmon R. "The British Investment Public and the Swan Land and Cattle Company, Limited." *Annals of Wyoming* 48, no. 2 (April 1976): 253-63.

Rico, Monica. "The Cultural Contexts of International Capital Expansion: British Ranchers in Wyoming, 1879-1889." *Antipode* 30, no. 2 (1998): 119-34.

Sherow, James E. *The Chisholm Trail: Joseph McCoy's Great Gamble*. University of Oklahoma Press, 2018.

Sherow, James E. "Joseph McCoy's Dream: Abilene, Kansas, and the Opening of the Great Cattle Drives Up the Chisholm Trail 150 Years Ago." *Kansas History* 40 (Summer 2017): 82-85.

Skaggs, Jimmy M. "Pecuniary Man: Attitudes of British Investors Toward the Western Range Cattle Industry." *Red River Valley Historical Review* 1, no. 1 (January 1974): 46-54.

Turrentine, Jackson, W. "British Interests in the Range Cattle Industry." In *When Grass Was King*, by Maurice Frink, W. Turrentine Jackson, and Agnes Wright Spring, 133-330. University of Colorado Press, 1956.

Walker, Don D. "History Through a Cow's Horn: Joseph G. McCoy and His Historical Sketches of the Cattle Trade." In *Clio's Cowboys: Studies in the Historiography of the Cattle Trade*, by Don D. Walker, 1-24. University of Nebraska Press, 1981.

WESTERN US: IRRIGATION/RECLAMATION

Brookings Institution, Institute for Government Research. *The U.S. Reclamation Service: Its History, Activities and Organization.* Service Monographs of the United States Government. No. 2. D. Appleton and Company, 1919.

Cannon, Brian Q. "Water and Economic Opportunity: Homesteaders, Speculators and the U.S. Reclamation Service, 1904-1924." *Agricultural History* 76, no. 2 (April 2002): 188-207.

Fiege, Mark. *Irrigated Eden: The Making of an Agricultural Landscape in the American West.* University of Washington Press, 1999.

Pisani, Donald J. *To Reclaim a Divided West: Water, Law, and Public Policy, 1848-1902.* University of New Mexico Press, 1992.

Pisani, Donald J. *Water and the American Government: The Reclamation Bureau, National Water Policy, and the West, 1902-1935.* University of California Press, 2003.

Romero, Tom I., II. "Ditches and Desirability: Regulating Race through the Flow and Quality of Immigration and the Application of Western Water Law in the Nineteenth and Early Twentieth Centuries." In *Beyond the Borders of the Law: Critical Legal Histories of the North American West*, edited by Katrina Jagodinsky and Pablo Mitchell, 162-200. University Press of Kansas, 2018.

Worster, Donald. *Rivers of Empire: Water, Aridity, and the Growth of the American West.* Oxford University Press, 1985.

WORLD WAR I

Buschman, Neil O. "The United States Food Administration During World War I: The Rise of Activist Government Through Food Control During Mobilization for Total War." PhD diss., Auburn University, 2013.

Capozzola, Christopher. *Uncle Sam Wants You: World War I and the Making of the Modern American Citizen.* Oxford University Press, 2008.

Clements, Kendrick A. *Hoover, Conservation, and Consumerism: Engineering the Good Life.* University Press of Kansas, 2000.

Cuff, Robert. "The Dilemmas of Voluntarism: Hoover and the Pork-Packing Agreement of 1917-1919." *Agricultural History* 53, no. 4 (October 1979): 727-47.

Cuff, Robert D. *The War Industries Board: Business-Government Relations during World War I.* Johns Hopkins University Press, 1973.

Gregg, Sara M. "From Breadbasket to Dust Bowl: Rural Credit, the World War I Plow-up, and the Transformation of American Agriculture." *Great Plains Quarterly* 35, no. 2 (Spring 2015): 129-66.

Hawley, Ellis. *The Great War and the Search for a Modern Order: A History of the American People and Their Institutions, 1917-1933.* 2d ed. Waveland Press, 1997.

Hawley, Ellis W. "Herbert Hoover, the Commerce Secretariat, and the Vision of an 'Associative State,' 1921-1928." *Journal of American History* 61, no. 1 (June 1974): 116-40.

Hochschild, Adam. *American Midnight: The Great War, a Violent Peace, and Democracy's Forgotten Crisis.* Mariner Books, 2022.

Johnson, Timothy. "Nitrogen Nation: The Legacy of World War I and the Politics of

Chemical Agriculture in the United States, 1916-1933." *Agricultural History* 90, no. 2 (Spring 2016): 209-29.

Kennedy, David M. *Over Here: The First World War and American Society*. 25th anniversary ed., Oxford University Press, 2004.

Moore, Thomas Lane, III. "The Establishment of the Federal Trade Commission, 1912-1918." PhD diss., University of Alabama, 1980.

Mullendore, William Clinton. *History of the United States Food Administration, 1917-1919*. Stanford University Press, 1941.

Nash, George H. *The Life of Herbert Hoover: Master of Emergencies 1917-1918*. W.W. Norton & Company, 1996.

Neiberg, Michael S. *The Path to War: How the First World War Created Modern America*. Oxford University Press, 2016.

Smith, James H. "Cultivating Intelligent Consumption: The United States Food Administration and Food Control During World War I." PhD diss., West Virginia University, 2015.

US Food Administration. Statistical Division. *Production of Meat in the United States and Its Distribution during the War*. 1919.

US Senate, Committee on Agriculture and Forestry. *Increased Production of Grain and Meat Products: Hearings Before the Committee on Agriculture and Forestry*. 7 vols. 65th Cong. (1918).

WORLD WAR II

Alacevich, Michele, Pier Francesco Asso, and Sebastiano Nerozzi. "The Shaping of Public Economic Discourse in Postwar America: The 1947 Meat Shortage and Franco Modigliani's Meat Plan." *Research in the History of Economic Thought & Methodology* 33 (January 2015): 3-42.

Backer, Kellan. "The Quartermaster Corps and World War II Army Subsistence." In *Food Across Borders: An Introduction*, edited by Matt Garcia, E. Melanie DuPuis, and Don Mitchell, 121-39. Rutgers University Press, 2017.

Backer, Kellen. "When Meals Became Weapons: American Food In World War II." In *Nature At War: American Environments and World War II*, edited by Thomas Robertson, Richard P. Tucker, Nicholas B. Breyfogle, and Peter Mansoor, 176-95. Cambridge University Press, 2020.

Backer, Kellen. "World War II and the Triumph of Industrialized Food." PhD diss., University of Wisconsin-Madison, 2012.

Bentley, Amy. *Eating for Victory: Food Rationing and the Politics of Domesticity*. University of Illinois Press, 1998.

Black, Brian. "Fueling the 'American Century': Establishing the US Petroleum Imperative." In *Nature At War: American Environments and World War II*, edited by Thomas Robertson, Richard P. Tucker, Nicholas B. Breyfogle, and Peter Mansoor, 116-46. Cambridge University Press, 2020.

Brilliant, Mark, and David M. Kennedy, eds. *World War II and the West It Wrought*. Stanford University Press, 2020.

Collingham, Lizzie. *The Taste of War: World War Two and the Battle for Food*. Allen Lane, Penguin Group, 2011.

Gardner, Martha N. "Battling Insects and Infection: American Chemical and Pharmaceutical Expansion During World War II." In *Nature At War: American Environments and World War II*, edited by Thomas Robertson, Richard P. Tucker, Nicholas B. Breyfogle, and Peter Mansoor, 275–97. Cambridge University Press, 2020.

Grove, Wayne A. "The Mexican Farm Labor Program, 1942-1964: Government-Administered Labor Market Insurance for Farmers." *Agricultural History* 70, no. 2 (1996): 302-20.

Heisler, Barbara Schmitter. "The 'Other Braceros': Temporary Labor and German Prisoners of War in the United States, 1943-1946." *Social Science History* 31, no. 1 (Summer 2007): 239-71.

Hurt, R. Douglas. *The Great Plains during World War II*. University of Nebraska Press, 2008.

Jacobs, Meg. "'How About Some Meat?': The Office of Price Administration, Consumption Politics, and State Building from the Bottom Up, 1941-1946." *Journal of American History* 84, no. 3 (December 1997): 910-41.

Kevles, Daniel J. "Enlisting the Laboratories: Science, Defense, and the Transformation of the High-Tech West." In *World War II and the West It Wrought*, edited by Mark Brilliant, and David M. Kennedy, 38-73, 195-202. Stanford University Press, 2020.

Mansavage, Jean. "For Land's Sake: World War II Military Land Acquisition and Alteration." In *Nature At War: American Environments and World War II*, edited by Thomas Robertson, Richard P. Tucker, Nicholas B. Breyfogle, and Peter Mansoor, 51-84. Cambridge University Press, 2020.

Robertson, Thomas, and Richard P. Tucker. "Introduction: Total War and American Nature." In *Nature At War: American Environments and World War II*, edited by Thomas Robertson, Richard P. Tucker, and Nicholas B. Breyfogle, and Peter Mansoor, 1-20. Cambridge University Press, 2020.

Robertson, Thomas, Richard P. Tucker, Nicholas B. Breyfogle, and Peter Mansoor, eds. *Nature At War: American Environments and World War II*. Cambridge University Press, 2020.

Smith-Howard, Kendra. "Soldiers of the Soil: Labor, Nature, and American Agriculture During World War II." In *Nature At War: American Environments and World War II*, edited by Thomas Robertson, Richard P. Tucker, Nicholas B. Breyfogle, and Peter Mansoor, 149-75. Cambridge University Press, 2020.

Takaki, Ronald. *Double Victory: A Multicultural History of America in World War II*. Little, Brown, 2000.

USDA, BAE. *A History of the Emergency Farm Labor Supply Program 1943-47*, by Wayne D. Rasmussen. Agriculture Monograph No. 13, 1951.

DATABASES AND CATALOGS

19th Century Historical United States Newspapers
19th Century Masterfile
ABI/INFORM Global
Access World News

404 BIBLIOGRAPHY

Accessible Archives
Ageconsearch.umn.edu
Agricola
Alt-Press Watch
American Historical Imprints
American Periodical Series (digital and microfilm)
Archive Finder
Census.gov/history/www/through_the_decades/
Catalog of US Government Publications
Core Historical Literature of Agriculture (CORE)
Early American Imprints
Early American Newspapers
Early American Periodicals
EBSCOhost
genealogybank.com
HarpWeek
HathiTrust Digital Library
Historical Statistics of the United States. Millennial Edition, 2006.
Home Economics Archive: Research, Tradition, History (HEARTH)
Index to USDA Agricultural Economic Reports
Index to USDA Agriculture Information Bulletins
Making of America
National Agricultural Library
newspaperarchive.com
ProQuest Congressional
ProQuest Dissertations & Theses
ProQuest Historical Newspapers
Readers' Guide Retrospective
USDA Food Availability (Per Capita) Data System
WorldCat

PERIODICALS AND NEWSPAPERS

Alternative Agriculture News
American Egg and Poultry Review
American Poultry Advocate
American Poultry Journal
Boston Globe
Chicago Tribune
Des Moines Register
Farm Journal
Farm Quarterly
Feedstuffs
Godey's Lady's Book
Meat and Live Stock Digest
Milwaukee Sentinel

National Hog Farmer
National Live Stock & Meat Digest
National Provisioner
New York Produce Review and American Creamery
New York Times
Poultry Science
Reliable Poultry Journal
Successful Farming
Wallaces' Farmer
Wall Street Journal
Washington Post

ILLUSTRATION CREDITS

All are public domain.

p. 15 *Bird's eye view of New-York & Brooklyn / drawn from nature & on stone by J. Bachmann.* New Jersey, New York City, Governors Island, New York Harbor, New York County New York State, ca. 1851. New York: Published by A. Guerber & Co. Photograph. https://www.loc.gov/item/90707101/.

p. 16 *Representation of the famous Washington market, New York City.* New York, 1853. https://www.loc.gov/item/2006682446/.

p. 23 US Census Office. *Statistical Atlas Prepared under the Supervision of Henry Gannett, Geographer of the Twelfth Census.* 1903. Plate 5.

p. 27 "Hog-slaughtering and pork-packing in Cincinnati." Double page of engravings from drawings by H.F. Farny. Published in *Harper's Weekly*, 1873 Sept. 6, 776-777. https://www.loc.gov/item/2004677270/.

p. 36 "The Communipaw Stockyards at Jersey City, New Jersey." *Frank Leslie's Illustrated Newspaper*, November 17, 1866.

p. 48 *Parcs a bestiaux cattle yard A view of the Chicago stockyards.* Chicago Illinois, 1871. https://www.loc.gov/item/2012647890/.

p. 53 *The modern colossus of rail roads* by Joseph Ferdinand Keppler. 1879. New York: Keppler & Schwarzmann. https://www.loc.gov/item/2014645351/.

p. 59 Townsend MacCoun. *An Historical Geography of the United States.* Silver, Burdett & Company, 1901.

p. 62 *The far west - shooting buffalo on the line of the Kansas-Pacific Railroad.* Great Plains, 1871. https://www.loc.gov/item/2004669992/.

p. 72 *Filling skins, sausage department, Armour's great packing house, Chicago, U.S.A. 1893.* New York: Strohmeyer & Wyman. https://www.loc.gov/item/89712084/.

p. 81 *Dreamland, Coney Island, New York City.* New York, ca. 1908. https://www.loc.gov/item/93506593/.

p. 83 *Watch the Professor.* 1906. N.Y.: J. Ottmann Lith. Co., Puck Bldg. https://www.loc.gov/item/2011645894/.

p. 91 *The meat market.* Carl Hassman, artist. 1906. N.Y.: J. Ottmann Lith. Co., Puck Bldg. https://www.loc.gov/item/2011645899/.

p. 92 *East Side women discussing price of meat during N.Y.C. Meat Boycott.* Apr. 1910. https://www.loc.gov/item/2004679521/.

p. 102 *In the heart of the Great Union Stock Yards, Chicago, U.S.A.* Chicago Illinois, ca. 1909. Copyright, 1909, by Kelley & Chadwick. https://www.loc.gov/item/89711602/.

p. 108 *Push Cart Market, East Side.* New York, ca. 1915. https://www.loc.gov/item/90709369/.

p. 112 *Be patriotic — sign your country's pledge to save the food.* Paul Stahr. United States, 1918. [New York: The W.F. Powers Co. Litho., ?] https://www.loc.gov/item/96515511/.

408 ILLUSTRATION CREDITS

p. 115 *Pigs is pigs we raised more hogs in 1918 than before the war : 1919 must show increase 15% ... will you raise your share?* 1914. [Wisconsin] : Wisconsin State Council of Defense

p. 124 "How 'Meat for Health Week' Was Put Over," *National Provisioner* 69, no. 2 (July 14, 1923): 23.

p. 127 *Grocery store of Fred Gauer, 117 Hare St., Baltimore.* Interior of Fred Gauer's grocery store, meat counter II. Photography by Theodor Horydczak. https://www.loc.gov/item/2019671669/.

p. 129 *Care of Meat in the Home,* USDA, Bureau of Home Economics, 1929. USDA Poster Collection, archive.org

p. 131 US, FTC, *Food Investigation: Report of the Federal Trade Commission on the Meat-Packing Industry*, 6 vols., 1919. Insert following p. 46.

p. 151 Quaker Ful-O-Pep Chick Starter. Advertisement appeared regularly in trade magazines. *Reliable Poultry Journal*, 1930.

p. 154 Purina Chicken Startena. Advertisement appeared regularly in trade magazines. *Reliable Poultry Journal*, 1926.

p. 157 *Poultry buyer's Negro truck driver loading the truck on the Enos Royer farm.* Sheldon Dick, photographer. Lancaster, Pennsylvania. 1938. https://www.loc.gov/item/2017790554/.

p. 159 *1941 Electric plucker removes every pin feather without a tear in the skin. 500 to 1000 birds could be plucked in a day by this method. Enterprise coop cannery. Coffee County, Enterprise, Alabama.* John Collier, Jr, photographer. 1941. https://www.loc.gov/item/2017820086/.

p. 162 *Shopper watching the weighing of a chicken in the Giant Food shopping center.* Marjory Collins, photographer. 1942. Washington D.C. United States District of Columbia. https://www.loc.gov/item/2017825567/.

p. 166 *Women with shopping carts, one with a baby, in the baked goods section of a Giant food store in Washington, D.C.* / Thomas J. O'Halloran, 1958. https://www.loc.gov/item/2023630508/.

p. 170 *Gene helps feed the hogs. Near Ames, Iowa.* Jack Delano, photographer. 1942. https://www.loc.gov/item/2017831239/.

p. 171 *Hogs on Fred Coulter's farm.* Grundy County, Iowa. John Vachon, photographer. 1940. https://www.loc.gov/item/2017810044/.

p. 174 *4 out of 10 Pigs Never Grow Up.* USDA. Office for Food and Feed Conservation, 1947. USDA Agriculture Poster Collection archive.org.

p. 231 *Boycott meat!: April 1-7, 1973.* [or 1974] New York Consumer Assembly, Sponsor/Advertiser. https://www.loc.gov/item/2016647144/.

p. 244 *Tractors, one flying the flag of the American Agriculture Movement, on their way to the U.S. Capitol, Washington, D.C., during the "Tractorcade" protests of February.* Warren K. Leffler, photographer. 1979. https://www.loc.gov/item/2021637306/.

p. 271 Lagoon. Photograph by Jeff Vanuga. USDA Natural Resources Conservation Service. 2011. USDA NRCS Photo Gallery. NRCSGA02036. Wikimedia.

p. 283 *Sows suckle their litter of piglets in the farrowing, or birthing, shed on Dean and Julie Folkmann's hog farm in Benton County, Iowa, near the town of Newhall, Benton County, Iowa.* Carol M. Highsmith, photographer. 2016. https://www.loc.gov/item/2016630244/.

INDEX

1970s, 232-35
Abilene (Kansas), 65
agribusiness, 181-83
Agribusiness Accountability Project, 224
Agricultural Adjustment Act (1933), 156
Agricultural Adjustment Administration, 156
agricultural crises, 1920s, 133-34, 137, 139; 1979-1985, 243-45
agriculture, 19th c. reform of, 24; and home market, 24
agriculture, alternative, 275-76
agriculture, organic, 225-26, 246-47, 278
agriculture, policy, 119, 155-56, 160, 168-71
agriculture, productivity of, 162, 169-70, 180
agriculture, subsidized, 89, 120-22, 155-56, 170-71
Alliance for a Clean Swine Industry, 271
American Agriculture Movement, 243-44
American Farm Bureau Federation, 135-37, 138-39
American Meat Institute, 217
American Meat Packers Association (AMPA), 104, 132
American National Live Stock Association, (ANLSA), 99, 100-05, 118-20, 134, 307n43
American Society for the Prevention of Cruelty to Animals (ASPCA), 42
Anderson, Andrew D., 202-03, 328n73
Angell, George T., 42
animal protein factor (APF), 172
antibiotics, 172-73, 222-23, 252, 334n43, 335n58
antitrust, 70, 93-94
A&P 178
Armour and Company, 31, 51-52, 71-72, 105-06
Armour, Philip, 30-32, 71-72
Armour, Simeon, 73
associationalism, 110

Barnum, Phineas T., 12, 13
beef consumption, 83, 164-66, 251-53, 294n3
beef, exotic, 279
beef, grass-fed, 263, 279-280
Beef Products Inc., 285
beef as symbol, 56
Beef Trust, 1888 hearings into, 71-74; attempt to nationalize, 130-32; blamed for cattle bust, 68-69; collusion, rationale for, 71-73; consent decree, 135; diversifica-

tion and investments, 82, 99; exposé of, 1902, 90; FTC report on, 131-32; and WWI, 113-14. *See also* American National Live Stock Association; meatpacking
Beltsville (MD), 95, 149
Benson, Ezra, 210
Bergh, Henry, 41-42
Berry, Wendell, 226
Borah, William, 109
Borland, William P., 105, 309n64
Boulder, (Colorado), 185
boycotts/protests, 91-92, 97, 107-09, 230-31
boxed beef, 194-95, 204, 206
Bradford, William, 6-7
Brand, Charles, 103, 104
Brand conference (USDA), 1915, 103-05
Brand, Stuart, 224
broiler industry, 1900-1920, 146-148; 1950s, 178-80; 1970s, 239; blackmarket in, 161; broiler prices, early 20th c., 147; broilers as loss leaders, 178-79; consumption, 254; Delmarva, 149-52; early 20th c., 147-48, 152; feeding stations, 147; in Georgia, 153, 156-60; hearings into, 180; Jewish influence on, 147; kosher markets, 147; livestock feed manufacturers and, 149, 157; poultry research, 148-49; production numbers, 152, 158, 160; supermarkets and, 178-79; USDA and, 149-51, 157-58
buffalo, 61-62
Bull's Head Tavern (New York City), 12, 18
Burke, E.L, 100, 119
Burroughs, Wise, 175-76
butchers, work described, 17-18, 39-41
Butz, Earl, 226, 234, 235
byproducts, 26-27, 70, 193

canals, 25
cancer, 211
Carson, Rachel, 212
Carter, James "Jimmy," 243
cattle, colonial period, 4-8; market weight, 1820s, 28; nutrition, 175-76; Ohio River valley, 27-28; producers, 1950s, 197-98; quality of questioned, 77; shortage of, 63, 95
cattle ranchers, 76-77, 98-99, 191
"cattlemen's frontier," 27-28
cattle trails, 12, 28, 64
Center for Consumer Freedom, 280-81
Center for Rural Affairs, 224
Center for Science in the Public Interest (CSPI), 254
chain grocers, 127-28. *See also* meat retail/wholesale; supermarkets
Chef's Collaborative, 280
Chez Panisse, 257

INDEX   411

Chicago (IL), 29-30
Chicken of Tomorrow competitions, 178
chickens, 144-46. *See also* broiler industry
Chipotle, 284
Christopher Columbus (hereford), 175
Cincinnati, 26-27
cities, fear of, 74-75, 86; food and, 14, 16; reform of 34, 37-38; unsanitary conditions in, 34-35
Cold War (1947-1991), 165, 168-69
Coleman, Mel, Jr, 282
Coleman, Mel, Sr, 259, 260, 263, 265
Coleman Natural Meats, 259-66, 267, 282
colonial America, 3-9
colonial meat trade, 8
Colorado State College of Agriculture and Mechanic Arts, 185
Commoner, Barry, 212, 220
Communipaw Abattoir, 35-37, 38
Community Food Security Coalition, 275-76, 287
ConAgra, 241-42
confinement, 145, 149, 177-78, 198-99, 201
consumer activism, 214
consumer economy, 87-89, 155, 163. *See also* paradox of plenty
consumerism, 214
Consumer Reports, 216
consumers, 1820s, 21; 1910s, 91-92, 107-09; 1950s, 170-71; 1960s, 213, 214; 1970s, 230-31; as collective, 214; entitlement, 96, 97-98, 120; food prices and; Great Depression and, 155; interests of, 106; policy for, 89, 103; role in economy, 55-56, 88, 89; WWI 116; WWII, 158, 163. *See also* consumer economy
contract farming, 180, 196-97
conversion rates, 178, 175
Corn Belt livestock production, mid-20th c., 197-99
Corn Belt Producers' Association, 117
corn-cattle-hog complex, 8, 25
corners, 31
corporate farms, 224, 248-50
corporations, 38. *See also* monopolies
Cotton, Joseph, 116, 119
countercuisine, 259
Crawford County Packing Company, 203
Crescent City Live Stock Landing and Slaughterhouse Company, 40
Cudahy Packing Company, 105
cycle of extravagance, 6

Davis, John, 181-82
DDT, 210
Delaney Clause, 209

Delmarva, 149-52. *See also* chickens; broiler industry
DeLorenzo, Mickey, 230
Denison (Iowa), 202
Denver (Colorado), 185
depressions, economic, 1890s, 74; 1930s, 154-56
DES daughters, 222
Diet for A Small Planet, 225
Diethylstilbestrol (DES), 174-77, 220-22
Division of Consumer Protection, 158
Division of Price Stabilization, 158
dressed beef, 41, 43, 54-55, 69-70. *See also* Armour and Company; Beef Trust; Swift & Company

Eastman, T.C., 43-44
E-Colo-Beef, 227-28
Egg McMuffin, 253
eggs, 144
Eli Lilly and Company, 176
Ellsworth (Kansas), 66
Engler, Paul, 252
entitlement, 5-7, 19-20, 56; criticism of, 112; urban, 96, 97-98; WWII and 163
environmental threats, 1950s, 208-09, 212
Erie Canal, 25
Escherichia coli O157:H7, 252, 268
exports, 8, 44, 50, 114

FAO (United Nations' Food and Agriculture Organization), 234, 337n15
factory farming, 141-42, 169, 220, 224
family farm, 169, 248
famine, 168, 232
farmers' markets, 276, 337n15
Farm Aid, 244
farm bill, 156, 245-46, 339n52
Farm Bloc, 138. *See also* American Farm Bureau Federation
Far West, 57-60. *See also* western US.
Federal Food, Drug, and Cosmetics Act (1938), 209
Federal Trade Commission, report on meatpackers, 106, 130-31
feedlots, cattle, 202, 209, 281, 326n30. *See also* Monfort Feedlots, Inc.
First Colony Farm, 236, 240
Food Additives Amendment (1958), 209
food, chemicals in 208, 209-10
food, as diplomacy, 168-69
food fads, 85-86
Food and Fuel Control Act, 110
food prices, 1910s, 86-87, 90-91; 1970s, 233, 234-45; explanations for, 86, 97-98; low, 257-58; consumer economy and, 87-88. *See also* boycotts/protests; consumer

INDEX   413

economy; paradox of plenty
food, as right, 163
food retail/wholesale, 126-27
foodways, early 20th c., 81-82, 83-85; mid-20th c. 164-65; 1980, 254-57; consumer niches, 256-57
Fort Collins (Colorado), 184, 185
Fourteenth Amendment, 40-41
frankfurters, 124-25
frontier, end of, 74

Gainesville (Georgia), 156, 179
Garst, Roswell, 176
Garza, Eligio de la, 265-66
General Executive Committee of Mechanics, Workmen, 21
General Motors Acceptance Corporation (GMAC), 88
genetics, 148
gestation stalls, 282-83, *ill.*, 283
Goldberg, Ray, 182
Gore, Thomas P., 119-20
grain shortage, 1970s, 232
Grand Trunk Railway, 49
Grand Union (supermarket chain), 262
grazing land. *See* western range
Great American Desert 59
Greater Northeast, 23, 296n30
Great Grain Robbery, 232-33
"great law of the movement of cattle," 63
Greeley (Colorado), 185
Green Revolution, 232
Guymon (Oklahoma), 272-74

Hammond, George, 44, 48, 51, 105
Harding, Warren G., 138, 139
Hard Times, Hard Tomatoes, 224
Harper, Mike, 241. *See also* ConAgra
Haw, Bill, 240-41. *See also* National Farms Inc.
Heard, Dwight B., 105, 118
heart disease, 210-11, 239n12-13
high cost of living, 87. *See also* food prices
hog production, colonial era, 4, 6, 7; Ohio River valley, 25-26; and confinement, 177-78, 198-99; Corn Belt, 197; corporate, 235, 240-41, 247-48, 273; debates about, 274; floods and, 272; North Carolina, 270-72; specification, 258; WWI, 114-16
Holman, Currier, 204, 205, 329n77
home market, 24, 80
Homestead Act 1862, 63
Hoover, Herbert, 138, 155; described, 110-11; as Food Administrator, 111-17, 121-

414 INDEX

420, 422; hog farmers and, 114-117; meatpackers and, 113-14; price fixing and, 115-16, 121-22; psychology of conservation, 111-12; surplus and, 112
hormones, 174-77
hot dogs, 215-18
Hotel Restaurant Institution industry (HRI), 166-68, 177
Houston, David, 102, 109, 137
Humane Society of the United States (HSUS), 284
hybrid poultry, 178

internal improvements, 24-25
International Live Stock Exposition, 78
Interstate Commerce Commission, 70
Iowa Beef Packing (IBP), 202-05, 328n73
Iowa State College, 176, 177
irrigation. *See* reclamation

Jack in the Box, 268
Jacobson, Michael, 254
Jastro, Henry, 101
Jewell, Jesse, 157-60, 179-80. *See also* broiler industry
John Morrell & Co., 249
Johnson, Hugh S., 139
Joseph Plan, 140

Kansas City, 31, 51
Kansas Pacific Railroad, 65, 66
Kellogg, J.H., 85
Kellogg, Will K., 85
Kellogg's Corn Flakes, 85
Kendrick, John B., 130, 134
Kennedy, John F., 213
Kenyon, William S., 130
Keys, Ancel, 211
Korean War (1950-1953), 169

labor, 55-56, 74-75
labor, agricultural, 98, 159
Lappé, Frances Moore, 225
lard, 26-27, 193
Lean Finely Textured Beef, 284-86
livestock shipping, 42-43
living wage, 55
Long, Stephen, 58
Loudermilk, Mary Tallulah Dickson Jewell, 156
Low-Input Sustainable Agriculture (LISA 1985), 247
Luter, Joseph III, 270

INDEX   415

Lux, Charles, 60-61, 75

manure management/lagoons, 199-201
Marquis de Morès (Amédée-Marie-Vincent Manca de Vallombrosa), 67-68
Massachusetts Society for the Prevention of Cruelty to Animals, 42
Mayer, Oscar Jr, 217
McCoy, Joseph, 64-66
McDonald's 167, 253, 254, 284
McGovern Report, 251
McLean, Malcolm, 235-236, 240
McNary-Haugen Act, 141
McNuggets, 254
McQuoid, Charles, 236-37
McRib, 253
meat consumption, 1900-1920, 83; 1940s, 162; 1950s, 164; campaign to increase, 123-24; colonial era, 5-6; foreigners' responses to, 18-19; New York City, 15, 294n5
meat, contaminated, 1950s, 109-210
meat inspection, 269
meat, nutritive value of, 4-5
meat, organic, 265-66, 276-78
meatpacking, Cincinnati, 26-27; described, 32-33, 35-37; mid-20th c., 205-07; late 20th c., 258; as urban nuisance, 32-33, 38. *See also* Beef Trust and specific companies
meat, preservation of, 5
meat retail/wholesale, 95-96, 128-30, 165-66, 194
Meeker, Arthur, 105, 106
Meredith, Edwin T., 140
microwave oven, 255-56
Miller, Henry, 60-61, 75
Monfort Brothers (company), 189
Monfort, C.K., 184, 185-86
Monfort of Colorado, Inc. (1970-1987), 231-32
Monfort family, early years, 184-89
Monfort Feedlots, Inc. (1930-70), 187-92, 195, 226-27
Monfort, Kenneth, 189, 190-91, 207, 231
Monfort, (Lillian) Edith (neé Shrum), 186
Monfort, Margery, 188
Monfort Packing Company, 192-96, 242-43
Monfort, Pella J. (neé Phipps), 184, 185
Monfort, Richard, 189-90
Monfort, Viola (neé Swanson), 190
Monfort, Warren, 184, 185-86, 190, 192, 323n7
monopolies, 21-22, 52, 70
Morrill Land Grant Act (1862), 63
Morris, Nelson, 43, 105

416 INDEX

Mrs. Gooch's Ranch Markets, 261
Murphy Farms, 270
Murphy, Wendell, 270, 272

Nader's Raiders, 214
Nader, Ralph, 212-220
National Agricultural Conference 1922, 139-40
National Anti-Food Trust League, 97
National Association of County Agricultural Agents, 136
National Farms, Inc. (NFI), 240-41, 248-49
National Live Stock and Meat Board, 123-124
National Organic Standards Board (NOSB), 266, 276
National Resources Defense Council (NRDC), 222
Native Americans, 4, 7, 60, 61-62
New England Fresh Meat Express, 50
Newer Nutrition, 125-26
New Image Grass Beef, 279
New Jersey Stockyard and Market Company, 35. *See also* Communipaw Abattoir
New Orleans, 39-40
New-York Board of Health, 37
New York Central Railroad, 30
New York (City), 13, 14-18, 20-22
New York City Board of Education, 124
New York Herald, 90, 91
Niman Bill, 263, 280
Niman Ranch, 263, 281-82
Nixon, Richard M., 215-16, 235
Norris, George W., 109

Office of Price Administration (WWII), 160, 190
Ohio River, 25
oil embargo, 233
Oliver, Jamie, 285
Omnivore's Dilemma, 281
organic food industry, 276

Packers-Stockyards Act 1921, 138-39
Palmer, Mitchell A., 135
paradox of plenty, defined, 87-89; described, 117, 119-20; USDA and, 89-90; management of, 139-41, 170-71
Peaceful Pastures, 277-78
Peek, George N., 139
Peek-Johnson Plan, 139-40
Pentagon, 167
pernicious anemia, 172-73
Petaluma (California), 147

Pike, Zebulon, 58
"pink slime." *See* Lean Finely Textured Beef
Plankinton, John, 31
Pollan, Michael, 279, 280, 281
pork consumption, 164, 253
Post Shredded Wheat Biscuits, 85-86
poultry cages, campaign against, 284
"practical farming," 224
public interest lobby, 220
Public Law 480, 171
public markets, New-York City, 13, 16-17, 20-23
quarantine, livestock, 65, 101
Quilted Giraffe, 258

race/racism, 20, 40, 59-60, 61, 74-75, 305n1
railroads, 25, 28-30, 45-47, n29/298
railroad/stockyard/slaughterhouse complex, 29-30, 32, 35, 45-47
Rath Packing Company, 176
reclamation, 75-77
Red Scare (WWI), 134-35
refrigerated rail cars, 47-48, 51
restaurant culture, 83-85, 89, 167-68
Riqles, A.E. de, 101, 102, 103-04
rights, 19-21, 39-41
Rocky the Range organic chicken, 264
Rodale, J.I., 225
Rodale, Robert, 225
Roosevelt, Franklin D., 155, 158
Roosevelt, Theodore, 76, 93, 98
Roth, Eldon, 285, 286
Russian Revolution 1917, 111, 134, 310n6

Salatin, Joel, 277-78
Salmonella, 208, 209
Schell, Orville, 263, 281
Schlosser, Eric, 281
Scientific American, 43
scientific proof, problem of, 221, 223
Seaboard Corporation, 272-73
Sherman Antitrust Act 1890, 73, 93
Silent Spring, 212
Silver, Gray, 138
Slaughterhouse Cases, 39-41
slaughterhouses, 26, 32-33, 37-38
Smithfield Foods, 270-71
Smoot, Reed, 139

418 INDEX

Soviet Union, 169, 232
specification buyers, 197, 258
Specific Pathogen Free livestock, 178
steamboats, 29
Steward, Ira, 55. *See also* living wage
Stilbosol, 176
Stockman Grass Farmer, 279
Strong, Josiah, 74
supermarkets, 165, 166, 312n11. *See also* meat retail
"surplus problem." *See* paradox of plenty
Swift, Edwin C., 50, 54
Swift, Gustavus F., 44-45, 47-49, 299n28
Swift & Company, 47-51, 54, 105, 196, 206-07, 242, 300n29
Sykes, A., 117-18

Taggert, Jon and Wendy, 279
Tennessee Valley Authority (TVA), 155
Truman, Harry, 168, 169
Tyson, Don, 237-39, 254-55
Tyson, John, 237
Tyson Feed & Hatchery (1947-1963), 237, 238
Tyson Foods (1963-) 239, hog production, 239-41, 254, 255

Union Stock Yard & Transit Co. (Chicago), 30, 78, 206
urban population, 14
urban growth and agriculture, 200, 201, 227
urbanites and agriculture, 227, 246, 248-49
USDA, authority, loss of, 235, 329n1; Beltsville, 95; early 20th c., 94-95; extension services, 136; factory farming and, 141-42; founded, 63; livestock shipping and, 42; organic foods policy, 261, 264, 265-66; relations with producers and packers, 77,78; rural depopulation, large farms, supported by, 160, 169. *See also* broiler industry, paradox of plenty
US Food Administration (1917-1919), 110. *See also* Hoover, Herbert

"value-added," 179, 239, 258
Vanderbilt, William, 52
vertical integration, 171, 179, 180, 192
Vitamin B12, 173
Vitamin D, 149
vitamins, 125-26

wage earners, 55
Wallace, Henry A., 140
Wallace, Henry C., 115, 117, 119-21, 138
War of 1812, 23
War of the Rebellion, 38, 63

Waters, Alice, 257, 280
Weld County (Colorado), 184
Western Grasslands Beef Alliance, 280
western range, 61-62, 77, 191, 325n27
Western Refrigerator Car Company, 43
western US, 58-62, 66-69, 76, 77
Whole Earth Catalog, 224-25
Wholesome Meat Act (1967), 218-20
Wickard, Claude R., 160
Wilson, James, 77, 90-91, 94, 98
Wilson, Lloyd, 192
Wilson, Thomas E., 132, 313n22
Wilson, Woodrow, 106, 109-10, 130
Winfrey, Oprah, 274-75
Winthrop, John, 4
World War I, 101, 117
World War II, 158-159, 160-63

yuppies, 256

ABOUT THE AUTHOR

Maureen Ogle is an historian living in Ames, Iowa. She is the author of several books, including *Key West: History of An Island of Dreams*, and *Ambitious Brew: A History of American Beer*.

She can be found at maureenogle.com or on Bluesky as @maureenogle.bsky.social

www.ingramcontent.com/pod-product-compliance
Lightning Source LLC
Chambersburg PA
CBHW060546080526
44585CB00013B/463